Praise from the Experts
for the Third Edition of
Allergy and Candida Cooking

"Sondra Lewis is an expert in the kitchen and a wise healer for those with food allergies and Candida. I have counseled tens of thousands of patients and numerous health care practitioners, and I constantly refer to **Allergy and Candida Cooking**. *This book is a detailed explanation of what food allergies, leaky gut and candida overgrowth are, and how they manifest in the body. No one I have found puts together all these concepts in one format. We are all individuals, and Sondra never forgets that. This is a brilliant production and a life saver for so many."*

—Michael P. Constantine, N.D., Clinical Consultant and Specialist
in Food Allergies, Candida and Gluten Intolerances

* * * * *

"A valuable therapeutic tool – fun to read and use – benefiting many of my patients."

—Ralph C. Lee, M.D.
Private Practitioner and Member of ACAM and ICIM

* * * * *

*"***Allergy and Candida Cooking** *is a distinct summary and effective therapeutic guide for patients with Candida-Related Complex and food sensitivities. The explanations for Candida-Related Complex and its correct control with dietary manipulation are crucial. The rotary diversified diet recommended is solid. The most important part of the book is the recipes, often the stumbling block for patients. Our office's master's degree nutritionist uses the book's principles. Sondra's book has been an immeasurable source of progress for my patients."*

—James A Hamp, M.D., F.A.C.S., F.A.A.O.A.
ENT Professional Associates, S.C.

* * * * *

*"***Allergy and Candida Cooking** *has been the most valuable diet resource for my patients with Candida-related illness. No other book more effectively answers the question, 'What can I eat?' The book is an invaluable resource of practical, easily implemented recipes for patients with Candida-related illness and multiple food sensitivities. It also supplies an easy to understand explanation of the nature and causes of Candida-related illness. This is the one essential book for patients engaging in a Candida treatment regimen. Without proper attention to dietary implementation, these patients cannot recover."*

—George F. Kroker, M.D.
Allergy Associates of La Crosse, WI

Praise Excerpts for the Earlier Editions!

"Finally, a complete guide for my patients and myself. I refer to it all the time."

Barbara Schiltz, Nutritionist

* * * * *

"The comprehensive information in **Allergy and Candida Cooking Made Easy** *will help many people with food allergies and Candida yeast infections, especially those recently diagnosed. I especially like the care you have taken in suggesting appropriate treats and snacks for each of the four days. In my experience, people won't stick with a diet that forbids all forms of fun foods. ... a very livable plan for eating one's way to recovery."*

—Marjorie Hurt Jones, R.N., author <u>The Allergy Self-Help Cookbook</u>

* * * * *

"Sondra Lewis' knowledge of Candidiasis and the treatments for it is very impressive. In **Allergy and Candida Cooking Made Easy** *she gives the medical background for problems related to Candidiasis and food allergies. I highly recommend this book to anyone with Candidiasis and/or food allergies who is eager to actually get well by improving their diet while enjoying what they eat."*

—Nicolette M. Dumke, author <u>Allergy Cooking with Ease</u>

* * * * *

"A superb book written by a person who's been there! **Allergy and Candida Cooking Made Easy** *serves as an invaluable resource for any person with yeast-related health problems. I especially recommend it for those who continue to experience problems even though they take antifungal medication, avoid chemical pollutants and take nutritional supplements."*

—William G. Crook, M.D., author <u>The Yeast Connection Handbook</u>

* * * * *

"If you were to gather a few books together for a library covering natural foods preparation, **Allergy and Candida Cooking Made Easy** *would be one of the best to add to your shelf. Many books have been written covering the field; however, this book occupies a unique place because of its ease of use, helpfulness and applicability and good basic coverage over a wide range of topics. It is especially valuable because it was developed through the personal needs and hands-on experience of the author. Highly recommended from beginner to expert!"*

—Larry Hendershot, Food Consultant

* * * * *

*"***Allergy and Candida Cooking Made Easy** *is the best cookbook I have seen on the subject of Allergy and Candida; much more detailed and has a larger variety of foods and recipes. The four day meal planning and recipes, using a wide variety of foods, makes meal planning much easier to follow. Thank you for a much needed book on Allergy and Candida."*

—Ross R., customer in WI

see pages 56 and 69 for additional customer reviews

Allergy and Candida Cooking

Understanding and Implementing Plans for Healing

THIRD EDITION

Sondra Lewis

with Dorie Fink

Canary Connect Publications

A Division of SOBOLE, Inc.

Coralville, Iowa

DISCLAIMER

This information is not intended to replace medical diagnosis or treatment, but rather to provide assistance in implementing a Candida-Control and/or Rotational Food Plan. Please consult your health-care provider for medical advice.

The publisher and authors declare that to the best of their knowledge all material in this book is accurate. We shall have neither liability nor responsibility to any person with respect to any loss or damage alleged to be caused, directly or indirectly, by the information contained in this book.

First edition was sold under the title, Allergy & Candida Cooking—Rotational Style by Sondra K. Lewis with Lonnett Dietrich Blakley (copyright 1995)

Second edition was sold under the title, Allergy & Candida Cooking Made Easy by Sondra K. Lewis with Lonnett Dietrich Blakley (copyright 1996)

Cover Design by George Foster, Foster & Foster, Inc.
Cover Illustration by Rachel Hein, Pea Patch Graphics
Illustrations by Rachel Hein (Pea Patch Graphics) and Christine Hicks

Published in United States of America by
Canary Connect Publications
605 Holiday Road, Coralville, Iowa 52241-1016
For ordering, see page 261.

ISBN-13: 978-0-9643462-6-0   ISBN-10: 0-9643462-6-5
First printing (spiral-bound), March 2005. Additional printing (spine-bound), September 2005.

Library of Congress Cataloging-in-Publication Data
The Library of Congress cataloged the earlier spiral-bound edition as follows:

Lewis, Sondra K.
   Allergy and candida cooking : understanding & implementing plans for healing / Sondra lewis, with Dorrit Fryling Fink.-- 3rd ed.
      p. cm.
   Summary: "Over 375 allergy-free recipes that correspond to a 4-day rotational food plan. Resources for understanding and implementing plans for healing for those with yeast overgrowth health issues including candida-related complex, fibromyalgia, chronic fatigue syndrome, endometriosis, inflammatory bowel diseases (IBS), ADD, food allergies, vaginitis, prostatitis, headaches, sinusitis and more"--Provided by publisher.
   Includes bibliographical references and index.
   ISBN-13: 978-0-9643462-4-6 (pbk. : alk. paper) 1. Food allergy--Diet therapy--Recipes. 2. Candidiasis--Diet therapy--Recipes. I. Fink, Dorrit Fryling, 1973- II. Title.

   RC596.L493 2005
   641.5'631--dc22

2005007407

Printed in United States of America
www.CanaryConnect.com

10 9 8 7 6 5 4 3 2

Table of Contents

CHAPTER FOUR
Understanding & Implementing
a Nutritional Support Program   39

CHAPTER FIVE
Understanding the Nature & Causes
of Food Allergies   51

CHAPTER SIX
Understanding & Implementing
the Mechanics of
a Rotational Food Plan   57

CHAPTER SEVEN
Cooking Within the Parameters
of the Food Plans   65

RECIPES

Acknowledgments

Everything that has gone in to making this book possible
— the knowledge and understanding of the material,
the foods, the people, the ideas, the healing itself —
has come from the Lord, my God, and His Son, Jesus Christ my Savior.

To Him be all praise and glory!

I wish to thank the following people for their direct and/or indirect help in making this book a reality:

My editors, Dorie and Lonnett, for taking my thoughts/words and turning them into smooth flowing pieces of "art";

To all those who came before me in the study of Candida-Related Complex, food allergies and eating on rotation for their knowledge, inspiring recipes, guidance and examples through their writings as well as through many kind words of assistance;

Special thanks to Drs. Crook and Kroker and others who encouraged and assisted me with all editions of this work;

Rachel and Chris for graphic illustrations that add life and fun to the words;

My health-care team;

The many "beautiful" people whom I have met during the journey of writing, revising and marketing this book who have offered their compliments, encouragement, information, guidance and support;

My husband, Bob, family and friends for their patience, encouragement, prayers and being part of my quality control and assurance team as "official tasters";

And a special tribute to my friend Patricia.

Preface

In the years when I was first diagnosed with Candida-Related Complex (CRC), food allergies, Chronic Fatigue Syndrome and Multiple Chemical Sensitivities (MCS), I was exhausted from the illness and overwhelmed at the thought of all that might be involved in healing. The prospect of remaining so sick – or, worse yet, getting sicker – was unbearable, so I began to learn all I could about my illness and the healing process.

It became clear that what I ate directly impacted my health. Not only had it lead to my illness, but it could be instrumental in my recovery. The prospect of finding ways to live without sugars, white flours and common food allergens was challenging, but the pieces began to fall into place. Using my background as an educator in Home Economics and my experience as an assistant manager in college food service, I began to develop a rotational food plan with corresponding recipes and I was encouraged by my results.

A few months later, I saw George Kroker, M.D. of La Crosse, WI for an evaluation. After examining my dietary sheets, he noted that he was impressed with my understanding and implementation of the dietary parameters required for healing and he encouraged me to turn them into a book. That effort became <u>Allergy and Candida Cooking Rotational Style</u>, published in 1995. In 1996, it was revised and became <u>Allergy and Candida Cooking Made Easy</u>. I chose the name Canary Connect for my publishing house because canaries were known to warn coal miners of danger. Those of us affected by CRC and MCS have come to regard ourselves as "canaries" for today's world. Since we respond more noticeably to the dangers of the typical North American diet and to chemicals around us, we "sing" our message of warning. We also "sing" to share with each other. I hope that the song of this book will speak to you and encourage you in your journey to lead a healthy, fulfilling life.

At one point, I was tempted to let the book go out of print, but the cries for more help and continued access to recipes and comprehensive information were too hard to ignore. Through my own healing process I had gained a much deeper understanding of the health challenges related to yeast overgrowth. My recommitment to writing included finding a "new look" for the book and an easier way for the reader to implement the healing strategies. I was also committed to providing detailed information about the causes of CRC and food allergies as well as the solutions

I soon saw this book as God's purpose for this point in my life – even down to working with Dorie, my editor for this edition.

Read, cook, eat and enjoy! May God bless you in your endeavors.

*"Every journey begins
with a single step."*
—Unknown

*"The common conception is
that motivation leads to action,
but the reverse is true. Action
precedes motivation.*

*"You have to prime the pump
and get the juice flowing,
which motivates you to work
on your goals.*

*"Getting momentum going is
the most difficult part of the
job, and often taking the first
step is enough to prompt you
to make the best of your day."*
—Robert J. McKain

*"Hold fast to dreams;
for if dreams die,
life is a broken-winged bird
that cannot fly. "*
—Lanston Hughes

**Recipe Illustrations on Covers
by Rachel Hein, Pea Patch Graphic**

Grilled Chicken Breast, page 131
Wild & Brown Rice with Herbs, page 167
Chili, page 110
Amaranth Crackers, page 178
Turkey & Carrot Tortilla Wrap, page 186
Salad Greens with Lemon-Oil Dressing, page 96
Amazing Sugarless Cookies, page 198

Implementing Your Healing Plan
How to Use this Book

I am a person who prefers to understand the whole picture before deciding if the book's material applies to me. Then I can see where I fit into the action suggested by the author.

This book offers just that. It is designed to provide you with the tools to understand the causes and implications of yeast overgrowth and food allergies. It investigates the strategies for reversing these conditions and helping your body to heal from damage that has occurred. It offers a step-by-step overall action plan for healing as well as two healing food plans (The Candida-Control Food Plan and The Rotational Food Plan). These plans allow for individual flexibility to achieve results.

To receive the full benefit from this book, I strongly recommend that you read Chapters One–Six in their entirety. A great way to do this is to read one chapter a day for 6 days/evenings. As you read, make notes in the margins or in a journal, regarding thoughts that seem to fit you. These could include symptoms you are experiencing, lifestyle healing strategies that seem appropriate and concepts that you want to think about further.

After reading the first six chapters, take a day off, resting your mind from health concerns. You have just spent a week reading and perhaps reading many new things – remember God rested on the 7th day. On this rest day, spend some time in prayer and listening to your God. If you are rested mentally and physically, deciding how to begin to implement the healing strategies is a bit less overwhelming. To make it even easier, there is a 4-step Action Plan in Chapter Two that is laid out for you step-by-step. Incorporate the concept of rest time between the action plan steps as well.

Before using the recipes, I suggest that you read Chapter 7 and the short introductions to each recipe section (pages 69, 94, 103, 112, 120, 127, 130, 142, 151, 160, 164 and 189). These few pages are filled with tips for understanding and using the recipes with ease. Also, the Appendices are filled with tools to help you easily find answers to your questions, especially if cooking is new for you.

Dealing with health-related issues can be overwhelming and exhausting, especially when you are not feeling well! Remember to read through this book one piece at a time. As we gain knowledge, we are more motivated and better equipped to move

> *"The man who removes a mountain begins by carrying away small stones."*
> —Chinese Proverb
>
> **Each step taken moves you closer to your desired result!**

into action. If you begin your journey with the attitude shown by the canary below—
"I may be backed into a corner, but I'm not giving up!"—you can achieve more than you
may have imagined. Remember that in some ways being in a corner is not a bad position
from which to start. The walls at your back protect you from that direction and the only
way you can go is forward. The canary shown just inside the back cover has used the tools
of commitment and knowledge to fight the battle against Candida-Related Complex and/or
food allergies and is doing well in his/her search for better health. Gather your resources
and begin the fight! You are in my prayers as I ask for success and encouragement for you
in this endeavor.

Sondra

Many facing health challenges such as Candida-Related Complex
and food allergies may feel discouraged and "cornered." If you begin
your healing journey with the attitude—

"I may be backed into a corner, but I'm not giving up!"

—more can be accomplished than you imagined.

CHAPTER ONE

Understanding the Nature & Causes
of Candida-Related Complex

On a daily basis, our bodies encounter numerous "invaders" which threaten to attack us with disease and infection. When healthy, our immune systems have the ability to ward off these threats and protect our bodies from invasion. However, when the immune system is weakened, chaos begins to reign. Often, the chaos goes undetected for quite some time. Eventually, enough disruption and destruction has taken place that our bodies begin to display an array of symptoms that indicate something is wrong. The symptoms are diagnosed and treated, sometimes without the root cause being discovered. Often, that root is an overgrowth of yeast. Because of the vast array of symptoms and potential complications, it is easy to misunderstand the nature of this yeast overgrowth or not to fully realize the impact it can have on our health. This misunderstanding, or incomplete understanding, then leads to inappropriate or incomplete treatment and, thus, the body is never given the chance to properly heal. This chapter seeks to demystify the process of yeast overgrowth by looking at the nature of yeast and its overgrowth and examining what causes that overgrowth to occur.

What is Yeast Overgrowth?

Yeasts, members of the Fungi Family, are part of the vegetable kingdom. In small amounts, they are necessary to the healthy function of our body by helping with digestion and the absorption of enzymes and vitamins.[1] When they live in harmony with other normal bacteria, yeasts are able to do the job they were created to do. However, given the right conditions, yeast, an opportunistic organism, multiplies easily and changes forms readily, becoming very invasive and destructive.[2] When allowed to grow freely, it is a vicious organism that can permeate and alter every organ function in the body, causing a vast array of symptoms (see next page). It is important to realize that while some symptoms are typical among most people who are experiencing an overgrowth of yeast, many symptoms vary significantly between individuals. Genetics, areas of illness and previous injuries may all leave certain parts of our body more vulnerable than others. Like a football player who feels his arthritis first in the knee that sustained an injury, we are most likely to feel the effects of yeast overgrowth in the areas of our body where we are most vulnerable.

Common Symptoms Associated With Yeast Overgrowth

Below is a list of common symptoms associated with yeast overgrowth.[3, 4, 5] As noted earlier, not all symptoms will be exhibited any one person.

Allergic Symptoms:

- acne
- asthma
- bronchitis
- chemical sensitivities (especially perfume and tobacco)
- dizziness
- earaches and itchy ears
- eczema
- eye irritation (burning and itching)
- food allergies and/or food cravings
- hay fever
- headaches
- hives
- middle ear infections (recurrent)
- mold allergies: symptoms flare up on damp days or in moldy places
- rashes
- sinusitis
- sore throat

Emotional & Mental Symptoms:

- anxiety, fretfulness, nervousness
- confusion
- concentration, lack of
- depression
- fatigue, lethargy, a "drained" feeling
- feeling overwhelmed
- "foggy brain," mental fogginess
- irritability
- insomnia
- loss of libido (loss of sexual drive)
- mood swings
- memory lapses, poor memory
- spaciness
- waking up tired in the morning

Gastrointestinal & Genitourinary Symptoms:

- abdominal pain/discomfort
- bloating/gas
- constipation alternating with diarrhea
- constipation
- diarrhea
- indigestion
- hormonal changes
- inflammations of the stomach lining and/or colon
- menstrual complaints, especially PMS
- nausea
- prostate problems
- urinary tract problems
- vaginal yeast infections

Other Physical Symptoms:

- appetite changes
- athlete's foot
- body odor
- canker sores/fever blisters
- diaper rash
- halitosis (bad breath)
- jock itch
- joint pain and/or swelling
- muscle weakness
- myalgias (muscular flu-like symptoms)
- nail fungus
- numbness, tingling
- rectal itching
- thrush (white coated tongue or white curdles in mouth)
- "tightness" in chest
- vision distortions
- weight loss or gain

What Causes Yeast Overgrowth?

As mentioned previously, small amounts of yeast are intended to live in our bodies in harmony with normal ("friendly") bacteria. The "friendly bacteria" are fragile organisms, which make up a vital part of a healthy immune system and are often described as the body's first line of defense. When the immune system is weakened, the friendly bacteria are affected. This upsets the delicate balance between friendly bacteria and yeast, giving the opportunity for yeast to overgrow. This yeast overgrowth thus weakens our immune systems further, creating a repeating cycle and a downward spiral in our health. A variety of factors can either weaken our immune system or in other ways affect the delicate balance of yeast and friendly bacteria, causing an overgrowth of yeast.

The factors that lead to yeast overgrowth are almost exclusively related to various forms of stress. Stress is perhaps the most underestimated and unrecognized culprit in hindering optimal health and it comes in various forms—physical, emotional and chemical. By putting our body in "alarm mode" stress keeps our immune systems on high alert, thus prohibiting our body from healing. Many stress factors in our lives are unavoidable. Yet, as they pile up, one by one, they place an increasingly heavy burden on our immune systems, and thus on our health.

Imagine for a moment that your body is like a river, your immune system is likened to the banks of the river and that the stress of life is likened to rain. As long as you do not have too much rain (stress), the river banks are designed to contain the flow of water. Likewise, our immune systems are capable of managing various stressors in life. But just like with the river, too much rain (stress) creates a flood state. Depending on how strong our immune system is and how many stressors are pouring in at once, we may be able to stop the overflow before it becomes too extensive. But if the overflow is allowed to continue, or if our immune system cannot manage the stressors quickly enough, the damage can become quite extensive (just like damage of a flood).

Some of us, by nature of our geographic location, occupation, temperament, culture, previous injuries, illnesses, genetics and circumstances while in utero (nutrition, exposure to chemicals, etc.), have rivers that are already quite full. Thus, some people face a flood stage early in life, while others may not experience flooding at all. The amount of damage created by a flood of stressors vary greatly from person to person. Thus, as we look at the stress in our lives, it is important to remember that they affect each of us differently at different points in our lives.

Physical Factors Affecting Yeast Overgrowth

Allergies and sensitivities, lack of restorative sleep, too much or too little exercise, illness and a lack of necessary nutrients are some of the physical strains that may impact our immune system. Allergies and sensitivities

Physical Factors

- Age
- Allergies and Sensitivities
- Diet Rich in Sugars and Refined Carbohydrates
- Lack of or Excess of Exercise
- Illness or Infection
- Nutritional Deficiencies
- Re-Infection by Sexual Partner
- Lack of Restorative Sleep

include reactions to foods, chemicals (i.e., fumes, scents, smoke and cleaning compounds) and inhalants (i.e., animal dander, molds, pollens and yeast). Allergies fight against the body's immune system and our ability to resist infection. Our twentieth-century American diet, rich in simple carbohydrates (i.e., refined sugars, white flours, white rice), artificial ingredients/products, "junk" foods and alcohol, encourages yeast overgrowth, not only by weakening the immune system, but also by directly feeding the yeast. Often sexual partners will both have yeast overgrowth but only one is diagnosed and treated, leaving a situation of re-infection. Our age even plays a factor. At birth, approximately 90% of the bacteria in the "gut" is friendly bacteria. Due to the lifestyle of North Americans, this number is reduced to about 15% by adulthood.[6]

Emotional Factors Affecting Yeast Overgrowth

Our immune systems are also burdened by emotional stress factors. Busyness, fear and suppressed emotions are some of the burdens that require the use of extra nutrients by our bodies, leaving the opportunity for us to become nutritionally depleted. This requires the immune system to work harder to protect our bodies against infection and the friendly bacteria are left unable to restrain the growth of yeast.

Emotional Factors
• Anger
• Anxiety
• Busyness
• Depression
• Fear
• Frustration
• Hormonal Changes
• Illness
• Loneliness
• Suppressed Emotions
• Worry

Chemical Factors Affecting Yeast Overgrowth

Air pollution, an overabundance of chemicals and additives in our food and water supply, tobacco usage and excessive use of medications, drugs and alcohol are all forms of chemical stress factors on our immune systems. Indoor air quality at home and work is affected by such things as air sanitizers, cleaning chemicals, formaldehyde-based products and second-hand smoke as well as insect sprays and lawn-care chemicals used around our homes.

Chemical Factors
• Air Pollution (including indoor air at home and work)
• Alcohol
• Drugs & Medications (Antibiotics, Birth Controls Pills, HRT, Steroids, Chemotherapy)
• Food Additives
• Herbicides/Pesticides
• Hormones
• Mercury and other Heavy Metals
• Radiation
• Tobacco Usage

Medications, steroids (including cortisone, prednisone, birth control pills and hormone replacement therapy [HRT]) immunosuppressive drugs (such as chemotherapy and radiation) and hormonal changes (during menstruation, menopause and pregnancy) all have the potential to suppress the body's ability to fight the overgrowth of yeast by either killing off the friendly bacteria or otherwise weakening the body's immune system. Bruce Miller, D.D.S., C.N.S., points out that steroids "nourish, stimulate and seem to make [yeast] more aggressive."[7] Ironically, stress itself can lead to increased chemical stress. "Many of the adrenal hormones produced when you are under stress are steroid molecules. Stress just feeds the problem and makes your symptoms worse."[8]

One type of medication that directly destroys the friendly bacteria is antibiotics. While antibiotics are very useful and important in treating bacterial infections, they kill off the friendly bacteria along with the harmful bacteria. The yeast, unharmed by antibiotics, is then allowed to grow out of control because the number of friendly bacteria has been reduced (see page 5). (This is why many women develop vaginal yeast infections after being treated with antibiotics.) Strengthening our bodies so that we do not harbor infection and require antibiotics in the first place is an important part of healthy immune system.

It is also important that we take antibiotics only when it is conclusively determined that a bacterial infection is present. Unwarranted use of antibiotics, or not taking antibiotics according to the prescribed instructions, may build a resistance to these medications on both an individual level and in society at large.

In addition to prescription antibiotics, we also consume antibiotics and steroids when we eat proteins from animals that have been fed commercial (non-organic) feed. Of the millions of tons of antibiotics used in North America, approximately half are found in animal feed.[9] Commercial feed contains antibiotics and steroids to prevent illness in animals and to help the animals gain weight in preparation for market. We do not take these antibiotics and steroids directly, but we ingest them because they are stored in the fat and protein cells of the animals. Poultry, meat, eggs and dairy products as well as farm-raised fish are foods that are at risk for containing antibiotics and steroids.

But medications are not the only chemicals we find in our food and water supply. Residues of herbicides and pesticides are found on many foods including fruits, vegetables and grains. The "run off" of these chemicals is also in our water. Food additives are used in abundance in processed and packaged foods to extend their shelf life. Increasingly high levels of mercury, an immunosuppressive agent, are being found, especially in cold water fish and drinking water. Another source of mercury is found in dental fillings. Scientific findings are showing that fungal infections may be linked to mercury hypersensitivity, including dental amalgam.[10]

What is Candida-Related Complex (CRC)?

The most common yeast found in humans is *Candida albicans*. Consequently, many people refer to *candida* when discussing yeast-related health problems. Some of the names that have been used to label this condition include: Chronic Candidiasis, Yeast Syndrome and Candida. George F. Kroker, M.D. of Lacrosse, Wisconsin, suggested Candida-Related Complex.[11] For simplicity, Candida-Related Complex (CRC) is used in this cookbook to describe any or all health problems attributed to the overgrowth of yeast.

Candida-Related Complex (CRC) is the complex of factors that make up the illness that results from an overgrowth of yeast. It is a chronic condition, which can cause extensive damage throughout the body. Because yeasts thrive in the warm, moist mucous membranes of our body, they are most often found in the digestive tract (including the esophagus), the genitourinary tract (including the vagina) and the sinuses. *Candida albicans* is also commonly found on the skin, in the form of eczema, diaper rash and jock itch. While most symptoms of yeast overgrowth are noticeable early on, they are often "simply annoying" and it frequently takes several years before the destruction is disabling enough to receive attention. Several factors may affect the severity of this systemic (or entire body) *candida* invasion.

Factor: The Release of Toxins

Candida albicans can exist in two forms. In normal conditions, it has a single, small round bud. When it divides, it breaks into two cells. However, when the yeast is growing out of control, it often begins to sprout an "arm" known as a hypha. This hypha then sends out pointed "branches," looking like a tree or shrub, and is known as mycelium.

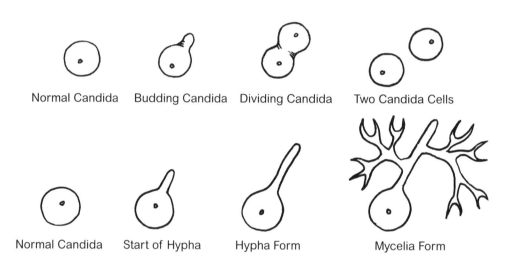

| Normal Candida | Budding Candida | Dividing Candida | Two Candida Cells |

| Normal Candida | Start of Hypha | Hypha Form | Mycelia Form |

These "branches" penetrate body tissues. When they do, they release 80 different chemical compounds (toxins) into our bodies.[12] The most toxic chemical released is acetaldehyde.[13] Zolton Rona, M.D. explains that acetaldehyde is a by-product of alcohol and produces many symptoms of alcohol toxicity.[14] It is very toxic to the brain[15] and produces many of the symptoms commonly described as "a hangover."[16] Don Colbert, M.D. notes that "acetaldehyde is related to formaldehyde ... [a] dangerous solvent" even to breathe. He likens the acetaldehyde production in our bodies to drinking liquid formaldehyde.[17] When acetaldehydes are produced, they can quickly get into the bloodstream. Their presence in the blood creates sensitivities to aldehyde odors (such as paints; glues and solvents; finger nail polish; and the insulation, carpets and pressed woods in many homes.) It is interesting to note that synthetic "progesterone [a component of birth control pills and often a part of hormone replacement therapy] alters the mucous membranes of the mouth, throat, lungs, vaginal vault and other mucous-lined passages. This alteration seems to make it easier for the 'roots' of the yeast to penetrate the lining" and release these toxins.[18]

Even more toxins are released when a yeast cell invades the wall of a white or red blood cell and causes the bacteria that has been collected by the white blood cell to be dumped back into the bloodstream.[19] A release of toxins also occurs when the yeast cell simply completes its lifecycle and dies.

The release of toxins puts a great strain on our liver, which tries to detoxify the compounds and protect our body from harm. When the liver is not able to process all of these toxins, they are stored in our body. As more toxins are stored, we become increasingly likely to experience allergic reactions to molds, pollens, scents, chemical fumes and/or smoke. These allergic reactions irritate the membranes and weaken the immune system, allowing the body to become more susceptible to infections (i.e., ear, sinus, throat, bronchial, bladder) that require the use of antibiotics and yeast is again encouraged to grow.

Factor: The Leaky Gut

When toxins irritate (inflame) the lining of the intestinal tract, they eat tiny holes through its protective lining. This causes the protective lining to break down, or erode, resulting in an increased permeability. This allows substances (yeast, pollens, undigested proteins, toxins) to pass or "leak" through, freely circulating into areas of the body where they normally would not go. This condition is known as "leaky gut" and triggers a state of continuous and prolonged stress on the immune system.[20, 21]

When toxins "leak" out of the gut, they by-pass the liver, providing the body with no chance to detoxify them. They can then migrate to other areas, such as the heart, joints and connective tissues, which adds stress by increasing the inflammatory process and often producing more body fluids.[22]

Factor: Other Illnesses

When our body is sick, or simply "fighting off an illness," and the immune system is focused on defending the body against the illness, good flora die and the yeast is allowed to multiply more easily. Consequently, people who are dealing with multiple illnesses or a specific, long-term illness, will have a more difficult fight against yeast overgrowth. It is also important to remember that even when minor infections occur in a person affected by yeast overgrowth, efforts to restrain continued overgrowth must be especially vigilant.

Factor: The Perpetual Cycle

The added stress created by the release of toxins, a leaky gut and other illnesses increases the burden on our immune system, perpetuating the continued overgrowth of yeast. The more widespread the yeast grows, the greater the extent of the body's reactions and the greater the stress.

As the earlier analogy of the river and the river banks implied, our bodies are designed to cope with some stress. Any one of the stress factors discussed in this chapter, in and of itself, might not pose much threat. And, when our bodies are healthy, our immune systems can handle several stressors at once. However, as the stressors continue to pile up and increase in duration and/or intensity, our immune systems begin to break down and situations are created which provide the opportunity for yeast to overgrow. These situations include the onset of infection, the depletion of nutrients and the release of toxins. They, in turn, increase the stress on our bodies by making us uncomfortable, keeping us awake at night, requiring various medications (steroids and antibiotics) and causing us to be fatigued, further depleting our stores of nutrients and releasing even more toxins. All of this added stress further weakens the immune system and the self-perpetuating cycle continues.

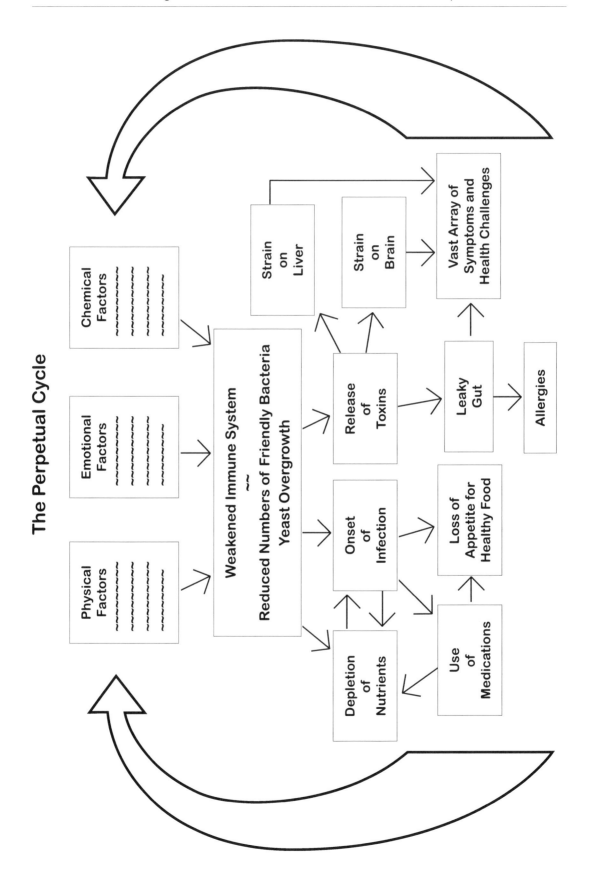

The Perpetual Cycle

As an additional piece of the cycle, ill persons often lose their desire for vegetables and animal protein, foods on which yeast does not thrive. Instead, they crave and often overeat foods on which yeast does thrive, particularly sugar-laden desserts and sodas. Women often experience these cravings a week prior to their menstrual period. For the health conscious person, food cravings may include honey, granola bars, whole-grain bread, cheese, dried fruit, nut mixes and peanut butter. Persons who follow a "junk food diet" may crave chocolate chip cookies, pizza, soda pop, alcoholic beverages or other foods made from refined carbohydrates (white flours and sugars). Because yeast thrives on sugar, these foods only add to the problem. The number of health problems increases and the cycle repeats again and again.

Yeast Visual

To better understand what happens in your body to cause an overgrowth of yeast, try this experiment using active dry yeast (bread yeast). Bread yeast and the yeasts found living in our bodies are different, but they desire the same living environment and have similar growth patterns. In a clear, two-cup measure, add one package of active dry yeast to one-half cup of lukewarm water (approximately 100–110°F.). Do not stir. Watch what happens over a three-minute period. Add one tablespoon of granulated sugar (again, do not stir) and watch. What you see is yeast in its inactive state and its reaction when given a warm, moist place to live and start to slowly grow. When fed sugar, it grows faster. In fact, within three minutes a population explosion occurs. After ten minutes, a thick layer of a rapidly growing yeast colony is found on top of the water. If the yeast is allowed to grow with further nourishment but the water becomes cold, the yeast stop reproducing. However, your digestive tract is always a dark, moist, warm place. So to control the yeast's growth in a weakened system where the friendly bacteria are reduced, omit foods on which yeast feeds (sweets and other simple carbohydrates) and include probiotic supplements (see pages 45–46), which enhance the friendly bacteria population.

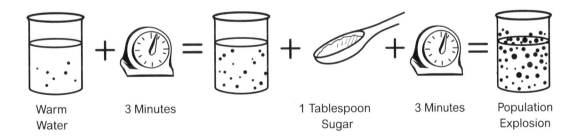

| Warm Water | 3 Minutes | | 1 Tablespoon Sugar | 3 Minutes | Population Explosion |

Who Discovered Candida-Related Complex (CRC)?

C. Orian Truss, M.D., an allergist and internist, first pioneered the connection between human illness and the yeast, *Candida albicans*. Other health-care professionals, including William G. Crook, M.D., have added additional research and information to the study of CRC. Their writings and research have greatly improved the understanding and treatment of the condition and led more medical professionals to accept the concept that yeast can cause health problems, bringing hope to thousands of desperate, distraught people.

Who Treats Candida-Related Complex (CRC)?

It is important to find a caring, nutritionally oriented health-care professional who has an understanding of the factors that can weaken the immune system and promote CRC. If needed, see www.canaryconnect.com for a listing of organizations that provide assistance in locating physicians who treat CRC.

Diagnosis of Candida-Related Complex (CRC)

Before diagnosing CRC, it is important to rule out other health challenges. If no conclusive diagnoses can be made, it is appropriate to pursue the diagnosis of yeast overgrowth. Patient history is key to making a correct diagnosis of CRC. Health-care professionals pay careful attention to the patient's history of medications (i.e., antibiotics, steroids, birth control pills) that upset the delicate balance between yeast and the friendly bacteria. They also consider the patient's symptoms, especially vaginal discharge or itching, itching or rashes around the genital/rectal area, nail fungus and/or "thrush" (a white coating on the tongue or white curds inside of the mouth). The patient's positive response to CRC treatments helps to confirm the diagnosis. There are also self-evaluation questionnaires that may help in the evaluation process (see www.canaryconnect.com).

Certain blood and stool tests are helpful in diagnosing CRC. The tests may include stool analysis for *candida*, abnormal bacteria and/or parasites, digestive markers and/or intestinal function. The blood tests measure antibodies, antigens and immune complexes. A list of laboratories that perform these tests is available on www.canaryconnect.com.

Understanding the Effects
of Yeast Overgrowth on Your Health

The list of symptoms often associated with CRC is numerous and complex (see page 4). But a listing does not often describe how one feels. Often, there is a general sense of "not feeling right" or the feeling that one is about to get sick. People with CRC tend to get "little" illnesses such as colds, the flu or respiratory viruses more frequently than those with a healthy immune system. Many people say that they are "sick and tired of being sick and tired." People with CRC may be labeled as hypochondriacs if they always talk about all their aches and pains. The symptoms may come and go as the body and mind adapt to feeling ill. Or the immune system may wax and wane as it struggles to deal with the demands placed upon it causing symptoms to appear and disappear. Often so many factors are involved that the symptoms are masked (such as with some food allergy reactions, see page 52).

One of the common complaints of people suffering from CRC is that they feel they are going to "explode" or "jump out of their skin." These feelings may also be accompanied by burning sensations and mood swings as well as feelings of spaciness. All of these symptoms are related to the central nervous system and are a direct result of toxins entering the bloodstream.[23]

The variety and number of toxins released into the bloodstream adds to the complexity and variety of symptoms. Dr. Bruce Miller points out that "each of these can affect different organ systems." He goes on to say that, "Other germs that attack our bodies just affect one system and produce one or two symptoms associated with that system. For instance, an intestinal virus generally releases one toxin which can cause nausea and diarrhea… *candida* releases not just one toxin,"[24] but more than 80![25] It is no wonder people with yeast overgrowth are often so tired! And, it makes sense that everyone with CRC will have a different combination of symptoms.

It is clear that the weakening of the immune system increases susceptibility to a variety of illnesses, allergies and health-related conditions (see next page). It also makes sense that the release of toxins can have a drastic impact on the liver and the brain, leading to an array of disorders. Of further importance is the fact that an overabundance of yeast causes inflammatory reactions which can be linked to asthma, heart disease, arthritis, Fibromyalgia, sinusitis and other inflammatory diseases. Depending on the extent of the overgrowth and the organ systems involved, the symptoms may seem almost insignificant, or they may be quite debilitating.

There are also certain illnesses that are likely to perpetuate yeast overgrowth. Dr. Zoltan Rona notes that "diabetes, hypoglycemia and other metabolic diseases [such as low thyroid] can be triggers for [yeast] proliferation."[26] Carol R. Dalton, N.P., and Hormonal Health Specialist, goes so far as to say that anyone experiencing frequent yeast infections should be checked for these conditions.[27]

"Diabetics frequently suffer from the effects of an overgrowth of yeast, particularly when blood sugar levels are not under control."[28] It is interesting to note that yeast thrives, especially in the vagina, when there are low levels of vitamin A in the body. Since the thyroid hormone is needed to convert the beta carotene in our food and supplements to vitamin A, it makes sense that people with a low-thyroid condition may not be making enough vitamin A and therefore may experience more yeast overgrowth.[29] As an example, when I took beta carotene supplements and ate carrots and sweet potatoes, my palms and eyelids would turn yellow, which is an indication that one is not converting the beta to vitamin A. Once I corrected a low-thyroid condition, I utilized the beta-carotenes in foods and supplements, which solved one challenge in my efforts to control yeast overgrowth.

Paul Faulk, D.C., notes that when an overgrowth of yeast breaks down the immune system, the adrenal gland system will eventually be fatigued. Since failure of the adrenal gland system negatively affects the formation of red blood cells, the spleen will also be fatigued. He goes on to note that when yeast "invades the spleen and the gall bladder, lupus-like symptoms are often produced."[30]

There is also evidence to show that cholesterol levels are directly linked to yeast overgrowth. Because cholesterol is one of the body's defenses against the toxins released by yeast, when high levels of yeast are present, the body produces more cholesterol. Zolton Rona, M.D., remarks that high levels of cholesterol are "a sign that something is wrong, not that [the cholesterol] has to be lowered by reducing cholesterol intake in the diet … studies support the fact that the use of antifungal therapies lowers cholesterol and reverses arteriosclerosis. Every cholesterol-lowering prescription drug is also antifungal."[31]

Illnesses/Health Challenges Related to Yeast Overgrowth

Below is a list of illnesses and health challenges that are often related to yeast overgrowth. A few have been explained in more detail in this chapter. For more information, consult "The Yeast Connection Handbook" by William G. Crook, M.D., and the "Complete Candida Yeast Guidebook" by Jeanne Marie Martin and Zoltan Rona, M.D.

• ADD/ADHD	• Hypoglycemia
• Addictions	• Immune Dysfunction
• Adrenal Exhaustion/Insufficiency	• Infertility
• AIDS	• Irritable Bowel Syndrome (IBS)
• Alcoholism	• Lupus (Systemic Lupus
• Arthritis	Erthematosus)
• Asthma	• Mercury and/or other heavy metal
• Autism	hypersensitivity and/or toxicity
• Cancer	• Mitral Valve Prolapse
• Chemical Sensitivities	• Mononucleosis
• Chronic Fatigue Syndrome	• MS
• Colitis	• Myasthenia Gravis
• Crohn's Disease	• Nutritional Deficiencies and some
• Diabetes	Nutrient Toxicity
• Eating Disorders	• Osteoporosis
• Eczema	• Pancreatic Enzyme Deficiency
• Endometriosis	• Parasitic Infections
• Fibromyalgia	• Premenstrual Syndrome, PMS
• Gastritis	• Prostatitis
• Gout	• Psoriasis
• Heart Disease	• SAD Disease
• High Cholesterol or very low	• Scleroderma
Cholesterol (under 150)	• Sinusitis (Chronic)
• Hydrochloric Acid Deficiency	• Thrush
• Hyper & Hypothyroidism	• Vaginitis
	• Vulvodyna (Vulvar Burning)

Summary

Yeast overgrowth is the direct result of a weakened immune system. When physical, emotional and chemical stress cause the immune system to be overworked and overburdened, friendly bacteria begin to die and the delicate balance between friendly bacteria and yeast is destroyed. No longer living in harmony with the friendly bacteria, the yeast begins to grow out of control, penetrating tissues and releasing toxins throughout the body. A vicious, self-perpetuating cycle begins. This cycle must be broken if full health is to be restored. Breaking that cycle takes time, patience and some creativity. In the next chapter, we look at ways to break that cycle as we begin our discussion of healing strategies for Candida-Related Complex.

CHAPTER TWO

Understanding & Implementing
the Healing Strategies
for Candida-Related Complex

In Chapter One we discussed the concept of the stressors in life being like the waters that fill a river and the immune system being like the river banks that contain those waters, provided they are high and strong and that the waters do not come too quickly. Those of us who experience yeast overgrowth experience a "flood stage." After a literal flood, there are two things to be done: 1) clean up the damage and 2) take measures to prevent flood damage from occurring again. The same is true when dealing with a yeast overgrowth: first we eliminate the yeast and toxins from the body tissues (the clean up) and, along side of that, build up the body's ability (immune system) to keep the yeast and toxins out (prevent future flooding).

This chapter introduces the healing strategies for both the clean up and the prevention of yeast overgrowth. Just as the type of equipment sent out to clean up after a flood depends on the nature and extent of the damage, so the healing strategies vary according to the individual. Not every strategy is necessary or appropriate for every person. A Healing Action Plan is outlined (see the next page) to provide a framework for healing.

Healing from Candida-Related Complex (CRC) involves both the elimination of yeast and toxins from body tissues and the strengthening of the immune system so that overgrowth does not happen again so easily. For a treatment program to be effective, it requires a multifaceted healing plan including "better nutrition, reduced stress, cigarette and alcohol cessation, aerobic exercise, spiritual and psychological therapy, a less contaminated/polluted environment, most often aggressive antifungal therapy"[1] and correction of "nutritional deficiencies, endocrine problems and food/chemical sensitivities."[2]

To help explain the purpose of a multifaceted healing plan, George F. Kroker, M.D. compares a person with CRC to one who has experienced a heart attack. During a heart attack, the entire cardiovascular system is involved and the attack is almost always the result of many years of wear and tear on the system. Therefore, a good cardiovascular physician not only focuses on the effects of a heart attack, but also on the underlying causes (i.e., high blood pressure, elevated cholesterol, history of smoking). Healing strategies include eliminating/lessening as many of these factors as possible to prevent a future heart attack.

Dr. Kroker views CRC as a "heart attack of the immune system" with immune system weakness and the underlying causes for it as the key factors. A very common scenario is one where the CRC patient had recurrent infections because of untreated allergies earlier in life. The use of antibiotics in treating these infections set up the patient to have more yeast-related problems. Simply treating CRC with a sugar-free food plan and antifungal medication may not be adequate if underlying issues such as allergies, exposures to chemicals at home and work, malnutrition and immune system weakness are not addressed.

Healing Action Plan

A Healing Action Plan is a way to organize the healing strategies to promote and maintain health. It incorporates strategies from two different categories: A) Lifestyle Changes (see pages 19–24) and B) Nutrition (see Chapters 3 and 4). In addition, there is a section on What to Do When You're Not Improving (see pages 24–26). Where you start, of course, depends on where you are in the process of attacking CRC and/or food allergies when you read this book (recently diagnosed, been at this for a while, thinking this could be your "problem"). There is also a synergistic factor between the healing strategies. For example, diet alone is not the answer for dealing with CRC or food allergies, but probiotics, nutritional supplements and antifungals without dietary restrictions do not work either. As Dr. Kroker describes, CRC is an attack on the immune system and many factors are involved. So, an effective action plan requires many strategies working together to reduce the "total load" on the immune system as well as to strengthen it directly. The river analogy continues: if we reduce the rain, we give the river banks a chance to do their job. Ideally, one could do everything (that is ideal for them) at once for maximum and fast healing. However, that in itself, could stress the body both physically and emotionally. Andrew Weil, M.D., notes that when a lifestyle change starts slowly and builds over time, the change can "take root and become an ongoing contribution to health."[3] Trying to do too many new things at once brings on an overwhelmed feeling which itself is a symptom of CRC. You may be doing several of these things already, or they may all be new. You may have considered several of these strategies before, or it may take awhile to decide that you want to give them a try. The important thing is to take things one step at a time, adding to what you have already established as you are able – physically and emotionally – to do so. Decide how much is best for you at each new step.

The Action Plan outlined is with the newly diagnosed person (or person exploring wellness) in mind. If you have already begun the healing processes, use the Action Plan as a guide for "filling in the gaps" and continuing on in your journey towards health.

Action Step 1: Belief That Healing Can Happen

Believing that healing is possible is essential and the first important step for recovery.[4] On your journey, you may experience periods of doubt and lack direction but choosing to be intentional about what you desire helps your focus. Establish your health goals and write affirmations to achieve them (see resource on www.canaryconnect.com to assist you).

A positive mindset helps you focus on healing. You can do everything here but if you do not have a positive attitude that healing is possible then none or very little will happen. Also, I feel that believing a strategy can have a positive effect is necessary. Take time to read the strategy descriptions, seeking to understand the theory behind them so that you have confidence to give them a try. If you need more information, seek out the resources offered on www.canaryconnect.com. Also, sign up for the FREE e-mail newsletter, e-CCNews (Canary Connect News).

Seek Warm Fuzzies

Reject Cold Pricklies

Seek support from understanding friends and family. Strive for warm fuzzies in your life and reject the cold pricklies that could bring you down. A warm fuzzy is a comforting hug (mental or physical) that lifts your outlook. A cold prickly is like that person who said to you, "It's all in your head. There's nothing wrong with you." Cherish warm fuzzies and seek them out at every opportunity.

Action Step 2: Avoidance of ...

To heal, there are several things to eliminate. For some (i.e., smoking, alcohol, steroids) it is advisable to be under doctor or clinical supervision. Of course, these cannot be eliminated overnight, but avoiding them has a major impact on your healing. Others (i.e., birth control pills, HRT) could be considered if you are not healing. (In most cases, omitting them causes more stress. Often the other healing strategies can overcome the effect these have on the body.)

<u>Alcohol and Tobacco Usage</u>: Alcohol feeds yeast. In addition, an excess of alcohol weakens our immune system and damages our liver, making it difficult for our bodies to handle toxins. Tobacco usage also weakens our immune system and irritates our sinuses. If you smoke, it is very important to quit as soon as possible. If you live with a smoker, it is equally important for him/her to not smoke in your living space.

<u>Antacids</u>: Antacids promote an acid-free environment in your digestive system, which encourages yeast growth. Stomach distress may not be caused by excessive acid at all, but the opposite condition—too alkaline an environment. An alkaline stomach does not provide the proper environment for digestion and therefore may allow undigested food particles to appear in your stool. Repeated occurrences of this situation can lead to constipation, diarrhea and nutrient deficiency. Pancreatic plant digestive enzymes or hydrochloric acid capsules may be recommended to aid in digestion as well as to combat yeast growth by returning your stomach to a proper acidic nature.[5] (See Improving Digestion, pages 21–22)

<u>Antibiotics and Steroids</u>: Since antibiotics destroy friendly bacteria, avoid their use unless absolutely necessary (page 7). Steroids nourish yeast growth, so make all efforts to avoid them. If you use steroids for medical conditions (such as for asthma), discuss with your physician how to gradually reduce their use. As mentioned in Chapter One, progesterone in birth control pills and hormone replacement therapy (HRT) is a steroid that encourages yeast growth and alters mucous membranes, making it easier for yeast to penetrate mucous linings. Of course, immediately discontinuing their use may bring on the additional stress (perhaps producing more steroid molecules) of an unplanned pregnancy or menopausal "hot flashes". If you are not improving after treatment for yeast overgrowth,

or if the overgrowth chronically returns, discuss natural methods of birth control or HRT with your physician. Also, note that plant-based progesterone preparations (available by prescription at compounding pharmacies) are a good alternative for HRT as they do not seem to have the same effect as the chemical-based hormones.

<u>Tight-Fitting Clothing</u>: Synthetic fibers and tight-fitting clothes used for exercise or dress (i.e., panty hose) create warm, moist places for yeast to grow. Instead, choose natural fibers that breathe and clothes that are not too tight.[6]

<u>Sugars</u>: This is discussed in Chapter Three and is a component of the next action step.

Action Step 3: Nutritional & Lifestyle Changes

Like the illustration on page 2, you are preparing for a battle and can win as the illustration on the last page depicts. Action Step 1 (positive attitude and being committed to doing the necessary actions) is your "sword" and you have begun handling the "roadblocks" by avoiding items listed in Action Step 2. Now, you are ready to begin Step 3: Nutritional (Food Plan and Nutritional Support) and Lifestyle Changes.

A. Candida-Control Food Plan—Stage 1 Outlined in Chapter Three

B. Nutritional Support Program—Foundation Basics (see Chapter 4, page 42)

C. Nutritional Support Program—Probiotics (see Chapter 4, pages 45–46).
Simply beginning a quality nutritional support program of the "basics" and probiotics often provides enough increased energy to continue forward with your healing strategies (i.e., carrying forth with your Stage 2 food plans and/or to initiate/increase an exercise program). Visit www.canaryconnect.com to order the recommended getting started package. If you prefer to discuss this package or order by phone, see page 261 for the phone number.

D. Optional: Lifestyle Changes (your choice). If you can emotionally handle more change now, choose one or two very easy healing strategies from the list of Lifestyle Changes (pages 19–24). Making dietary changes might be all some people can handle, but do think about how one little thing might help you handle the other stressors. Some examples on how to implement easy Lifestyle Changes are:
  • Eliminating pollens, dust, dander, molds and toxic chemical exposures in your home to reduce the "total load" on your immune system. A good air purifier solution is only a few clicks away on www.canaryconnect.com.
  • Asking a friend for a referral or scanning the yellow pages to be only one phone call away from the healing effects of a bodywork appointment.
  • Hanging a few notes around your home/workplace to remind you to breathe, chew slowly, pray, laugh, meditate, etc., is a very easy way to reduce stress, improve digestion or increase your oxygen intake, creating a natural antifungal.

Action Step 4: More Nutritional & Lifestyle Changes

Once you feel comfortable with Action Step 3 being a regular part of you daily routine, it is time for Action Step 4. Even if you are not ready for Stage 2 of the Food Plan, at least continue adding nutritional support as outlined and additional lifestyle changes.

A. Candida-Control Food Plan—Stage 2   Outlined in Chapter Three

B. Nutritional Support Program—Fiber   Your fiber intake most likely is increasing as you follow the dietary guidelines but it is almost impossible to consume enough fiber from food. It only seems wise to use a fiber supplement(s) of your choice. (See Chapter 4; page 46 for more information.) Start with a low dose and gradually add more each day. Take fiber supplements with plenty of pure water and spread out the amount taken throughout the day.

C. Nutritional Support Program—Antifungals   Advance purchase your antifungal approach so you are ready to begin it about 1 week after beginning Stage 2 of the Candida-Control Food Plan. See Chapter Four for choice options. Often your physician may prescribe his/her recommendation. If you desire, you may request a specific test (see www.canaryconnect.com for info) from your health-care professional to determine which antifungals are best for your specific type of yeast overgrowth.

D. Lifestyle Changes   Choose another easy or more complicated healing strategy from the list of Lifestyle Changes (see section beginning at bottom of page).

Continuing with Nutritional & Lifestyle Changes Action Steps

A. Candida-Control Food Plan   Continue with Stage 2 as outlined in Chapter Three, moving on to Stage 3 when it is the appropriate time for you.

B. Nutritional Support Program   Add **Essential Fatty Acids** and **Antioxidants** to your nutritional wellness program. It is easy to add flax to your program by including it as a "condiment" flavoring to steamed vegetables or raw vegetable salads. Depending upon your symptoms, add the **Target Support** supplements for additional healing (see Chapter 4).

C. Nutritional Support Program—Healing Leaky Gut   Usually one takes antifungals for about three (3) weeks. I recommend <u>that</u> <u>everyone</u> <u>take</u> supplements to heal leaky gut for at least a month following their antifungal treatment. See Chapter Four and www.canaryconnect.com for more details.

D. Lifestyle Changes   Continue to incorporate lifestyle changes into your normal routine. These changes help you immensely to prevent future *candida* overgrowth (also see Chapter 3, Stage 4: Prevention).

Lifestyle Changes to Use in the Action Plan

Lifestyle changes are activities that, for the most part, only take a little initiative and implementation and, with repetition, can become a habitual part of your routine. They focus on one of the following aspects of health: eliminating toxins and excess yeast; healing from the damage of yeast; reducing physical, emotional or chemical stress; and improving digestion. Focusing on these aspects of health strengthens the immune system, allowing your body to heal while also working to prevent future overgrowth. Each strategy is listed in alphabetical order (not by order of importance even though they are numbered).

Not all of the strategies are necessary for everyone. If you find that a particular strategy is causing excessive stress for you, it may not be beneficial to your healing (at this point or even ever). While other people can give you good feedback about how they see you responding to treatment, you know your body best and only you can listen to your body and make the best decisions for you. As you read through the healing strategies, note those that sound like they would be a good fit for you and your health concerns.

1. Bodywork Therapies

There are many different types of bodywork therapies. Highlighted below are two of the most popular forms, which are helpful for healing as well as for general health maintenance. For resources of other helpful bodywork therapies, see www.canaryconnect.com.

<u>Chiropractic Care</u>: Spinal misalignment can cause nerve interference and block the nerve impulses required for healing. Since nerves control all body functions (including immune system responses), structural stress weighs on the immune system and inhibits its proper operation. Several symptoms associated with CRC (i.e., headaches, sinus problems, allergies, fatigue, thyroid malfunction, constipation, diarrhea, indigestion, adrenal exhaustion) can also be warning signs of spinal misalignment. Also, spinal subluxations (vertebral dysfunction) can actually increase or facilitate nerve function which can be as damaging as inhibiting nerve function. This is especially important with allergies. A hyperactive nerve may cause an increase in immune system function thus creating an allergic response to a harmless substance such as pollen. This is often what leads to adrenal fatigue since the adrenal glands get over-stimulated for an extended period of time and basically "wear out." Regular chiropractic care is important to the healing process because it naturally restores proper nervous system function, reducing multiple symptoms and, thus, reducing stress. This helps the immune system to be stronger.

<u>Massage</u>: Therapeutic massage, including Shiatsu and Swedish massage, enhances circulation, aiding in the release of toxins. Massage relaxes the muscles, tendons and ligaments, allowing better range of motion, stress-reduction, increased blood flow and renewed energy. Since the circulatory system delivers nutrients to all parts of the body and removes toxins and waste, the increased efficiency resulting from therapeutic massage can greatly aid the body's healing process. By integrating regular massage into your health care routine, you enhance the effectiveness of all treatments, including conventional and alternative therapies.

"Healing Crisis"

There are times when the body is not ready for deep cleansing, especially when one is in a weakened state. Rapid cleansing can cause a "healing crisis." For example, one might feel headaches, tiredness, muscle aches or other symptoms similar to having the flu. A "healing crisis" can result from any healing strategy such as a deep massage. When you realize you are experiencing a "healing crisis" it is best to recognize it, identify the source and attempt to slow it down. In the case of a "healing crisis" brought on by a massage, drink plenty of water, giving the body a chance to flush out the excess toxins. Take care in cleansing to understand what your body is ready for. Sometimes a healing crisis can be a good thing that takes you to the next step in the healing process. Get the support of your medical advisors to help understand what is best for you.

2. Breathing Exercises

Dr. Andrew Weil says that, "Breath is a master key to health and healing."[7] In his writings, Weil offers easy breathing exercises, starting with a simple technique of noticing the contours of your breath cycle. This breath work is good for stress reduction, sleeping, meditating, improving digestion and oxygenating the body (oxygen is a natural antifungal).

3. Digestion Improvement

The purpose of digestion is to break down food so it can be easily absorbed and utilized by the body. Eighty percent (80%) of our immune system is contained in the intestinal tract.[8] In order for the body to have nutrients for healing, improving digestion is the most important healing strategy for CRC along with strengthening the immune system[9] (also targeting the intestinal tract). Some symptoms of poor digestion include indigestion, heartburn, burping, bloating, gas, abdominal cramps, bad breath, body odor, coated tongue, constipation and diarrhea. Even if digestion is normal, some individuals require digestive aids during CRC treatment.[10] "Undigested proteins, to which yeast and other allergens attach themselves ... often enter by way of the digestive tract. One way to prevent this is to take plant enzymes" before meals[11] as well as two hours after meals.[12]

Plant (pancreatic) enzymes function in both the acidic environment of the stomach and the alkaline environment of the intestine.[13] These enzymes include protease to break down protein, lipase to break down fat, amylase to break down starch and other carbohydrates, lactase to break down milk sugar and alpha-galactosidase to help prevent gas from forming when eating gas producing foods (i.e., beans, broccoli, cabbage). See www.canaryconnect.com for product recommendations.

In addition to using plant digestive enzymes, other things that improve digestion include:

- Honor your food and mealtimes with prayer and thanksgiving.
- Eat sitting down, practicing proper posture.
- Be intentional about having a nicely set table, pleasant conversation and/or peaceful music.
- Eat at a moderate pace. Chew food thoroughly, moving it from one side to the other, as digestion begins in the mouth. In a sense, this holds true for drinking a food product as well. One can not actually chew a food drink but you can consume it slowly, holding each swallow in your mouth for a time.
- Be mindful while eating, experiencing flavors and textures. This creates more self-respect and peace inside your body as well as in your digestive tract.
- If you, on occasion, eat "on the run," at your desk or the like, try your best to be mindful and chew thoroughly.
- Do not overeat.
- Do not eat when angry, upset or hurried as emotional upsets disturb digestion.
- Eat plenty of fiber daily (see Chapter 4).
- Drink plenty of quality water throughout the day but not too much with meals.
- Drink warm or cool beverages with meals as ice-cold drinks slow down digestion.
- Achieve and maintain adequate nutrient levels (see Chapter 4).

- Correct imbalance of intestinal flora—reducing yeast overgrowth and enhancing friendly bacteria (see Probiotics—Chapter 4).
- Heal leaky gut (see pages 25 and 49).
- Exercise to strengthen the muscles used in digestion and elimination. Avoid excessive physical exertion immediately before or after meals. However, a short, relaxing walk enhances digestion.
- Eating three square meals daily with no snacking is helpful for some while others do better with 5–6 smaller meals per day.
- Eating a balance of protein, carbohydrates and fats at each meal is helpful for some while a few do best following "Food Combining" principles (see Chapter 3).

If these measures do not solve your digestive disorder, I recommend special testing. See www.canaryconnect.com for more information and resources on diagnostic testing.

4. Exercise

Medical studies are proving that the lack of an exercise routine is one of the underlying causes of many health challenges. Regular exercise improves energy, increases circulation, improves digestion and relieves stress. It raises the brain's serotonin levels, which in turn reduce fatigue and improve our mood. When exercise is aerobic in nature, it creates more oxygen in the body, providing an environment in which *candida* cannot thrive. Also, sweat created during aerobic exercise aids in toxin elimination during treatment and helps the body release toxins lodged in the muscles. (Remember the importance of breathing and maintaining good posture during exercise.)

Before starting any exercise program, seek the advice of your physician, physical therapist and/or personal trainer for an individualized, monitored program. Choose an exercise time when your energy is routinely the highest. Begin slowly and increase gradually. An overall program consists of four parts:

1. Stretching
2. Weight training
3. Aerobic weight-bearing exercise (most experts agree walking is the best)
4. Gentle bouncing on a mini trampoline (5–15 minutes daily)

> "People who cannot find time for recreation, are obliged sooner or later to find time for illness." —John Wannamaker
>
> **What's Your Recreation Passion?**

5. Nasal Irrigation

One of the body's first lines of defense against disease is the thin layer of mucus lining our nasal passages. A nasal douche or irrigation is a natural, non-toxic, easy, effective and inexpensive way to keep this mucus layer moist, clean and healthy. It cleans the nasal passages of dusts, molds, pollens, chemicals, cleaners, fragrances, formaldehyde, smoke and other airborne contaminants that coat the mucous membranes. Nasal and sinus congestion, irritation and inflammation are also greatly reduced to allow for the healthy tissue of the nostrils to operate optimally. For detailed instructions, see www.canaryconnect.com.

6. Restorative Sleep! Oh, So Important!

Restorative sleep is becoming more highly recognized in achieving and maintaining health. Many with CRC, Fibromyalgia, Chronic Fatigue Syndrome, Chemical Sensitivities and/or other related health challenges have difficulty getting the appropriate rest and sleep they require to heal. They have difficulty falling asleep, problems waking up once asleep and/or wake up feeling they have not slept a wink. Our bodies heal and rejuvenate during the sleeping cycle. Did you know that your adrenals recover most while asleep those two plus hours before and after midnight?

My Personal Story: To overcome sleep difficulties, I use a clock with a sundown feature. The sundown feature slowly lowers the light level over a 30-minute period and then turns off to let you fall asleep gently. Most often, I am asleep within 15 minutes. On the occasion that I do not fall asleep by the time the light goes out, I reset the sundown feature for more time. If I wake up in the night and do not return to sleep immediately, I also reset the sundown feature. In the morning, the light gradually increases in intensity until it reaches full brightness. Then there is a gentle buzzer.

7. Stress-Reduction Techniques

Stress is modern-day "buzz" word in our culture when it comes to health issues and for very good reasons. As mentioned in Chapter One, stress puts the body into an "alarm mode" and does not allow the immune system to heal. Many of the adrenal hormones produced when under stress are steroid molecules, which encourage yeast growth. Prolonged physical stress robs the body of B-vitamins. In addition to B-complex, other supplements help the body to cope with stress. The amino acid, L-theanine facilitates the generation of alpha waves associated with an alert but relaxed state. The herb, ashwagandha enhances the body's ability to adapt to stress. A natural plant sterol, Beta-Sitosterol helps to blunt the adrenal hormones produced during physical stress. (See www.canaryconnect.com for resource.)

Along with supplements, a regular practice of other stress management techniques is essential. I suggest prayer, personal Bible study, laughter, regular exercise, enough restful sleep each night, breathing exercises, progressive mental relaxation, meditation, visualization, talks with an understanding friend and balancing your time indoors and outdoors, especially getting plenty of sunlight. To create a healthy body and lifestyle that resists stress and disease, take steps to add some of these practices to your daily and weekly routines. William G. Crook, M.D. recommends adopting a lifestyle with 15 to 20 minutes per day of meditation, breathing exercises and relaxation.[14]

8. Toxin Challenges on the Immune System

Chemicals in the air, water and food weaken our immune systems, especially when our livers are over burdened with toxins produced by yeast overgrowth. Many physicians[15, 16, 17] include reducing your toxin load as part of an overall CRC treatment program.

Food: Consuming meats and poultry raised on steroids and antibiotics destroys friendly bacteria. Instead, choose naturally-raised meats (and the dairy products) and poultry (and the eggs) raised without the use of antibiotics and growth hormones. Many times these foods have another advantage because the animals are often fed organically-raised grains.

Choose wild fish caught in "safe" waters since farm-raised fish can contain high levels of mercury, PCBs, pesticides and herbicides (see page 160). Choosing organically grown fruits, vegetables and grains as much as possible lowers the chemical burden on your immune system. In addition, organic foods often have a higher nutritional value because the soils from which they are grown are richer in nutrients than other soils. This is due, in part, to the fact that organic farmers rotate their crops to control insect infestation, which keeps single crops from depleting the soil of any one set of nutrients. Also, especially if you have food allergies, look for products that say "contains no GMO (Genetically Modified Organisms) ingredients."

Water: It is important to drink 8 or more glasses of water throughout each day. However, our drinking water supply often contains high levels of mercury and chemical "run off" from pesticides and herbicides used on farm fields and homeowners' lawns. In addition, city tap water contains chlorine and possibly fluoride, which generally depress thyroid function and the overall immune system.[18] Instead of drinking tap water, consider drinking some type of "purified" water, such as water that has gone through reverse osmosis, been distilled or is bottled (preferably in glass or hard plastic). If using bottled water, research the source of the water as all bottled waters are not purified and may contain pesticides or other contaminants found in regular tap water. Also, consider using toothpaste without fluoride. (See resource on www.canaryconnect.com for water filter and toothpaste)

Household Cleaners: The fragrances and chemicals breathed in from a variety of cleansers (i.e., chemical-based laundry detergents, dish detergents, multipurpose cleaners, fabric softeners, air sanitizers) add extra stress to the liver. Instead, use fully biodegradable, natural, plant-based cleaners (see www.canaryconnect.com for links to excellent cleaners) to lighten the load on your liver and to improve the indoor air quality.

Indoor Air Quality: In 1995, the Environment Protection Agency said that Indoor Air Quality was the number one environmental health concern. The pollution indoors is often 5–100 times higher than outdoor air pollution. To strengthen your immune system, lighten the load on your liver and improve indoor air quality, use a low-maintenance air purifier that filters/neutralizes pollens, dander, dust, dust mites, chemicals, molds, bacteria and viruses in your home and, if possible, in your workplace. (See www.canaryconnect.com for an excellent resource.)

Cookware: To reduce the toxic load, gradually replace aluminum, copper and non-stick coated cookware (formaldehyde-based) with stainless steal, cast iron, high quality enamel-baked and/or glass bake and cookware. Use a microwave oven less often or not at all as studies show that 90% of antioxidants are destroyed in microwave-cooked foods.[19, 20] If you use a microwave, do not use plastic dishes or plastic wraps to cover foods when cooking as the microwaves cause the chemicals from the plastics to leach into the food.[21]

What to Do When You're Not Improving

If your symptoms have not gone away after implementing the approximate 2-month Action Plan outlined earlier in this chapter, consider the following strategies:

1. Check to ensure you are following the basics:
- Proper attitude
- Avoidance of things that feed yeast (see pages 17–18)
- Taking enough of the right kinds of absorbable supplements (including probiotics and antifungals) (see Chapter 4)
- Following Stage 2 of Food Plan strictly and long enough (see Chapter 3)

2. Allergy Testing & Desensitization

Allergies fight against the body's immune system and one's ability to resist infection. For the immune system to be strengthened, it may be necessary to address the issue of allergies.

Mold Allergies: Allergies in general are a major problem for many people with CRC, but mold allergies seem to be the most problematic. It can be very difficult to distinguish between an allergic reaction and symptoms of yeast overgrowth. For example, a symptom (such as itching or burning eyes) can result from an allergic reaction to an airborne mold OR from a yeast overgrowth. Therefore, it is important to seek testing and treatment for allergies, especially to molds and the *candida* yeast.

Food Allergies: Many persons with CRC are sensitive to certain foods, additives and/or preservatives. Often food sensitivities and allergies are the result of your body's immune defense system reacting to the presence of incompletely digested food particles outside the gastrointestinal tract. Healing the leaky gut (see section below) and reestablishing proper intestinal flora (see Chapter 4, Probiotics) has a powerful effect on reducing food allergies. However, during this healing process it is best to avoid eating allergenic foods and to eat other foods on a rotational basis in order to lighten the load on your immune system (see Chapters 5 and 6).

Chemical Sensitivities: Many people with CRC are sensitive to chemicals, especially fragrances and formaldehyde-based products. Once normal yeast and friendly bacteria levels are restored and the yeast is no longer producing acetaldehyde toxins in the body, (Chapter 1, page 8) many allergic reactions to formaldehyde products will subside. However, it is best to avoid excessive and repeated exposure to these chemicals and products in order to aid the body in healing and prevent future overgrowth.

3. Healing Leaky Gut

Leaky gut is a common condition for those with CRC (see Chapter 1, page 9). It is important to promote healing in the gut because a healthy gastrointestinal lining is essential for keeping unwanted toxins and food particles from penetrating the wall and entering the bloodstream. It also is a key factor in proper digestion of food and absorption of nutrients. It is vital to the health of the immune system and liver.

Clearing the body of the overabundance of yeast, reestablishing friendly bacteria, following healing food plans discussed in this book and using nutritional supplements discussed in Chapter Four, all have great benefit to healing the leaky gut. However, if you are not healing consult further info on www.canaryconnect.com.

4. Improving Digestion

Since digestion can impact virtually all of your body's systems, try focusing more on ways to improve digestion (see pages 21–22 and resources on www.canaryconnect.com).

5. Liver Support & Detoxification

The liver is one of the most important, multifaceted and underrated components of the gastrointestinal system and is known as the body's primary filter/detoxification site. It makes bile to help with the digestion of fats and manufactures 1000 plus enzymes that are used in the digestion and absorption of nutrients. The liver also makes and controls some of the body's hormones. Many with CRC find that their liver function is very poor and/or that their liver is burdened by many toxins. Strategies that support liver function include:

- Drinking plenty of "purified" water to assist with flushing toxins
- Improving digestion and assimilation so that important nutrients reach the liver
- Increasing your intake of soluble and insoluble fiber (see Chapter 4, page 46)
- Regular aerobic exercise (aid in toxin elimination)
- Diminishing exposure to chemicals (i.e., pesticides; herbicides; paints; fuels; formaldehyde; solvents; industrial chemicals; chemicals/toxins in water, food, swimming pools and hot tubs)

If the liver is not able to clean the toxins from the blood, the stored toxins weaken our immune system. However, before intensive healing of the liver begins, it is IMPORTANT to make sure that the intestinal lining is healthy (see Healing Leaky Gut, pages 25 and 49) since a leaky gut can allow toxins being released from the liver to re-enter the bloodstream. For further assistance, consult resources on www.canaryconnect.com.

6. Parasites, Abnormal Bacteria & Other Illnesses

Often, if people are not improving, it is because the yeast overgrowth is a symptom of a root illness. That root illness may be a parasitic or abnormal bacterial infection, a metabolic disease (i.e., diabetes, hypoglycemia, low thyroid) or mercury or other heavy metal toxicity. If so, it is important to address these problems before one can successfully fight the yeast overgrowth. (See resources on www.canaryconnect.com.)

7. Re-infection

If you are not healing or are experiencing recurrences, it is possible that your sexual partner has CRC, so it is recommended that he/she seek treatment.

Summary

There are many healing strategies for CRC and they all work together. Think of them as a team of players. Not all players are needed all the time, but it is valuable to understand the advantages of each strategy to devise the most effective "game plan." That being said, there are two (2) team players that are essential to any CRC game plan: 1) a Candida-Control Food Plan and 2) quality food supplements. These components are so important that they are each given their own chapter (Chapters 3 and 4).

CHAPTER THREE

Understanding & Implementing
the Candida-Control Food Plan

Perhaps it seems unfortunate that foods can instigate the unwanted growth of *candida* yeast. The good news is that food can also be instrumental in eliminating excess *candida* from the body and preventing future overgrowth. If we reduce our intake of foods that feed *candida*, the yeast begins to starve and die. If, at the same time, we eat foods that nourish our bodies, we begin to strengthen our immune system, thus aiding the healing process and helping to maintain health. Because implementing a healing food plan is such an important yet challenging task, this chapter looks at ways to choose and stick with a plan despite the challenges.

A healing food plan is the single most important part of treatment for Candida-Related Complex (CRC), yet it can be the most difficult. Implementing a healing food plan usually involves a change in eating patterns and requires some thoughtful planning. Because processed foods contain many ingredients and chemicals that hinder good health, a healing food plan also requires making more foods "from scratch," which means more involved food preparation (see next paragraph for relief from this sentence). Changes can be difficult, planning overwhelming and preparation draining, especially for those already fatigued from CRC. On top of all of this, the person entering into a CRC food plan is faced with cravings since eliminating sugars (an important part) causes the yeast to "scream" for more. When a person with CRC says, "I just can't handle giving up all sugars," or, "I need my bread," there is a very real sense in which this is true. The yeast inside the person cannot live without these foods and can therefore make life rather miserable for the person in whom it is residing.

The task of beginning and continuing with a healing food plan is not impossible. In fact, while it may seem daunting at first, if carefully examined, it is found to be quite manageable and can be incorporated into your life. This chapter and Chapter Six lay out ways to organize your thoughts and make planning less overwhelming. The recipe section has several "Quick & Easy" recipes. There are also many Helpful Hints throughout the recipes and appendices that minimize your preparation time. Often, simply getting started with Stage 1 of the Food Plan and proper basic nutritional supplementation (see Chapter 4) brings enough relief from symptoms that you have the motivation and energy to continue with the treatment strategies appropriate for you to heal. The more yeast you get rid of, the sooner you will get better.

The Candida-Control Food Plan

A Candida-Control Food Plan focuses on eliminating foods that *candida* yeast thrives on. It is helpful to organize the plan into four stages: 1) Preparing to Win the Fight, 2) The Fight, 3) Challenging the Results and 4) Prevention. The dietary treatment for CRC is unique to the individual and it is therefore appropriate to make adjustments based on your personal needs. At the same time, this plan is devised to be general enough that anyone interested in treating CRC is welcome to use the plan "as is" with the expectation of success.

Stage 1—Preparing to Win the Fight

This stage is designed to give you time to prepare mentally and physically for Stage 2, The Fight. It is important to gather your resources, experiment with new foods and develop a battle plan. The easiest way to begin is to read over the foods allowed in Stage 2. Compare these foods with your current diet and compose a plan to gradually increase the foods that are allowed in Stage 2 and decrease the foods that are to be eliminated. The primary goal is to eat nutrient-dense meals while reducing foods that are processed, refined (especially sugars and white flour), packaged, fortified (see page 32), artificial, moldy (i.e., cheese, peanuts) and/or that contain dairy products or yeast. (Yeast-containing foods do not promote *candida* growth[1], but they are removed from Stage 2 of the plan because those with CRC often have allergies to yeast and its cousin, mold. Also, Gail Burton says that, "All yeasts have estrogen receptors and give off female hormones ... causing hormone imbalances."[2]) The process of reducing your consumption of these foods prepare you to eliminate them completely during The Fight (Stage 2). Ideally, this takes about 2–4 weeks; taking more than 4 weeks is not recommended.

Examples:

Currently Eating	Plans to Make the Change	Goal to Eat
Fruited and sugar-sweetened yogurt every day for breakfast	Purchase plain unsweetened yogurt to mix with the sugared variety, beginning with half/half, then $3/4/1/4$ then go to plain mixed with unsweetened fresh/ frozen fruits and liquid stevia OR enjoy Yogurt Smoothie (page 100)	No yogurt for at least the first 2 weeks of Stage 2, then after passing (yogurt, soy and fruit) food challenges, enjoy Yogurt Smoothie occasionally
Only eating 2 servings or less vegetables/day	Use Pilaf recipes to increase vegetables as well as whole-grains; good breakfast idea, especially during Stage 2	Eat 4-6 servings of a wide variety of fresh low-carb vegetables/day
Eating several sugar-laden desserts/week	Plan ahead to have fresh fruit available for dessert + make a carob cake with stevia as a good sub for chocolate	Eliminate all sugary desserts

Breakfast is an easy place to eliminate a lot of sugar and experiment with the tastes of "new" grains/nongrains. Hot cereal such as oatmeal, oat bran and brown rice can be enhanced by garnishing them with real or Clarified Butter, unrefined oils (i.e., flax), cinnamon, Nut Milks and dry roasted nuts/seeds (i.e., pecans, almonds, sunflower seeds, pumpkin seeds).

As you make dietary changes throughout Stage 1, begin eating a wide variety of foods and, if possible, do not eat the same food two days in a row. Also, it is best to begin omitting the common food allergens (i.e., wheat, corn, egg, dairy, soy) (see Chapter 5) and, of course, omit eating the foods that you know or suspect are food allergens for you.

As you begin to adjust your diet, also take the time to learn about some of the foods allowed in Stage 2 that may be new to you (see Appendix D). Check to see if they are carried in your local grocery store or health food market (if you cannot find something, the store manager is likely to be quite willing to order it for you). Begin to purchase these items so that you are not burdened by shopping and locating food items once The Fight has begun.

Stage 2—The Fight

This 4–6-week time period is when much of the yeast overgrowth is replaced with friendly bacteria because you are cutting off the yeast's food supply and taking probiotics (See Action Step 3C on page 18 and Probiotics on pages 45–46). The Fight time varies with each person. It is best to plan to be in this stage for 4–6 weeks, however, some can begin the next stage in only 3 weeks.

When possible, it is best to purchase organic and/or natural foods because this limits exposure to chemicals (herbicides and pesticides), antibiotics, steroids, chemical-based additives and foods with genetically modified organisms (GMO).

The beverage of choice for at least Stage 2 (but most likely all stages) is "purified" water (see pages 24 and 26), however, other beverages are acceptable (some in moderation). See pages 100–101 for some herbal tea and other options.

Stage 2 of the Candida-Control Food Plan is outlined in detail on the next three pages. For assistance in choosing Stage 2 recipes see page 68 for an explanation of the Stage 2 symbols and guidance included with the recipes. For Stage 2 meal planning ideas see Appendix C.

Wise Choice for Cooking Vegetables

When cooking vegetables, lightly steaming them is the method of choice. By bringing a small amount of water to a boil and immediately reducing the heat, you will allow the vegetables to gently cook, while retaining the vast majority of their nutrients. Boiling or using a pressure cooker reduces the nutrients quite substantially (47–66%).[3] Using a microwave can reduce the antioxidants by as much as 95%.[4]

Protein: A Crucial Building Block

Protein supplies are depleted very quickly when fighting CRC.[5] Because protein is required for the production of antibodies (to fight disease), enzymes (to digest food), tissue (for repair and growth) and hormones, it is an essential part of a healing food plan. Simply being low (not deficient) in a single amino acid (the building blocks of protein) can lower the response of your immune system by 30%.[6] In addition, protein supplies your body with energy and helps to regulate the pH level in your body (see page 37).[7]
Because protein is so vital to the healing process, it is important to help your body utilize the protein you ingest (through food, protein powders and/ or amino acids). Quality digestive enzymes are often a good choice (see page 21 and www.canaryconnect.com for resources).

Candida-Control Food Plan — Stage 2

Foods Allowed to Eat Freely (unless allergic)

<u>Vegetables</u> – fresh or frozen (not canned):

Amaranth greens	Cucumber	Radish
Artichoke	Daikon	Scallions
Arugula	Dandelion	Shallots
Asparagus	Eggplant	Spinach
Basil	Fennel	Sprouts, all kinds
Beet Greens	Garlic	Spaghetti squash
Bok choy	Kale	Squash, summer varieties
Broccoli	Kohlrabi	(i.e., crookneck, patty
Brussels Sprouts	Kohlrabi greens	pan, summer, zucchini)
Cabbage	Leek	Tomato
Carrots (raw only)	Lettuce, all kinds	Turnip
Cauliflower	Mustard greens	Turnip Greens
Celery	Okra	Watercress
Chard	Onion	
Cilantro	Parsley	
Collard	Peppers, all kinds	

<u>Legumes</u>

Adzuki beans		Navy Beans
Black turtle beans	Green Beans	Peas, edible pod varieties
Garbanzo beans	Kidney beans	Pinto Beans
	Lentils (green & brown)	Split Peas

<u>Fats</u> – unrefined and cold-pressed

Olive and coconut oil are ideal because they are antifungals. All other oils, except peanut oil, are acceptable, however, I do not recommend canola (because is a GMO food), corn and soy (because they are common allergens).

<u>Nuts/Seeds and their Butters</u> – purchase raw

Almond	Macadamia Nut	Sesame
Brazil Nut	Pecan	Sunflower
Filbert	Pine Nut	Walnut
Flaxseed	Pumpkin	

<u>Fish</u> – buy fresh/frozen, wild fish is best (not farm-raised). See page 160 for guidelines.

Cod	Orange Roughy	Sole
Flounder	Pollack	Etc.
Halibut	Salmon	

<u>Poultry</u> – organic or free-range

Chicken	Eggs	Turkey
Cornish Hen	Goose	Etc.
Duck	Pheasant	

Candida-Control Food Plan — Stage 2 (continued)

Foods Allowed to Eat Freely (unless allergic) continued

Red Meats – organic or wild game

Antelope	Pork (only uncured &	Veal
Beef	unsmoked)	Venison
Buffalo	Rabbit	Etc.
Lamb	Squirrel	

Sweeteners

Stevia, pure powdered form or liquid (watch ingredients)
Food grade vegetable glycerin (watch ingredients)

Foods Allowed in Limited Amounts (unless allergic)

Vegetables

This list varies according to every author/nutritionist/physician who recommends CRC diets. Usually these foods just need to be eaten in moderation during Stage 2 because their sugar content is higher than other vegetables.

Beet	Parsnip	Squash, winter varieties
Carrot (cooked in	Potatoes	except spaghetti (i.e., acorn,
moderation)	Pumpkin	butternut, pumpkin)
Celeriac (celery root)	Rutabaga	Sweet Potatoes

Legumes

Flat Beans	Peas, green shelled	Tofu
Lima beans	Soybean	Soy and other protein powders

Fats

Butter: Clarified Butter (see recipe and Appendix D) and/or unrefined oils are the better option during Stage 2. If you use unclarified butter, use in moderation.

Whole Grains/Nongrains & Starches

This is a difficult area to advise as everyone is different. It depends upon how severe your CRC seems to be and if food allergies are involved. I suggest that you omit the common food allergens (wheat and corn) and gluten-containing grains (see page 235) for at least a couple of weeks during Stage 2. This leaves the below foods. If you are following the 4-day rotation outlined in Appendix B, you have at least one grain/nongrain for each day.

Amaranth	Brown Rice (omit brown	Arrowroot Starch
Buckwheat	rice pasta, see page 38)	Tapioca Starch
Millet	Teff	Kudzu
Oat (see page 235)	Wild Rice	
Quinoa		

Candida-Control Food Plan — Stage 2 (continued)

Foods to Avoid During Stage 2

<u>Sugars & Sugar-containing Foods</u>: Candies, desserts, pastries, soft drinks, cookies, cakes, stuffing and anything refined and/or with a high sugar content. Read all labels of packaged foods to make sure there are no hidden sugars: brown, granulated, powdered, evaporated cane juice, dextrose, fructose, galactose, glucose, glycogen, lactose (milk sugar), maltose, mannitol, monosaccharides, polysaccharides, raw cane juice, sorbitol, sucrose, Sucanat (organic raw sugar), molasses, maple sugar/syrup, date sugar, honey, turbinado sugar.

<u>Milk & Milk-Containing Products</u>: Dairy is a common allergen and contains lactose, a simple carbohydrate which feeds the yeast. It is therefore omitted at least until you improve. Often organic plain unsweetened yogurt is tolerated during Stages 1, 3 and 4.

<u>Artificial Foods</u>: Sweeteners, preservatives, colorings, oils and other artificial foods.

<u>Black Pepper</u>: It is hard to digest.

<u>Caffeine-Containing Foods</u>: Coffee, tea, chocolate

<u>Fruits</u>: All fruits and fruit juices are best to avoid during Stage 2. However, unsweetened cranberry juice and freshly squeezed lemon juice are okay in moderation. If you find it too difficult to avoid all fruits, it is highly recommended to avoid moldy fruits (i.e., melons, grapes, strawberries, berries) and high glycemic fruits (i.e., bananas, pineapple, watermelon) as well as all canned, dried and juiced fruits. If you do choose to consume limited amounts of fruits that can be peeled, it is important to remove the peel during this stage, as the peel often harbors molds.

<u>Yeast and Moldy Foods</u>:

- Fermented or aged products (i.e., alcoholic beverages, cheese, cream of tartar, cider, root beer, malted foods)
- Vinegar-containing foods* (i.e., catsup, mustard, sauces, salad dressing, pickled vegetables)
- Moldy foods (i.e., mushrooms, malted foods, dried fruits, fruits that tend to mold quickly)
- Processed and smoked with nitrates (i.e., luncheon meats, hot dogs, sausage)
- Yeasted bread products (especially during the early part of Stage 2)
- Peanuts (including peanut oil and peanut butter) and pistachios. Both harbor fungus.
- Leftovers: Molds quickly grow on leftovers so eat them within 24 hours or freeze them immediately.

*Raw apple cider vinegar is tolerated and beneficial for some, but is still best to avoid during the early weeks of Stage 2.

<u>Miscellaneous Foods</u>:   Foods that are instant, processed, refined, fortified, "junk" and containing trans fatty acids. Fortified foods use synthetic nutrients (see page 40), which are toxic to the body.

Stage 2 Yeast Challenge. If your symptoms have cleared after following Stage 2 of the Food Plan for at least 2 weeks, you can do a yeast food challenge with Brewer's yeast (bread yeast) or vinegar. Watch closely for immediate and delayed reactions. If you do have reactions, continue to avoid yeast and moldy foods for 6 months in addition to

working with a health care professional to desensitize your body to yeast and molds. If you do not seem to have reactions, continue trying other yeast/moldy foods (i.e., catsup, sauces, salad dressings, mushrooms, tempeh, miso, apple cider vinegar) as well as gradually increasing amounts of each. See Stage 3 for more details about food challenges.

Stage 3—Challenging the Results

This stage gradually moves you from The Fight to Prevention. Your body's response to Stage 2, and the decrease and then absence of symptoms, helps you to know when you are ready to move into Stage 3. You may experience a favorable response to the Stage 2 food plan treatment in as few as ten days to two weeks. However, it is important to remember that although your major symptoms may disappear, the yeast overgrowth was probably well established before it was identified, and will have tenacious "roots" that take some time to remove. Persistence with the Stage 2 food plan and with other treatment protocols (discussed in Chapters 2 and 4) for at least 4-6 weeks (some require several months) is key to regain and maintain good health. If, after several weeks, most symptoms remain, or if, after several months, any symptoms persist (even minimally), move to "What to Do When You're Not Healing" (Chapter 2, pages 24–26) before entering Stage 3.

Once your symptoms have been cleared for at least 2-3 weeks, it is time to gradually challenge your body's response to individual foods. This tells you which ones may be tolerated. If you have not done the yeast challenge, it is a good one to try first.

Basically a challenge involves choosing a food that you have not eaten in at least two weeks. Many begin by challenging fruits. It is easier to sort out possible reactions if only one variable is challenged at a time. In the example below, a small peeled apple was selected. For the next 48 hours nothing else was challenged.

Keep a notebook to record the foods challenged and any noticeable reactions experienced, delayed or immediate (see example below). Also record other possible causes of the reaction such as environmental or stress factors (i.e., a headache could be a response to a food you are challenging, or it could coincide with a poor night's sleep the night before). If you are chemically sensitive, it is better to try food challenges at home.

Day Date	Time	Food and Form Eaten	Amount Eaten	Reaction & Possible Cause
8/25	10 am	Peeled apple	small size	no reaction for 2 days

After the approximate 48-hour period, if no reactions have been noticed, you can add the selected food to your list of allowed foods. In addition, the next time you try apple you may want to expand the challenge by eating the peel and again waiting 48 hours to check for immediate and/or delayed reactions.

Once a food challenge is completed and no further reactions are noticed, you may select another food. This time you may wish to select a cherry, blueberry or some other fruit with skin that you would not peel OR perhaps a totally new food category such as gluten grains.

After you have been able to eat many foods without noticeable reactions and have continued to do so without yeast-related symptoms for at least a month during Stage 3, try small amounts (i.e., 1–2 teaspoons) of alternative sweeteners such as agave nectar, brown rice syrup, raw honey and pure maple syrup.

When experimenting with yeasted foods, fruits and alternative sweeteners, I cannot emphasize enough how important it is to try only a small amount of one at a time and to wait for both immediate and delayed reactions (at least 48 hours) before trying a larger amount or another food.

If, during any challenge, a reaction is noticed, it is likely that either your body is not yet able to handle the increased intake of "sugars" OR food allergies are present. If a single food is suspected, eliminate that food for a while. If the reactive foods are high in carbohydrates and/or "sugars" (i.e., fructose, lactose), staying in Stage 2 for a while is advised. If multiple types foods are suspected, it is reasonable to assume there are food allergies and a rotational food plan (see Chapter 6) is strongly advised.

Stage 4—Prevention

Many of the treatments chosen for dealing with CRC become lifestyle changes, something that is implemented into everyday life. Nowhere is this as true as with the Candida-Control Food Plan. Stage 3 proves that life continues beyond Stage 2. A preventative diet adheres to the Healthy Eating Pyramid. This pyramid suggests that "sugars" and white refined foods are to be eaten only sparingly, that daily exercise, whole-grain foods, fruits and vegetables and plant oils are the foundation of the pyramid and that vitamins are recommended for most people.[8] Choosing to cook instead of eating prepared foods gives you control over quality (i.e., organic, additives, hidden ingredients). These preventative habits go a long way to providing your body with the necessary nutrients to maintain a strong immune system. They also help to keep the *candida* yeast from regaining ground and beginning to overgrow.

It is good to note that people who suffer from CRC are always more susceptible to recurrences. Knowing how to pay attention to the early warning signs and when to re-enter Stage 2 for a time is a valuable tool that also helps you to maintain good health.

* * * * * *

Battle Hints: Tips for Getting Through "The Fight"

- Prepare to fight the cravings: You may find it helpful to hide or give away foods you are not allowed to eat. If other family members desire them, move them to a cupboard that you do not open. If you are cooking for other family members, look for recipes in this book that they will enjoy too, or let them eat carry-out. Do whatever is necessary so you are not tempted to eat non-allowed foods.
- Listen to your body and avoid eating any foods you are craving, even if they are listed as acceptable foods. Chances are that you are allergic to the food or that it promotes yeast growth (e.g., fruit, sugars, breads) and the yeast is "yelling" for it.
- Retrain your taste buds. Remember that "new" foods may not taste good because *candida* clouds your taste buds and brain. After the initial healing (may be as little as 10 days), food cravings and feelings of denial begin to diminish. Also, try different

combinations. For example, you might not like teff cereal, but you might enjoy teff as a breading for chicken or fish. Continue to experiment, making a game of it.

- Plan meals with two words in mind: THINK VEGETABLES. Scan The Veggies section of the recipes (page 69–94) and choose a variety of vegetables to satisfy your taste buds. Complete your meals with small amounts of meat, beans and/or grains.

- Use alternative grains/nongrains to add breads to your meals. Dropped biscuits take only 5–6 minutes to prepare and 10 minutes to bake (page 174–175). Griddle breads (page 184–185) are a quick and easy way to add sandwiches to your meals.

- Skins of fruits and vegetables accumulate mold during growth. Scrub/wash the skins of all vegetables and fruits with biodegradable cleaner before peeling or cutting to avoid spreading the mold. (My recommendation for vegetable wash is a very diluted solution of Shaklee Basic H®. In a large bowl of water, I use only a half squirt of a mixture of $1/4$ teaspoon of Basic H in 1 pint of water. See www.canaryconnect.com for ordering. I also use this to wash grains before cooking.)

- Dispose of any fruit or vegetable with evidence of mold.

- Adjusting your food plan with the seasons may be necessary. For example, it was important for me to eat fewer fruits and other simple carbohydrates when it was rainy, damp and moldy outside for several days. Now that I do not have CRC health issues, this is not as much of a problem for me but I do notice that it enters into the "total load" factor in staying healthy in general. Keeping a food diary helps you notice these insights.

- Sometimes persons with CRC react to flours but have no problem eating the whole grain. There are two reasons for this reaction:
  1. The oil in flour stored at room temperature starts to deteriorate and mold multiplies.
  2. The surface dirt, mold and pollens that are removed when washing the grain before cooking were not removed before the grain was ground into flour.
  Before you give up on flours and baked goods, try purchasing freshly ground flour and freezing it immediately. If this does not help, try grinding your own flour (see recipe for making White Buckwheat Flour for tips on handling the grain before grinding).

- Read all labels when buying foods to check for "hidden" ingredients.

- Ground nuts/seeds are easier to digest than the whole nut/seed. If you have a sensitive digestive system, you may find it necessary to omit all nuts/seeds in the beginning stages of the food plan. In addition, CRC sufferers may not be able to tolerate supermarket nuts and seeds because of mold growth. I recommend organic nuts and seeds purchased directly from the grower. (See resource on www.canaryconnect.com.)

- Choose alcohol-free flavorings/extracts; read the labels for other hidden ingredients.

- Enjoy breakfast! This can be the hardest meal to plan. Some ideas include:
  —Hot cereal (see page 28 – Stage 1 – for ideas)
  —Steamed rice with cinnamon, ginger, curry powder and/or nuts
  —Denver Eggs with rice or potatoes (page 128)
  —Hard cooked eggs (page 127)

- Use the many Quick & Easy recipes (easily located by this symbol) and the Quick & Easy meals (see Appendix C) to minimize time and energy spent cooking.

- Use quick cooking pastas and grains/nongrains (i.e., millet, quinoa, buckwheat).
- Be creative with snacks. Try raw vegetables, a small peeled apple or pear (when appropriate), celery sticks with nut butters (avoid peanut butter) or tahini, raw (dry-roasted) nuts/seeds (i.e., almonds, filberts, pecans, sunflower seeds, pumpkin seeds). See Appendix C for more ideas.
- Enjoy your meals and make them attractive on the plate. Relax before, during and after your meals to aid digestion. Eating slowly and chewing every bite also aids digestion. In order to relax before a meal, try to plan and prepare some things in advance (i.e., prepare fresh vegetables for cooking ahead of time to avoid being rushed during meal preparation).
- Everyone is different and only you can listen to your body and make the best decision for you. Since Candida-Related Complex (CRC) often clouds your ability to concentrate and make decisions, keep a notebook to record the foods you are eating. Record date, time, food eaten, amount eaten and any noticeable reactions experienced as well as any possible other causes such as environmental factors.

Day/ Date	Time	Food & Form Eaten	Amount Eaten	Reaction & Possible Cause
8/25	6 pm	Ground Beef Patty Corn w/ margarine Sliced Tomatoes	1 medium 2 large ears 1 large	headache began approximately 30 minutes after meal that lasted for 2 days—suspect corn and margarine

- Some tips for eating at a restaurant or banquet:
  1. Plan ahead. Call ahead for the menu, particularly if you are attending a banquet.
  2. Skip the appetizer.
  3. Order unflavored mineral water instead of wine or a mixed drink. Consume carbonated water only on occasion as it interferes with the absorption of calcium.
  4. Use oil and a squeeze of lemon for salad dressing. Ask what comes on the salad before ordering to avoid bacon bits, croutons, cheese, etc.
  5. Order animal protein without sauce—broiled dry is the best choice. Grilled or broiled steak, chicken or fish is a good option. Check that no marinades or breadings are used. Take your own Clarified Butter and have the restaurant use it instead of their vegetable shortening in preparing your dinner. Also, ask them to scrape the grill to remove most of any remaining shortening and/or food products.
  6. Order steamed vegetables instead of bread. Take your own muffin, bread or dessert.
  7. Order your baked potato dry and take your own Clarified Butter or flaxseed oil. If you usually enjoy your baked potato with sour cream, try substituting Sunflower Mayo or Creamy Italian Dressing. Also, do not eat the potato skin.
  8. If you can tolerate herbal tea, sip a cup while others are eating dessert. Or eat slowly, more slowly than the others at your table, so you are still enjoying your meal while they are having dessert.

Considering & Integrating Other Healing Food Theories

Low-Carb Theory

Some health-care professionals suggest a low-carbohydrate food plan, ranging from 60–100 grams of carbohydrates per day. Consume these carbohydrates evenly throughout the day and gradually increase the amount as you improve.

Potential problem: A prolonged high-protein/low-carbohydrate food plan may cause problems for individuals with CRC in the form of persistent fatigue, weakness, excessive weight loss and/or malnourishment, all of which hinder exercise. Also, prolonged high-protein consumption can cause kidney failure and excessive red meats can be a problem for those with inflammatory health issues (see page 142, intro to Red Meat recipes).

Potential problem: Complex carbohydrates aid in the prevention and treatment of high blood pressure and heart disease, osteoporosis and digestive disorders. As quoted in The Yeast Connection Cookbook, Sidney M. Baker, M.D., said that "eating a diet rich in complex carbohydrates is the best way to promote normal bowel flora in the person who has some immune dysfunction."[9]

Often the better solution is to choose only complex carbohydrates (i.e., whole grains/ flours, beans, higher carbohydrate vegetables) over the simple carbohydrates (i.e., fruit, sweeteners, refined flours).

Gluten Theory

The gluten in gluten grains converts readily to glucose in the body, which feeds the *candida* yeast[10] (see Appendix D for more information about gluten). In addition, some grains are common food allergens.

For these reasons, choose only the gluten-free grains during Stage 2 of the Candida-Control Food Plan, adding gluten grains gradually during Stage 3. Test the grains carefully as you introduce them and watch for immediate and delayed reactions (see pages 52–53).

Blood Type Theory

This theory outlines that the lectins in foods react differently with each of the blood types and therefore set up the body for various health issues. Even though this does not address food allergies and/or yeast overgrowth directly, some with CRC and/or food allergies have seen improvement to their overall health by choosing foods that are compatible with their blood type while others see no improvement or a worsening of overall health issues. It is most certainly not the complete answer but it is at least worth considering.

Acid/Alkaline Theory

Both acidic and alkaline environments are necessary for health. While many health problems result from an environment that is too acidic, it is also true that many health problems are the result of an environment that is too alkaline – not acidic enough. (Ironically, the symptoms can be very similar, see "Avoidance of Antacids" in Chapter 2.) Our various body tissues and fluids have specific pH levels (the degree of acidity) necessary for optimal health. If one part of our body is too acidic, other parts will try to compensate, often becoming too alkaline. Discovering and providing what your body needs can be instrumental in helping your body to heal.

Food Combining Theory

Some people advocate the use of food combining, a strategy that combines foods that are digested in a similar fashion, so as to make the digestive process easier. While resources for more detailed information about this theory can be found on the web at www.canaryconnect.com, the basic guidelines are as follows:

- Eat fruit by itself
- Eat proteins (i.e., meat, dairy, fish) separately from starches (i.e., grains, flours, sugars)
- Eat beans separately from dairy and meat

Perhaps the biggest complication with food combining comes for those who have hypoglycemic tendencies. Eating a high glycemic food, like a banana, without other foods can cause brain fog and fatigue shortly after eating. If you choose to practice food combining, it may be possible to keep your blood sugar levels stabilized by only eating the lower-glycemic carbohydrates and fruits (i.e., blueberries, cherries, cranberries).

Glycemic Index Theory

The glycemic index (GI) is an alternative way to classify/rank foods containing carbohydrates. It assists diabetics in using foods to control their blood sugar (glucose) by noting how individual foods affect blood sugar levels. The carbohydrates in foods that digest faster have a higher glycemic index. The theory for those with CRC is that higher-glycemic foods might also tend to feed the yeast since they raise blood glucose levels. In contrast, the lower-glycemic foods digest more slowly, releasing glucose gradually into the bloodstream, not satisfying the yeast. The advice is not to stop eating higher GI foods but to eat them in smaller portions and in combination with low GI foods so that the glycemic load (GL) is low. Glycemic load refers to how a particular serving size affects the body by "the quantity of carbs that enters the bloodstream."[11]

When I classified the foods to eat freely and those to eat in limited amounts, I took GI and GL into consideration. (These also factored into considerations for Stage 2 recipes and menu ideas found later in the book). Recipes with brown rice pasta were not included in Stage 2 because it has one of the highest GI rankings of all foods (a 92 out of 100) and has a high GL ranking as well.[12]

Summary

Though dietary changes and restrictions can be difficult and overwhelming, they are crucial to the movement towards health; the rewards are well worth the sacrifice. No matter what other healing strategies you employ, if the food supply to the yeast is not cut off, the other strategies will have little long-term benefit. At the same time, choosing nutrient-rich foods provides your immune system with ammunition for The Fight. Nonetheless, it is not often possible to get the quantity of nutrients required from food alone. Thoughtful additions of quality supplements maximize your efforts to bring healing and maintain good health. This strategy is discussed in the next chapter.

CHAPTER FOUR

Understanding & Implementing
a Nutritional Support Program

The healing strategies for yeast overgrowth consist of killing off the excess yeast and strengthening the immune system so that the yeast is no longer allowed to grow out of control. To accomplish these tasks, a strong nutritional support program is essential. Dr. Bruce Miller says that, "Therapy is directed at holding yeast growth down while nutritional supplements, diet and lifestyle changes encourage the healing of your altered metabolic processes and immune defense systems."[1] We discussed lifestyle changes (Chapter 2) and dietary changes (Chapter 3). In this chapter, we explore a nutritional program that kills off the excess yeast and supports the immune system, therefore enhancing the effectiveness of the other healing strategies. Nutritional supplementation works at the cellular level, targeting problems at their source. The material presented in this chapter provides a basic structure for selecting the types of supplements your body needs. For specific recommendations, please visit www.canaryconnect.com.

Food Supplements: What They Are
and Why They Are Important

Food supplements are exactly that – nutrients from food-based sources that supplement your diet. They do not take the place of a healthy diet but, rather, they enhance a healthy diet, allowing the healthy food you eat to be used more effectively. Many wonder why these supplements are needed – shouldn't we be able to get everything we need from food itself? The answer is "no" and the reason is comprised of several factors:

- **Greater demand (quantity):** Yeast overgrowth depresses the immune system, thus requiring a greater quantity of nutrients than a healthy immune system.
- **Difficulty with absorption:** Yeast overgrowth interferes with the body's ability to absorb nutrients, thus increasing intake needs.
- **Depleted nutritional value of food:** The nutritional values of food are often not what we expect. Long periods of storage, shipping conditions, processing and some cooking methods deplete foods of many nutrients. Broccoli containing high amounts of calcium when picked may have little calcium left when it actually reaches your plate. In addition, a recent study showed that farming practices can lower the nutritional value of food. The study showed that produce grown today often has less nutritional value than when it was grown in 1950, sometimes by as much as 38%.[2]

- **Limited diet:** In order to promote healing, the Candida-Control Food Plan (especially Stage 2) restricts foods, even some that are considered healthy. For those with food allergies, the dietary intake is restricted even more. These restrictions limit some of your body's access to key nutrients and, thus, supplements are beneficial.
- **Starting point:** Because of the factors listed above, your body has likely been deprived of necessary nutrients for quite some time. Supplements provide the jump start necessary to catch up.

How to Choose Quality Food Supplements

The quality of the food supplements we choose has a dramatic impact on their effectiveness. Because a body infested with yeast has difficulty absorbing nutrients, it is extremely important to avoid synthetic supplements and to choose food supplements that are "bio-available" (readily absorbed by the body). It is also important that they have the correct amount of the nutrients. Quality supplements are—

- **From natural sources:** food and plant-based (not synthetic); free of artificial colorings, artificial sweeteners and artificial preservatives; co-factors found with the nutrient in nature must be present in the supplement (i.e., see vitamin E, page 44). Since there is no industry standard to define the term "natural," it is important to select a company with integrity you can trust.
- **Processed appropriately and without alcohol and chemicals:** some processing methods, alcohol and chemicals kill the natural enzyme life and destroy nutrients.
- **Made from quality raw materials:** pure and organic,[3] picked at peak time of maximum nutritional quality. It is also good to look for products that use non-GMO (Genetically Modified Organisms) ingredients – especially if you have food allergies.

Food-Based Supplements and Food Allergies
My Personal Story

Because of my food allergies, I avoided food-based supplements for over 10 years, instead using a variety of "hypoallergenic" synthetic vitamins/minerals. During that time, my nutrient levels continued to decline, especially the zinc, calcium and friendly bacteria. While my health had stabilized, it had not improved. I finally decided I needed to give the food-based supplements a try. The positive impact on my health was unmistakable. Within two months, the friendly bacteria levels increased from 0 to between 2+ and 3+ (4+ is the highest test level). Also by two months, the symptoms from the severe zinc deficiency (i.e., allergies and depression) were lifting and later tests showed my levels of zinc and other nutrients (many of which had been low) were in the normal range. In just four months, my blood calcium levels went from being very low to being in the normal range. Also, I was not suffering with stomach aches after taking the supplements as I had been with the synthetic brands. Having nutrients that were easily accessible to my body was exactly what I needed. Since supplement companies with good integrity offer a 100% money back guarantee, it is well worth the try!

- **Manufactured by a company with strict quality control:** conducts testing to confirm:
    - o bio-availability (how quickly it disintegrates and is absorbed)
    - o what percentage of the nutrients are getting from the mouth to the bloodstream and body cells
    - o that the supplement contains exactly what is on the label
    - o that all raw materials are pure and that they are free from pesticides, fungicides, herbicides, heavy metals (i.e., mercury) and other toxins
    - o that the product is fresh and remains fresh under proper storing conditions and for guaranteed time period as indicated on the label (expiration date)
- **Manufactured by a company with high integrity:** committed to scientific research (not marketing research) and the company's research is published in peer-reviewed scientific medical journals (i.e., American Journal of Clinical Nutrition, Journal of American Medical Association, FASEB Journal), not just advertising journals
- **Backed with a 100%-satisfaction guarantee**

"Priority"

"Those who cannot find the resources for good nutrition eventually experience illness."
—Sondra Lewis

"Bio-availability"

An independent study by the Today Show on NBC looked at how quickly multi-vitamins disintegrated. One brand disintegrated in 17 minutes. The others took 50 minutes to $4^1/_2$ hours[4] — long enough to have passed through the digestive tract and be eliminated from the body without ever being used! For nutrients like folic acid, which need to be absorbed while still in the stomach, every minute counts!

"The Cost Factor"

It is hard enough to choose quality supplements, decide which ones to take and integrate them into your daily routine. To factor in the seemingly high cost is often another source of concern and dismay. The healing that supplements provide, however, will in the end, reduce the amount of money necessary for medications, doctors' visits and other treatments for illness. Remember, your body responds best when healing strategies are added gradually. Taking one step at a time allows your budget to adjust as well.

- - - - -

Dr. Bruce Miller points out that, "A strong program of supplementation could cut billions from the medical costs of our nation...a nation that can afford to spend 30 million dollars on candy for its children on one Halloween night can afford food supplements for the children and themselves throughout the year."[5]

- - - - -

"We talk too much about the cost of good nutrition and too little about the cost of bad nutrition."[6]

Supplements for the Action Plan

As suggested in the Healing Action Plan (page 16), it is highly recommended that supplements be introduced gradually to your daily routine. This gives your body a chance to adjust to the new healing agents and allows you to more easily notice the effects. The supplements discussed in this chapter are divided into the following categories:

1) Foundational Basics
2) Probiotics
3) Fiber
4) Antifungals
5) Essential Fatty Acids (EFAs)
6) Antioxidants
7) Healing the Leaky Gut
8) Target Support (digestive, liver and immune system support and inflammation reducing supplements)

1) Foundational Basics

The foundational basics do what their name suggests: they are the basic nutrients that provide the foundation for healing and prevention. If the basics are not in place, your body has difficulty absorbing and fully utilizing other supplements. While each of these basic supplements is foundational to healing, it is important to introduce them one at a time.

The basics consist of:
- **a multi-vitamin/mineral**
- **additional B-complex**
- **extra vitamin C**
- **extra vitamin E (with selenium)**
- **extra zinc**
- **calcium with magnesium (especially for women)**
- **iron**

<u>Multi-Vitamin/Mineral</u>: A good multi-vitamin/mineral is important for everyone. The basic guidelines include choosing one that contains 100% of the Daily Value (DV) of most key vitamins and minerals. Some nutrients (i.e., calcium, magnesium) are too bulky to compact them into a pill small enough to swallow.

<u>B-Complex</u> (thiamin, riboflavin, niacin, B_6, folate/folic acid, B_{12}, biotin and pantothenic acid) is very important, because many aspects of CRC specifically deplete the body of the B-vitamins. First of all, friendly bacteria produce a large portion of our bodies' biotin. When an overgrowth of yeast reduces the number of friendly bacteria, biotin production is also reduced.[7] Furthermore, many of the things that allow yeast to overgrow (i.e., antibiotics, corticosteroids, birth control pills, sugar, refined carbohydrates, alcohol, stress) also deplete the body of the Bs.[8, 9] Even without yeast-related health issues involved, it is hard to maintain adequate amounts of the B-vitamins in the body. These vitamins are easily lost or destroyed in storage, shipping, handling and cooking. Because they are water soluble, they also leave the body easily, requiring regular replenishment.

Yet, these vitamins are essential building blocks for healing. Not only do they lift our mood, helping us to cope with the challenges of healing, they strengthen the immune system; reduce sugar cravings; help the body to cope with stress; aid in the growth of red blood cells; regulate the use of fat, protein and carbohydrates; and bind with toxins produced by dying yeast, which helps to reduce the symptoms of die off (see page 47). In addition, B-vitamins help convert food into energy; without them, our energy levels are lower. They also provide important support to the liver and other organs. The broad base of support that the Bs provide, and the lack of an adequate supply of B-complex in a person with CRC may be one of the reasons CRC patients have such a vast array of symptoms. Finally, when biotin "is present in ample quantities,"[10] yeast is much less likely to convert to the invasive, mycelium form.[11]

The B-vitamins should be taken only as a complex, and not as single vitamins (i.e., do not take only biotin). These vitamins work together and they need each other to do their jobs properly. If you increase one without increasing the others, the one you increase may enlist the help of the others (even though ample supplies are not there), thus depleting the body's stores of the ones you are not increasing. The end result is an increased deficiency.

A Note About Yeast in Supplements

Since some supplements include a yeast component, it is important to understand how to use these supplements during CRC treatment. Ingesting yeast does not cause the yeast in the body to grow,[13] so simply having an overgrowth of yeast is not reason to avoid it. However, many people with CRC have, or develop, an allergy to yeast.[14] Consequently, it is possible that a reaction will occur when yeast-containing products are taken. To challenge this, take the yeast-containing supplement at a time when you are not trying any other new foods, supplements or healing strategies. Also make sure that you are not having new exposures to molds and chemicals. If you tolerate the supplement well for 3-7 days, you can assume that it is safe for you. If the supplement causes a reaction, consider the type of supplement described below.

- - - - -

Dr. Bruce Miller suggests that those with yeast allergies choose supplements that "have been processed in such a way as to kill the yeast and remove the part ... that causes the most allergic reactions" or to treat the objectionable parts of the yeast organism and "render them harmless."[15] (Many people react to the cell wall of the organism, but not to the cytoplasm of the cell.[16]) An example of a supplement treated appropriately for someone with CRC would be a B-complex containing Brewer's or torula yeast. Any part of the yeast not removed or treated during processing dies in the acidic environment of the stomach where B-complex is broken down for use in the body.[17]

<u>Vitamin C</u>: Because it is water-soluble, Vitamin C should be taken evenly throughout the day to maintain adequate levels. (A sustained-release formula is great for this provided the release is timed properly and synthetic materials are not used.) It is also depleted by stress (including infection, fatigue, anxiety, extreme temperature changes), alcohol, smoking and birth control pills.[12] Vitamin C is a natural antihistamine and stimulant of white blood cells,

providing help with allergies and viral infections. It also strengthens adrenal function. It should always be taken with a bioflavonoid and is most effective against allergies when in a buffered form. Being a weak acid, high doses of vitamin C kill yeast, bacteria and parasites.[18] In addition to increasing the absorption of many other nutrients (including iron and calcium), vitamin C is an antioxidant and works to make vitamin E more effective. Together they "stimulate the immune system to be more aggressive against yeasts, fungus and other invaders."[19]

Vitamin E with Selenium: Sometimes called the nutrient in search of a disease,[20] vitamin E has been proven to enhance the immune system and to help heal tissue. Vitamin E is actually a complex, like the Bs, and is most beneficial when derived from natural vegetable sources. Unlike their synthetic counterparts, these natural sources offer all of the known forms of vitamin E.[21] Vitamin E is fat soluble, offering great protection for cell membranes and is most effective when taken with selenium and vitamin C. Selenium is also important in aiding detoxification,[22] stimulating the response of antibodies[23] and producing thyroid hormone, three important benefits for those with CRC. Since it is easily depleted from soils that are overused, supplementation is becoming increasingly important.[24]

Zinc (15–30mg/day beyond the 15mg provided by a multi-vitamin): With antioxidant properties and involvement in more than 90 enzymatic reactions,[25] zinc can be very beneficial to healing the gut. Zinc is also instrumental in allowing for rapid cell division.[26] This is beneficial in the repair of tissues, further aiding the healing of the gut. Since zinc is intricately involved in strengthening the immune system, it is key in the production of "T-cells,"[27] it is a beneficial aid to healing and helps to ward off colds and viruses while also diminishing the impact of allergies. Bruce Miller, D.D.S., C.N.S., says that "to get over the candida problem as quickly as possible, do not skimp on the zinc."[28]

Calcium and Magnesium: Working in balance with each other, calcium and magnesium interact with cells and help the muscles to contract and expand (deficiencies can lead to leg cramps, common to CRC). Proper amounts of calcium can help in the reduction of lead toxicity[29] and can promote restful sleep. Because calcium is involved in hundreds of enzymatic reactions, it is a crucial element to have for healing.[30] Deficiencies in both calcium and magnesium can lead to nervousness, irritability, fatigue, stronger PMS symptoms, poor concentration and depression. Yet, yeast infections are known to specifically interfere with the processing of magnesium within the body.[31] Because your body can only absorb a certain amount at a time, it is best to take your calcium/magnesium supplements a few hours before or after your multi-vitamin so that you receive the most benefit from both sources.

Iron: A reduced amount of iron in the bloodstream often results in general fatigue and weakness. You only have to be <u>low</u> in iron for these symptoms to present themselves; you do not need to be anemic. Other symptoms may include heartburn, diarrhea, headaches, dizziness, overall itching, heart palpitations and a sore tongue.[32] The range of symptoms comes from the fact that iron is required to carry oxygen to the body's cells. Not only is this oxygen an important antifungal, but it is also required in large amounts when the immune system is engaged in a battle. You do not want to fight CRC without an adequate means to transport the oxygen to where it needs to go. Iron absorption is increased when consumed with vitamin C. Since iron is a mineral that can be toxic if taken in quantities too large, it is important to refrain from self-diagnosing an iron deficiency and to obtain blood work before adding extra iron to your regimen.

2) Probiotics

Probiotics are the friendly bacteria that support the immune system and help the body to keep the growth of yeast in proper balance. They are required to reestablish the normal flora balance in your digestive tract. Probiotic means "for life." Common forms of friendly bacteria include *Lactobacillus acidophilus* (*L. acidophilus* or *L. dophilus*) and *Bifidobacterium bifidum* (*B. bididum* or *L. bifidus*). Probiotics are intimately and actively involved in our overall health, enhancing the body's immune response to protect us from numerous diseases.

A healthy population of these friendly bacteria allows them to convert food to organic acids, keeping the pH of the gut slightly acidic, which is very healthy. They like and live best in an acidic environment, just the opposite of what yeast needs to survive. This results in the crowding out/ starving of *candida* and other bad bacteria.

> ### The Potency of Probiotics
>
> People have said that though probiotics are beneficial in treatment, they cannot kill off excess yeast without the aid of an antifungal. That is true of many probiotics. However, a quality probiotic, with proper encapsulation, is potent enough to eradicate some yeast. Consequently, die-off symptoms (see page 47) are likely when beginning a quality probiotic (see www.canaryconnect.com for resource). Several of my clients have found this to be true and it was the case for me as well. I have actually had clients, with mild to moderate CRC symptoms get rid of the excess yeast without using antifungals because the probiotics were so effective.

Benefit is also received from the fact that "minerals such as calcium, zinc and iron can become bound to fiber. When the probiotics ferment (eat) these fibers, the minerals are released for the body's use."[33] Probiotics also produce bacteriocins (killer chemicals), which target bad bacteria (i.e., yeast, *E. coli*).

Probiotics are very fragile and die quickly in heat, light, air, moisture and stomach acid. Some companies guarantee a culture count at the time of manufacture, but by the time it reaches your intestines, it may actually contain no cultures. Choose a probiotic that guarantees live bacteria to your intestines by having an encapsulated delivery system to protect the bacteria until they reach the intestines. Because probiotics may produce die-off symptoms (see page 47) it is important to start slowly and increase gradually. Often, the healing dosage is 2–4 times the dosage listed on the bottle. Later, a maintenance dosage is usually no more than two doses/day.

Some probiotics can be found naturally in foods, especially in whole milk products, including yogurt, milk, butter and sour cream. However, the live bacterial cultures die very easily and may not ever arrive in your intestines. And, since milk intake may be limited (milk sugars are avoided during at least Stage 2 of the Candida-Control Food Plan and many with CRC are allergic/sensitive to milk), food is not a reliable source for probiotics.

That being said, some foods can enhance the growth of friendly bacteria and prevent the spread of bacterial infections. These foods and food supplements are usually high in chlorophyll, presenting a green color and include alfalfa, barley green, chlorella, spirulina, green Kamut® and blue green algae. They also boost energy levels and the immune system.[34]

FOS (fructo-oligo-saccharides), a white powder that is half as sweet as sugar and very simple to use, is another natural probiotic enhancer (often referred to as a "prebiotic"). Because the FOS molecule is too large to be recognized and digested by the body, it reaches the intestines intact where it can be broken down and used by the beneficial bacteria. At the same time, FOS cannot be used by *candida*, other yeasts, salmonella, *E. Coli.*, or certain other harmful bacteria.[35, 36, 37, 38] Due to this characteristic, FOS is often beneficial in the treatment of leaky gut syndrome as well as CRC. However, if you test positive for abnormal bacteria such as *Klebsiella* pneumonia and certain other bacteria, it is recommended to omit using FOS until after treatment since some of these bacteria feed on the FOS.[39] After successful treatment for abnormal bacteria, many people can use FOS as a probiotic enhancer without the return of *Klebsiella*. However, it is important to do subsequent testing for confirmation.

3) Fiber

Fiber is particularly beneficial to those healing from CRC because it binds with toxins – those already in the body and those produced when the yeast dies (*candida* die off). This bonding prevents the toxins from being reabsorbed into the body and helps to reduce the burden placed on the liver. Fiber also works to help "friendly bacteria" become reestablished in the colon.[40]

It is important to get a balance of soluble and insoluble fiber. The soluble fiber combines with water which dilutes the toxins[41] and slows the digestive process so that starch and sugars are not absorbed as quickly. The insoluble fiber is the part that serves as a natural laxative, helping the stool to become bulky and to move through the system more quickly, aiding in the removal of toxins from the body.

Most health organizations, including the National Cancer Institute, recommend about 30g/day of fiber.[42, 43] However, the average American only gets 5–10 grams.[44] Though all plant-based foods contain fiber, it is very difficult to get enough fiber from food. Also, since processing removes fiber, most of the highly processed foods that are so readily available contain very little fiber. Therefore, a quality supplement containing a balance of soluble and insoluble fiber is important. Possible sources include: rice and oat bran, psyllium seed and husk, pectin, fruit and oat fibers, cellulose, fennel seed and soy fiber. According to Leo Galland, M.D., "The best tolerated and safest fiber is pure microcrystalline cellulose (not even methyl cellulose)."[45] It is important to start slowly, taking note of your bowel function and increasing fiber amounts daily until regular elimination and stools of proper consistency are obtained. Because fiber may slow the absorption of medications, it is wise to take these one or two hours after consuming a large amount of fiber.

4) Antifungals

Depending on your sensitivities, you may need to rotate the antifungals that you use, taking each one only every other day, every third day or even every fourth day.

Prescription Antifungals:

Treatment of CRC generally requires the use of one or more antifungals to kill the yeast. Dr. Crook, expert in identifying and treating CRC claims that, prescription antifungals "literally punch holes in *candida* cell membranes ...keeping them from multiplying and raising large families. The azole drugs [Diflucan, Sporanox and Nizoral] may also keep the little round yeast cells from putting out branches (mycelia)."[46] Talk with your doctor about implementing the use of prescription antifungals. The ideal time to do this is about 2 weeks after beginning Stage 2 of the Candida-Control Diet. For prescription antifungals to be effective, they generally need to be taken for 2–6 weeks.

Non-Prescription Antifungals:

Garlic: has wonderful antifungal properties as well as being a natural antibiotic. It has properties that are anticarcinogenic, antiparasitical, antiviral and anti-inflammatory. It helps to prevent heart disease and lower cholesterol, removes toxins from the body, stimulates the immune system, stops the reaction of free radicals and regulates blood sugar. It is important to use a supplement that is processed under temperature-controlled conditions so that the allicin in the garlic (the active component that fights *candida*) is not destroyed.[47] Use with parsley to deodorize breath.

Coconut Oil and Olive Oil: If you are able to tolerate these every other day, simply alternating between the two will provide a good antifungal base. Bruce Fife says that, "Coconut oil is...a natural antibacterial, antiviral, antifungal and antiprotozoal food."[48]

Bentonite: "Acts like a sponge in drawing toxins and other waste out of the intestine."[49]

Caprylic Acid: Derived from coconut, caprylic acid is readily absorbed so time-released or enteric coated formulas help to provide gradual release throughout entire intestinal tract.[50]

Tannalbit: Zinc tannins are effective in reducing intestinal yeast.[51]

"Die Off"

Healing is a process and that involves many ups and downs. With CRC, one common experience is a temporary worsening of symptoms as you succeed in killing off or starving out the overpopulation of yeast. This reaction, called die off, is the result of your body reacting to the toxins and products given off by the yeast cells as they die. The greater the amount of yeast destroyed, the worse these symptoms can be. It may take several days for the body to rid itself of the resulting dead yeast. As the yeast dies off, your body is able to continue moving towards health, so be assured that this is part of the healing process.

- - - - -

To ease these die-off symptoms, Dr. William G. Crook recommended beginning with the strict sugar-free diet for a week or so before beginning antifungals.[52] Other things to reduce these symptoms include the use of liver supportive supplements (such as milk thistle), antioxidants (especially Vitamin C to the extent your bowels are able to tolerate it), B-complex, extra probiotic and extra fiber supplements.

Citrus Seed Extract: discourages *candida* from growing in the intestinal tract. Zolton Rona, M.D. claims that these extracts "can be as effective as nystatin and caprylic acid for gut fungal overgrowth."[53] They are also beneficial in treating parasites. Paramicocidin is a supplement derived from grapefruit seed extract and is sometimes available through health food stores or health care professionals.

Coenzyme Q$_{10}$: helps the body to maximize the use of oxygen, a natural antifungal

B-Complex (including PABA, folic acid and biotin): "PABA is synthesized by friendly bacteria in healthy intestines. [It] is essential for the breakdown and utilization of proteins as well as the formation of red blood cells. It stimulates intestinal bacteria to produce folic acid, which has a strong antifungal effect."[54] Biotin helps to reduce the growth of *candida*.

Psyllium (source of fiber): cleans out fecal buildup[55] and "flushes the gastrointestinal tract of fungi and their mycotoxins."[56]

Foods That Can Be Considered as Natural Antifungals (important that they be organic and free of chemicals from processing):

"Green foods" rich in chlorophyll (i.e., alfalfa, barley green, chlorella, spirulina, blue green algae, green Kamut®) also, **kelp, dulse and seaweed**: rich in iodine and selenium which are able to inactivate fungi[57]

Oils: olive oil, castor oil, peppermint oil, oil of oregano, fish oils, borage oil, evening primrose oil, black currant seed oil, flaxseed oil, coconut oil, tea tree oil

Pau D'Arco Tea: best ingested on an empty stomach, this nutritional tea may be enjoyed warm or cold and helps to reduce yeast growth (see page 101)

Soy: the isoflavones are antifungal

5) Essential Fatty Acids (EFAs)

Candida expert Dr. William Crook says that "almost without exception, physicians treating patients with yeast-connected health problems have used EFA supplements as an essential part of their treatment program."[58] EFAs including Omega-3 (eicosapentaenoic acid/ EPA) and Omega-6 (gamma linolenic acid/GLA) fatty acids are available in vegetable forms (flax seed oil, evening primrose oil, GLA and borage oil) and animal form (fish oils). These essential fatty acids are important for reducing inflammation and rebuilding cells. They also help to reduce cholesterol, regulate hormones and fight infection.

Flax: A good source of EFAs, it is recommended that one to two tablespoons of flaxseed oil be taken each day.[59, 60] It may be taken by itself, but because most oils are not palatable in their individual forms, it is easier to include the flaxseed oil on the food you eat. Its tasty, buttery flavor is good poured on pancakes, muffins, potatoes and vegetables. When using flaxseed oil for its nutritional properties, do not add it before cooking because the oil losses its beneficial factor when heated above 300°.[61]

Fish Oils: Choose fish oils that are mercury-free. The company should be able to verify that the raw materials were also tested for mercury and rejected if even trace amounts of this heavy toxin were found. Simply adding a substance that prevents the mercury from being absorbed by the body is not sufficient or advised.

6) Antioxidants

An antioxidant is a "substance that scours the body for unstable oxygen molecules called free radicals, which can cause cell damage."[62] Antioxidants are found in dark green and orange vegetables as well as in whole grains. Some of the best antioxidants are vitamins C and E and the carotenoids.

<u>Vitamins C and E</u>: see pages 43–44

<u>Carotenoids</u> (lutein, zeaxanthin, lycopene, astaxanthin, alpha carotene and beta carotene) and <u>Flavonoids</u>: These helpful nutrients aid in detoxification of the liver and increase immunity.[63] One of the most common carotenoids, beta carotene, has several powerful properties when helping the body resist disease:

> ### Another Danger of Synthetic Supplements
>
> Synthetic vitamin A supplements can be toxic, especially for those with a poor functioning liver. A natural vitamin A causes no toxic effects.[64]

- It is an extremely powerful stimulant to your immune system;
- It blocks cell-damaging free radicals and acts as a reservoir for vitamin A;
- It promotes the growth and activity of fighting cells;
- It aids in the development of healthy mucous membrane tissue, providing support to the immune system and making these tissues strong and less likely to be invaded by the fungal form of *candida*.

Interestingly, the absorption of vitamin A is often blocked by antibiotics and cholesterol lowering drugs.

7) Healing the Leaky Gut

Healing the leaky gut is extremely important to the overall healing from CRC and/or food allergies. Carol Dalton, N.P., goes so far as to say that attempting to detoxify the liver before the gut is repaired could be dangerous, as toxins that are released from the liver could permeate the intestinal wall and circulate throughout the body.[65]

She suggests thinking of supplements that support the integrity of the gut lining "as a glue or cement to plug up the microscopic holes caused by the *candida*."[66]

<u>L-Glutamine</u> is an amino acid that promotes the growth and repair of tissue in the intestinal tract. In addition, it works to regulate the pH level in the body and aid in the reduction of free-radicals and inflammation. It can be found in animal and plant protein, though it is often destroyed during cooking.

<u>DGL (deglycyrrhizinized licorice)</u> maintains the integrity of the gut lining.

Often people with leaky gut use one or more of the anti-inflammatories listed on the next page to reduce inflammation in the gut, which synergistically works with the healing supplements.

8) Target Support

Depending upon your symptoms, the following may be helpful.

<u>Digestive Enzymes:</u> Digestive plant-based enzymes help break food down and allow for a more complete absorption of nutrients. They also help to prevent constipation, bloating and digestive discomfort. Also, if food is only partially digested, it can ferment into alcohol and sugar which feeds the yeast, or can putrefy and produce additional toxins leading to inflammation.[67] (For more info, see Improving Digestion, pages 21–22.)

<u>Anti-inflammatories:</u> Inflammation is often a chronic problem for people with CRC. Not only are tissues in the gut inflamed by the overgrowth of yeast, the many toxins in the body cause inflammation throughout the various organ systems. Arthritic and asthmatic symptoms are some of the most notable examples. While many of the lifestyle changes made to treat CRC help to reduce inflammation, there are some foods and food-based supplements that will aid this process as well and promote overall healing.

Garlic: see page 47
Grape Seed Extract: reduces histamine production which helps to reduce inflammation triggered by allergic responses[68]
Ginger Tea: soothes and repairs gastrointestinal tissues that have become inflamed by CRC

EFAs: see page 48
Bilberry: has anti-inflammatory and anti-bacterial properties
Alfalfa: a rich source of many healing properties, including anti-inflammatory properties and is a natural antihistamine
Vitamin C: see pages 43–44

<u>Liver Support:</u> Visit www.canaryconnect.com for suggestions and resources related to testing liver function as well as finding dietary, nutritional and herbal support.

<u>Immune System Support:</u> While all supplements indirectly support the immune system by reducing the stress of infection and inflammation, helping to eliminate toxins from the body, supporting the growth of friendly bacteria, delivering oxygen and/or repairing cells, some supplements target the immune system directly. Vitamin C with bioflavonoids, zinc and Echinacea are especially helpful. Coenzyme Q_{10} is another vital compound in the human body that helps to boost immunity and support energy production in every cell including the heart.

<u>Saw palmetto:</u> is important for men with prostatitis associated with yeast infections.[69]

Summary

When our bodies are affected by yeast overgrowth, quality nutrient support is necessary for our bodies to heal. Despite this requirement, our bodies are often deficient in nutrients – we do not have the minimum maintenance amount, let alone the extra supply to begin healing. It is important to eat a nutrient-dense diet, however, this is not enough. We need supplements that are easily absorbed and safe for us to process and use. Choosing to integrate quality supplements into daily life is a crucial step in the journey towards health.

CHAPTER FIVE

Understanding the Nature & Causes of Food Allergies

Food allergies and sensitivities can be very difficult to recognize and diagnose. They produce a variety of symptoms and reactions, both immediate and delayed. These reactions can be clearly linked to offending foods, additives and preservatives, or they can be "hidden" or "masked." Often, the reactions stem from a condition called leaky gut. Because leaky gut is often both the result of yeast overgrowth and the perpetuator of yeast overgrowth, CRC and food allergies often go hand-in-hand. This chapter describes what food allergies are, how they evolve, how they manifest themselves, how they are diagnosed and how they are treated.

What is a Food Allergy?

An allergy is an individual's adverse response to a substance that does not typically cause a problem for others. Common allergens include dust, pollen, animal dander, food and chemicals. For someone with a weakened immune system, the underlying cause of CRC, repeated exposure to a substance can eventually cause the immune system to reach a state where it cannot deal with the exposure and often the result is allergies. This scenario is even more likely in those with a predisposition to allergies based on family history. Allergies sometimes appear relatively late in life, however, thinking back, you may remember the subtle effects of allergies since childhood.

The most common food allergens are those foods eaten frequently. The typical American diet includes one or more servings of beef, chocolate, citrus, corn, egg, milk or dairy products, peanuts, shellfish, soy, tomato, wheat and yeast each day. If you read the labels of prepared foods, many of these ingredients are in common foods such as salad dressing, catsup, pancake syrup, breakfast cereal, breads, snack cakes, chips and granola bars.

When you eat foods to which you are allergic, lymphocytes or white blood cells release proteins called immunoglobulins. These immunoglobulins then react with other cells in the body (i.e., tissues of the nose, lungs, skin, digestive tract), releasing histamines that produce symptoms or allergic reactions.

Food allergies are either fixed or cyclical. Fixed food allergies usually appear early in life, often the first time the food is consumed. The reactions are very strong, often potentially dangerous and appear soon after contact with the food. The allergy has a lifelong pattern, is very unlikely to disappear and the food always needs to be eliminated. Fish, tree nuts and peanuts are three common fixed food allergens. Often, people who react to fish and/or nuts need to avoid all fish and/or nuts but have no other food allergies. However, this cookbook deals with the description, causes and treatment of cyclical food allergies.

Cyclical Food Allergies

Cyclical reactions are much different from fixed food reactions in that you may or may not notice a reaction, may not notice the reaction every time you eat the food or the reaction may vary each time the food is consumed. The level of reaction may range from quite weak to severe, is seldom dangerous and may depend upon how much or how often you eat the food. For example, eating one cup of popcorn once a week may not cause you any noticeable reaction. But if you eat an increased amount (let's say four cups of popcorn once a week) or if you increase the frequency (one cup of popcorn each day), an immediate or a delayed reaction may occur.

A cyclical food reaction can be either masked or unmasked. An unmasked reaction occurs soon after eating a food and it is easy to identify which food causes the reaction. The most common reaction is a masked cyclical reaction and often it occurs many hours after eating the food. Many times no connection is made between your health problems and the foods you eat. Symptoms do not necessarily occur or worsen at the time the food is consumed. Repeated, oftentimes daily, consumption of a food to which you are allergic may cause symptoms to become chronic or, ironically, to temporarily disappear. Instead of feeling poorly when consuming a food allergen, you may feel slightly stimulated (may be a good feeling), crave the food and/or feel worse if you avoid eating it for a couple of days. A craving often leads to over-consumption or a feeling that the craved food is needed to maintain good health. This pattern is called a "food addiction."

An example of how a food allergy becomes masked is as follows:[1] If a person allergic to wheat has avoided it for ten days or longer, they will probably have a definite, recognizable, immediate or delayed reaction if they eat wheat or a wheat product. However, if they continue to eat wheat every day, the reaction occurs but at a lesser level of severity. Eventually the reaction is no longer noticed or associated with eating wheat and has therefore become masked or hidden. These masked reactions become chronic ailments. When this acute stage is reached you may crave the foods you are allergic to and/or often feel better when you eat them.

To unmask a food allergy, begin by completely avoiding the suspected food(s) for two weeks. Read all food labels to be sure you are omitting all sources of the suspected food(s). Corn, wheat and soy are good examples since they are hidden ingredients in commonly consumed foods. The list of suspected foods includes the common food allergens as well as foods you normally eat more than two times a week. After your chronic symptoms have cleared, eat a small amount of one of the suspected foods. Use a notebook to record date, time, food eaten, amount eaten and any reactions experienced as well as any other possible causes (i.e., environmental factors, lack of sleep,

Common Cyclical Food Allergens
wheat
milk/dairy products
eggs
corn
soy

excessive stress). The body's response may be readily noticeable and/or unexpected. Watch for immediate as well as delayed reactions. A delayed reaction can occur in as little as 30 minutes after eating the food or as long as up to 48 hours later.[2] A delayed reaction is caused by the fact that it takes time for the allergens to travel through the bloodstream and encounter the sensitized cells in the body. If you have an immediate or delayed reaction, avoid eating the food for three to six months before trying it again.

FOOD
AND
REACTION
DIARY

If no reactions have been noticed after this 48 hour period, expand the challenge by eating a larger amount or eating the food two or three times in one day. Again, wait 48 hours to check for immediate and delayed reactions. Use your notebook to record your responses.

Day/ Date	Time	Food & Form Eaten	Amount Eaten	Reaction & Possible Cause
8/25	8 am	scrambled eggs with butter	2 large	Mild headache 2 hours following breakfast lasting until mid-afternoon. Itchy rectum around noon on 8/26. Suspect the butter as well as the egg. Next time try using Clarified Butter or oil.

What Causes Food Allergies?

Food sensitivities are the result of the body's immune defense system reacting to the presence of incompletely digested food particles outside the gastrointestinal tract. To understand this, let us first look at how the gastrointestinal tract works. The gastrointestinal tract is a hollow tube, which stretches from the mouth to the rectum and includes the esophagus, stomach and small and large intestines. It is designed to break down food into usable particles and separate them from waste materials to be eliminated from the body. The usable particles are allowed to enter the bloodstream where they provide the nutrients needed for proper body function. In a healthy system, the permeability of the gut allows only the beneficial substances to get through.[3]

Unfortunately, many factors can cause the gut lining to become inflamed and to break down or erode, resulting in an increased permeability. This allows substances such as incompletely digested food particles and toxins to freely circulate ("leak") into areas of the body where they normally would not. The body recognizes these substances as "foreigners" and signals the immune system to attack and make antibodies against them. If the attacked substance is a food particle, the body then recognizes the food as a foreign substance and a food sensitivity has developed. As stated in Chapter One, this condition is known as leaky gut syndrome and triggers a state of continuous and prolonged stress in and on the immune system.[4]

> *"Little by little the bird builds its nest."*
> —French Proverb

Some causes of gut inflammation that can result in "leaky gut" include:

- Candida-Related Complex
- Use of antibiotics
- Use of non-steroidal, anti-inflammatory drugs, including aspirin, Motrin®, ibuprofen, Advil®, Aleve® and Naprosyn® (Tylenol® is not included in this category)
- Eating foods to which you are already allergic
- Stress, hurried meals, anxiety, fatigue, etc.
- Alcohol consumption
- Chemotherapy/radiation

Since a leaky gut can lead to food allergies and food allergies can contribute to continued or increased gut inflammation, this becomes a self-perpetuating cycle unless steps are taken to correct the gut condition (page 49) and deal with the food allergies.

Typical Allergic Reactions to Food

Allergic reactions to foods are numerous and complex. The following are typical reactions.[5,6] However, not all symptoms may be exhibited and they may vary depending upon the food.

Respiratory Symptoms:

• dry mouth • ear infections • ringing in ears	• rubbing nose all the time • sensitivity to odors • wheezing/coughing/asthmatic reactions

Gastrointestinal Symptoms:

• gain in weight • craving for food, alcohol or tobacco	• constipation • colic	• diarrhea • stomach upset

Genitourinary Symptoms:

• chronic bladder irritation • bedwetting	• premenstrual tension • menstrual cramps

Skin Symptoms:

• sweating • blushing • eczema	• outer ears hurt • bright red ear lobes • diaper rash

Systemic Symptoms:

• fluid retention in any part of body • unexplained fluctuation of weight	• muscle/joint swelling, redness and pain • backache • fatigue	• dark circles under eyes • leg aches • muscle aches • hyperactivity

Cardiovascular Symptoms:

• abnormal heart rhythms	• severe chest pain	• heart palpitations

Cerebral Symptoms:

• migraine headaches or chronic headaches • changes of mood: lack of ability to concentrate; feelings of sadness, weariness, frustration, animation, euphoria, aggressiveness, anger, panic, violence, silliness and/or "spaciness" • inappropriate laughter • crying spells	• depression • constant anger • impairment of speaking and reading ability • lack of coordination • loss of balance • excessive hunger or thirst • sleepiness or insomnia • phobias, delusions, hallucinations • amnesia • convulsive seizures	• blackouts • psychosis such as manic depression or schizophrenia • night terrors: scream in the middle of night, eyes open staring • "Jeckyll and Hyde" reaction • make clucking noise • see a difference in handwriting just after eating a food or meal

Diagnosis of Food Allergies

A clinical ecologist, internist or allergist who treats food allergies can perform tests to aid in determining food allergies, including skin prick, sublingual and/or blood tests. Two blood tests are commonly used: the IgE test measures immediate or rapid reactions and the IgG test measures "hidden" or delayed-onset reactions. See www.canaryconnect.com for a listing of labs that perform these and other helpful diagnostic tests.

Naturopaths, chiropractors, acupuncturists, massage therapists, physical therapists and other bodywork health-care practitioners can use several different forms of "muscle testing" or Applied Kinesiology to determine specific food allergies. This science involves testing an arm or leg muscle's strength resistance. The practitioner exerts light, brief pressure on the back of the hand, wrist or lower arm or leg. When a reaction is encountered, the decreased muscle strength allows the arm or leg to be moved out of position. The item being tested may be held by the patient, the practitioner may touch specific reference points on the body or the practitioner may communicate with the body by asking questions regarding specific substances. Even patients themselves can learn and perform "muscle testing," however, it is often not as accurate as testing done by someone who has been trained.

Some health-care professionals closely supervise a special fasting, elimination and rare food diet to aid in determining food allergies.[7]

Another important step in the diagnosis of food allergies is to determine if the symptoms are the result of a food allergy or food intolerance. While a food allergy is an over-reaction of the body's immune system, food intolerance does not involve the immune system. Food intolerances are usually caused by an enzyme deficiency that hinders digestion. Common examples are dairy products or beans. However, if a high quality, complete digestive enzyme (see page 21) is taken 15 to 30 minutes before eating the food, no symptoms occur. This can be confusing since food intolerance symptoms, such as intestinal discomfort, often resemble those of a food allergy.[8]

Treatments for Food Allergies

While continuous, long-term treatments are essential in dealing with food allergies, there are some short-term measures, which can help during a reaction.

- Drink $^1/_4$ teaspoon of baking soda mixed with $^1/_2$ cup purified water. You may need to repeat the dose.
- Drink buffered, corn- and citrus-free vitamin C powder dissolved in purified water.
- Use Alka Seltzer Gold, which is often available only by special order through a pharmacy.
- Use Alka-Aid or Bi- or Tri-Salts preparations. These often contain sodium and potassium bicarbonates.

Long-term treatments are the first line of defense in dealing with food allergies and are used to eliminate or control the effects of the reactive foods.

Some practitioners offer desensitization sublingual drops or shots to build the body's natural defense system and lower allergic reactions. Other practitioners offer bodywork allergy treatments. (If needed, see www.canaryconnect.com for a listing of organizations that provide assistance in locating health-care practitioners who treat food allergies.)

Along with some type of desensitization, complete healing requires healing the leaky gut. Visit www.canaryconnect.com for resources that outlines the underlying causes and plans for healing "leaky gut" as well as nutritional healing strategies for the immune system.

Summary

Strengthening the immune system, healing the leaky gut and helping your body to receive and utilize necessary nutrients are important strategies in treating food allergies (outlined in Chapters 2–4). However, it is equally important to eliminate or limit offending foods by using a rotational food plan. This plan provides an effective means of controlling food exposures and allowing the immune system to recover and heal from the effects of a food before it is eaten again. The rotational food plan is discussed in the next chapter.

_____

"My 8 year old son uses the rotation with ease. He simply turns to the foods for the Day and finds out what to eat for breakfast."

—Judy Beuter, customer in IA

"I found this cookbook to be just what I needed for planning meals for my family to keep our food allergies from increasing. Problems with Candida have affected five generations of my family."

—Jo Ellyn O., customer in TX

CHAPTER SIX

Understanding & Implementing
the Mechanics of
a Rotational Food Plan

Candida-Related Complex (CRC), often goes hand-in-hand with leaky gut syndrome[1] as well as allergies to individual foods, additives and preservatives. Therefore it is important to diversify the foods used in the Candida-Control Food Plan. One way to diversify is by rotating. This is especially advantageous during the early weeks and months of the CRC treatment program when the body is weakest and there is a greater chance of developing food allergies. In addition, following a rotational food plan can assist in identifying hidden food allergies and thus aid in recovery.

The purpose of this chapter is to explain how a food rotation system is developed and to give you tips on how to implement one. The rotational plan is already set-up in this cookbook (Appendix B) along with meal planning ideas (Appendix C) and supporting recipes. The rotational guidelines outlined in this chapter provide an understanding of the food selections used in the recipes, assist you to make adjustments in the outlined rotation plan to fit your dietary needs or, if necessary, offer the tools necessary to create your own rotational plan.

Rotary Diversified Food Plan—What & Why

The rotary diversified food plan was first developed in 1934 by Dr. Herbert J. Rinkel. It is used by people who have food sensitivities, are healthy members of a family prone to food allergies or by health-conscious individuals who like the diversity of rotating.[2] A rotational food plan is a controlled way to eat that accomplishes three main goals:

1. It helps in the treatment of current food allergies by allowing the body to recover from the effects of a food before it is eaten again.
2. It lessens the chances of developing additional food allergies.
3. It aids in identifying foods that could be causing problems.

Using a rotational format when starting a Candida-Control Food Plan can also be beneficial since feelings of deprivation may surface when many favorite foods are omitted from one's eating patterns. To compensate, the frequent response is to overeat a substitute for the omitted food(s). However, overeating an individual food increases the chances of developing a sensitivity to it. For example, I substituted rye crackers and popcorn for wheat, my first-known food allergen. Within two months an allergy to rye and corn developed, so I incorporated rice cakes. Soon an allergy to rice developed. Since a rotational format regulates exposure to an individual food, it can help prevent this cycle.

Eating on Rotation

Through a rotational food plan, you control exposure to foods that can cause cyclical food reactions. A 4-, 5-, 6-, 7- or 8-day rotational food plan may be used. Whichever cycle length is used, each food eaten on a particular day is not eaten again until that day repeats in the rotation. In the sample 4-day rotation outlined in Table A, the broccoli and brown rice on Day 1 are not eaten again until the following Day 1, with three days in between. In the sample 5-day rotation in Table A, broccoli and brown rice are eaten on Day 2 and are not eaten again until the next Day 2 with four days between consumption.

TABLE A

Four-Day Rotation

Day 1	Day 2	Day 3	Day 4	Day 1	Day 2	Day 3
broccoli	cod	carrot	orange	broccoli	cod	carrot
brown rice	lettuce	turkey	beans	brown rice	lettuce	turkey

Five-Day Rotation

Day 1	Day 2	Day 3	Day 4	Day 5	Day 1	Day 2
quinoa	brown rice	amaranth	buckwheat	beans	quinoa	brown rice
spinach	broccoli	tomato	carrot	asparagus	spinach	broccoli

Four days are generally long enough to move food through the complete digestive tract and eliminate the waste part from the body. Persons with chronic constipation may need a cycle longer than four days. In this case, I suggest using an 8-day rotation. This allows maximum time for food to move through the system and, after becoming healthier, switching to a 4-day rotation is easy. Often a 4-day rotation is long enough for some foods but not for others. In this instance, use the basic 4-day rotation but rotate specific foods every eight days. Table B illustrates this with carrot and cauliflower eaten once in eight days, whereas the other foods are eaten every four days.

TABLE B

Day 1	Day 2	Day 3	Day 4	Day 1	Day 2	Day 3	Day 4
br. rice	lettuce	**carrot**	beans	br. rice	lettuce	**cauliflower**	beans

What is a "Day"?

While a day is usually defined as the meals you eat between sunrise and sunset (breakfast, lunch, dinner), for the purposes of a rotational food plan this 24-hour period can be adjusted to fit individual needs.

Someone who has difficulty preparing breakfast may prefer to use extras (leftovers) from dinner the previous evening and would define a rotational day as lunch, dinner and breakfast the following morning.

If you work outside the home and carry lunch, you may wish to define the day as dinner, breakfast and lunch. This pattern allows you to prepare extra servings for your next day's lunch while preparing your evening meal.

Basically a "day" consists of any 24-hour period and the meals consumed during that time frame. This can be from midnight to midnight, 3 p.m. to 3 p.m. or any other cycle that works for you. With planning, you can easily and successfully maintain the rotation while enjoying nutritious, delicious meals.

Steps for Implementing a Rotational Food Plan

Step 1: Believe in Your Success

You might recall that a positive attitude is the first action step in the Healing Action Plan (Chapter 2). It is also the key ingredient to your success here. You may be feeling deprived because you are limited by food allergies. Instead, take those lemons and make lemonade, as in many ways a rotational diet offers you more variety than other dietary plans.

Step 2: Planning

Planning is a key task when following a rotational food plan. Planning takes time up front but it simplifies:
- Meal preparation
- Creation of rotational menus
- Adding diversity, including many different types of proteins, vegetables and whole grains/nongrains to your diet, thus nourishing your body
- Making your mealtimes colorful, relaxing and fun
- Developing a shopping list that enables you to:
    —purchase what you need and
    —decrease impulse buying of nonessential or improper foods

> ### My Favorite P's
>
> I think of planning as I think of prayer. Practicing prayer, especially before making decisions, makes life easier to handle because it requires you to slow down, identify your needs and wait/listen for a response.
>
> Likewise, planning smoothies your path, making it easier to know what's for dinner and what to get at the store. It also saves preparation time in the kitchen.

When I first began using a rotational diet, I was encouraged to eat simple meals [i.e., meals with only two (meat/vegetables; starch/vegetables) or three (meat/starch/vegetables) components]. When implementing a major dietary change, it often feels easier to cook the individual foods separately—i.e., grill the chicken breast, cook the brown rice and steam the broccoli. While these meals may have their disadvantages (boring when eaten for extended periods and often make extra clean-up), the extras can be used to creatively prepare an easy breakfast and a lunch to carry to work. Some of these ideas are included in the menu plans on pages 60–61.

On the other hand, using the same foods that one might cook separately, you can create casserole-style meals and hearty complete meal soups, many of which can be frozen for future quick meals. Often these meals are prepared in one pan, streamlining the clean-up process. Also, they introduce you to a variety of new flavors through the combination of flavors when foods are cooked together. Using complementary-flavored foods can also help eliminate the need to use condiments (i.e., catsup), which might otherwise be used on foods cooked separately. Finally, the food's appearance is often enhanced when the different colors and textures are combined.

While casserole-style meals do not always involve fewer cooking utensils, they sometimes add the advantage of providing time to clean-up the preparation pans/dishes and kitchen while the casserole is cooking. This time can also be used for relaxing before the meal (a good technique for improving digestion).

Step 3: Getting Started with the Rotational Food Plan

Since this book includes an already-developed rotational plan, corresponding recipes and menu planning ideas, one could choose menus and recipes, purchase food supplies, set a date and begin all at once. But for many of us, that is more than we can handle when healthy, so how can we expect that of ourselves when symptoms of food allergies are sapping us of energy and concentration?

A better approach is to begin with one or two categories of foods from the rotational food plan (Appendix B). You can begin with any category you like but I prefer beginning with "grains and flours" and "higher carbohydrate vegetables," as the two categories interrelate (i.e., a bean or legume flour and the actual legume) and both categories have many common allergens so beginning there can offer a relief of symptoms, making it easier to continue forward with additional changes.

As you are creating menu plans for the next 4–8 days, begin with choosing one or two foods from the categories you selected for each of the 4 days and create your menu around those foods without concern for foods in the other categories. However, when possible, do not eat the same food two "days" in a row. Table C has taken one food per day of the rotation in Appendix B. The sample menus below Table C provide four days of meals that rotate these four foods. (Other foods are added without regard to rotation.)

TABLE C

Day 1	Day 2	Day 3	Day 4
brown rice	potato	quinoa	beans

Day 1: (Dinner) **brown rice** with beef & broccoli stir-fry. (Breakfast) use extra **brown rice** and stir-fry it with almonds. (Lunch) create a salad with a few reserved strips of stir-fried beef, spinach, broccoli, tomato and Easy "C" Dressing.

Day 2: (Dinner) **potato** with grilled chicken breast and gravy (use arrowroot to thicken) and tossed salad with Garlic-Lemon-Oil Dressing. (Breakfast) use extra **potatoes** and cook with scrambled eggs. (Lunch) use extra grilled chicken and gravy, adding broth and vegetables (i.e., onions, celery) to create a soup.

Day 3: (Dinner) **Basic Quinoa** with Baked Fish and Sautéed Zucchini & Sunflower Seeds (Breakfast) enjoy extra baked fish and zucchini. (Lunch) use extra **quinoa** in 3 Color Salad.

Day 4: (Dinner) grilled pork chop, Navy **Beans** & Broth and Sautéed Green **Beans** & Pumpkin Seeds. (Breakfast) dice up extra pork chop and scramble with eggs. (Lunch) use extra navy and green **beans** to create a soup.

Note that while the four foods selected for rotation (in bold) are eaten four days apart, all other foods are consumed no more often than every other day.

For the next four days, you can repeat these or choose to make adjustments.

When you are ready to move on (I suggest you do this in 8 to 16 days: 2 or 4 repetitions of the 4-day cycle), add another food category such as animal protein. When planning meals, choose foods to rotate from this new category and add them to the foods from the previous categories, without concern to rotating foods in the remaining categories. This allows you time to become accustomed to your food plan and successfully adjust to the new dietary lifestyle before proceeding. Always remember to avoid eating any food two "days" in a row.

As you continue to add new categories to your rotation, you may find it helpful to refer to Appendix C for meal planning ideas and guidance on how to use them.

Step 4: Personalizing a Rotational Food Plan

Depending upon your food allergies and other dietary restrictions, as well as availability of certain foods and likes/dislikes, it may be necessary to adjust the rotational food plan outlined in Appendix B OR to develop a completely new one. Below are the steps to follow:

Adjusting the Rotational Food Plan

1. Photocopy the food plan and two copies of the blank form found in Appendix B.
2. With a pencil, cross out all foods you cannot eat due to food allergies or other dietary restrictions. Indicate the time frame for seasonal foods (i.e., asparagus, artichoke, fennel).
3. Evaluate whether the foods remaining are enough for each day to have a balanced diet. Look for a cross section of protein sources, grain or higher carbohydrate vegetables and low carbohydrate vegetables as well as fruits and sweeteners (once you can add them to your food plan).
4. If there are not enough foods on some days and plenty on other days, follow the basic "Rotation Guidelines" (see page 62) and begin moving foods from one day to another.

Creating a Rotational Food Plan

Choose foods to which you are not allergic and begin assigning them days following the principles outlined in the "Rotation Guidelines" (see page 62). Use the form in Appendix B as a format. To accomplish this, proceed through the food categories in the following order:

1. Start with Grains, Flours & Baking Foods and Higher Carbohydrate Vegetables such as: root vegetables (i.e., potatoes, parsnips, turnips, sweet potatoes), squashes (i.e., pumpkin, acorn, butternut) and legumes (i.e., peas, lentils, dry beans).
2. Then proceed with Animal Protein and/or other protein sources (i.e., beans, nuts, seeds, amaranth, quinoa).
3. Next consider the Lower Carbohydrate Vegetables (i.e., celery, tomato, spinach, leeks).
4. Finally add nuts, seeds, herbs, spices, fruits and sweeteners. As you consider nuts, seeds and vegetables, also decide on an oil for each day.

Rotation Guidelines

Guideline 1: Eat the same food item no more often than every fourth day.

In Table B (pg. 58), a food (i.e., beans) is eaten each Day 4, allowing three days in between.

Guideline 2: Within a rotation, food families are also rotated.

Foods are grouped into botanical food families based on their biological origin. Each food family is assigned a name and a number for identification. Food families are rotated because foods in the same family tend to share common allergens and could cause similar reactions. Eating brown rice on Day 1, spelt on Day 2, oat on Day 3 and millet on Day 4 is eating a member of the Grass Family every day, and so is not proper food rotation. Table D illustrates how all foods from an individual family are eaten on an assigned day.

TABLE D

Day 1 Grass Family	Day 2 Lily Family	Day 3 Mustard Family	Day 4 Legume Family
brown rice	garlic	cauliflower	peas
spelt	onion	Brussels sprouts	pinto bean
oat	leeks	broccoli	garbanzo bean
millet	asparagus	cabbage	lima bean

A complete listing of food families can be found in Appendix A. This listing also includes nonedible plants; someone allergic to a weed or plant may also be allergic to the foods in that family group. For example: if allergic to pigweed, be cautious of amaranth; if allergic to poison ivy, be cautious of cashews, pistachios and mangoes; if allergic to lamb's-quarters, be cautious of quinoa, spinach, chard and beets; and if allergic to ragweed, be cautious of lettuce and other members of the Composite Family, especially during ragweed season.

Guideline 3: Different foods within a food family may be rotated every other day.

As explained in Guideline 1, within a 4-day rotation a particular food is eaten at least four days apart. However, Guideline 3 allows different foods in the same food family to be eaten two days apart. Table E (next page) illustrates that each food chosen is eaten every four days, yet separate foods in a food family are eaten two days apart (i.e., Grass Family foods, brown rice and spelt are on Day 1 and oat and millet on Day 3). This allows for more flexibility and variety in planning meals.

One exception to Guideline 3 involves three foods from the Grass Family. Wheat, spelt and Kamut® are closely related and should always be assigned to the same day; not divided two days apart. If you have a wheat allergy, a food challenge for spelt and Kamut® is recommended (see pages 33–34 and 53–54).

Persons with severe food allergies may need additional restrictions to the 4-day rotation:

1. Do not repeat foods or food families twice within one day unless at the same meal (i.e., if you have brown rice for breakfast, do not eat it, or any member of the Grass family for lunch or dinner).
2. Do not incorporate Guideline 3 into your rotation.

TABLE E

Day 1	Day 2	Day 3	Day 4
Grass Family	**Lily Family**	**Grass Family**	**Lily Family**
rice	garlic	oat	leeks
spelt	onion	millet	asparagus

Mustard Family	**Legume Family**	**Mustard Family**	**Legume Family**
broccoli	garbanzo bean	cauliflower	peas
cabbage	lima bean	Brussels sprouts	pinto bean

Guideline 4: Foods may be moved to another day using the following examples:

<u>Example 1</u>: Moving foods on a permanent basis. To move cabbage, a member of the Mustard Family, from Day 1 to Day 2, you must move other Mustard Family foods from Day 1 to Day 2. This also requires the moving of the Mustard Family foods on Day 3 to Day 4 so that foods from the same family are still eaten 2 days apart.

<u>Example 2</u>: Use "Floating Foods" to allow for creativity and flexibility. A "floating food" (as marked with asterisk/double asterisk in Appendix B) is a food that is used in recipes on both Days 1 and 3 or Days 2 and 4. These are not flagged in the recipes. Since most are used in small amounts, I do not concern myself with this break in rotation but if you do, just consume at least six days apart, as Table F indicates.

TABLE F

Day 1	Day 2	Day 3	Day 4	Day 1	Day 2	Day 3
	oregano		no oregano		no oregano	

Day 4	Day 1	Day 2	Day 3	Day 4	Day 1	Day 2
oregano		no oregano		no oregano		oregano

<u>Example 3</u>: While "Floating Foods" are minor foods to change in the rotation, there may be other more significant foods that you desire to temporarily move in order to accommodate favorite recipes or food combinations. Any food may be temporarily moved between Day 1 and 3 or Day 2 and 4 to allow for creativity and flexibility. As an example, wild rice (a Day 3 food) is used in Wild & Brown Rice with Herbs (a Day 1 recipe). Wild rice pasta can be used in All-in-One Salad for Day 3 (see Table G). To assist you, a cross (†) is used in the recipes to indicate when a "floating food" is used. You can move any food by following Guidelines 1, 2 and 3. Just remember, when moving a food, it is important to avoid eating it for four days before eating it again.

TABLE G

	Day 1	Day 2	Day 3	Day 4
Cycle 1:	Wild & Brown Rice w/ Herbs		omit wild rice	
Cycle 2:	omit wild rice		Wild Rice Pasta in All-in-One Salad	

<u>Example 4</u>: Allow "Fun Foods" to brighten your day. "Fun Foods" are foods with no other or only a few other foods in their family. These foods can be moved with ease, when allowing three days between the times you consume them. The "Fun Foods" (that do not have an assigned day in this rotational plan) are listed at the beginning of Appendix B. For example, Brazil and macadamia nuts are each a member of a different food family with no other foods in their family so they can be freely used as "milk" options in recipes on all four days provided they are not used again until three more days have passed. These foods are not flagged in the recipes.

<u>Example 5</u>: Move foods on an occasional temporary basis. Perhaps you would, on occasion, like to eat asparagus with scrambled eggs on Day 1. The Lily Family, of which asparagus is a member, is assigned on Days 2 and 4 as illustrated in Table E (page 63). To temporarily move asparagus from Day 4 to Day 1, omit eating all foods from the Lily Family on Day 4 before and Day 2 after you eat asparagus on Day 1. In addition, omit eating asparagus on the Day 4 after you eat it on Day 1 (see Table H). On the next repeat of the rotational cycle return to eating foods from the Lily Family as Table E illustrates.

TABLE G

Day 1	Day 2	Day 3	Day 4	Day 1	Day 2	Day 3	Day 4
	Lily Family		Lily Family	Lily Family	Lily Family		Lily Family
	eat garlic and/or onion		omit all	eat asparagus	omit all		eat leeks omit asparagus

<u>Example 6</u>: Choose to substitute other foods rather than move foods. Sometimes moving foods is more difficult than creatively substituting. Carefully evaluate any move to be sure it does not cause too many problems and consider adapting the recipe to use foods assigned on a particular day before attempting a move. For example, I substituted garbanzo beans for brown rice (a Day 1 food) in Stuffed Green Peppers (a Day 2 recipe).

Time to Cook, Eat & Enjoy!

Now that you have an understanding of CRC and food allergies, as well as their treatments, it is time to begin enjoying the recipes in this cookbook. Health and well-being are enhanced by using of a wide variety of foods. Introduce yourself to several "new" foods by reading Appendix D: Know Your Ingredients. Each day of the rotational food plan has supporting recipes and meal planning ideas. The recipes may use unfamiliar "new" foods, but they have only slight changes in flavor and texture. It will not be long before your taste buds will not crave the original. Learn to enjoy the flavors of "new" foods combined with old favorites.

After using a rotational food plan, you may soon be able to safely tolerate foods that previously caused moderate to severe reactions. This is possible because the body's immune system had an appropriate rest period. You may regain tolerance to some foods in as little as 3–4 weeks; for other foods it may take 2–6 months or longer. You soon will realize that good, tasty and nutritious meals are a natural part of your every day life.

CHAPTER SEVEN

Cooking Within the Parameters
of the Food Plans

A variety of flavorful recipes with low-allergenic ingredients is the biggest help to implementing a healing food plan. These recipes are designed to follow the 4-day rotation outlined in Appendix B: Rotational Food Plan. Included with the recipes are: an indication of each recipe's assigned Day in the rotation, Helpful Hints, Equipment Tips and Serving Suggestions. The recipes are divided into the following sections:

The Veggies: Cookery & Salads
Salad Dressings/Condiments/
    Beverages/Miscellaneous
Bean Cookery
Soups
Sandwiches
Entrées: Eggs

Entrées: Poultry
Entrées: Red Meats
Entrées: Italian
Entrées: Seafood
Whole Grain Cookery
The Sweets

Vegetarian recipes are found throughout (see Recipe Index). Before beginning the cooking, I suggest that you read "About the Recipes" and the short introductions to each recipe section.

About the Recipes

The recipes emphasize "traditional" foods and tastes so that all family members may enjoy the same food plan. Only a few recipes contain common food allergens (i.e., wheat, corn, soy, egg, dairy products). Wheat is totally omitted unless you count the wheat alternatives, spelt and Kamut®. If an ingredient is new to you, consult Appendix D: Know Your Ingredients, or the vegetable section at the beginning of "The Veggies: Cookery & Salads" (see pages 70–81).

Before beginning a recipe, read through it to be sure you have all the ingredients. The recipes are formatted with an amount column on the left, an ingredient column on the right and a small space in between. This allows you to move your finger down the list of ingredients very quickly to see if you have the ingredients before you start. If you do not usually keep a specific food product on hand or know you have a limited amount of an ingredient, a quick glance to the left lets you check the amount listed in the recipe. This format allows you to check the list quickly without constantly moving your eyes back and forth.

The recipe instructions use a numbered, step-by-step outline. At first glance, some of the recipes may appear complicated, however, most of the time it is just the opposite. The length offers an easy step-by-step guide to prepare the recipe. This is especially helpful for beginners. Also, the numbered outline helps you to keep your place as you prepare the recipe.

Oven temperatures are denoted in the recipe just before the numbered list of directions.

Baking dish sizes are also noted just before the numbered list with an indication if the dish is to be prepared (i.e., oiled, floured). If it just mentions the dish size, then the recipe is to be baked without oiling the dish OR the oiling process is included as one of the recipe steps (i.e., Pizza Crust, page 151).

To reference other recipes in this cookbook, the recipe title is capitalized (i.e., Clarified Butter). You can locate the recipe that is being referenced by looking in the Recipe Index if the page number is not indicated.

There is a page at the back of this book to use for indicating your favorite recipes or other notes regarding the recipes.

A few of the recipes were created by another person or adapted from another cookbook. These credits are included on page 210.

A Word About the Ingredients:

Occasionally the recipes include an ingredient that breaks rotation. These ingredients are marked with a cross (†) along with an explanation on how to accommodate the break in rotation.

Your particular health situation and personality will dictate how strictly you adhere to the rotation or how freely you make substitutions (see Appendix G: Substitutions).

To avoid corn in baking powder, the leavening agent used most often in these recipes is a combination of unbuffered vitamin C crystals and baking soda. When purchasing the C crystals, be sure to ask (if the label does not say) for the source so that you avoid ingredients that are high food allergens (i.e., corn). See Appendix G for additional information and other substitute options.

All recipes using grains and their flours are referring to the whole grain and its whole-grain flour. For space considerations, the phrase "whole-grain" was omitted. For example, spelt flour can now be purchased as white (refined) spelt flour, but the recipes in this book were developed using whole-grain spelt flour.

A Word About Utensils & Preparing to Cook:

My favorite utensil for stirring batters (i.e., pancakes, muffins, tortillas, crackers) is a heat resistant rubber spoonula, which is a rubber spatula that is curved more like a spoon and is resistant to melting so it can be used to stir hot foods (i.e., stir-fries, sauces, soups).

Before beginning actual recipe preparation, set up your mixing and/or cooking area. This may involve clearing away extra items on your counter to make space. At first this may seem time consuming, but once you have practiced it a few times it will become "old hat" and you will appreciate the time saved. As you read through the recipe, take note of the various preparation equipment and gadgets needed. For example to prepare muffins, in the mixing area have the following: recipe, ingredients, dry cup measures, measuring spoons, 1-cup liquid measure, table knife (for leveling ingredients), mixing bowl, rubber spoonula (or other utensil for mixing), whisk and muffin tins. In the baking area have the following: preheated oven, timer, toothpicks (for testing doneness), cooling rack and sharp knife (for removing muffins from tins).

When setting out recipe ingredients in the mixing area, you might like to organize them in the order listed in the recipe (which is the order you use them during preparation). After using each item, set it aside to put it away later. Use a table knife or other straight edge to mark your place in the recipe. These techniques are especially helpful if you are interrupted (i.e., child asking a question, phone call).

A Word About the Terms:

To shorten preparation and cooking time of many skillet casserole meals follow the **"Chop & Drop"** and **"Slide, Season & Cook"** methods.

"Chop & Drop" is a method to sauté vegetables in oil. It consists of slicing/dicing/chopping vegetables, beginning with the vegetable that takes the longest to cook. Begin sautéing the first vegetable while you dice the next vegetable in the order listed on the recipe. For example (Spaghetti Meat Sauce recipe): The recipe reads, "In large skillet, 'Chop & Drop' vegetables in order listed." First chop the onions and drop them in the skillet with oil. Turn heat source on medium and begin sautéing onions while you dice the green peppers (the next ingredient in recipe). Repeat until all vegetables are in the skillet. Stir the sautéing vegetables with each addition (or more often as needed) to cook them evenly.

For recipes using ground meat, the **"Slide, Season & Cook"** method is employed soon after adding the last vegetable. First, slide the sautéed vegetables to one side of skillet. Add ground meat to other side and sprinkle seasonings evenly over meat and vegetables. Stir often to brown meat and cook vegetables evenly, keeping the meat and vegetables somewhat separated. Once the meat is cooked, stir vegetables and meat together.

Definitions for other cooking terms used in the recipes may be found in Appendix E: Cook's Glossary.

A Word About Measuring:

Measurements in these recipes are provided as a guide. It is a good rule of thumb to use the quantities suggested the first time a recipe is prepared. Once you get to know a recipe, adjust the quantities according to your tastes and preferences.

Accurate measuring is important in some of the recipes, especially for baked goods with gluten-free grains (see Appendix F: Measuring How To's).

When preparing a fraction of ($1/2$, $1/4$) or multiplying (doubling, tripling) a recipe, first calculate the measurements of the ingredients. Write these amounts in the margin of the cookbook.

> *"Laughter is by definition healthy."* —Doris Lessing

Symbols to Guide You

 Helpful Hints (also called Hints, Sondra's Thoughts, Sondra's Hints) include:
  • Things that are not required to make the recipe but help the
    preparation go more smoothly
  • Tips for storing, freezing and reheating
  • Substitutions
  • Sondra's favorite ingredients to use

Sometimes the hints are written in a box off to the side while other times for short "one-liners" the chef hat and hint is noted at the end of the recipe directions.

 Steps Involved serve two purposes:
  1. Provide a list of the tasks involved, seeing at a glance what is required
  2. Serve as a quick guide once you become familiar with a recipe

Sometimes they are written in a box, placed off to the side of the recipe. Sometimes preparation is so short, the recipe box is placed right by the directions.

 Equipment Tip: highlights helpful equipment for preparing the recipe

 Serving Suggestion: highlights serving ideas

☑ **Pre-Prep:** This symbol indicates that the item or step in the recipe should be done prior to preparing the recipe. (In some cases, you can prepare this ingredient as you prepare the recipe, but realize that it will take much longer to complete the recipe.) For example, to cook beans (page 105), the recipe indicates to pre-prep the washing and soaking of the beans. This needs to be done in advance since the beans need to soak overnight. In contrast, the Vegetarian Lasagna (page 158) recipe tells you to pre-prep the lasagna noodles. The noodles do not need to be prepared in advance but to make the recipe less physically draining, the noodles can be prepared ahead of time.

Often these pre-prep steps are very simple. For example, the extra rice, chicken and broth left from a dinner can be frozen in the amount needed for a soup to be prepared four days later.

Symbols Placed to the Left of the Recipe Title Include:

S_2 indicates that the recipe is compatible with the guidelines for Stage 2 of the Candida-Control Food Plan (pages 30–31).

S_{2C} indicates that the recipe can be used during Stage 2 if care is taken to select the correct choice of ingredient(s) (i.e., All-in-One Salads).

S_{2L} indicates that the recipe can be used during Stage 2 in limited amounts (i.e., Baked Sweet Potato).

S_{2CL} indicates that the recipe can be used during Stage 2 if care is taken to select the correct choice of ingredient(s) and it is eaten in limited amounts (i.e., Basic Grains).

For further guidance see notes written near the yield of the individual recipes.

Quick & Easy: indicates that the recipe takes 30 minutes or less to prepare.

 Easy: indicates that the recipe is not difficult to prepare, but either the preparation time and/or the cooking time takes longer than 30 minutes.

 Quick & Easy w/ Pre-Prep: indicates that the recipe can be prepared in 30 minutes or less if you have the pre-prep item prepared in advance.

 Easy w/ Pre-Prep: indicates that the recipe is not difficult to prepare, especially if you have the pre-prep item completed in advance.

Summary

If you are new to cooking, it will take some time, as well as mental energy, to learn some of the techniques involved. If you tackle it bit by bit, however, you will find that what once felt overwhelming soon feels like second nature. Go slowly, focusing on the types of foods that are comforting for you. Is there a food you are missing or craving? Make it your project this week to learn how to make an appropriate substitute (and most often that substitute is in this book). Is there a particular meal (i.e., breakfast) that is especially daunting? Look thru the recipes of that variety and take the time to experiment. Soon a vast array of aromas and tastes will fill your kitchen and satisfy your taste buds while offering healing.

"Sondra has done a great deal of testing. ... the type of book I needed when first diagnosed with Candida and food allergies."

—Elva Waters, customer in IA

RECIPES

The Veggies
Cookery & Salads

The versatile vegetables are the core of the Candida-Control Food Plan. I even recommend that readers plan menus around vegetables. Choose the vegetables first and then decide what would taste good with them.

Vegetables can be served in a variety of ways (i.e., in casseroles, stir-fries, soups, salads or side dishes—cooked or raw). My favorite ways are lightly steamed and stir-fried (on the crispy side). An easy way to have vegetable broth for soups/casseroles is to freeze any remaining water after simmering veggies. For a rotational veggie broth, freeze liquid in jars marked Day 1, Day 2 .... Thaw before use.

S₂ Artichoke (Globe) (Composite Family, #80, Day 2 Vegetable)

Though low in calories and cholesterol, artichokes are abundantly rich in nutrients, (i.e., fiber, calcium, iodine, folate, magnesium, chromium, manganese, potassium, vitamin C). They strengthen heart activity and neutralize some toxins. Easy to digest, they also aid in some digestive disorders, increase energy and improve liver and gallbladder function. Select tight and heavy artichokes.

Globe Artichoke

1. Trim off stem flush with bottom of artichoke. Cut top off about 1 inch down and cut tips of leaves off with scissors. Drizzle lemon juice on cut edges.

2. Steam bottom-side-up in about 1 inch of simmering water for 30–45 minutes, depending upon the size. Season with salt while cooking. To test for doneness, tug on a leaf; it should release with just a little resistance.

 Eat artichokes by removing leaves, starting with outer-most leaves. Dip leaf base in a mixture of melted butter or Clarified Butter and freshly squeezed lemon juice and scrape the vegetable "meat" off with your teeth. When you come to the center (heart), remove the "fuzz" with sharp knife and savor the "heart." It is the best!

S₂ Asparagus (Lily Family, #11, Day 4 Vegetable)

Asparagus is a rich source of nutrients, providing ample amounts of vitamin A, B-complex, C, E, potassium, zinc, rutin and glutathione (an important anticarcinogen). Asparagus is helpful in treating rheumatism, edema, constipation, membrane irritation and gout and works to reduce mucus and phlegm.

1. Remove woody, fibrous texture portion near opposite end of tip by either of the following methods:
   - Hold on to spear tip. Place paring knife blade against bottom end. Apply gentle pressure against spear while moving up the spear a small distance at a time. Soon you will feel the difference in texture as you move past the woody portion and into the tender part of the spear. This will happen when your knife blade cuts easily into the spear. Cut off and discard this woody portion.
   - Hold both ends of a spear and flex it (bow it down). It will naturally break at the junction between the woody and tender part.

2. Cut tender portion into 6-inch lengths for spears and 1-inch lengths for cuts/tips.

3. Wash pieces thoroughly to remove sand and dirt.

4. **For Spears:** Arrange spears in top portion of steamer pan or in a steamer basket. Sprinkle with salt. Cover and steam for 10–15 minutes or until tender. Time will depend on spear diameter. Check water level about every 5 minutes so it does not boil dry.

   For Cuts/Tips: Cook as described above for spears or place in saucepan with small amount of boiling water. Sprinkle with salt. Cover and simmer for 5 minutes or until tender.

continued ...

continued ...

For Roasted Spears: Preheat oven to 400°. Using your hands, lightly coat asparagus with oil. Place single layer in heavy skillet with oven proof handles. Roast until tender, about 5–7 minutes, turning asparagus half way through cooking time. Time will depend on spear diameter.

Asparagus Spears
with Tips

 If you use a cast iron skillet, preheat skillet in oven while preheating oven or begin cooking during preheating process and allow about 5 extra minutes of roasting time.

S$_{2L}$ Beets (Goosefoot Family, #28, Day 3 Vegetable)

Though high in natural sugars, beets are very healthy for the liver and aid both circulation and the relief of constipation. Beets are usually served cooked (seasoned with coriander), however, they are delicious served raw on salads, especially small, fresh-picked beets.

1. Cut off stem and greens. Scrub beets thoroughly. Wash the greens separately and use only if they are crisp.

2. **Cooking peeled beets:** Peel beets. Slice or dice. In saucepan with small amount of water, simmer beets for 10 minutes seasoned with salt and coriander. Add greens and cook 10 minutes longer or until beets are tender.

   Cooking whole unpeeled beets: In saucepan, simmer beets in enough salted water to cover them until tender (about 1 hour). Transfer to cold water. Remove skins and stems (most will slip off easily). Follow directions for peeled beets except simmer only until greens are tender.

Beets
with Greens

S$_2$  Bok Choy (Mustard or Cruciferious Family, #36, Day 1 Vegetable)

Bok choy has broad white or greenish-white stalks with loose, dark green leaves and is an excellent source of vitamins A and C. It looks like a cross between celery (stalk) and collards (leaves). Bok choy has a pungent fragrance and taste, especially when eaten raw, but becomes milder when cooked.

Recipe Ideas:

1. Add to stir-fries, stews, soups, casseroles (i.e., Chicken Spaghetti/Pizza Sauce or Skillet Chicken Noodle Casserole) and egg dishes (i.e., Scrambled or Denver Eggs).

2. Serve raw in salads.

To Prepare:

Wash stalks and leaves. Chop stalks into small pieces. Cut leaves with scissors or tear into small pieces.

A Single Stalk
and Leaf

S₂ Broccoli (Mustard or Cruciferious Family, #36, Day 1 Vegetable)

With twice as much vitamin C as an orange and almost as much calcium as whole milk, broccoli has many health benefits for the person needing to limit dairy and/or citrus intake. An added benefit is that the calcium is more absorbable than that found in milk. A versatile vegetable to serve, it has benefits for the eyes and contains good levels of selenium and vitamins A, E and C, making it a good antioxidant. Broccoli can be enjoyed raw or cooked. Lightly steamed it is an elegant side dish or a pleasant addition to stir-fries, casseroles and pilafs.

Method to prepare fresh broccoli for casseroles, stir-fries or as a steamed side dish.

1. Cut off florets. Peel stalk portion with vegetable peeler or paring knife to remove fibrous outer bark. The outer bark is a little darker green and you can see the fibers in this woody covering. The inner tender stalk is a lighter green and has a smooth, even texture.

Broccoli Florets
with Stem

2. **For Cuts**: Cut stalk into medallion (disk) pieces and floret portion into bite-size pieces.
   For Spears: Cut both stalk and floret portion into strips.

3. Soak pieces in salted water for 5 minutes to kill hidden pests. Drain, rinse again.

4. **For Side Dish:** Place in saucepan with small amount of boiling water. Sprinkle with salt. Cover and simmer for 3–5 minutes. Serve immediately as overcooked/mushy broccoli is bitter.

   For Stir-Fry or Salads: Blanch or lightly steam, 1–2 minutes. Cool to room temperature for stir-fry or chill for salad.

S₂ Brussels Sprouts (Mustard or Cruciferious Family, #36, Day 3 Vegetable)

Soak in salted water for 30 minutes. Drain. Remove wilted outer leaves. Trim the flat bottom end, leaving whole. Cut an "X" in this bottom about ¹/₄ inch deep to cook the inside quickly and evenly. Cook covered in a small amount of salted water for 8–12 minutes or until desired tenderness. I prefer to simmer them less time and stir-fry them with chopped walnuts in a little coconut or grapeseed oil and season with coriander.

Brussels Sprouts

S₂ₒₗ  Carrot (Carrot Family, #65, Day 3 Vegetable)

Carrots

A very versatile vegetable, carrots can be enjoyed raw, cooked in casseroles, soups and stir-fries or as a side dish. If eaten with the peel, they are a great source of carotenoids, including Vitamin A. Because of their diuretic nature, they help to prevent constipation and alleviate indigestion. When cooked, carrots have higher sugar levels. Therefore, cooked carrots are listed to be eaten in moderation during Stage 2 of the Candida-Control Food Plan.

S₂ Collards (Mustard or Cruciferious Family, #36, Day 1 Vegetable)

Collards, a non-heading cabbage with broad, smooth, dark green leaves and fairly long stems, have a strong, somewhat bitter flavor, but are milder than other varieties of greens. They are an excellent source of vitamins A and C, iron, calcium, magnesium, potassium and folic acid.

S₂ ☑ Bare Bones Collard Rolls (Day 1 Recipe)

1–3 medium	collard leaves (per roll)
your choice	Day 1 foods (i.e., cooked fish, brown rice or cooked chicken chunks*)
seasoning	dill weed, ground cumin or dry mustard

1. Heat and/or prepare filling.

2. For each roll, wash 1–3 medium to large collard leaves. Trim any bad spots and thick portion of center rib.

3. In skillet large enough to hold leaves without folding (if necessary, it is okay to fold stack of leaves one time), bring small amount of water to boil. Place stack of collard leaves in pan, season, cover and simmer for 15 minutes until tender. Check water level about every 5 minutes so it does not boil dry.

Collard Leaf

4. Using two slotted spoons/spatulas for support, transfer stack of cooked leaves onto a heat resistant surface (such as cutting board, large platter). (If leaves were folded, unfold.) Spoon your choice of filling onto center of top leaf. Sprinkle with seasonings. Carefully pick up edge of 1–3 leaves (depending on sturdiness of leaves and/or personal preference for amount of "greens"). Using fingertips, roll leaves around filling (move quickly to avoid being burned). Transfer finished roll to serving plate and continue with remaining leaves. Serve immediately.

*Temporarily move collards to Day 3 and fill with flaked salmon, cooked turkey chunks and/or millet.

S₂ Eggplant (Nightshade or Potato Family, #74, Day 2 Vegetable)

A member of the nightshade family, eggplant comes in a variety of colors and sizes/shapes. The smaller the berry, the firmer and sweeter it is likely to be. Because 90% of the fruit is water, it is low in calcium and most minerals, though it is a good source of potassium. Eggplant should be used within 2 days of purchase to retain the sweet flavor and is best baked or simmered since it absorbs oil very readily.

Sondra's Hints: Several Day 2 recipes list thinly sliced, peeled eggplant. Since small pieces of cooked eggplant resemble the appearance and texture of sliced sautéed mushrooms, I cut them accordingly:

- For a long slender eggplant, peel and thinly slice.
- For pear-shaped variety, peel, cut into strips (similar to size of slender eggplant) and then slice thin.

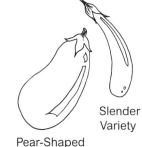

Slender
Variety

Pear-Shaped
Variety

S₂ 🕐 Fennel (Carrot Family, #65, Day 1 Vegetable)

Fennel is a wonderful plant for people with CRC. Sweet fennel, with its licorice-like taste can be prepared as a vegetable and enjoyed cooked or raw. Its leaves make a nice garnish. Wild fennel, on the other hand, provides us with an herb (its leaves) and a seasoning (its seeds). Used to flavor a variety of grains from bread and crackers to pies and desserts, the wild fennel seeds are sometimes served as a digestive aid after a meal. They alleviate intestinal gas and mucus in the lungs. They are also anticarcinogenic.

To Serve: Fennel is my new favorite vegetable. Within about 2 months of seeing the vegetable prepared on my favorite Food Network show, I began adding it to many Day 1 recipes, such as Pilaf, Skillet Chicken Noodle Casserole, Chicken/Broccoli Mac'n Cheese-Less and Chicken Stir-Fry.

Fennel
with Fern-Like Top

To Prepare: After washing, cut off the stem portion. Cut the globe portion into fourths, remove the core and slice or dice so it is ready to use in recipes or to add to salads. Discard the stem portion but mince the fern-like top as a garnish for the dish or to add at the last minute of cooking.

S₂ 🕐 Garlic (Lily Family, #11, Day 2 or 4 Vegetable)

Garlic has many health benefits including its antibacterial, anticarcinogenic, antifungal and antiparastical properties (see page 47 for more information). Adding garlic cloves in the last few minutes of cooking provides the greatest health benefit. Since the flavor is released while cooking, you may choose to mix some garlic in at the beginning of the cooking process and save some to add at the end.

Many recipes use fresh garlic cloves. However, you may substitute powder or dehydrated forms of garlic. Use ⅛ teaspoon for 1 clove. Garlic salt is not recommended.

Mincing Fresh Garlic:

1. Separate cloves of garlic from bud (head).
2. Lay clove on cutting board. Place large knife blade over it. Pound knife blade hard with "heel" of hand to crush garlic and loosen the peel. Remove peel.

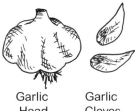

Garlic   Garlic
Head   Cloves

3. Using a chef's knife, rock blade back and forth to finely mince. To rock, use fingers of left hand to hold tip of blade firmly on cutting board. With right hand, lift blade from board to rock up and down several times across the garlic. Stop on occasion to remove garlic from blade. Gather garlic into pile on cutting board and repeat rocking procedure. If left-handed, use reverse hands.
4. To release more garlic flavor, gather in pile on cutting board. Place flat side of chef's knife over garlic and gently smash pieces.

S₂ Green Beans   (Legume Family, #41, Day 4 Vegetable)

Green beans are a versatile vegetable, satisfying when steamed and served alone or as a tasty addition to stir-fries, soups and baked dishes. A diuretic, green beans help with diabetes and are a good source of vitamins A, B, calcium and potassium.

S₂  Sautéed Green Beans & Pumpkin Seeds   (Day 4 Recipe)

In skillet (w/ lid), steam frozen (or fresh stemmed) green beans in small amount of water (2 minutes for frozen or 4 minutes for fresh). The trick is to have no or very little water remaining. Drain any remaining water away, keeping beans in skillet. Add a drizzle of Day 4 oil, squeeze of fresh orange (optional), sprinkle of salt, pumpkin seeds and sliced leeks as desired. Sauté to desired doneness, stirring often. (I prefer them slightly crunchy.)

Green Beans

S₂  Greens

As a vegetable side, greens can be cooked as described below or ribbon cut (see page 136) and added to casseroles, soups or stir-fries.

1. Wash greens. Trim away any bad portions. You may prefer to remove the tough center rib (often stronger, more pungent portion) from rather large leaves (i.e., collards, kale). Tear or cut leaves into small pieces as desired.

2. In saucepan, bring small amount of water to boil, add greens, sprinkle with salt (and/or the Day's seasoning). Cover and simmer as chart below indicates. Check water level often, so it does not boil dry.

3. If desired, drizzle with the Day's oil. Serve immediately.

4. Greens are a quick and easy way to add flavor and nutritional value to pasta or grains.

Amaranth Leaf

Green	Food Family	Day	Minutes to Simmer
Amaranth	Purslane (#30)	Day 2	10–15 min.
Beet Greens	Goosefoot (#28)	Day 1	5 min.
Chard	Goosefoot (#28)	Day 1	5–7 min.
Collards	Mustard (#36)	Day 1	15 min.
Dandelion	Composite (#80)	Day 4	5 min.
Kale	Mustard (#36)	Day 3	15–20 min.
Kohlrabi Greens	Mustard (#36)	Day 3	5–7 min.
Spinach	Goosefoot (#28)	Day 3	3–5 min.
Turnip Greens	Mustard (#36)	Day 1	5–7 min.

Dandelion

Chard Leaf
with Stem

S₂ 🕐 **Kale & Cauliflower** (Mustard or Cruciferious Family, #36, Day 3 Recipe)

Kale and cauliflower create a nice blend of flavors to serve as a side dish with Quick & Easy meals for Day 3. Since kale is packed with nutritional value, especially lutein and zeaxanthin, chlorophyll, calcium, iron and vitamins A and C, it is a nice complement to cauliflower which has a lower nutritional value than other members of the Mustard Family (#36). The many varieties of kale are available year round. Kale eases lung congestion and has healing benefits for the stomach, liver and immune system, making it a superb vegetable for those with CRC.

1. Wash kale thoroughly. If large, you may desire to remove rib. Tear or ribbon cut into smaller pieces.

2. Place kale in saucepan with small amount of boiling water. Sprinkle with salt. Cover and simmer for 10–15 minutes. Check water level about every 5 minutes so it does not boil dry.

3. Add washed cauliflower florets, sprinkle with salt and simmer covered for 3–5 minutes longer until cauliflower is tender. Serve immediately.

Kale Leaf

S₂ 🕐 **Kohlrabi** (Mustard or Cruciferious Family, #36, Day 3 Vegetable)

Kohlrabi is another vegetable that can be of great benefit to a person with CRC. It is good for specifically treating Candida as well as viral infections. Because it helps to regulate blood sugar, it is also useful in treating hypoglycemia and diabetes. Much like a cross between a radish and a cucumber in taste, it is great shredded on salads or sliced for munching. Before eating, remove the tough skin at the base and peel the entire bulb. It is a great addition to stews and soups. Some even eat it stuffed! It is sweetest when small (tennis ball size) and the leaves may be enjoyed much like collards or kale (see greens recipe on page 75).

Kohlrabi with Greens

S₂ 🕐 **Leeks** (Lily Family, #11, Day 4 Vegetable)

Leeks are a mild cross-like taste of onions and garlic. They are high in sulfur and also an excellent source of carotenoids, lutein and zeaxanthin. The leaves and bulb can all be enjoyed in soups, salads, stir-fries, pilafs and casseroles.

1. Remove any wilted, dried or spongy portions. Rinse to remove surface dirt/sand.

2. Cut in half lengthwise. Lay cut side down on cutting board. Slice at desired thickness, working from open end toward root end, tossing root. Place slices in bowl of water. The remaining sand will naturally fall to bottom. Remove leeks and drain.

3. Freeze unneeded portion in a food storage bag. To prevent freezer burn, first spin dry in salad spinner.

Yield: 1 medium leek yields ~1 cup sliced leeks

Leeks

S₂ Onions/Scallions   (Lily Family, #11, Day 2 Vegetable)

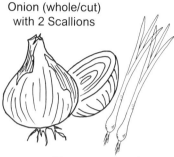

Onion (whole/cut)
with 2 Scallions

The low-cal onion is a tasty and healthy way to add flavor to almost any dish. The onion is an antibiotic, antifungal and antiviral agent. It also has anti-inflammatory and anticancer properties and, because of its high sulfur content, it is useful in eliminating heavy metals and parasites. It also lowers cholesterol. There are many varieties of onions; the sweeter ones have a higher sugar content.

Scallions *(sometimes referred to green onions) are the immature onion and have most of the same nutritional benefits of onions, though they are richer in some vitamins and minerals. Scallions are a great digestive aid and make foods with a high fat content more digestible. Use from green tip to root.*

 Freeze unused chopped/sliced leeks or onions without blanching.

Parsnips   (Carrot Family, #65, Day 3 Vegetable)

A staple in Europe before being replaced by the potato, parsnips are members of the carrot family. Because of their strong sweet and nutty flavor, they should be used sparingly in soups and stews. They can be well enjoyed prepared as you would prepare potatoes. Good for the stomach and liver, they also help to improve bowel function. Best in late fall and early winter, parsnips should be firm and fresh or they lose their flavor.

It is best to choose young, tender parsnips. If using large parsnips, remove the pithy center before cooking.

Add parsnips to winter stews and soups (such as Millet or Quinoa Turkey Vegetable Stew and, my favorite, Turkey Parsnip Soup) and/or serve as described below.

1. Scrub, peel and slice. Place in saucepan with small amount of boiling water or Turkey Broth. Sprinkle with salt. Cover and simmer for 15 minutes until tender. Check water level often so it does not boil dry.

2. If desired, whip with hand blender. Serve plain or season with flaxseed oil and/or caraway seeds.

Parsnip

S₂ Peas with Pods   (Legume Family, #41, Day 4 Vegetable)

Because the sugars in peas start converting to starch as soon as they are picked, peas protected by a pod stay sweeter for much longer. Sugar snap peas and snow peas have edible pods that are good sources of vitamins A and B, as well as calcium and potassium.

Sugar Snap
Peas

Enjoy raw for snacks, in stir-fries or lightly steamed OR prepare like Sautéed Green Beans & Pumpkin Seeds (page 75).

S₂ 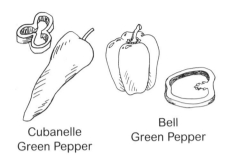 Peppers (Nightshade or Potato Family, #74, Day 2 Vegetable)

Sweet peppers come in a variety of colors. Generally, the lighter the color, the milder the taste. This is true of the mild Cubanelle, my favorite pepper for stuffing. The red bell is the most flavorful and the most nutritious. Peppers are one of my favorite vegetables, especially raw, when fresh from my garden. I also enjoy freezing stuffed peppers to enjoy the summer abundance year round.

Cubanelle
Green Pepper

Bell
Green Pepper

S₂ₗ Pumpkin (Gourd Family, #79, Day 2 Vegetable)

Helping to regulate blood sugar and ease asthma, pumpkin is a good addition to a healthy diet. It is rich in vitamin A and potassium. Its pureed form can be greatly enjoyed in pies, soups and breads. The commercially available pumpkin seeds are actually from a special kind of pumpkin grown in South America and benefit colon health. They are a great source of protein, Omega-3 fatty acids, iron, zinc, phosphorus and vitamin D. They also contain calcium and vitamin B. Easier to digest if they are lightly roasted, they add a nice crunch to stir-fries and salads.

Pumpkin Puree (Day 2 or 4 Vegetable)

Method 1—for Small or Large Pumpkins

1. Wash pumpkin, remove stem and cut in half crosswise. Cut threads with scissors. Scoop out seeds and threads.
2. Rinse pumpkin. Place cut sides down in large casserole dish(es). Add water to depth of $1/4$ inch. Bake at 350° for 45–60 minutes until pulp of pumpkin is fork tender. Add more water if needed, do not allow dishes to become dry.
3. Remove from oven and allow to cool enough to handle it.

Pumpkin

4. Use a large spoon to remove pulp from shell. If desired, blend pumpkin pulp in blender. Measure pumpkin in desired amounts and freeze.

Method 2—for Small Pumpkins (such as Sugar Pumpkins)

This method is for pumpkins that will fit in a large slow cooker (approx. $2^3/4$ pounds).

1. Wash pumpkin and remove stem. Place pumpkin in slow cooker with about 6 cups of water. Water level should cover approximately $3/4$ of the pumpkin. Cook on high for $3^1/2$–4 hours or until pumpkin is tender when pushed in with a spoon.
2. Remove carefully with two large spoons and set on cutting board to cool.
3. Remove pulp as described in Step 4 of Method 1.

Yield: a $2^3/4$-pound sugar pumpkin yields ~3 cups of pumpkin puree

S₂ Radishes (Mustard or Cruciferious Family, #36, Day 1 Vegetable)

The radish has a distinctive flavor that sweetens when cooked. With antifungal and antibacterial properties, it is an excellent choice for a snack and an easy way to add flavor to salads and soups. Even the greens provide a nutritious addition to stir-fries and soups. Daikon radishes are a pearly long white root that can be as long as your arm. They have antibacterial, antifungal and anticarcinogen properties. They also contain decongestants and diuretics.

Daikons without tops

Radishes with Greens

Rutabaga (Mustard or Cruciferious Family, #36, Day 3 Vegetable)

Rutabaga, a relative of the turnip, has all of the nutritional properties of turnips plus vitamin A. It is stronger in flavor than the turnip but is a great aid in liver detoxification. (I guess I need to reconsider my low taste impression of rutabaga. I welcome you, my readers, to share your rutabaga recipes [as well as any recipe] with me so I can share with others via the free e-CCNews; visit www.canaryconnect.com to sign up.)

S₂  Spinach (Goosefoot Family, #28, Day 3 Vegetable)

A tasty addition to salads, sandwiches, soups and casseroles, spinach can be enjoyed raw or cooked. Because it easily absorbs flavors and spices, it enhances many dishes with more than its own flavor. It is rich in vitamin C, calcium, phosphorus and protein. It also contains some iron. Spinach eases constipation. Winter spinach has a stronger taste than spinach grown in the summer months.

A Bunch of Spinach

S₂ Squash—Summer Varieties (Gourd Family, #79, Day 2 Vegetable)

An indigenous vegetable of the Americas, squash comes in several varieties. The summer squashes (i.e., zucchini and patty pan squash) tend to be rich in vitamins A and C and potassium. Cooking brings out their mild flavor; they are most flavorful when small. Patty pan squash can be temporarily moved to Day 4 to make it a delightful addition to Sautéed Green Beans & Pumpkin Seeds (page 75).

S₂ Sautéed Squash & Sunflower Seeds (Day 2 Recipe)

1 tablespoon	olive oil
¹/₂ cup	diced red pepper
2 cups	sliced summer squash
2	scallions, sliced
as desired	salt, Day 2 seasonings and seeds

In skillet, sauté vegetables and seeds in oil for 5–7 minutes until desired doneness (season with salt and/or Day 2 seasonings). Serve immediately.

Zucchini Squash

Crookneck Squash

Patty Pan Squash

S₂ₗ Squash—Winter Varieties (Gourd Family, #79, Day 2 and 4 Vegetables)

The winter varieties, including spaghetti, acorn and butternut squash, are low in sodium, have more complex carbohydrates and more beta carotene than their summer counterparts and are as rich in vitamins A and C, potassium, iron, riboflavin, carotenoids and magnesium. They are beneficial for treating diabetes and digestive disorders.

Sondra's Hints

Cooked squash may be frozen. Wrap in serving-sized portions.

- - - - -

To Reheat: Thaw squash at room temperature for a couple of hours or in the refrigerator for several hours. Heat covered in a 300° oven until warm.

- - - - -

For Pizza: Thaw squash (see "To Reheat"). Top pizza with thin layer to resemble cheese-like appearance. Do not use too much squash, as the flavor will seem too sweet and not spicy enough (see page 152).

S₂ Spaghetti Squash
(Day 2 Vegetable)

Spaghetti squash has a sweet flavor. It is delicious served with butter or flaxseed oil and Day 2 seasonings (i.e., basil, garlic) as well as with tomato or white sauce.

1. Cut squash in half lengthwise. With scissors, cut strands that attach to the seeds, then scoop seeds out. Sprinkle inside with salt and other seasonings as desired.

2. Place in shallow baking dish, cut side down. Add water to depth of ¹/₂-inch. Bake at 350° for 30–45 minutes until shell yields to gentle pressure and inside is fork tender. Remove from oven and allow to cool 5 minutes. It may be cooked whole but generally takes twice as long to bake.

3. With 2 table forks, pick at the squash as it separates from shell into strands that resemble spaghetti. Place desired amount on plate and top with sauce and/or seasonings.

Pulling out Strands of
Spaghetti Squash

S₂ₗ 🕐 ✓ 15 Minute Butternut Squash Soup (Day 4 Recipe)

¹/₄ cup	sliced leeks		¹/₂ tsp.	sea salt
1 Tbsp.	safflower oil		³/₄ tsp.	allspice
			¹/₄ tsp.	ground cloves
1 pkg.	frozen winter squash, thawed (10 oz.) OR		1 cup	Macadamia or Brazil Nut Milk (page 101)
1 cup	✓ Pureed Butternut Squash* (page 191)			

Sauté leeks in oil until tender. Whisk in squash, seasonings and milk. Cook until thickened, stirring almost constantly. Freeze extra.

Serve as appetizer or dessert.

*May substitute pureed sweet potato or pumpkin.

Yield: 1³/₄ cups   7 (¹/₄ cup) servings)   Enjoy a serving occasionally during Stage 2.

S₂L Sweet Potato   (Morning-Glory Family, #70, Day 4 Vegetable)

Sweet Potato

Sweet potatoes are higher in sugar than white potatoes. However, they are also rich in Vitamins A and C, carotenoids, calcium and thiamine. They are often considered medicinal for the kidneys and the stomach, though eating too many can cause indigestion. Being the only member of a food family, you may move them to any day of the rotation with ease.

S₂L Baked Sweet Potato   (Day 4 Recipe)

My favorite way to fix sweet potatoes is baked. Scrub and dry the skins, rub the Day's oil on the skin, pierce a couple of times with a fork and bake in 400° oven for about 30–45 minutes, depending upon size. Serve with flaxseed oil.

During Stage 2 choose small-sized sweet potatoes.

S₂L Sweet Potato Chips   (Day 4 Recipe)

1. Wash and peel sweet potatoes. Thinly slice between ¹/₁₆- and ¹/₈-inch thick.

2. Fill bottom of steamer pan with at least 2 inches of water. Heat to boiling. Add potato slices to steamer pan insert. Cover and cook over boiling water until tender (3–5 minutes). Immediately transfer to ice cold water to chill.

3. Place slices (single layer) on dehydrator trays. Sprinkle lightly with sea salt. Dehydrate for 7–8 hours at 140° until crisp. Check doneness by cooling a chip to taste.

4. Cool and store chips in freezer until ready to eat.

 Makes a great snack but do not eat too many as the dehydration process concentrates the sugars.

S₂ Turnip   (Mustard or Cruciferious Family, #36, Day 1 Vegetable)

Turnip with Greens

Turnips are a wonderful anticarcinogenic and a good source of vitamins B and C as well as potassium, phosphorus and calcium. Their flavor softens as they are cooked and easily absorbs other flavors (especially chicken broth), making them a great addition to casseroles and soups. Eaten raw, such as grated for a salad, turnips are a good digestive aid. They also reduce mucus and phlegm. Turnip greens, milder than kale and mustard greens, should be lightly cooked before eating.

Sondra's Thoughts

Scrub the skins of all vegetables and fruits before peeling or cutting to avoid spreading mold, which may have accumulated on the surface during the growth or storage process. For cleaner, see page 35.

"Carry-Over Cooking"

When preparing a meal, and you notice the steamed vegetables finishing faster than the rest of the meal, simply remove them from the heat source, drain liquid off and allow them to "carry-over cook" in the covered saucepan.

S₂ Stir-Fry Vegetables

Day 1	Day 2	Day 3	Day 4
broccoli cuts/florets, blanched	zucchini or summer squash, slant cut	cauliflower florets, blanched	asparagus cuts, blanched
cabbage, chopped	onion, sliced	Brussels sprouts, sliced, blanched	leek, sliced
celery, slant cut	green pepper strips	carrots, slant cut	any variety of peas, blanch if desired
salad turnips, sliced	eggplant, peeled, thin strips	kohlrabi, peeled, sliced	*Jerusalem artichoke, sliced thin
diakon radish, sliced	amaranth greens, torn	kale (small leaves are best), torn	cashew pieces
fennel, sliced	*grape or cherry tomatoes	*spinach, torn	pumpkin seeds
water chestnuts, sl.	sunflower or pumpkin seeds	filberts, chopped	safflower or soy oil
bamboo shoots	olive or sunflower oil	walnuts, chopped	*fresh garlic, minced
bok choy, sliced	*fresh garlic, minced	grapeseed, walnut, or coconut oil	
collards, torn			
*chard, torn			
almonds, sliced			
pecans, chopped			
sesame/almond oil			

*Hold these "last minute" vegetables until end of cooking time.

Preheat skillet on medium; I prefer cast iron.

1. Prepare ingredients in amounts desired.
2. In skillet, stir-fry vegetables and nuts/seeds in oil with the Day's seasonings. Stir often to cook evenly; best if left crunchy. Add "last minute" vegetables. Cook 30–60 seconds longer, stirring often. Serve immediately.

Stir-fry in oil w/ seasonings
Add "last minute" veggies
Serve immediately

S₂ Celery Soup (Day 1 Recipe)

2 cups   diced celery
2 cups   water
scant ¼ tsp.   sea salt

Combine ingredients in saucepan and simmer for 30 minutes. Blend soup in blender OR use immersion blender (page 116) until very smooth. Season with dill if desired.

Yield: 2 cups   2 servings

Celery

The ability to beat the odds lies within us all.

S₂ₗ Pilaf (Day 1 or 3 Recipe)

1 cup	dry grain—brown rice, millet, quinoa
as desired	broth—chicken, turkey or vegetable
~2 cups	vegetables (see "Thoughts" below)
as desired	nuts/seeds, seasonings and garnishes (see "Thoughts" below)
as needed	Day's oil

1. Rinse and cook grain according to Basic Grains (page 165) except add about ¹/₄ cup more cooking liquid and, if desired, replace half of the liquid with vegetable or poultry broth. If you are not using broth, add a couple of teaspoons of the Day's oil.

2. In skillet (I prefer cast iron), lightly sauté your choice of vegetables in the Day's oil, adding some vegetables and nuts at the end of the cooking time. Time the sautéing to be finished just as the grain finishes cooking. Add sautéed mixture to cooked grain, stir, cover and allow to "rest" at least 5 minutes before serving.

Yield: Rice or Millet: 4¹/₂ cups Quinoa: 6 cups During Stage 2 enjoy smaller servings.

Sondra's Thoughts

Rice Pilaf for Day 1: Cook rice in half chicken broth/half water. For veggies, I enjoy the combo of diced fennel and celery, sliced water chestnuts and ribbon cut (page 136) chard with ¹/₂ cup broken pecans (adding chard and pecans at the end of cooking time). Garnish with fresh minced parsley. Serve with Chicken Loaf Patty and chicken broth pan drippings.

- - - - -

Quinoa Pilaf for Day 3: Cook quinoa in half vegetable or turkey broth/half water. For veggies, I enjoy the combo of diced carrots, sliced cauliflower and 1–2 handfuls of baby spinach leaves with ¹/₂ cup or more coarsely chopped walnuts (adding spinach and walnuts at the end of cooking time). Serve with Turkey Loaf Patty and broth pan drippings.

- - - - -

Millet Pilaf for Day 3: Cook millet in half turkey broth/half water. Prepare and serve the same as Quinoa except use 1 teaspoon of caraway seeds instead of walnuts.

Meal Preparation Tips

Complete a meal by using the sautéing skillet to cook Chicken/Turkey Loaf Patties. The trick is to grind (if needed), mix up the meat mixture and shape the patties (lay shaped patties on baking sheet) while grain and vegetables are cooking.

As soon as you move the sautéed vegetables to cooked grain, add a small amount of the Day's oil to hot skillet and immediately transfer patties using a metal spatula. Cook for about 4–5 minutes per side, adding a drizzle of oil to the topside of patty just before flipping.

- - - - -

For an added touch of flavor, add about a cup of broth to skillet after removing cooked patties. Whisk broth while heating to remove the pan drippings. Serve these drippings over meat patty and pilaf.

S₂ Italian Eggplant (Day 2 Recipe)

1 pear-shaped	eggplant, peeled and sliced ¹/₂-inch thick
¹/₂ cup	tomato puree
1 cup	water
¹/₄ cup	finely diced green pepper
¹/₄ cup	finely chopped onion
¹/₄ teaspoon	sea salt
¹/₄ teaspoon	dried minced garlic
¹/₂ teaspoon	dried basil

> Layer eggplant
> Combine sauce ingred.;
>   pour over eggplant
> Bake

Oven temperature—350°.
Preheating not necessary.

1. Layer eggplant in covered, shallow baking dish. (Cut slices to fit.)

2. In 2-cup measure, combine remaining ingredients. Pour evenly over eggplant. Bake covered for 30–40 minutes or until eggplant is tender.

Yield: 4 servings

Pasta Sauce Version: For a fast, even easier version of Italian Eggplant, combine ³/₄ cup each prepared pasta sauce and water to replace all sauce ingredients in recipe. Bake as directed above. Yield: 4 servings

 Sprinkle shredded mozzarella or Parmesan cheese on top of serving for non-CRC family members.

S₂  Pesto

Traditionally pesto contains cheese, however, it is tasty without. I love these recipes served with each Day's pasta or cooked vegetable OR used as dip for raw vegetables.

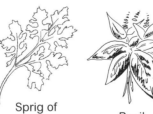

Sprig of Parsley

Basil

Bunch of Cilantro

Arugula Leaves

	Day 1	Day 2	Day 3	Day 4
¹/₄ cup toasted nuts	almonds	pine nuts	walnuts	macadamia
2 cups measure packed	flat-leaf parsley	basil	cilantro	arugula

In food processor (or blender) pulse chop the Day's nut and veggie with ¹/₂ teaspoon of salt and 2 cloves of fresh garlic on Day 2 and 4. Stream in 2–4 tablespoons of the Day's oil while continuing to blend. Add and mix in ¹/₄ cup water.

Yield: ³/₄ cup

S₂ₗ 🥣 Spicy "Shake & Bake" Potatoes (Day 2 Recipe)

Use this recipe to avoid the preservatives and large amount of oil in the packaged products. Try the spice combinations listed or create your own "flavor."

2 teaspoons	olive oil
2 cups	1/2-inch cottage-sliced peeled potatoes (quarter lengthwise and slice; if using fingerling potatoes, simply slice)
2 tablespoons	potato starch
1/4 teaspoon	sea salt

Seasoning Combo Choices:

1/4 teaspoon	garlic powder
1/8 teaspoon	ground cayenne (red) pepper

OR

1/4 teaspoon	garlic powder
1/4 teaspoon	dried leaf oregano
1/8 teaspoon	dried marjoram

OR

1/4 teaspoon	garlic powder
1/2 teaspoon	chili powder
1/8 teaspoon	dried leaf oregano

> Recipes
> Prepare potatoes
> Mix coating
> Drain potatoes; coat
> Bake
> Serve immediately

Preheat oven to 425°. Add oil to stainless steel baking pan. Spread evenly.

1. Prepare potatoes. Cover with water.
2. In a small bowl, combine potato starch, salt and your choice of seasonings.
3. Drain potatoes and immediately add to plastic food bag. Add spice mixture. While holding bag closed with as little air in bag as possible, quickly toss to evenly coat potatoes.
4. Pour potatoes into prepared pan. Spread out evenly. Bake for 25–30 minutes until potatoes are tender. Serve immediately.

Yield: 4 servings   During Stage 2, enjoy these occasionally.

S₂ₗ ⏱ Fried Potatoes (Day 2 Recipe)

3 medium-sized	potatoes
1/4–1/2 cup	each: diced onions and green peppers
1 tablespoon	butter or Clarified Butter (page 97)
1 tablespoon	olive oil

> Recipes
> Prepare potatoes
> Heat oil; melt butter
> Add veggies and
>   seasonings; cook

1. Wash, peel and slice potatoes (~1/4-inch thick slices). Cook 1–2 minutes in steamer pan.
2. Preheat electric skillet to 350°. Heat oil; melt butter. Add vegetables and season, if desired, with salt and cayenne pepper. Cook for about 10 minutes, turning as needed. Turning less often will create brown, crispy potatoes.

Yield: 4 servings   During Stage 2, enjoy smaller servings or on occasion.

S₂ₗ Cream of Potato Soup (Day 2 Recipe)

2 cups	diced, peeled potatoes
¼ cup	finely chopped onions
½ teaspoon	sea salt
2 tablespoons	potato starch
2 tablespoons	chopped Brazil OR macadamia nuts
3 cups	liquid (potato broth and water)

1. In saucepan, simmer potatoes, onion and salt in small amount of water until potatoes are almost done. Drain in colander, reserving liquid.

2. Combine starch, nuts and ¼ cup of liquid in blender. Blend on highest speed for 1–2 minutes until well blended, stopping to scrape sides and bottom as needed. Add remaining liquid and blend a few seconds longer. Pour mixture into potato saucepan. Cook until mixture thickens, stirring constantly for smooth mixture.

3. Add potatoes and cook until tender. Taste, add more salt if desired.

Yield: 5 cups   2 servings   During Stage 2, enjoy smaller servings or on occasion.

> Simmer potatoes; drain
>
> Blend nut mixture; add; cook
>
> Add potatoes, cook

Mac'n Cheese-Less (Non-rotating Recipe[†])

2 cups	macaroni—spelt, Kamut®, br. rice		1 tsp.	sea salt (divided)
2 Tbsp.	sesame seeds		1 tsp.	onion powder[†]
	OR		½ tsp.	garlic powder[†]
¼ cup	nuts—cashew, Brazil, macadamia		1 Tbsp.	fresh lemon juice
			1¼ cups	water (divided)
¼ cup	diced red peppers[†]		2 Tbsp.	sesame oil
	OR shredded carrots (Day 3 food)		2 Tbsp,	flour—same as pasta

1. In saucepan, bring water to boil. Add macaroni and ½ teaspoon of the salt; cook until slightly under *al dente*. Drain.

2. Meanwhile, in blender, finely chop nuts/ grind seeds. Add pepper/carrot; blend. Add remaining ½ teaspoon of the salt, seasonings and juice with small about of the water. Blend until smooth, stopping to scrape sides/bottom as needed. Add remaining water. Blend before adding to skillet in Step 3.

> Cook macaroni
>
> Blend nut/seed mixture
>
> Prepare roux
>
> Add ingred. & cook in stages; "rest"
>
> Serve immediately

3. In skillet, prepare roux (whisk flour in oil, cooking for a minute). Stir in nut mixture. Cook to thicken, stirring often. Add pasta and cook for about 1 minute. Remove from heat, cover and let "rest" for 2 minutes for sauce to set up and coat macaroni.

Yield: 4 cups   4 servings   A great recipe to enjoy during Stage 1 when omitting cheese.

[†]*This amazing, delicious recipe does not fit the rotation as outlined in this cookbook. However, I enjoy it on Day 1 without concern regarding the foods assigned to Day 2 or 3.*

S₂L Creamed Potatoes (Day 2 Recipe)

3 cups	diced, peeled potatoes
3 tablespoons	finely chopped onion
3 tablespoons	finely diced green peppers
1/2 teaspoon	sea salt
2 tablespoons	potato starch
2 tablespoons	chopped Brazil or macadamia nuts
1 1/4 cups	liquid (potato broth and water)

Simmer potatoes; drain

Blend nut mixture; add; cook

Add potatoes, cook

Prepare same as Cream of Potato Soup (previous page), adding peppers in Step 1. If mixture is too thick, add a small amount of water.

Yield: 3 1/3 cups   3 servings   During Stage 2, enjoy smaller servings or on occasion.

S₂ Italian Vegetables (Day 2 Recipe)

1 tablespoon	olive oil
1 cup	chopped onion
1 1/2 cups	diced peeled eggplant
1 1/2 cups	diced zucchini/summer squash (peel if desired)
2 cloves	fresh garlic, minced
1/2 teaspoon	sea salt
1/2 teaspoon	dried basil
1 teaspoon	dried leaf oregano
1 (15 oz.) can	diced tomatoes (see "Hints")
1 cup	water

1. In skillet with lid, "Chop & Drop" vegetables, garlic and seasonings.

2. Add tomatoes (hand crush as pour into skillet) and water. Bring to boil, reduce heat and cover. Simmer 5–10 minutes or until vegetables are tender and flavors blended.

Yield: 3 1/2 cups   3 servings

"Chop & Drop"

Add puree/water; simmer

Freeze extra

S₂ Italian Nightshade
(Day 2 Recipe)

Prepare same as above in Italian Vegetables, using 2 cups each eggplant and green peppers for onion/eggplant/squash.

Yield: 3 1/2 cups   3 servings

Sondra's Hints

For an extra "kick," use fire-roasted diced tomatoes.

- - - - -

May substitute 1/2–1 cup of tomato puree for diced tomatoes.

Yields: 2 1/2–3 cups

S₂ Zucchini or Okra with Tomato (Day 2 Recipe)

1 tablespoon	olive oil
1 cup	chopped onion
2 cups	sliced zucchini or summer squash
	OR
1 cup	sliced okra
1 clove	fresh garlic, minced
1/8 teaspoon	sea salt
as desired	dried seasonings (i.e., summer savory, leaf oregano, basil)
1 (15 oz.) can	crushed/diced tomatoes
	OR fire-roasted diced tomatoes

Sauté veggies
Add tomatoes;
simmer

In skillet or saucepan, sauté vegetables, garlic and seasonings in oil until at least onions are tender. Add tomatoes (hand crush while pouring into skillet). Bring to boil, reduce heat, cover and simmer for 5–7 minutes to blend favors.

Serve over baked potatoes and fish.

Yield: 2 1/2 cups   2 servings

S₂CL Perfect Pasta—Tips & Techniques

For Mio Amore Amaranth and Ancient Harvest Wheat-Free Quinoa Pasta:*

1. In saucepan, bring 1 1/2 cups of water to boil. Add 1/2 cup pasta and some salt. Bring back to boil. Immediately remove from heat, cover and let stand for 8–10 minutes.

2. If serving hot, drain and serve immediately or add to soup/stew and serve immediately. If using in cold salad, drain, immediately chill in ice water, drain and gently toss in salad.

For Mio Amore Wild Rice and Rye Pasta:

1. In saucepan, bring 1 1/2 cups of water to boil. Add 1/2 cup pasta and sprinkle with salt. Bring back to boil. Reduce heat. Gently boil for 7–8 minutes until *al dente*. Stir occasionally.

2. Follow Step 2 above.

Follow package directions for the following pastas:

Eden Foods Kudzu & Sweet Potato Pasta   100% Buckwheat Soba Noodles
Eden Foods Mung Bean Pasta   Various Kamut®, Rice and Spelt pastas

During Stage 2, enjoy small servings of gluten-free pastas (i.e, amaranth, buckwheat, sweet potato, mung bean, quinoa, wild rice). Omit brown rice pasta (see page 38). Yield:

Amaranth: 1/2 cup = 1/2 cup   Mung Bean: 1.2 oz. = 1 cup
Buckwheat: 2 oz. = 2/3 cup   Quinoa: 1/2 cup = 1 cup
Kamut®, Rice and Spelt: 1/2 cup = 1 cup   Rye: 1/2 cup = scant 1 cup
Kudzu/Sweet Potato: 1.2 oz. = scant 1 cup   Wild Rice: 1/2 cup = 2/3 cup

Special Note: Overcooking these gluten-free pastas makes them mushy.

S₂c All-in-One Salads

Grain/Nongrain Choices:	Day 1	Day 2	Day 3	Day 4
¹/₂ cup cooked pasta (recipe on page 88)	spelt, br. rice or Kamut®	amaranth	wild rice, rye, or quinoa	mung bean
¹/₂ cup cooked grain/nongrain	brown rice	amaranth	millet or quinoa	buckwheat

Protein Choices:

~3 ounces baked/broiled seafood	halibut	cod, pollack	salmon	haddock orange roughy
¹/₂ cup diced roasted meat	chicken	beef buffalo	turkey	pork venison
2 hard boiled eggs, diced	chicken			
1 cup cooked beans, drained		garbanzo lima		kidney, navy or black

Vegetable & Seasoning Choices:

¹/₂ cup cooked vegetables		diced potatoes		fresh or frozen peas
2 cups shredded or small pieces of fresh vegetables (blanch asparagus, broccoli and cauliflower for 1–2 minutes)	celery broccoli cabbage turnip, radish	peppers zucchini cucumber onion	beet cauliflower carrots kohlrabi	pea pods bean sprouts asparagus leeks
season as desired with sea salt and/or the Day's seasonings				
fresh "greens" (optional)	Swiss chard	lettuce	spinach	sorrel

Dressing Choices (see pages 94–96):

¹/₄–¹/₂ cup "Mayo"	Almond	Sunflower or Creamy Ital.	Filbert	Macadamia or Cashew
¹/₃ cup Creamy Veggie Dressing	Cabbage	Zucchini	Carrot	
1 recipe Easy "C" Dressing	Sesame	Sunflower	Grapeseed	Safflower

1. Prepare your choice of ingredients and dressings. In bowl, gently toss all ingredients except "greens" and dressing. Add dressing and mix to coat all ingredients. Chill.

2. Serve on a bed of "greens" or tear leaves and mix into salad along with more dressing just before serving.

 May complement salad with crackers, muffin or biscuit.

 Sondra's Thoughts

Rice pasta is weak on flavor, so I add a little extra dry mustard to Almond "Mayo" for that day.

- - - - -

Because of their distinctive flavors, I do not recommend combining salmon and quinoa.

Yield: 2¹/₂–3 cups, complete meal for 1 person   There are many choices above that can be enjoyed during Stage 2. Some ingredients listed are to be consumed in limited amounts, however, the amounts listed seem to be low enough to enjoy during Stage 2.

S₂  ☑ Chef Salad

Day 2	**Day 3**
lettuce, assorted variety, torn	spinach, torn
radicchio, shredded	carrots, shredded
cucumbers and/or zucchini, sliced	beets, shredded
tomato wedges	cauliflower, sliced or in florets, lightly
green peppers, in strips or diced	steamed or blanched, chilled
red onions, sliced or diced	kohlrabi, peeled, shredded
sunflower seeds	*radishes, salad turnips or bok choy,
garbanzo beans, drained	shredded or sliced
cod or pollack, flaked	walnuts or filberts, chopped
cooked roast beef, diced or in strips	*eggs, hard-cooked, diced
Lemon-Oil Dressing	salmon, flaked
Creamy Dressing (Zucchini)	cooked turkey, diced or in strips
Easy "C" Dressing (Sunflower)	Creamy Dressing (Carrot)
Creamy Italian Dressing	Easy "C" Dressing (Grapeseed)
	Filbert "Mayo"
	*foods temporarily moved from Day 1
Salad Dressing recipes on pages 94–96	

Prepare and toss your choice of vegetables and protein sources in amounts desired. Top with your choice of dressing. Serve with crackers, biscuits or muffins for a complete light meal, especially nice on a hot summer day.

S₂ₗ 🕐 ☑ 7 Layer Salad (Day 4† Recipe)

4 cups	torn lettuce†
1 cup	frozen peas, thawed
1/4 cup	sliced leeks
1/2 cup	diced cucumber (peel if desired)
1/2 cup	diced green pepper†
1 pound	fresh pork side, thickly sliced
1/3 cup	☑ Macadamia Nut "Mayo" (page 95)

> Prepare veggies
> Cook pork; crumble
> Layer ingredients
> Chill

1. Prepare vegetables and "Mayo".

2. Cook pork, salt as desired while cooking. Drain on paper towel. Cool and crumble.

3. In a 8–10-inch square dish, layer ingredients evenly in the order listed above—lettuce thru pork.

4. Pour "Mayo" over top of salad. Cover and refrigerate an hour to blend flavors.

Yield: 4 servings   Enjoy in limited amounts during Stage 2 or limit/omit the peas.

†These foods are assigned to Day 2; omit them on Day 2 before and after eating on Day 4.

S₂ ☑ Coleslaw (Day 1 Recipe)

1 cup	shredded or finely chopped cabbage
1/4 cup	diced celery
1/4 cup	☑ Almond "Mayo" (page 95)
	OR
1/2 recipe	Easy "C" Dressing (Sesame) (page 94)
as desired	sea salt, fresh parsley, dill weed

Combine
Chill

Combine and chill.

Yield: 1 cup   2 servings

S₂ ☑ Kidney Bean Salad (Day 2† Recipe)

1 1/4 cups	☑ cooked kidney beans,† drained
1 cup	diced cucumber (peel if desired)
1/2 cup	diced green pepper
1/4 cup	☑ Sunflower "Mayo" (page 95)
1/4 teaspoon	onion powder
1/4 teaspoon	sea salt

Combine
Chill

1. Prepare beans by following steps 1–3 of Kidney Beans for Chili (page 110), using only 1/2 cup dry beans and 1 cup of water.

2. Combine all ingredients and chill.

Yield: 2 1/2 cups   5 servings

†*Kidney beans are assigned to Day 4; omit them on Day 4 before and after eating on Day 2.*

S₂L ☑ Potato Salad (Day 2 Recipe)

2 cups	diced peeled potatoes
1/2 teaspoon	sea salt
2/3 cup	diced green or red pepper
2/3 cup	diced cucumber (peel if desired)
2 tablespoons	finely chopped onion
	OR
1/2 teaspoon	onion powder
1/3 cup	☑ Sunflower "Mayo" (page 95)

Cook potatoes;
   chill
Combine
Chill

In saucepan over medium heat, simmer potatoes and salt in small amount of water until tender. Drain and chill. Add remaining ingredients. Stir and chill. Sprinkle with paprika, if desired.

Yield: 2 1/2 cups   5 servings

During Stage 2, enjoy small servings of potato salad occasionally, especially at a picnic.

S₂ₗ ☑ Cucumber & Pea Salad (Day 4 Recipe)

1 cup	fresh or frozen peas, thawed and drained
1 cup	sliced cucumber (peel if desired)
1/2 cup	sliced leeks
1/8 teaspoon	sea salt
1/3 cup	☑ Macadamia or Cashew "Mayo" (page 95) OR
1 recipe	Easy "C" Dressing (Safflower) (page 94)
as desired	fresh sorrel

Gently toss prepared vegetables with salt. Add dressing, mix, and chill. If desired, serve on a bed of sorrel.

Yield: 2 cups   4 servings   Enjoy a small serving of Pea Salad occasionally during Stage 2.

A Page of Easy
Combine &
Chill Salads

S₂ Day 4† Mixed Vegetable Salad

2 cups	cucumber and/or zucchini slices†
2 tablespoons	sliced leeks
as desired	sprouts
2 recipes	Easy "C" Dressing (Safflower) (page 94)

Combine ingredients and chill.

Yield: 2 cups   2 Servings

†Zucchini is assigned to Day 2; omit it on Day 2 before and after eating on Day 4.

☑ Apple Salad (Day 3 Recipe)

1 small	apple, diced (~2/3 cup)
2 tablespoons	chopped walnuts
2 tablespoons	☑ Filbert "Mayo" (page 95)

Combine and chill.

Yield: 2/3 cup   1 serving

☑ Vegetable/Apple Salad
(Day 3 Recipe with Variations)

1 medium	apple, diced (~1 cup)
1/2 cup	shredded carrot
2 tablespoons	chopped walnuts
3 tablespoons	☑ Filbert "Mayo" (page 95)

Combine and chill.

Yield: 1 1/2 cups   2 servings

Variations

Add 1–2 tablespoons finely flaked coconut.

- - - - -

Add 1 cup of fresh torn spinach and more "Mayo."

- - - - -

Use 1/4 cup diced celery for half of the carrots. Omit eating celery on Day 1 before and after eating this variation on Day 3.

Quinoa Salad (Day 3 Recipe)

1 cup	☑ Basic Quinoa (page 165), chilled
1/2 cup	finely diced apple
1/3 cup	shredded peeled carrot
few sprigs	fresh parsley (optional)

Combine and chill.

Yield: 1 1/3 cups firmly packed   1 serving

Three Easy
Combine &
Chill Salads
AND
Simple Stir-Fry

S₂ₗ ☑ 3 Color Salad (Day 3 Recipe)

3/4 cup	☑ Basic Quinoa (page 165), chilled
1 cup	shredded peeled carrot
~1 cup	fresh spinach, torn, loosely packed

Combine and chill. Serve within 24 hours.

Yield: 1 serving

Although raw carrots are listed in the foods to eat freely, 1 cup of carrots may be more than what some can handle during Stage 2. I would choose to decrease the carrots and increase the spinach.

Hint!

Use more or less of each food for salad or stir-fry.

S₂ₗ ☑ 3 Color Stir-Fry (Day 3 Recipe)

If you desire warm over cold, stir-fry 3 Color Salad in small amount of Day 3 oil until spinach wilts and the chill is gone.

The carrots in this stir-fry are cooked minimally, however, I would follow the same guidelines as described in the above recipe during Stage 2.

S₂ Day 2 Mixed-Vegetable Salad

2 cups	diced Day 2 veggies (i.e., zucchini, summer squash, cucumber, peppers)
2 tablespoons	finely chopped onion OR
1/2 teaspoon	onion powder
2 recipes	Easy "C" Dressing (Sunflower) (page 94) OR
1/3 cup	☑ Sunflower "Mayo" or Creamy Italian Dressing (page 95)

Combine and chill.

Yield: 2 cups

Sprout Salad (Day 4 Recipe)

1 can	unsweetened pineapple chunks (20 oz.)
1 pkg.	alfalfa sprouts (4 oz.)
$1/4$ cup	raw pumpkin seeds

Combine and chill for a few hours to blend flavors.

The pineapple provides a wonderful complementary flavor.

Yield: 6 servings

RECIPES

Salad Dressings/Condiments
Beverages/Miscellaneous

Condiments and salad dressings are the little "extras" that add flavor and variety to our food. Because they routinely contain sugar and vinegar, they can be a challenge when using the Candida-Control Food Plan, especially Stage 2. However, these recipes offer quick and easy ways to prepare and store "the extras," helping you to stick to the Food Plan. Likewise, having some fun, nutritious beverages in your repertoire allows for enjoyable snacks and easy additions to quick meals.

Freshly squeezed lemon/lime/orange juice or unbuffered vitamin C crystals often work to replace vinegar in your favor condiments recipes.

S$_2$ Easy "C" Dressing

	Day 1	Day 2	Day 3	Day 4
1 teaspoon oil	sesame	olive or sunflower	grapeseed	safflower
1 tablespoon	water			
$1/8$ teaspoon	unbuffered vitamin C crystals			
1–2 pinches seasonings	dill weed	onion powder basil	cilantro caraway seed	tarragon

 In a small bowl, whisk together your choice of oil and seasonings with water and "C" until it dissolves. If desired, substitute 1–1$1/2$ teaspoons of freshly squeezed lemon, lime or orange juice for C crystals.

Yield: 1 serving

S₂c  "Mayo"

Amount	Ingredient	Day 1	Day 2	Day 3	Day 4
$^1/_2$ cup	nut or seed	almonds	sunflower seeds	filberts	macadamia or cashews
1 tablespoon	flour or starch	Kamut®, spelt or brown rice	arrowroot or potato starch	tapioca or cornstarch	kudzu
$^1/_4$ teaspoon	sea salt				
1 teaspoon	unbuffered vitamin C crystals				
1 cup	water				
as desired	seasoning	$^1/_2$ teaspoon dry mustard	$^1/_4$ teaspoon garlic powder	caraway seed cilantro	tarragon

1. In blender, blend nuts/seeds on highest speed for 1–2 minutes, stopping to scrape sides and bottom as needed. For smoother texture, add flour/starch and blend on highest speed 1 more minute. Add remaining ingredients, except seasonings. Blend on highest speed for a minute.

> Recipes
>
> Blend nut/seed mixture
> Add seasonings
> Cook; chill

2. Pour mixture into saucepan. Add seasonings. Cook over medium heat, stirring constantly with whisk until mixture is thick yet smooth.

4. Chill. If too thick, add more water. May be stored in refrigerator for a week or frozen.

 Flour, starch and seasonings may be easily interchanged to customize your rotation.

Yield: 1$^1/_3$ cups During Stage 2, choose the following thickeners: brown rice flour, arrowroot starch, tapioca or kudzu.

S₂  Creamy Italian Salad Dressing (Day 2 Recipe)

Prepare Sunflower "Mayo" (recipe above). Stir in the following seasonings and chill.

2 teaspoons dried leaf oregano
1 teaspoon dried basil
$^1/_4$ teaspoon sea salt
$^1/_4$ teaspoon garlic powder
Yield: 1$^1/_3$ cups

> *"The time to relax is when you don't have time for it."*
> —Sydney J. Harris

S₂ Creamy Dressing

Yield/Servings	Day 1 1/3 cup/1	Day 2 1 cup/4	Day 3 1 cup/4
vegetable	1/3 cup shredded cabbage, packed	1 cup diced peeled zucchini	1 cup shredded peeled carrots
water	1/4 cup	1/2 cup	1/2 cup
oil	1 teaspoon sesame	1 1/2 t. sunflower	1 1/2 t. grapeseed
unbuffered vitamin C crystals	1/4 teaspoon	1/2 teaspoon	1/2 teaspoon
sea salt	1 pinch	2 pinches	2 pinches
optional ingredients	1/4 t. dry mustard 1/2 t. sesame seeds	garlic and/or onion powder, as desired	1/2 teaspoon caraway seed

 In blender, blend all ingredients, except Day 2 and 3 optional ingredients, on highest speed for 1–2 minutes until smooth, stopping to scrape sides/bottom. Pour into jar/bottle. For Day 3, add caraway seeds; shake. Chill. For Day 2, add seasonings just before serving.

Yield: see above

S₂ Lemon-Oil Dressing
(Day 2 Recipe)

Mix 2 teaspoons of Day 2 oil with 1 teaspoon of freshly squeezed lemon juice.

S₂ Garlic-Lemon-Oil Dressing (Day 2 Recipe)

Heat 2 Tbsp. of olive oil with 1 clove fresh garlic (cracked) over low heat to fuse the garlic flavor into the oil. Cool. Remove garlic. Mix oil with 1 Tbsp. fresh lemon juice.

Lemon Juice—Tips on Preparing

 Wash lemons, roll on counter using pressure (to get the juices flowing), cut in half crosswise and squeeze by hand or juicer. Remove large pulp pieces and seeds. Save time by juicing several at once, pouring juice into ice cube trays and freezing for later use. (After frozen, cubes may be stored in plastic bag).

 Sondra's Thoughts

Serve Day 1 recipe within a couple of hours.

- - - - -

Day 2 and 3 recipes may be frozen or stored in refrigerator for a week.

- - - - -

Day 2 recipe can be made with frozen zucchini. Freeze zucchini in 1 cup amounts. Blend ingredients for a few seconds; then allow to thaw for a minute or so. Repeat process until zucchini is thawed and blended smooth.

Pancake or French Toast "Maple Syrup" (Day 3 Recipe)

1 teaspoon	alcohol-free maple extract
2–4 ounces	100% pure vegetable glycerin
as desired	FOS or stevia (stevia breaks rotation but minor)

Combine ingredients and serve over pancakes.

S_2 Catsup (Day 2[†] Recipe)

1 (6 oz.) can	tomato paste
$1/2$ cup	water
$1/8$ teaspoon	sea salt
$1/2$ teaspoon	onion powder
$1/2$ teaspoon	dried leaf oregano
$3/8$ teaspoon	unbuffered vitamin C crystals
	OR
1 tablespoon	fresh lemon juice (reduce water by 1 tablespoon)
$1/8$ teaspoon	each: garlic powder, ground cloves, ground cumin[†] and dry mustard[†]

> Combine
> Chill
> Freeze extra

Combine ingredients and chill. Dilute with water if desired.

Yield: ~1 cup

[†]*These seasonings are assigned to Day 1. This minor break in rotation is not a concern for most.*

S_2 Clarified Butter (Day 2 Recipe)

In skillet, heat 1 stick of unsalted butter to a slow boil until it foams well. Remove from heat and cool until milk solids fall to bottom of pan or float to top. Carefully skim off floating white milk solid residue and discard. Gently pour clear yellow liquid into a glass jar with a tight-fitting lid. Discard residue on bottom.

> Heat butter
> Chill slightly
> Skim off solids
> Store in glass jar

Yield: ~$2/3$ cup

Sondra's Thoughts

Using a skillet or pan that is small enough to allow melted butter to have a little depth works best to facilitate the separation process.

- - - - -

To maintain freshness and prevent mold formation, keep container tightly closed and always use a clean utensil. Store in refrigerator. This is firm when cold yet will soften quickly at room temperature. Soften only the amount you wish to use.

- - - - -

Clarified butter is also available commercially under the product name Ghee.

S₂ Avocado

Though really a fruit, avocados are often treated like a vegetable. Their high fat content makes them smooth and creamy in nature, lending themselves nicely to dips and spreads. People who have trouble digesting other fats are often able to assimilate the fats in avocados. Avocados contain good amounts of protein, potassium and vitamin E.

- Mash for guacamole, dips and spreads
- Slice and serve on crackers
- Dice and use in salads

S₂ Guacamole (Day 2† Recipe)

1 medium	ripe avocado†
2 tablespoons	chopped onion
2 tablespoons	diced green pepper
1/4 teaspoon	chili powder
1 clove	fresh garlic, minced
2 pinches	sea salt
2 pinches	unbuffered vitamin C crystals
1 small	tomato, diced (optional to include)

Blend ingredients
Stir in tomatoes
Cover; chill
Freeze extra (see Hints)

Cut avocado in half lengthwise, remove pit and scoop flesh into a food processor or blender. Add remaining ingredients except tomato. Blend to desired consistency. Transfer to bowl and stir in tomatoes. Cover and chill.

 Serve as a dip with crackers. Or, omit tomatoes and serve with Tacos, Enchiladas, Taco Pizza or Beef Fajitas.

 Guacamole may be frozen without tomato. Freezing causes avocado to darken slightly. To lighten, stir in a pinch of vitamin C crystals before serving.

Yield: ~2/3 cup without tomato   6 servings

†*Avocado is a Day 3 food but I don't concern myself with the minor break in rotation.*

S₂ Picante Sauce (Day 2 Recipe)

1/2 (28 oz.) can	tomato puree
1 cup	water
1/4 cup	finely diced green pepper
2 tablespoons	finely chopped onion
1 teaspoon	chili powder

1 tsp.	dried leaf oregano
1/2 tsp.	sea salt
1/2 tsp.	dried minced garlic
1/4 tsp.	dried red pepper flakes

In saucepan, combine all ingredients. Bring to boil, reduce heat and gently boil for 10 minutes to blend flavors and reduce sauce to 2 cups. Stir often, especially at end. Chill.

Gently boil
Chill
Freeze extra

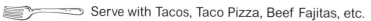 Serve with Tacos, Taco Pizza, Beef Fajitas, etc.

Yield: 2 cups   8 servings

☑ **Raspberry Pear Jam** (Day 1 Recipe)

2 cups	frozen raspberries (thawed)
2 cups	☑ Pear Sauce (page 102)
2 tablespoons	flour—brown rice, spelt or Kamut®

Combine fruits and flour in deep saucepan. Cook on medium-high for 5–10 minutes until thickened, stirring almost constantly with whisk to prevent burning.

Yield: 1^1/3 cups

> Combine
> Cook, stirring constantly
> Freeze extra

 Rhubarb Jelly (Day 4 Recipe)

2 cups	diced rhubarb
^{1}/4 cup	honey
	OR
^{1}/4 teaspoon	stevia powder with ^{1}/4 cup water
^{1}/8 teaspoon	sea salt
^{1}/2 teaspoon	kudzu starch

> Combine; cook
> Add kudzu; thicken
> Cool
> Freeze extra (see "Hints")

1. Combine all ingredients except kudzu in saucepan. Cover and cook on low for 5 minutes or until rhubarb is tender. Stir occasionally during cooking process.

2. Add kudzu and continue to cook, stirring constantly, until thickened. Cool.

 This jelly is delicious for breakfast or a snack on toasted Buckwheat Bread (page 181).

 Freeze stevia version using Ice Cube Tray method. The honey version may be frozen in a jar; it doesn't freeze solidly, so it's easy to scoop out.

Yield: 1 cup

S$_2$ **Dry Roasted Nuts/Seeds**

Soak your choice of nuts/seeds overnight in refrigerator in enough water to cover. Drain water and pour nuts/seeds into shallow baking dish. Spread to be only single layer. Bake at 250° for 30 minutes, stirring occasionally. Cool. When completely cool, store in tightly closed container in freezer. Remove as needed for snacks, "Milks" or recipes.

 Ice Cube Tray Freezing Hint!

A great way to freeze extra condiments, lemon juice, jelly/jams, sauces, salad dressings, nut milks is to freeze in ice cube trays. After frozen, remove and store frozen cubes in food storage bag. Thaw as needed.

 Helpful Hints

Nuts are better tolerated by those in the early treatment stages of CRC if they are dry roasted.

Also to assist with digestion, soak nuts and seeds overnight before roasting.

Spritzer Beverages

Ingredients	Grapefruit (Day 2)	Cranberry (Day 4)	Orange (Day 4)	Cranberry-Orange (Day 4)
chilled unflavored carbonated water	1 (12 ounce) bottle			
chilled or partially frozen, unsweetened juice	$1/4$ cup grapefruit concentrate	$1/2$ cup cranberry	$1/4$ cup orange concentrate	$1/4$ cup orange concentrate + $1/2$ cup cranberry
Yield: 2 servings	$1^3/4$ cups	2 cups	$1^3/4$ cups	$2^1/4$ cups

Combine ingredients. If desired, add few drops of liquid stevia. Serve immediately.

 ## Soy Protein Shake (Day 4 Recipe)

1 cup	ice cold water
2 tablespoons	Shaklee Instant Protein® Soy Mix* OR
2 tablespoons	Ener-G Pure Soy Quick
1 tablespoon	carob powder (or more) OR
$1/4$ teaspoon	your choice of alcohol-free flavoring
7 drops	liquid stevia

> Blend
> Add stevia to taste
> Serve chilled
> OR
> Heat for warm drink

Blend your choice of ingredients in blender or battery-operated mixer until dissolved. Taste. If desired, add more stevia. Serve immediately chilled or heat for a hot drink.

Yield: ~1 cup   1 serving

 ## Yogurt Smoothie (non-rotating recipe)

Great "on the go" breakfast during the early stage of omitting sugars and flours.

$1/4$–$1/2$ cup	fruit (fresh or thawed frozen)
$3/4$ cup	plain, unsweetened yogurt (6 oz.)
2 Tbsp.	Shaklee Instant Protein® Soy Mix*
5 drops	liquid stevia

 In blender, blend fruit until smooth. Add and blend remaining ingredients with $1/4$–$1/2$ cup of cold water until well mixed. Drink immediately or chill overnight.

 I prefer $1/2$ cup of all fruits except only $1/4$ cup for blueberries. Lower fat yogurt requires less water.

Yield: $1^1/2$–$1^3/4$ cups

*To purchase, see www.canaryconnect.com

S$_2$  "Milks"

^{1}/$_4$ cup   nuts (i.e., almonds, Brazil, cashews, filberts, macadamia)
OR

2 tablespoons   seeds (i.e., pumpkin, sesame, sunflower)

1 cup   water

1. Blend dry roasted nuts or seeds in blender on highest speed until they become a fine powder, about 1–2 minutes, stopping to scrape sides and bottom as needed. (Brazil and macadamia nuts will only become finely chopped.)

2. Add ^{1}/$_4$ cup water and blend on highest speed until well blended, stopping to scrape sides and bottom as needed. Add ^{3}/$_4$ cup water and blend a couple of seconds longer. Chill. Add salt if desired. Stir before serving. Use "Milks" to flavor hot cereals or serve with cold cereals.

Yield: slightly over 1 cup   8 servings

Blend nuts/seeds
Add water/blend in stages
Freeze extra (page 99)

Blender

I recommend a blender with a heavy duty motor (perhaps 700 watts). A wide, detachable jar base is also handy.

S$_2$ Pau D'Arco Tea

To prepare, boil 4 cups of water in saucepan. Add 1 heaping tablespoon of bulk tea. For a sweeter flavor, add an optional few leaves of fresh basil. Remove from heat, cover and allow to steep for at least 20 minutes. Pour steeped tea through fine mesh strainer to remove leaves. Store in refrigerator or insulated container. Drink unsweetened, warm or cold. For more information, see page 48.

Hot Beverage Options
Experiment with steeping herbs and spices of your choice or add alcohol-free extracts to warm water.

Dacopa Beverage (Day 2 or 4)

Dacopa is a hot beverage similar to coffee. Made from dahlia root, it is a member of the Composite Family, #80. Prepare according to package directions.

> *"Things do not change—we do."*
> —Henry David Thoreau

Yogurt Delights (Day 2 Recipe)

Add any of the following to plain, sugar-free, organic yogurt.

- Alcohol-free vanilla extract
- Puffed amaranth, serve immediately
- Sliced cucumbers (peel if desired)
- Fresh or frozen (thawed) blueberries. Omit eating blueberries on Day 4 before and after enjoying this variation on Day 2. Other fruits can be used, see guidelines to temporarily or permanently move foods on pages 63–64.

 Pear Sauce (Day 1 Recipe)

1. Choose ripe but not overly ripe pears. Wash, peel, core, quarter, rinse and drain.

2. Run fruit through Champion Juicer set up for homogenizing. To prevent fruit from darkening, add about $1/4$ teaspoon of unbuffered vitamin C crystals for each 2 cups of sauce. Add more as needed, stirring after each addition. In saucepan, cook on low for 10 minutes, stirring often to prevent sticking.

> Prepare pears
> Process pears; cook w/ vit. C
> OR
> Cook pears w/ vit. C; blend
> Freeze

OR

2. To prevent fruit from darkening, add $1/4$ teaspoon unbuffered vitamin C crystals for each 2 cups of quartered pears. Add more as needed, stirring after each addition. In saucepan, cook on low until soft, stirring often to prevent sticking. Blend in blender or press through a canning sieve or food mill.

 For pancake topping, dilute 2 tablespoons of pear sauce with 1 tablespoon water and heat before serving.

Yield: 5 pounds pears yields ~$5^1/2$ cups of sauce

 Pear Sauce Sweetener (Day 1 Recipe)

Recipes in this cookbook are developed with a ratio of 1 cup Pear Sauce cooked down to $2/3$ cup Pear Sauce Sweetener.

After preparing Pear Sauce, cook in saucepan on low to thicken. Sauce will darken as it becomes thicker. Stir often to prevent sticking, especially at end. Cool. Freeze in portions needed for recipes.

Yield: 1 cup Pear Sauce yields $2/3$ cup of sweetener

> Using Pear Sauce, cook to thicken
> Cool
> Freeze for later

RECIPES

Bean Cookery

Beans are one of the easiest foods to prepare. They may take a long time to cook, either on the stove or in a slow cooker, but the actual "hands-on" time is very low in comparison with many other foods.

Beans are an inexpensive and good source of nutrients, including complex carbohydrates, protein, magnesium, calcium, potassium, zinc, several B-vitamins and fiber and are low in fat. Canned beans without syrup or other added ingredients can be an option in some recipes but my opinion is that you sacrifice "big flavor" for only a little of "hands-on" time and some advanced planning. The recipes in this section provide flavorful ways to prepare beans for eating as a side dish or to incorporate in other recipes.

Basic Bean Cookery

Store dry beans tightly covered in a cool dry place. Before using, sort through them, discarding any shriveled beans or debris. The following are general rules of thumb for cooking beans:

Beans—Prepare for Cooking

The first 3 steps can easily be accomplished in about 5 minutes the night before you plan to cook the beans. Step 4 will take about 2 minutes immediately before cooking.

1. Measure and place dry beans in large bowl. For 2 cups of dried beans, an 8-cup bowl is a perfect size.

2. To remove surface mold, dirt and/or other debris, add enough water to cover beans. Stir them with a spoon or with your hand. Skim off beans and debris that float to the top. Drain in colander, discarding water. Repeat procedure with fresh water two or three times until the water is clear.

3. Return beans to large bowl and fill with water (enough to allow beans to double). Place container in refrigerator and allow beans to soak for 8–12 hours.

   If you don't have 8 hours to soak the beans, use the following procedure:
   - Place rinsed and drained beans in a large pot. Cover with water.
   - Bring to a boil and cook for 2 minutes.
   - Remove from heat, cover and let stand for 1 hour.
   - Drain water, thoroughly rinse and drain beans again.

4. Before cooking beans, drain off soaking water. Thoroughly rinse again to remove the filmy (starchy) substance that formed when soaking. Repeat until water is clear.

Testing Beans for Doneness*

Use one of these to test for doneness. Discard test beans after completed.

- Remove a few beans to spoon. Blow on them. If the skins burst, the beans are done.

- Put a slightly cooled bean in your mouth and press it against the roof of your mouth. If you are able to break it up with your tongue without using your teeth, the beans are done.

- Bite into a slightly cooled bean. If it is tender without firm resistance, the beans are done.

As described by Marjorie Hurt Jones in Mastering Food Allergies newsletter "Bean Cookery," Mastering Food Allergies, Vol. IV, No. 3, issue 33 (March 1989), 1.

General Tips When Cooking Beans

- Lentils and split peas do not need to be presoaked but it may be done to assist with eliminating intestinal gas (except for red lentils which should not be soaked).

- If you soak too many beans, drain and freeze them in a food storage bag. Pull from freezer and cook as directed.

- Cook beans until tender but not mushy.

- If beans finish cooking earlier than you plan to serve them (i.e., an hour or so early), turn slow cooker setting to low or off for a while. Turn heat on near serving time to reheat beans to serving temperature.

- Many factors, such as variety, maturity, age and moisture content of beans affect the cooking time. Even the kind of water you use can affect the cooking time (i.e., beans take longer to cook in hard water).

Helpful Hints

The bean recipes prepared in a small (~1 quart) slow cooker may be doubled or tripled for cooking in a standard-sized slow cooker.

- - - - -

Freeze unsalted cooked beans in portions for recipes or to serve as a side dish. Label with the amount of salt needed. Add salt when reheating.

Options for Helping to Alleviate Intestinal Gas

You may not need to use all of these. Along with soaking the beans (see Prepare for Cooking on previous page), the most helpful seem to be the first two listed:

- IMPORTANT! Add salt listed in recipe within the last ten or fifteen minutes of cooking. For additional assistance, add appropriate proportion of salt only to the amount of cooked beans to be served. Freeze leftover beans unsalted and add salt when reheating.

Kombu

Kombu is a seaweed that provides wonderful flavors and nutrients to any dish that is baked or simmered. It also helps with the digestion of beans.

- Take a good quality, comprehensive digestive enzyme 20–30 minutes prior to eating.

- Begin soaking beans earlier in the day. After two hours, drain and rinse beans and add new soaking water. Repeat procedure every two hours or so throughout the day. Continue to soak beans overnight as Step 3 (previous page) describes.

- Add kombu to beans while cooking.

- Start cooking soaked beans by simmering on stovetop for 30 minutes with no seasonings added. Drain and rinse beans thoroughly. Transfer to slow cooker and follow recipe directions.

Cooking Beans on Stovetop

The recipes in this cookbook are designed for cooking beans in a slow cooker. If you prefer to cook beans on the stovetop, use the following method:

1. Place soaked, rinsed and drained beans in a large kettle.
2. Cover with approximately 3–4 inches of water.
3. Bring to a boil, reduce heat and simmer for appropriate time (see chart below).

Type of Legume	Simmering Time	Type of Legume	Simmering Time
Anasazi Beans	$1^1/_2 - 2^1/_2$ hours	Lima Beans	45 – 90 minutes
Adzuki Beans	$1^1/_2 - 2^1/_2$ hours	Mung Beans	2 – 3 hours
Black Turtle Beans	$1^1/_2 - 3$ hours	Navy Beans	2 – 3 hours
Black-eyed Peas	$1 - 1^1/_2$ hours	Northern Beans	2 – 3 hours
Garbanzo Beans (Chickpeas)	2 – 3 hours	Pinto Beans	$1^1/_2 - 2$ hours
Kidney Beans	2 – 3 hours	Soybeans	$2^1/_2 - 3$ hours
Lentils, Green	1 – 2 hours	Split Peas	1 – 2 hours
Lentils, Red (do not soak)	25 minutes		

S₂ ✓ Garbanzo Beans & Broth (Day 2† Recipe)

2 cups	dry garbanzo beans
5 cups	water
5–6	bay leaves† (optional)
1 cup	chopped onion
4 cloves	fresh garlic, minced
1 teaspoon	sea salt

Standard-sized slow cooker.

> Recipes
>
> Combine
> Slow cook
> Remove bay leaf; add salt
> Freeze extra

1. ✓ Prepare Beans for Cooking (page 103).
2. Combine and cook all ingredients except salt on HIGH for $4^1/_2$–5 hours OR on LOW for 10–12 hours until beans are tender.
3. Remove bay leaves and stir in salt about 10–30 minutes before serving.

- Serve as side dish. • Use in Day 2 recipes (i.e., Minestrone Soup).
- Drain and serve on salad, using broth in Zucchini Salad Dressing.
- Temporarily move garbanzo beans to Day 4 for Beans & Beans.

Yield: $6^1/_2$ cups

†Bay leaves are assigned to Day 3. I don't concern myself with this minor break in rotation.

S₂ ☑ Black Beans & Sauce (Day 4† Recipe)

1 cup	dry black beans
1 (3-inch)	kombu
2 cups	water
1/4 cup	fresh minced cilantro† (optional)
1 medium	diced green pepper† (optional)
1/2 cup	sliced leeks
1/2 teaspoon	sea salt

Small-sized slow cooker.

Recipes

Combine
Slow cook
Add salt
Freeze extra

1. ☑ Prepare Beans for Cooking (page 103).
2. Combine and cook all ingredients except salt on LOW for 8 hours or until beans are tender.
3. Stir in salt about 10–30 minutes before serving.

 Serve as side dish or use in recipe below.

Yield: 3¹/₂ cups

†See note at bottom of page.

Hint

If doubling the recipe, prepare in standard-sized slow cooker.

Cook on HIGH for 4–4¹/₂ hours OR on LOW for 8 hours.

S₂C ⏱ ☑ Tofu & Asparagus in Black Bean Sauce (Day 4† Recipe)

1 clove	fresh garlic, minced
1/2 teaspoon	safflower oil
1–1¹/₂ cups	fresh or frozen asparagus cuts and tips
7/8 cup	☑ Black Beans & Sauce† (~1/4 of above recipe) (7/8 cup = 3/4 cup + 2 Tbsp.)
1/4 pound	soft or firm tofu (optional) drained and cubed

Recipes

Sauté garlic
Add asparagus; simmer
Add beans and tofu; heat

1. In skillet, sauté garlic in oil until soft.
2. Add small amount of water, bring to boil, add asparagus and sprinkle of salt. Cover and simmer until almost tender (approx. 5–10 minutes).
3. Add beans and tofu. Cover and heat to serving temperature, stirring as needed.

Yield: 2¹/₂ cups, complete vegetarian meal for 1

†Green pepper is assigned to Day 2; omit it on Day 2 before and after eating on Day 4. Cilantro is assigned to Day 3. I don't concern myself with this minor break in rotation.

"Let us train our minds to desire what the situation demands."
—Seneca

S₂ **Lentil Casserole** (Day 4† Recipe)
Three Variations: Lamb, Pork, Vegetarian

¹/₂ cup	dry lentils (rinsed and drained)
3–4 cups	fresh stemmed or frozen green beans
¹/₂ cup	sliced leeks
²/₃ cup	water (use ³/₄ cup for vegetarian variation)
¹/₄ teaspoon	ground cayenne (red) pepper†
2 (6 oz.)	lamb or pork chops, trim excess fat (optional)
1 teaspoon	dried rosemary† (with lamb version)
¹/₄–¹/₂ tsp.	sea salt

> Recipes
>
> Layer ingredients
> Cook
> Add salt to mixture
> and chops; cook
> 10 more minutes

Prepare in oven using a covered casserole dish or use standard-sized slow cooker.

1. Layer lentils, beans and leeks. Sprinkle with cayenne. Add water. If using, layer chops on top and sprinkle with rosemary. Cover.

2. Bake in oven at 350° for 1³/₄ hours OR cook in slow cooker on HIGH for 4–5 hours OR on LOW for 8–9 hours until lentils and meat are tender.

3. Temporarily remove chops. Add at least half of salt and stir. Return chops and sprinkle with additional salt. If all liquid has been adsorbed, add more water. Cover and cook for 10 minutes longer.

 Recipe may be easily doubled or cut in half.
Single serving can be cooked in small-sized slow cooker.

Serves 2

†Rosemary and cayenne are assigned to Day 2; omit them on Day 2 before and after eating on Day 4.

S₂ ☑ **Baked Beans** (Day 4 Recipe)

2 cups	dry navy beans
3¹/₂ cups	water
1 cup	sliced leeks
1¹/₂ teaspoons	dried basil
1 teaspoon	paprika
1 tablespoon	safflower oil
1¹/₂ teaspoons	sea salt

> Recipes
>
> Slow cook
> Add salt
> Freeze extra

Standard-sized slow cooker.

1. ☑ Prepare beans for cooking (page 103).

2. Combine all ingredients except salt and cook on HIGH for 5–6 hours OR on LOW for 10–12 hours until beans are tender, stirring beans occasionally.

3. Stir in salt about 10–30 minutes before serving.

Yield: 6 cups 12 (¹/₂-cup) servings Although these beans are allowed freely during Stage 2, I recommend that they are served with other foods in suggested serving amounts.

S₂ ☑ Mexican Medley Beans (Day 4 Recipe)

¹/₄ cup each	dry beans—black, kidney, pinto, adzuki, navy
	OR
1¹/₄ cups	dry beans—any combination
2 cups	water
1 3-inch	kombu
1 cup	sliced leeks
2 cloves	fresh garlic, minced
1¹/₄ teaspoons	chili powder
¹/₈ teaspoon	dried leaf oregano
2 pinches	dried red pepper flakes
¹/₂ teaspoon	sea salt

Small-sized slow cooker.

1. ☑ Prepare Beans for Cooking (page 103).

2. Combine and cook all ingredients except salt on LOW for 10–12 hours or until beans are tender.

3. Stir in salt about 10–30 minutes before serving.

 Sauce thickens and flavors are enhanced if allowed to cool. When reheating, add more water as needed.

Yield: 3¹/₄ cups

Recipes

Combine
Slow cook
Add salt
Freeze extra

Hint

If doubling the recipe, prepare in standard-sized slow cooker.

Cook on HIGH for 5–6 hours OR on LOW for 10–12 hours.

S₂ ☑ Veggie Chili (Day 4† Recipe)

1¹/₂ cups	fresh stemmed or frozen green beans
³/₄ cup	☑ Mexican Medley Beans (above)
	OR
1 cup	☑ Tomato-Free Chili (page 109)
1 cup	diced zucchini† (peel if desired)
	OR
¹/₂ cup	sliced okra†
¹/₈ teaspoon	sea salt

Hint

Preparing this recipe with Mexican Medley Beans creates a hearty vegetarian meal.

Either way, this recipe provides a great way to "sneak" veggies into one's diet.

 In saucepan, bring small amount of water to boil. Add green beans, cover and simmer for 3 minutes. Add remaining ingredients, cover and simmer for 5–10 minutes. Add more water as needed.

Yield: 2¹/₂ –3 cups   1 serving

Zucchini and okra are Day 2 foods, omit them on Day 2 before and after eating on Day 4.

S₂ ☑ **Tomato-Free Chili** (Day 4 Recipe)

¹/₂ cup each	dry beans—black, kidney, pinto, adzuki, navy
	OR
2¹/₂ cups	dry beans—any combination
5 cups	water
2 (3-inch)	kombu
2 cups	sliced leeks
4 cloves	fresh garlic, minced
2¹/₂ teaspoons	chili powder
¹/₂ teaspoon	dried leaf oregano
¹/₄ teaspoon	dried red pepper flakes
1¹/₂ teaspoons	sea salt
1 pound	ground pork or venison

Recipes

Slow cook beans
Cook meat
Add meat and salt; cook
Freeze extra

Standard-sized slow cooker.

1. ☑ Prepare Beans for Cooking (page 103).

2. Combine and cook all ingredients except meat and salt on LOW for 10–12 hours OR on HIGH for 5–6 hours until beans are tender.

3. In skillet, cook meat until done, stirring often to chop and brown evenly. Stir meat and salt into cooked beans. Cook on LOW for another hour OR on HIGH for an extra 30 minutes.

 Sauce thickens and flavors are enhanced if allowed to cool. Add more water as needed when reheating.

Yield: 9 cups   4–6 servings

S₂ ☑ **Navy Beans & Broth** (Day 4 Recipe)

2 cups	dry navy beans
3¹/₂ cups	water
1 teaspoon	sea salt

Recipes

Slow cook
Add salt
Freeze extra

Standard-sized slow cooker.

1. ☑ Prepare Beans for Cooking (page 103).

2. Cook beans and water on HIGH for 2¹/₂–3 hours OR on LOW for 6¹/₂–7 hours until beans are tender.

3. Stir in salt about 10–30 minutes before serving.

Serve as side dish or use in Day 4 recipes (i.e., Beans & Beans or Quick Bean Soup).

Yield: 6¹/₂ cups   13 (¹/₂-cup) servings

Although beans are allowed freely during Stage 2, I recommend that they are served with other foods in suggested serving amounts.

S₂ ☑ Kidney Beans for Chili (Day 2† Recipe)

1¹/₂ cups	dry kidney beans†
1 cup	chopped onions
1 clove	garlic, minced
3 cups	water

Small-sized slow cooker.

1. ☑ Prepare Beans for Cooking (page 103).
2. Combine all ingredients and cook on LOW for 7–8 hours until beans are tender.

Yield: 4 cups

†*Kidney beans are assigned to Day 4; omit them on Day 4 before and after eating on Day 2.*

S₂ 🕐 ☑ Chili (Day 2† Recipe)

2 tablespoons	olive oil
2 cups	chopped onion
2 cups	finely diced peeled eggplant
1 cup	diced green pepper
1 med-size	jalapeño pepper, diced fine
1 pound	lean ground beef or ground buffalo
1¹/₂ teaspoons	sea salt
2 teaspoons	chili powder
2 (14 oz.) cans	diced tomatoes (fire-roasted or regular)
4 cups	☑ cooked Kidney Beans† (recipe above), drained (reserve broth)
~1 cup	broth from beans

> **Recipes**
>
> "Chop & Drop"
> "Slide, Season & Cook"
> Add ingredients; simmer
> Freeze extra

1. In large skillet, "Chop & Drop" vegetables in order listed. "Slide, Season & Cook" meat and seasonings, stirring often.

2. Pour tomatoes into a bowl and hand crush them into a chunky salsa-like mixture. Add tomatoes, beans and broth to skillet. Stir, bring to boil, reduce heat, cover and simmer for at least 15 minutes, stirring occasionally. Add more broth if needed.

Yield: 10 cups   6 servings

†*Kidney beans are assigned to Day 4; omit them on Day 4 before and after eating on Day 2.*

Sondra's Thoughts

Garnish with diced onions and/or peppers. Since reheating enhances the flavors, I prepare the chili earlier in the day, chill it and reheat for dinner. Also, even though it breaks rotation, I like to add two bay leaves while cooking beans and 1 teaspoon ground cumin when cooking chili.

A Substitute for Jalapeño Pepper

¹/₂ tsp. more chili powder
1 tsp. dried leaf oregano
and
¹/₂ tsp. dried red pepper flakes

S2c ☑ Lentil or Split Pea Soup (Day 4† Recipe)

1 cup	dry lentils or green split peas
2–3	bay leaves† (optional)
2 cups	water
1/4 cup	sliced leeks
1 clove	fresh garlic (optional), minced
1/4 teaspoon	sea salt

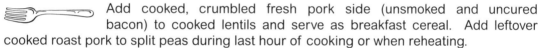

Combine
Slow cook
Add salt
Freeze extra

Small-sized slow cooker.

1. ☑ Prepare lentils/peas for cooking (see Prepare Beans for Cooking on page 103).

2. Combine all ingredients except salt and cook on LOW for 5–5¹/₂ hours (lentils) OR 6¹/₂–7 hours (green split peas) until tender.

3. Remove bay leaves and stir in salt about 10–30 minutes before serving.

Add cooked, crumbled fresh pork side (unsmoked and uncured bacon) to cooked lentils and serve as breakfast cereal. Add leftover cooked roast pork to split peas during last hour of cooking or when reheating.

Lentils do not need to be soaked overnight, but I prefer to do so.

Yield: Lentil Soup, 3 cups   3 servings
Although lentils are allowed freely during Stage 2, I recommend that they are served with other foods in suggested serving amounts.

Yield: Split Pea Soup, 3¹/₂ cups   3 servings
During Stage 2 enjoy this soup in limited amounts (i.e., ¹/₂ cup serving)

†Bay leaf is assigned to Day 3. I don't concern myself with this minor break in rotation.

S2 ☑ Beans & Beans (Day 4† Recipe)

2 cups	fresh stemmed or frozen green beans
1 cup	☑ Navy Beans & Broth (page 109)
	OR
1 cup	☑ Garbanzo Beans & Broth† (page 105)
1/8 teaspoon	sea salt

In saucepan, bring small amount of water to boil. Add green beans, cover and simmer for 3 minutes. Add beans with broth and salt. Cover and simmer for 5–10 minutes.

Yield: 3 cups   2 servings

†If using garbanzo beans, omit eating them on Day 2 before and after eating them on Day 4.

RECIPES

Soups

Soups are a wonderful, warm comfort food in the winter, as well as a quick light meal in the dog days of summer. Soups can provide a hearty meal or an elegant appetizer. A great way to use "the extras," soups are also nice to prepare in large quantities, freeze and then enjoy, especially on those "no time" and/or "low energy" days. With an endless combination of vegetables and protein sources, they can provide a nutrient-rich addition to any menu. Use these recipes and your imagination to enjoy a vast array of flavors.

Many soups (as well as other recipes) include broths prepared from the method recipes in this cookbook. There are also delicious, preservative-free brands that you can substitute, creating only minor breaks in rotation.

S₂ₗ Creamy Tomato Soup (non-rotating recipe)

Tomato soup is a favorite comfort food for children and adults. This quick & easy recipe offers a dairy-free version with garnish ideas to suit everyone's tastes.

4 cups	water		2 Tbsp	tomato paste
1/2 cup	Shaklee Instant Protein® Soy Mix			(~1/5 of 6 oz. can)
1 med.	onion, coarsely chopped		2 Tbsp.	arrowroot starch
1 rib	celery (optional), coarsely chopped		2 Tbsp.	olive oil
1 clove	garlic, cracked		3/4 tsp.	salt
3 cans	diced tomatoes (15 oz. cans)		5–10 drops	liquid stevia

1. In saucepan, whisk Soy Mix in water. Heat on medium-low, stirring occasionally.

2. Blend onions, celery and garlic in food processor or blender until finely chopped (divide ingredients in batches if processor/blender is small). Add remaining ingredients except stevia. Blend as smooth as desired. Carefully pour into heating soymilk. Stir to combine. Continue heating on medium-low, stirring often until soup comes to a gentle simmer for at least 5 minutes. Stir in stevia as desired for sweetness.

Prepare/heat "milk"
Blend ingredients
Simmer
Freeze extra

 Stir desired garnish options into each bowl (i.e., Pesto, cayenne). For the non-CRC person, also garnish with shredded cheese and/or black pepper.

Yield: 9¹/₂ cups 4–6 servings

During Stage 2, soy should be enjoyed only on occasion, however, this recipe makes a wonderful comfort food during Stages 1, 3 and 4.

S₂L ☑ Turkey Parsnip Soup (Day 3 Recipe)

3¹/₂ cups	water
1 cup	☑ Turkey Broth (page 134)
1¹/₂ cups	☑ cooked turkey chunks (pgs. 130/134)
1¹/₂ cups	thinly sliced or diced carrots (peel if desired)
³/₄ cup	thinly sliced or diced peeled parsnips
¹/₄ teaspoon	sea salt
as desired	fresh spinach leaves, torn OR Pesto (page 84)

A Page of Easy Combine & Simmer Soups

In saucepan, heat all ingredients, except spinach/Pesto, to boiling. Reduce heat, cover and simmer for 10 minutes or until vegetables are tender. Garnish servings with spinach or Pesto.

Yield: 4¹/₂ cups   2 servings Both the carrots and parsnips are limited during Stage 2.

S₂CL ☑ Turkey Kale Soup (Day 3† Recipe)

3¹/₂ cups	water
1 cup	☑ Turkey Broth (page 134)
1¹/₂ cups	☑ cooked turkey chunks (pages 130 & 134)
2 (packed) cups	torn kale (small pieces)
1 cup	thinly sliced or diced peeled parsnips OR diced peeled turnips† or rutabaga
2 teaspoons	dried cilantro (omit with turnip and rutabaga variations)
¹/₄ teaspoon	sea salt

In large saucepan, heat all ingredients to boiling, reduce heat, cover and simmer for 15–20 minutes or until vegetables are tender.

Yield: 5 cups   2 servings Using turnip makes this an unlimited Stage 2 recipe.

†Turnips are assigned to Day 1; omit them on Day 1 before and after eating them on Day 3.

S₂L ☑ Turkey Quinoa Soup (Day 3 Recipe)

4 cups	water
1 cup	☑ Turkey Broth (page 130)
¹/₄ cup	whole quinoa, rinsed and drained 2–3 times
1¹/₂ cups	☑ cooked turkey chunks (pages 130 & 134)
1¹/₂ cups	thinly sliced or diced carrots (peel if desired)
¹/₄ teaspoon	sea salt
as desired	fresh spinach leaves, torn OR Pesto (page 84)

In saucepan, heat all ingredients, except spinach/Pesto to boiling. Reduce heat, cover and simmer for 15 minutes or until ingredients are tender. Garnish servings with spinach or Pesto.

Yield: 5 cups   2 servings   Both the carrots and quinoa are limited during Stage 2.

S₂ ✓ Minestrone Soup (Day 2 Recipe)

3 cloves	fresh garlic, minced
2 teaspoons	olive oil
1 (28 oz.) can	diced tomatoes (unsalted)
1 cup	coarsely chopped onion
1½ cups	✓ Garbanzo Beans & Broth, drained (unsalted) (page 105)
2 cups	liquid (bean broth and water)
½ teaspoon	each: dried leaf oregano, dried basil and dried marjoram
1¾ teaspoons	sea salt

> **Recipes**
> Sauté garlic
> Simmer soup
> Add salt
> Freeze extra

Vegetables of your choice (tested combinations are as follows):

Version I: 2 cups each: peeled and diced eggplant and zucchini

Version II: 1 cup diced green peppers, 1 cup sliced okra and 2 cups amaranth greens, torn into small pieces

1. In 5-quart pot, sauté garlic in oil until soft. Add remaining ingredients except salt. Heat to boiling, reduce heat, cover and simmer for 3 hours, stirring occasionally.

2. Stir in salt about 10–30 minutes before serving. May be frozen.

Serve as complete meal or complement with Baked Cod and kiwi.

Sondra's Thoughts: I have prepared this in a slow cooker, but the flavor was not as good as it was using the simmering method described above.

Yield: 6½ cups   A delicious and perfect soup for Stage 2.

S₂CL ✓ Vegetable Beef Soup (Day 2 Recipe)

2 cups	tomato juice
2 cups	✓ Beef Broth (page 143)
1 cup	diced zucchini or summer squash (peel if desired)
1 cup	diced peeled eggplant
1 cup	✓ diced cooked roast beef (page 143)
1 cup	diced peeled potatoes OR
1 cup	✓ Garbanzo Beans & Broth (page 105)
as desired	Pesto (page 84)

In large saucepan, heat all ingredients except Pesto to boiling, reduce heat, cover and simmer for 25–30 minutes or until potatoes and eggplant are done. If desired, garnish servings with Pesto.

Yield: 6 cups   3 servings   Use the bean option to make the soup unlimited during Stage 2.

S₂CL ☑ Nightshade Beef Soup (Day 2 Recipe)

2 cups	tomato juice (unsalted)		1 cup	diced green peppers
2 cups	☑ Beef Broth (page 143)		¹/₂ tsp.	dried summer savory
2 cups	diced peeled eggplant		¹/₄ tsp.	sea salt
1 cup	diced cooked roast beef			

1 cup   diced peeled potatoes
         OR
1 cup   ☑ Garbanzo Beans & Broth (unsalted) (page 105)

 In saucepan, heat all ingredients to boiling, reduce heat, cover and simmer for 25–30 minutes or until potatoes and eggplant are tender.

Yield: 6 cups 3 servings Use the bean option to make the soup unlimited during Stage 2.

S₂L ☑ Egg Drop Soup (Day 3† Recipe)

1 cup	☑ Turkey Broth (page 134)
1 cup	water
2	eggs,† beaten
¹/₂ cup	thinly sliced carrots (peel if desire)
¹/₈ teaspoon	sea salt
¹/₂ cup	fresh spinach leaves, torn small

> Simmer liquids
> Add egg
> Simmer with
>   carrots and salt
> Garnish w/ spinach

1. In saucepan, heat turkey broth and water to simmer (just at boiling point).

2 While stirring broth, gradually pour beaten egg in by a thin stream. Add salt and carrots. Simmer until carrots are warm but slightly crispy.

3. Garnish serving bowl with spinach.

 Serve with muffin, biscuit or crackers.

Yield: 2 cups 1 serving Enjoy this delicious soup on occasion during Stage 2.

†Eggs are assigned to Day 1; omit them on Day 1 before and after eating on Day 3.

☑ Garbanzo Bean & Potato Soup (Day 2 Recipe)

1 cup	☑ Garbanzo Beans & Broth (page 105)
1 cup	diced peeled potatoes
2 tablespoons	diced green pepper
¹/₄ teaspoon	dried summer savory
¹/₈ teaspoon	sea salt

In saucepan, heat all ingredients to boiling, reduce heat, cover and simmer for 15 minutes or until potatoes are done. (For crunchy peppers add them during last couple minutes of cooking.)

Yield: 2 cups 2 servings

S₂c Cream of Broccoli or Cauliflower Soup (Day 1 or 3 Recipe)

	Broccoli (Day 1 Recipe)	**Cauliflower** (Day 3 Recipe)
1 cup	water	
³/₈ teaspoon	sea salt	
2 cups—fresh or frozen	broccoli cuts/florets	cauliflower florets
2 tablespoons	chopped macadamia or Brazil nuts	
2 tablespoons	flour (br. rice/Kamut®/spelt)	tapioca starch or cornstarch
1 cup	water	
seasoning, as desired	¹/₄ teaspoon dill weed	¹/₂ teaspoon cilantro

1. In saucepan, bring first measure of water to boil, add vegetable and salt, reduce heat, cover and simmer 5–7 minutes.

2. While vegetable cooks, blend nuts, flour or starch and ¹/₃ cup of water in blender, stopping to scrape sides and bottom of blender jar as needed.

3. Add remaining ²/₃ cup of water and most of cooked mixture to blender jar. Blend on lowest speed to desired consistency. Pour back into saucepan. Add seasoning. Heat to thicken, stirring often.

OR

3. Pour blended mixture and remaining ²/₃ cup water into cooked vegetable mixture (still in saucepan). Remove pan from heat source. Puree soup to desired consistency, using an immersion blender. Add seasoning. Heat to thicken, stirring often.

Yield: 2³/₄ cups 2 servings During Stage 2, use brown rice flour or tapioca starch as thickener options.

Immersion Blender

A handheld blender offers a safe, easy way to blend foods in the cooking pan.

Cook vegetable
Blend nut mixture; add; heat
For chowders, add fish as heating
Freeze extra

S₂c Chowder (Day 1 or 3 Recipe)

For a Day 1 Chowder, prepare Cream of Broccoli Soup. Add 6–8 oz. of flaked cooked Day 1 fish (i.e., halibut, sole, tuna) when adding dill.

For a Day 3 Chowder, prepare Cream of Cauliflower Soup.
Add 6–8 oz. of flaked cooked Day 3 fish (i.e., flounder, salmon) when adding cilantro.

Serve with crackers, biscuit or muffin for a quick, complete light meal.

Yield: 3²/₃ cups 2 servings For Stage 2, use thickener as indicated above.

S₂ 🕐 Cream of Asparagus Soup (Day 4 Recipe)

2 cloves	fresh garlic, minced
1/2 cup	sliced leeks
2 teaspoons	safflower oil
3 cups	fresh or frozen asparagus cuts and tips
2 cups	water (divided)
1/2 teaspoon	sea salt
2 tablespoons	chopped macadamia nuts or cashews
2 teaspoons	kudzu starch
1/8 teaspoon	tarragon

Recipes
Sauté garlic/leeks
Cook asparagus
Blend nut mixture; add; heat
Freeze extra

1. In saucepan, sauté garlic and leeks in oil until soft.

2. Add asparagus, 1 cup water and salt. Bring to boil, reduce heat and cover. Simmer for 15 minutes or until asparagus is tender.

3. Follow Steps 2 and 3 of Cream of Broccoli or Cauliflower Soup (previous page).

 Serve with Orange Roughy for complete light meal.

Yield: 3 cups   2 servings   This delicious easy recipe is perfect for Stage 2.

S₂C 🕐 ☑ Grilled Chicken Broccoli Soup (Day 1 Recipe)

as needed	sesame oil
8 oz.	raw chicken breasts/tenders (cut into small chunks)
2 cups	☑ Chicken Broth (page 134)
4 cups	fresh or frozen broccoli cuts/florets
2 tablespoons	flour—brown rice, spelt, Kamut®
2 cups	water
as desired	sea salt, dill weed and/or cumin

Recipes
Sauté chicken
Cook and puree broccoli
Add chicken
Prepare roux; add to soup; heat
Freeze extra

1. Season chicken with salt and seasonings. In skillet, sauté chicken in oil, stirring to brown evenly.

2. While chicken is cooking, bring broth, broccoli and your choice of seasonings to boil in large saucepan. Reduce heat, cover and simmer for 7–10 minutes or until broccoli is tender. Remove pan from heat. Puree soup to desired consistency, using an immersion blender.

3. Transfer cooked chicken to blended soup. In the skillet, prepare a roux by adding the flour and 1 tablespoon (or more) of oil. Whisk to blend. Cook for 1–2 minutes. Gradually add water while whisking to blend in the chicken drippings. Transfer thickened mixture to soup and heat to serving temperature.

Yield: 5 cups   2 servings
Use brown rice flour and you have a delicious complete meal perfect for Stage 2.

S₂ ☑ Chicken Collard Soup (Day 1 Recipe)

6 cups	☑ Chicken Broth (page 134)
2 cups	water
2 cups	collard greens (use approx. 5 medium-sized leaves, torn)
4 cups	chopped cabbage
2 cups	☑ cooked chicken chunks (pgs. 130 & 134)
¹/₂ teaspoon	dill weed

In saucepan, heat all ingredients to boiling, reduce heat, cover and simmer for 15–20 minutes or until vegetables are tender.

Yield: 8 cups 4 servings

A Page of Easy Combine & Simmer Soups

S₂CL ☑ Chicken Rice or Turnip Soup (Day 1 Recipe)

2 cups	☑ Chicken Broth (page 134)
¹/₂ cup	☑ cooked brown rice OR diced peeled turnips
¹/₂ cup	diced celery
¹/₂ cup	☑ cooked chicken chunks (pages 130 & 134)
¹/₈ teaspoon	each: sea salt and dill weed
as desired	Pesto (page 84)

Sondra's Thoughts

For a grilled chicken taste, sauté 1 pound raw chicken breast chunks as described in Step 1 of Grilled Chicken Broccoli Soup (page 117). Add chicken to soup during the last 5–10 minutes of simmering time. Then to skillet add about ¹/₄ cup of water, whisking to blend in the chicken drippings. Add mixture to soup.

In saucepan, heat all ingredients (except Pesto) to boiling, reduce heat, cover and simmer for 10–15 minutes or until vegetables are tender. Garnish servings with Pesto.

 May substitute 4 ounces raw chicken breasts chunks for cooked chicken. Follow directions in "Sondra's Thoughts."

Yield: 2 cups 1 serving During Stage 2, enjoy this recipe using turnips. However, the brown rice option should be okay when following the serving size suggested.

S₂L ☑ Turkey Soup (Day 3 Recipe)

3 cups	water
1 cup	☑ Turkey Broth (page 134)
1¹/₂ cups	☑ cooked turkey chunks (pgs. 130 & 134)
2 cups	diced carrots (peel if desired)

¹/₄ teaspoon sea salt
For garnish, use torn fresh spinach leaves OR Pesto as desired

In saucepan, heat all ingredients (except garnish) to boiling. Reduce heat, cover and simmer for 10–15 minutes, or until carrots are tender. Garnish each serving with spinach OR Pesto.

Yield: 4 cups 2 servings The amount of cooked carrots might be slightly too much during Stage 2, though you may consider enjoying a half serving.

☑ **Turkey Barley Soup** (Day 3 Recipe)

5 cups	water
1 cup	☑ Turkey Broth (page 134)
1/4 cup	dry pearled barley
1 1/2 cups	☑ cooked turkey chunks (page 134)
1 1/2 cups	thinly sliced or diced carrots (peel if desired)
1/2 teaspoon	sea salt
as desired	fresh spinach leaves, torn OR Pesto

Simmer barley

Add turkey & carrots; simmer

Garnish servings

Freeze extra

1. In large saucepan, bring water, broth and barley to boil, reduce heat, cover and simmer for 50 minutes.

2. Add remaining ingredients, except garnish. Simmer 10–15 minutes until carrots and barley are tender.

3. Garnish each bowl with fresh spinach OR Pesto.

Yield: 5 1/2 cups   2 servings

 ☑ **Turkey Quinoa Pasta Soup** (Day 3 Recipe)

1 cup	☑ Turkey Broth (page 134)
1 cup	water
1 cup	sliced peeled carrots
1/2 cup	fresh or frozen small cauliflower florets
1/2 cup	☑ cooked turkey chunks (pages 130 & 134)
as needed	sea salt
1/2 cup	wheat-free quinoa pasta

Simmer

Cook & add pasta

1. In saucepan, combine all ingredients except pasta. Simmer until vegetables are almost tender.

2. Cook pasta (Perfect Pasta, page 88); add. Serve immediately. Do not overcook.

 Prepare only amount to be served because quinoa pasta turns to mush when reheated.

Yield: 3 cups   1 serving

S₂ ☑ **Quick Bean Soup** (Day 4 Recipe)

2 cups	fresh stemmed or frozen green beans
1/2 cup	☑ Navy Beans & Broth (page 109)
1/2 cup	☑ diced, cooked roast pork

 In saucepan, bring 1/2 cup of water to boil. Add green beans and desired amount of salt, cover and simmer for 3 minutes. Add beans and pork, cover and simmer for 5–10 minutes to blend flavors. Add more water as needed.

Yield: 3 cups   1 serving

RECIPES

Sandwiches

Sandwiches make wonderful meals. The recipes in this section are written to be served on "breads" but they can also be served without (i.e., lettuce wraps, taco salads, vegetarian patties complemented with vegetables). Be creative and allow sandwiches to remain a part of your diet.

S₂L ☑ Garbanzo or Black Bean Patties
(Garbanzo–Day 2 / Black Bean–Day 4 Recipe)

1 ¹/₂ cups	☑ Garbanzo Beans & Broth (pg. 105)
	☑ OR Black Beans & Sauce (pg. 106)
	OR
1 (15 oz.) can	unsalted garbanzo OR black beans
2 tablespoons	flaxmeal
¹/₄ cup	ground seeds—sunflower for garbanzo; pumpkin for black bean
2 tablespoons	flour—garbanzo bean OR black bean
¹/₄ teaspoon	garlic powder

Drain beans
Cook flax mixture
Mash beans
Combine all ingred.
Form, season and
  cook patties
Freeze extras
  uncooked

1. Drain beans, reserving liquid. Add water to broth to yield ²/₃ cup for garbanzo beans or ¹/₂ cup for black beans.

2. In saucepan, bring ¹/₄ cup liquid and flaxmeal to a boil. Reduce heat and simmer for 3 minutes, stirring almost constantly. Set aside.

3. In bowl, mash beans and remaining liquid with hand potato masher. Add flax mixture and remaining ingredients. Stir to blend.

4. To form and cook patties, follow Step 5 for Lentil Patties (next page).

 Sondra's Thoughts

Warm beans mash easier.

- - - - -

If using canned beans, sauté a little fresh garlic, onion or leeks in oil and add to bean mixture.

- - - - -

Also see "Thoughts" on next page.

 For Garbanzo Bean Patty, serve as sandwich on Amaranth Bun or Garbanzo Bean Griddle Bread. Garnish with zucchini, tomatoes, sunflower greens, lettuce, Sunflower Mayo and/or Catsup. For Black Bean Patty, serve and garnish as described in Lentil Patties (next page).

Yield: 4 (4-inch) patties Although beans are not limited during Stage 2, I would limit these if served with bread.

S₂L Lentil Patties (Day 4 Recipe)

1 cup	dry green lentils
2¹/₂ cups	water
¹/₂ cup	sliced leeks
¹/₂ teaspoon	cayenne pepper† (optional or use other seasonings)
2 tablespoons	flaxseeds
2 tablespoons	green lentil flour
¹/₂ cup	pumpkin seeds, ground
as desired	sea salt and safflower oil

Rinse/drain lentils

Cook and mash lentils

Add other ingredients

Form, season and
  cook patties

Freeze extras
  uncooked

1. Rinse and drain lentils. Presoaking not necessary; if you choose to do so (Prepare Beans for Cooking, page 103), use ¹/₂ cup less water in recipe.

2. In saucepan, combine lentils, water, leeks and cayenne. Bring to boil, reduce heat, cover and simmer for 30–35 minutes or until lentils are tender. Stir occasionally.

3. Add flaxseeds and cook for 3 minutes, stirring almost constantly. Remove from heat.

4. Mash beans with hand potato masher. Add flour and pumpkin seeds and stir to combine. If too thick to form together, add small amount of water.

5. With a ¹/₂-cup measure, dip mixture onto lightly oiled, preheated griddle. Using heat-resistent rubber spatula, flatten and shape into 4-inch patty. Season with salt and cook about 5 minutes per side until golden brown. Add additional oil to griddle as needed with repeat batches.

Serve on a Buckwheat "Hamburger" Bun or Day 4 Griddle Bread. Spread with Day 4 Mayo. Garnish with sliced cucumbers or sprouts.

Yield: 6 (4-inch) patties   Although lentils are not limited during Stage 2, I would limit these if served with bread.

†Cayenne is assigned to Day 2; omit it on Day 2 before and after eating on Day 4.

Freezing & Cooking the Extras

Measure and dip mixture onto baking sheet. Flatten and form into 4-inch patty. Repeat to use all mixture. Place in freezer. After frozen, transfer patties to food storage bag and keep frozen until ready to cook. It takes 15 or more minutes to cook from frozen state. Turn often to brown/cook evenly.

Sondra's Thoughts

Serve these "Patties" with the Day's vegetables for a complete meal.

- - - - -

If lentils are too small to mash with potato masher, puree about ²/₃ of mixture in food processor or blender.

- - - - -

A smaller 2¹/₂-inch patty (use a ¹/₄-cup measure) serves nicely on griddle bread cut into fourths. Garnish as above.

☑ **Sandwich Ideas**

Bread * Choices:	Day 1	Day 2	Day 3	Day 4
Griddle Breads (page 184)	Brown Teff	Amaranth Garbanzo Bean	Quinoa	Lentil, Bl. Bean Buckwheat
☑ Tortillas (pg. 186)	Brown Teff, Spelt, Kamut®	Amaranth	Quinoa	Buckwheat White Bean

☑ **Spread Choices:**

	Day 1	Day 2	Day 3	Day 4
"Mayos" (page 95)	Almond	Sunflower	Filbert	Macadamia or Cashew
Other spreads		butter, Ghee Catsup, Cr. Italian Dressing		

☑ **Filling Choices:**

	Day 1	Day 2	Day 3	Day 4
Meats	roasted or grilled chicken	roast beef or buffalo minute steak Sloppy Joes	roast turkey grilled turkey breast	roast pork, venison or lamb pork cutlet
Fish (page 160)	Poached/Grilled/Broiled Fish Fillet for the Day			
Vegetarian (pages 120, 121 and 125)	almond butter tahini	Garbanzo Bean Patty	filbert butter	Black Bean or Lentil Patty Lentil Sloppy Joes cashew butter
"Salads" (page 126)	Chicken, Tuna or Egg		Salmon Turkey	Tofu and Cucumber

Topping & Seasoning Choices:

	Day 1	Day 2	Day 3	Day 4
Vegetables (leaf, sliced, or shredded)	chard cabbage radish	tomato, onion cucumber lettuce green pepper	spinach, kale kohlrabi carrots avocado	leeks cucumber sorrel
Sprouts	cabbage radish	sunflower greens	barley millet	alfalfa buckwheat mung bean clover, lentil
Chopped nuts or seeds	pecan, almond sesame seeds	pumpkin or sunflower seeds	walnuts filberts	cashews
Seasonings	Choose from those assigned to the Day			

 *For prepared Breads/Flat Breads, visit www.canaryconnect.com for resources. Use Pancakes or cut Griddle Breads in fourths for small-sized sandwiches for children.

☑ **Fajitas**

Bread* Choices:	Day 1	Day 2	Day 3	Day 4
Griddle Breads (page 184)	Brown Teff	Amaranth Garbanzo Bean	Quinoa	Lentil, Bl. Bean Buckwheat
☑ Tortillas (pg.186)	Brown Teff, Spelt, Kamut®	Amaranth	Quinoa	Buckwheat White Bean

Meat Choices:

	Day 1	Day 2	Day 3	Day 4
6-8 oz., skinless, boneless, cut into thin strips	chicken breast or thighs	beef or buffalo (use round or minute steak)	turkey breast	venison round steak or pork cutlets

Vegetable Choices:

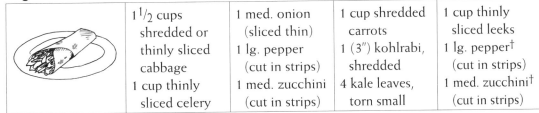

	Day 1	Day 2	Day 3	Day 4
	1 1/2 cups shredded or thinly sliced cabbage 1 cup thinly sliced celery	1 med. onion (sliced thin) 1 lg. pepper (cut in strips) 1 med. zucchini (cut in strips)	1 cup shredded carrots 1 (3") kohlrabi, shredded 4 kale leaves, torn small	1 cup thinly sliced leeks 1 lg. pepper† (cut in strips) 1 med. zucchini† (cut in strips)

Oil Choices:

as needed	Use oil the Day's oil

Seasoning Choices:

use as desired with sea salt	dill cumin fresh parsley	savory, oregano chili powder fresh basil/garlic	caraway seed coriander fresh cilantro	tarragon chili powder fresh garlic

 If using venison, soak in salted water in refrigerator for a few hours or overnight to remove the wild game taste, rinse and drain.

 In preheated skillet, sauté meat in oil, stirring often to brown evenly (while cooking, season as desired). Add vegetables, salt and seasonings. Stir often while cooking to desired tenderness (best if crunchy).

To Serve: Spread 3/4 cup of filling in center third of "bread" about 1 inch from one side (Diagram A). Fold the 1-inch edge side over first, then fold the 1/3 side edges over the filling (Diagram B). Hold with both hands to eat.

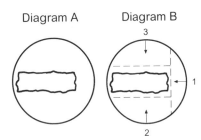

Diagram A   Diagram B

 May garnish Day 2 Fajitas with fresh diced tomatoes.

Yield: ~3 cups filling   4 (8–9-inch) fajitas

†*These foods are assigned to Day 2; omit them on Day 2 before and after eating on Day 4.*

*For prepared Flat Breads, see resources on <u>www.canaryconnect.com</u>

S₂L   ☑ Tacos (Day 2 Recipe)

1 pound	lean ground beef OR buffalo
1 cup	chopped onion
2 cloves	fresh garlic, minced
1/2 teaspoon	sea salt
1/2 teaspoon	each: dried leaf oregano and chili powder
1/4 teaspoon	red pepper flakes
1 (8 oz.) can	tomato puree OR sauce
as needed	☑ Day 2 Tortilla OR Griddle Bread (pgs. 186 & 184–185)
as needed	Toppings: fresh diced tomatoes (stir in some chili powder and oregano if desire an extra "kick"), shredded lettuce, diced onions, Guacamole and/or Picante Sauce

1. In skillet, cook meat, onion, garlic and seasonings until done, stirring often to brown evenly. Add puree or sauce. Stir and simmer for 10 minutes.

2. Prepare toppings while meat mixture is cooking.

To Serve: Layer prepared ingredients on 1/2 of tortilla or griddle bread. Fold and enjoy.

Yield: 2¹/₄ cups   9 (¹/₄ cup) servings

During Stage 2, I suggest that you limit yourself to one serving served as a taco and enjoy the rest served with lettuce and other toppings as taco salad.

Cook meat, etc.
Add puree; simmer
Prepare toppings
Freeze extra

S₂L 🥣 ☑ Lentil Tacos (Day 4† Recipe)

1 cup	dry green lentils
2¹/₂ cups	water
1/2 cup	sliced leeks
1/4 teaspoon	garlic powder
3/4 teaspoon	each: dried leaf oregano† and chili powder†
1/4 teaspoon	red pepper flakes
1 (6 oz.) can	tomato paste†
1/2 teaspoon	sea salt
as needed	☑ Day 4 Tortilla OR Griddle Bread (pages 186 and 184)
as needed	Toppings: see list in Tacos recipe above

Rinse/Drain lentils
Simmer lentils, etc.
Add paste and salt; simmer
Prepare toppings
Freeze extra

1. Using all ingredients except breads and toppings, follow directions for Steps 1–3 as described in Lentil Sloppy Joe recipe on next page.

2. Prepare toppings while lentil mixture is cooking.

To Serve: Layer lentil mixture and other toppings as described in Tacos recipe above.

Yield: 3 cups   12 (¹/₄ cup) servings   During Stage 2 follow same guidelines as above.

†These foods are assigned to Day 2; omit them on Day 2 before and after eating on Day 4.

Sloppy Joes (Day 2 Recipe)

1 pound	lean ground beef OR buffalo
1/2 cup	chopped onion
3/4 teaspoon	sea salt
1/2 teaspoon	dried leaf oregano
1/4 teaspoon	garlic powder
1/8 teaspoon	cayenne (red) pepper
1 (6 oz.) can	tomato paste
1 can	water (use tomato paste can)

Cook meat, etc.

Add paste and water; simmer

Freeze extra

1. In skillet, brown meat, onion and seasonings, stirring often to cook evenly.

2. Stir in tomato paste and water. Simmer uncovered for 10 minutes, stirring frequently.

 Serve on Day 2 breads (i.e., Tortilla, Griddle Bread, Amaranth Bun). Garnish with sunflower greens and/or chopped onions.

Yield: 2 1/2 cups   10 (1/4 cup) servings

 ## Lentil Sloppy Joes (Day 4† Recipe)

1 cup	dry green lentils
2 1/2 cups	water
1/2 cup	sliced leeks
1/2 teaspoon	dried leaf oregano†
1/4 teaspoon	garlic powder†
1/8 teaspoon	cayenne powder†
1 (6 oz.) can	tomato paste†
1/2 teaspoon	sea salt

Rinse/drain lentils

Simmer lentils, etc.

Add paste and salt; simmer

Freeze extra

1. Rinse and drain lentils. Presoaking not necessary; if you choose to do so (Prepare Beans for Cooking on page 103), use 1/2 cup less water in recipe.

2. In saucepan, bring all ingredients except tomato paste and salt to boil. Reduce heat, cover and simmer 30–35 minutes or until lentils are tender. Stir occasionally.

3. Stir in tomato paste and salt. Simmer uncovered for 10 minutes, stirring frequently.

 Serve on Day 4 breads (i.e., Tortilla, Griddle Bread, Buckwheat Bun). Garnish with sprouts and/or thinly sliced cucumber.

Yield: 3 cups   12 (1/4 cup) servings

†These foods are assigned to Day 2; omit them on Day 2 before and after eating on Day 4.

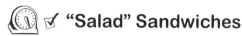 ☑ **"Salad" Sandwiches**

Choose appropriate Day's vegetable, mayo and seasoning according to protein selected.

Tuna or Salmon Salad (Tuna–Day 1 / Salmon–Day 3[†] Recipe)

8 oz.	☑ tuna OR salmon fillet (poached w/ $^1/_4$ teaspoon salt, flaked, chilled)
$^2/_3$ cup	diced celery OR shredded carrots
2	☑ hard-boiled eggs,[†] diced (optional to include)
few sprigs	fresh parsley OR cilantro, minced (optional to include)
$^1/_4$ cup	☑ Almond OR Filbert "Mayo" (page 95)
to taste	sea salt

Yield: 1$^1/_2$ cups without egg   2 cups with egg   Perfect for 4 wraps.   2 Servings

Due to the high mercury content in tuna, I suggest to omit tuna during Stage 2. See guidelines on page 160 for salmon.

S$_{2CL}$ Egg Salad (Day 1 Recipe)

2	☑ hard-boiled eggs, diced
$^1/_3$ cup	diced celery
few sprigs	fresh parsley, minced (optional to include)
2 tablespoons	☑ Almond "Mayo" (page 95)
to taste	sea salt

Yield: 1 cup   Perfect for 2 wraps.   During Stage 2 limit serving as a sandwich. See "Mayo" for guidelines in choosing thickener.

S$_{2C}$ Chicken or Turkey Salad (Chicken–Day 1 / Turkey–Day 3[†] Recipe)

$^1/_2$ cup	☑ diced, cooked chicken OR turkey chunks (pages 130 & 134)
1	☑ hard-boiled egg,[†] diced (optional to include, especially for turkey)
$^1/_3$ cup	diced celery OR shredded carrots
few sprigs	fresh parsley OR cilantro, minced (optional to include)
3 tablespoons	☑ Almond OR Filbert "Mayo" (page 95)
to taste	sea salt

Yield: 1 cup   Perfect for 2 wraps.   Same guidelines as on above recipe.

Tofu & Cucumber Salad Sandwich (Day 4 Recipe)

$^1/_2$ pound	soft tofu, drained
2 cups	diced cucumber (peel if desired)
2 tablespoons	☑ Macadamia OR Cashew "Mayo" (page 95)
$^1/_8$ teaspoon	sea salt
$^1/_8$ teaspoon	unbuffered vitamin C crystals
$^1/_4$ teaspoon	dried tarragon

Yield: 2 cups   Perfect for 4 wraps   2 Servings

continued ...

continued ...

Directions for "Salad" Sandwich Recipes on previous page.

Combine your choice of ingredients and chill.

Serve as salad on a bed of fresh "greens" of the day. Or serve as wrap sandwich (using tortillas or griddle breads) with fresh "greens" and/or sprouts of the day.

†*Eggs are assigned to Day 1; omit them on Day 1 before and after eating on Day 3.*

RECIPES

Entrées: Eggs

The inexpensive egg is generally quick and easy to prepare and offers high-quality protein with a wide variety of nutrients, including high amounts of vitamins A and E as well as riboflavin and folate. Proper handling of eggs is critical to reduce the risk of salmonella poisoning: keep refrigerated at all times; discard cracked/broken eggs; and cook completely, scrambling until no liquid remains and baking (i.e., soufflés) until a knife inserted comes out clean. The recipes on the next few pages are delicious options for those without egg sensitivities.

S_2 🕐 Hard-Boiled Egg:

To prepare perfect hard-cooked eggs, gently place cold eggs in saucepan with enough room temperature water to cover them. Bring to gentle boil, remove from heat source, cover and allow hot water to "carry-over cook" for 15 minutes. Refrigerate in uncracked shell until use.

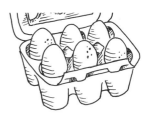

S_2 🕐 Scrambled Eggs with Bok Choy
(Day 1 Recipe)

1. Prepare desired amount of bok choy (page 71).
2. In skillet, sauté prepared bok choy in small amount of oil until tender.
3. Add slightly beaten eggs and dill, cumin, parsley and/or salt. Stir while cooking as with scrambled eggs.

Serve immediately.

Sauté bok choy
Scramble with eggs and seasonings
Serve immediately

Bok Choy

S_{2L} Denver Eggs (Day 1 Recipe)

2 cups	finely chopped cabbage
1 cup	diced celery
1/2 cup	chopped bok choy (page 71)
as desired	ground cumin, parsley, dill weed, sea salt
1 cup	cooked brown rice, chilled
4 large	eggs, slightly beaten

Preheat skillet (my preference is cast iron).

1. Sauté vegetables (seasoned as desired) in sesame oil, stirring often until desired doneness (I prefer slightly crunchy).

2. Add rice and mix. Pour eggs evenly over mixture. Cook while stirring quickly until eggs are done and rice is heated. Serve immediately.

> Sauté vegetables
> Mix in rice
> Add eggs and scramble
> Serve immediately

Yield: 2 Servings During Stage 2, you might consider using less rice in this recipe.

Breakfast Brunch Squares (Day 1 Recipe)

2 3/4 cups	cubed bread (use purchased yeast-free spelt, Kamut® or rice bread† OR Kamut® or Spelt Bread on page 182)
2 cups	fresh or frozen broccoli cuts
1/4 cup	hulled sesame seeds
1/4 cup	flour—brown rice, spelt, Kamut®
3/4 teaspoon	sea salt
1 cup	water
4 large	eggs

Preheat oven to 350°. Oil bottom and sides of 8-inch stainless steel baking pan with 1 teaspoon of oil. Glass is not recommended, as it tends to stick.

> Layer bread and broccoli
> Blend seed mixture
> Pour over bread and broccoli
> Bake
> Serve immediately

1. Evenly layer cubed bread and broccoli cuts in prepared pan.

2. Blend sesame seeds, flour, salt and about 1/3 cup of water in blender on highest speed until well blended, stopping to scrape sides and bottom as needed. Add remaining water and eggs. Blend on lowest speed ONLY for a couple of seconds. Pour liquid mixture evenly over broccoli and bread cubes. Lightly push any floating broccoli or bread cubes down into the mixture.

3. Bake for 45–50 minutes until egg mixture is set. Cut into squares and remove from pan with stiff metal spatula. Serve immediately.

Yield: 4 servings

†Some brands of bread may contain ingredients that break rotation.

Egg (Cheese-Free) Soufflé (Day 3† Recipe)

2 extra-large	eggs,† separated (yolks in large bowl & whites in mixer bowl)
1 teaspoon	grapeseed oil
$1/4$ cup	tapioca starch, measure packed (see Step 2)
$1/8$ teaspoon	sea salt
1 tablespoon	water
$3/4$ teaspoon	homemade baking powder (recipe below)

Preheat oven to 350°. Oil bottom/sides of 9-inch glass baking dish with 1 tsp. of oil.

1. Set bowl of egg whites in sink of warm water, stirring occasionally to warm them to room temperature. With electric mixer, beat room-temperature-whites until stiff. Set aside.

2. Scoop starch into $1/4$ cup dry measure, rounded up. Tap edge with knife a few times to pack. Level off. Place in separate bowl and stir with whisk to incorporate air back into starch.

3. In separate bowl, beat yolks with whisk. Add salt, water, tapioca starch and stir to combine. Add baking powder and stir. Fold in stiff egg whites.

4. Pour into prepared baking dish; spread evenly. Bake for 15 minutes or until a toothpick inserted in the center comes out clean.

Prepare egg whites
Measure starch
Beat egg yolks
Combine ingredients in stages
Bake
Serve immediately

 Makes a delicious, grain-free breakfast or serve with vegetables for light lunch or brunch.

Yield: 2 Servings
Cream of tartar used in the baking powder is the caution ingredient for Stage 2.

†*Eggs are assigned to Day 1; omit eggs on Day 1 before and after eating on Day 3.*

 Sondra's Hints

To remove soufflé from pan, use sharp knife to cut edges away from side of dish and then cut into 4 squares. Use stiff metal spatula to serve.

- - - - -

Soufflé rises to approximately $1\frac{1}{4}$ inches high and then falls to about 1 inch.

Homemade Baking Powder
(To be used in Egg Soufflé Recipe)

1 teaspoon	baking soda
2 teaspoons	tapioca starch
2 teaspoons	cream of tartar

Combine all ingredients and store in airtight container until needed.

Combine
Store for future

Yield: 5 teaspoons

RECIPES

Entrées: Poultry

As discussed in Chapter Three, protein is very important to healing. Poultry can offer low-fat, high quality protein to your healing food plan. Also, many of the following casserole-style recipes offer delicious, quick and easy ways to incorporate more high-fiber vegetables, whole grains and grain alternatives into family meals.

S₂ Cooked Chicken or Turkey Chunks (Day 1 and 3 Recipes)

Some recipes in this section (as well as some soup and salad recipes) call for cooked chicken or turkey chunks. There are a variety of ways to prepare them for use in recipes or serve with other foods for a meal:

Poaching
Using boneless, skinless chicken or turkey portions (breasts, tenders or thighs)

Cut meat into bite-sized chunks. In saucepan or small skillet with lid, bring to boil 2 cups of liquid per pound of meat (or follow liquid amount in recipe). If recipe does not indicate type of liquid, use broth (chicken, turkey or vegetable) OR water OR 50/50 combination of broth and water. Carefully slide meat portions into boiling liquid, season with salt and the Day's seasonings (fresh or dried), reduce heat, cover and simmer for 10–15 minutes (internal temp. of 180°). Remove meat, reserving created broth for recipe or freeze for future.

Poaching
Using bone-in chicken & turkey pieces, see "Sondra Hints"

Roasting Poultry Pieces

Sondra's Hints

If poaching serving-sized pieces, allow cooked meat to "rest" for 5 minutes on cutting board before cutting into bite-sized pieces.

- - - - -

Q&E Poached Meal
Poach serving-sized pieces (bone-in or boneless) with the Day's veggies/seasonings.

My favorite combos are:

Chicken breast with—
 Celery, fennel, chard and/or turnips
 Fresh or dried dill, fresh parsley and/or ground cumin

Turkey breast with—
 Fresh spinach or kale and parsnips
 Fresh cilantro or ground coriander

Roast poultry wings, drumsticks, thighs and/or breast halves for a meal, creating cooked chunks with the leftovers (see Roasted Poultry & Broth on page 134).

Grilled/Sautéed
Using boneless, skinless chicken or turkey portions (breasts, tenders or thighs)

For Chunks: Cut meat into bite-sized chunks. In skillet, stir-fry chicken, sprinkled with seasonings, in oil, stirring often to brown evenly. Transfer cooked meat to soup or casserole. To skillet, add about $1/4$ cup of water, whisking to blend in the grilled drippings. Use this mixture as a liquid in soup or casserole.

For Fillets: In skillet (or grill pan, see "Hints" at right), grill meat (seasoned with salt and the Day's seasonings) in oil for about 5 minutes on each side until golden brown. (Timing depends upon thickness of fillet.) Transfer cooked meat to serving plate and add about $1/4$ cup of water to skillet, whisking to blend in the grilled drippings. Pour this broth-like mixture over fillets. Mmm.

Sondra's Hints

For fillets as pictured on front cover, use a cast iron **grill pan**. Drizzle oil on fillet, season and place seasoned side down in pan. Oil and season second side.

- - - - -

If you desire thinner fillets, place breast in plastic food storage bag, lay bag flat on counter and pound using heavy skillet (I do not recommend using cast iron for pounding).

Method Recipe to Create Raw & Cooked Poultry Chunks and Smaller Sections to Roast or Poach

Purchasing a whole turkey (or chicken) and cutting it up yourself is often the most economical way to enjoy naturally-raised (without pesticides, herbicides and growth stimulates) poultry (especially turkey). It also allows you to freeze the meat in portions for family-sized meals. The following steps outline an efficient and manageable method to make use of as much of the meat as possible. Part of this process includes preparing cooked turkey chunks from the carcass.

1. If possible, begin with a fresh turkey. Otherwise, partially thaw turkey under refrigeration (i.e., for only two days rather than four). Remove giblet bag (usually tucked inside carcass). Clean turkey as described in Step 1 of Roast Poultry and Broth (page 134).

2. Using knife (I prefer trimmer), remove neck, wings and complete legs (drumstick and thigh). To remove the neck, cut below last bone just above bird's body and refrigerate for later. To remove the wings and complete legs, move the wing or leg to locate the joint connection, which is the separation point. Cut to remove pieces at this point. If desired, separate drumstick and thigh between joints. As you disconnect neck, legs, thighs and wings, rinse and refrigerate in large bowl until ready to package.

Equipment Needs

Large cutting board
(NOT wooden)

Sharp knives (carving, trimmer and fillet)

Plastic food wrap and/or food freezer bags

Butcher paper

continued ...

... continued

3. Using a trimmer knife, cut along ribs to disconnect back portion from breasts. Using a carving knife, cut along each side of breastbone to remove two breast portions. Refrigerate back portion and the breastbones. If you are going to roast the breast portions, rinse and refrigerate with skin on. If you would like breast meat for fillets, nuggets or strips, remove skin/fat (as much as possible). Rinse, dry and place unwrapped in freezer (semi-frozen meat cuts easier) while you continue.

4. Optional Step: If you desire more raw turkey chunks, remove skin and fat from back section and/or thighs. Then using a small carving knife, remove as much meat as possible from back portion, cut into chunks and refrigerate. Using fillet or carving knife, carve meat from thighs into strips. Then cut strips into bite-sized chunks and refrigerate. (Omit this step if you desire more cooked turkey chunks.)

Sondra's Hints

Since Step 2 is "hard" work, I recommend using no larger than a 12–15 pound turkey.

- - - - -

For less "fighting" the turkey sliding around, I recommend that you leave turkey in sink while doing Step 2.

- - - - -

Cutting cross-grain of the breast portion creates a tender cut, especially with the fillets.

- - - - -

Keep all pieces of turkey cool while handling other pieces.

5. Salt remaining carcass, neck, thighbones and breastbones. Simmer in large pot (breaking carcass to fit) or roast in covered roaster with approx. 2 cups water until meat is so tender that it begins to fall off the bones. Separate meat from broth (see Roasted Poultry and Broth on page 134 for handling broth). Cool meat enough to pull/cut meat off bones. Package and freeze meat in portions desired for recipes using cooked poultry chunks.

6. Using a fillet knife, remove the breast tenders from breast portions. (The tenders are the underneath portion of the breast, are slightly pink in color, separate easily from the breast and are the best portion for stir-fry). Using fillet or carving knife, cut breast portions cross-grain in thin or thick-cut fillets, strips or nugget portions. Package and freeze (with meat from Step 4) in desired servings (8 oz. chunks equals 1 cup).

7. To freeze wings, legs, thighs and/or breasts, place each piece in a food freezer bag, closing down tightly around meat OR wrap tightly with plastic food wrap. Then wrap with butcher paper. Mark each package (name and date). Freeze.

Yield: ~15# turkey provides 2 wings, 2 (~2#) Leg/Thigh, 1 (~2#) skin-on breast half, ~14 oz. breast tenders, ~1$^3/_4$# raw chunks/strips and 1$^1/_2$ cups cooked chunks

 ## Oven or Skillet Fried Turkey Nuggets (Day 3 Recipe)

1 cup	barley flour
1 teaspoon	each: sea salt and coriander
1 pound	raw turkey chunks (see method above)

continued ...

... continued

For Oven Fried versions, preheat oven to 450° and oil stainless steel baking dish with approximately 2 teaspoons of oil per 8 oz. of meat. **For Skillet Nuggets**, preheat skillet; I prefer cast iron.

Preheat oven or
    skillet
Prepare coating
Coat nuggets
Bake or skillet fry

1. In bowl, combine flour and seasonings.
2. Place slightly moistened turkey nuggets in plastic food bag. Add small amount of flour mixture, hold closed (without extra air in bag) and shake to coat.
3. **For Oven Nuggets:** place in prepared baking dish. Reduce heat to 400°. Bake for 20–25 minutes (internal temperature of 180°).
4. **For Skillet Nuggets:** add a fair amount of oil to preheated skillet. Add nuggets. Cook for approximately 10 minutes, stirring often brown evenly.

Store extra unused coating mixture in freezer for future use.

Yield: 4 servings

Chicken/Turkey Loaf/Patties (Day 1 or 3 Recipe)

Choose appropriate Day's grain and vegetable according to poultry selected.

1 pound	ground chicken or turkey breast
$1/2$ cup	(uncooked) Kamut® or spelt flakes
	OR regular rolled oats
$1/2$ cup	diced celery
	OR shredded carrots
$1/2$ cup	liquid—water OR ☑ Broth
$1/2$ teaspoon	sea salt

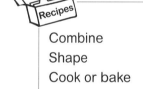

Combine
Shape
Cook or bake

Preheat oven to 350°.

In large mixing bowl, combine ingredients. Shape into 9 muffin cups ($1/3$ cup each), drizzle tops with oil and bake for 20–25 minutes. OR, form into 4 patties and cook in skillet with small amount of oil. (Patties are my favorite served with Pilaf, page 83).

Yield: 4 servings   The brown rice option mentioned in "Hints" would allow this recipe to be a Stage 2 recipe.

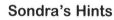

Sondra's Hints

Loaves or patties may be mixed, shaped and refrigerated to cook later.

- - - - -

If desired, substitute $1/4$ cup of cooked brown rice for Day 1 flakes and use only $1/4$ cup of liquid.

Preparing Ground Poultry

It is easy to grind your own ground chicken or turkey from boneless, skinless breasts in food processor. Cut meat into approximately $1/2$-inch chunks. Place about $1/2$ pound in food processor with metal blade. Pulse a few times until it is ground. Add remaining $1/2$ pound pulse until cut into small cubes, but not as finely ground.

S₂ Roast Poultry & Broth

	Day 1	Day 3
Your choice of poultry	7–8 pound roasting hen OR 3–4 pound chicken	12–15 pound turkey hen
sea salt	1–2 teaspoons	1–2 tablespoons
water	1–2 cups	2–3 cups

1. Remove giblet bag (usually tucked inside carcass). Rinse bird inside and out, removing pin feathers and any remaining organ meats inside the cavity. Rub inside and outside of bird with salt. Tuck wings under back of bird or sew wing tips to breast skin. Tie legs together with heavy cotton string.

2. Place bird on rack in stainless-steel roasting pan. Add water. Insert meat thermometer into thickest portion of breast meat (not touching a bone). Cover and roast at 350° until internal temperature reaches 180°. See chart below for approximate roasting time. If bird is not browning to your liking, roast uncovered for the last 30–60 minutes.

7–8 pound chicken roasting hen	$2^{1}/_{2}$ to 3 hours	
3–4 pound chicken	$1^{3}/_{4}$ to 2 hours	
12–15 pound turkey hen	$3^{1}/_{2}$ to 4 hours	

3. Remove from oven, uncover and allow to "rest" for 10–15 minutes before carving.

Cooked Chicken or Turkey Chunks: After meal, pull/cut meat off bones. Package and freeze meat in desired servings (8 oz. chunks equals 1 cup). Break carcass to fit into large pot, add 1–2 cups of water and simmer until meat falls off bones. Separate meat from broth (handle broth as described below). Package and freeze meat.

Chicken or Turkey Broth: Strain broth through fine-meshed strainer and chill. After chilled, remove solid fat layer on top (or use a broth/fat separator, see below), measure broth into desired portions needed for recipes (usually 1 cup) and freeze.

Broth Yield: 6–7 cups for roasting hen; 3–4 cups for chicken; 9–11 cups for turkey

Broth/Fat Separator

Add broth to separator. Notice the broth settles to the bottom. Pour off small amount of fat in the spout. Pour broth into container to freeze. Toss remaining fat at bottom. Some separators also have a filter.

Sondra's Hints

Poultry broth and cooked poultry chunks can also be created by simmering bony portions (i.e., neck, wings, back pieces) in salted water until meat is tender. Reserve meat and broth as described above.

S₂C ☑ Creamed Turkey on Rye Toast (Day 3 Recipe)

1 pound	ground turkey breast
¹/₂ teaspoon	sea salt
1 cup	☑ Turkey Broth (page 134)
1 cup	water
2 cups	kale (torn or cut into small pieces, measure loosely packed)
2 tablespoons	tapioca starch OR cornstarch

1. In skillet, cook turkey and salt until done, stirring often to brown evenly.

2. Add broth, water and kale. Heat to boiling, reduce heat, cover and simmer for 15–20 minutes or until kale is tender.

3. In small bowl, whisk together starch with extra ¹/₄ cup of water. Add and cook to thicken.

Brown turkey
Simmer kale
Mix/add thickener

 Serve over toasted 100% sourdough rye bread or Day 3 biscuits.

Yield: 3 cups   4 servings   During Stage 2, use tapioca starch for the thickener and serve over a Quinoa Biscuit.

☑ Sesame Goulash (Day 1 Recipe)

1 pound	boneless, skinless chicken breasts (cut into bite-sized pieces)
³/₄ teaspoon	sea salt
1 cup	diced celery
1 cup	☑ Chicken Broth (page 134)
¹/₄ teaspoon	ground cumin OR dill weed
1 cup	elbow macaroni—br. rice, spelt, Kamut®
2 cups	shredded cabbage
1²/₃ cups	water
¹/₄ cup	flour—br. rice, spelt, Kamut®
¹/₄ cup	hulled sesame seeds

Stir-fry chicken and celery
Add broth; deglaze
Add ingredients; cook
Add/cook seed mixture

1. In skillet, stir-fry chicken and salt in small amount of oil, stirring often to brown evenly. Dice and add celery, continue to stir-fry until meat is done.

2. Add broth slowly while stirring to deglaze chicken drippings. Add cumin or dill, macaroni, cabbage and water. Bring to boil, reduce heat, cover and simmer for 6 minutes or until pasta is slightly under *al dente*.

3. Blend flour, sesame seeds and ¹/₃ cup of extra water in blender on highest speed until well blended, stopping to scrape sides and bottom as needed. Add to skillet and cook, stirring constantly until mixture thickens.

Yield: 6 cups   4 servings   The pasta prevents this recipe from being a Stage 2 recipe.

☑ **Skillet Chicken Noodle Casserole** (Day 1 Recipe)

1^1/$_2$ cups	dry noodles or rotini—brown rice, spelt, Kamut®
1 cup	☑ Chicken Broth (page 134)
^{3}/$_4$ cup	water
8 oz.	raw chicken breast chunks
1^1/$_2$ cups	diced fennel
1 cup	diced celery
1^1/$_2$ cups	broccoli cuts
2 leaves	chard, ribbon cut (see "Hints")
^{3}/$_4$ teaspoon	sea salt (divided)
as desired	fresh or dried dill
as desired	ground cumin
2 tablespoons	flour—brown rice, spelt, Kamut®
1–2 tablespoons	☑ ground sesame seeds (measure packed, see "Hints")

Cook pasta

Simmer chicken

"Chop & Drop"

Blend thickener; add

Combine all; finish
   cooking

1. In saucepan, cook pasta in boiling water until *al dente*, following package directions. Add ^{1}/$_4$ teaspoon of the salt when adding pasta to boiling water. Drain and set aside for use in Step 4.

2. In large skillet, bring broth to boil, add chicken chunks and ^{1}/$_4$ teaspoon of the salt, reduce heat, cover and simmer.

3. "Chop & Drop" vegetables to skillet of simmering meat in order listed. Sprinkle with remaining ^{1}/$_4$ teaspoon of the salt and desired seasonings. Simmer for about 3 minutes after adding broccoli or until chicken is cooked and vegetables are at least 1 minute under desired tenderness. (I prefer the vegetables slightly crunchy.)

4. In a small bowl, whisk together flour, ground seeds and ^{1}/$_4$ cup of water (seeds are optional but they offer a richer taste and creamier appearance). Add flour mixture and noodles to skillet. Cook and stir for 1–2 minutes to thicken sauce, blend flavors and finish cooking vegetables.

Yield: 4–4^1/$_2$ cups   2 Servings

This is a great recipe during Stage 1 but the pasta prevents this recipe from being a Stage 2 recipe.

Sondra's Hints

To Ribbon Cut: Fold each chard leaf in half lengthwise, slice off center rib, pile up both leaf halves, tightly roll lengthwise and slice crosswise to make ribbon-like pieces.

- - - - -

Ground Sesame Seeds: To save time, grind 1 cup in blender or processor/chopper, store in freezer and measure packed.

- - - - -

Mix and match your choice and amounts of Day 1 vegetables to suit your tastes. Begin your preparation with vegetables that take the longest to cook (i.e., fennel and celery).

- - - - -

Best served immediately but can be gently reheated, adding water if needed.

- - - - -

Recipe can be easily divided for one serving or multiplied to serve a larger family.

Pasta Primavera (Day 1 Recipe)

1 ounce	spaghetti or angel hair pasta—brown rice, spelt, Kamut®
1 teaspoon	sesame or almond oil
3-4 oz.	raw chicken breast strips
3^1/$_2$ cups	Day 1 vegetables
as desired	sea salt, dill weed, ground cumin and/or almonds

Method 1—Dry

Preheat electric skillet or wok to 350°.

1. In saucepan, cook broken spaghetti or angel hair pasta in boiling water until *al dente*, according to package directions (add salt while cooking). Stir occasionally. Drain and set aside for use in Step 3.

Cook pasta
Brown and season chicken
Add vegetables; cook
Add sauce, if desired
Add pasta
Serve immediately

2. In skillet/wok, stir-fry chicken, sprinkled with seasonings, in oil, stirring often to brown evenly. Add vegetables, almonds and another sprinkle of seasonings. Cook to desired tenderness, stirring often.

3. Add drained pasta and stir constantly until well mixed and at serving temperature. Serve immediately.

Method 2—With Sauce

Additional Ingredients:

1 tablespoon	✓ ground sesame seeds (measure packed, see "Hints" on page 136)
1 tablespoon	flour—br. rice, spelt, Kamut®
^{1}/$_2$ cup	water

My Thoughts

My favorite vegetables to use in this recipe are:
1^1/$_2$ cups fresh broccoli cuts
1^1/$_2$ cups chopped cabbage
^{1}/$_2$ cup slant-cut celery

Follow Steps 1–2 from in Method 1 above.

3. In a small bowl, whisk together ground seeds, flour and water.

4. Add drained pasta and sesame mixture to chicken and vegetables in wok. Stir constantly until sauce thickens and coats all ingredients. Serve immediately.

Yield: 2^1/$_2$–3 cups   Serves 1   The pasta prevents this recipe from being a Stage 2 recipe.

S₂CL ✓ **Chicken Rice Casserole**
Tuna Noodle or Rice Casserole (Day 1 Recipes)

For rice versions follow Skillet Chicken Noodle Casserole (previous page), substituting pasta with 1 cup of cooked brown rice. For tuna versions, substitute water for chicken broth, simmer fresh tuna steak in salted water, remove and flake and add to simmering vegetables (Step 3).

The Chicken Rice Casserole version is okay for Stage 2 on occasion. The pasta and tuna prevents the other variations from being a Stage 2 recipe.

S₂c Oven Fried Chicken (Day 1 Recipe)

¹/₂ cup	flour—brown teff, brown rice, spelt, Kamut®
¹/₂ teaspoon	sea salt
¹/₂ teaspoon	ground cumin
	OR
¹/₄ teaspoon	dill weed
8 pieces	chicken, skin removed

Preheat oven—450°.

Oil baking dish or follow "Crispier Method" in "Hints".

1. Rinse chicken and pat with paper towel, leaving slightly moist.

2. In small bowl, combine your choice of flour and seasonings. Add small amount to food storage bag, add a piece of chicken, hold closed (without extra air in bag) and shake to coat. Place in baking dish, bone side down. Repeat for each piece, adding more coating as needed.

3. Reduce heat to 400°. Bake for 50–60 minutes (internal temp. of 160°–180°). Smaller or "bony" pieces take less time.

During Stage 2, use brown teff flour (my favorite) or brown rice flour.

Rinse chicken
Prepare coating
Coat chicken
Bake
Freeze extra

Sondra's Hints

Crispier Method: Bake chicken on wire rack (place inside pan) and omit oiling pan. For even crispier chicken, increase oven temp. to 450° during final 10 minutes.

- - - - -

The taller the sides on the baking dish, the less likely the fat will splatter in oven.

- - - - -

My favorite is brown teff flour with cumin.

- - - - -

If using pieces of chicken with less meat (i.e., back, wings), reduce seasonings or double flour then sprinkle a little salt on larger pieces.

- - - - -

Freeze extra coating for future use.

S₂L ☑ Turkey Quinoa Pasta Stew (Day 3 Recipe)

1 cup	☑ cooked turkey chunks (pages 130 & 134)
1 cup	☑ Turkey Broth (page 134)
1 cup	water
1 cup	kale (small pieces, measure loosely packed)
2 cups	cauliflower florets (small)
2 tablespoons	tapioca starch (optional)
1 cup	dry quinoa pasta (cook as directed in Perfect Pasta, page 88)

Cook vegetables & turkey in liquid
Prepare and add thickener (optional)
Cook & add pasta

continued ...

... continued

1. In covered saucepan, combine all ingredients except pasta and starch. Simmer until vegetables are almost tender (about 10 minutes).
2. If using starch, whisk with an extra $1/2$ cup water. Add to stew, stirring continuously until sauce thickens.
3. Just before serving, add cooked pasta and stir gently. Heat to serving temperature.

Serve with raw carrot sticks and Quinoa Biscuits. Prepare only amount to be served because quinoa pasta turns mushy when reheated.

Yield: $4^1/2$ cups   2 servings   During Stage 2, enjoy this on occasion.

S₂c Country Fried Chicken & Gravy (Day 1 Recipe)

8 pieces	chicken, skin removed
$1/2$ cup	flour—brown rice, spelt, Kamut®
1 tablespoon	sesame oil
to season	sea salt

Ingredients for Gravy:

2 cups	water
2 tablespoons	flour—brown rice, spelt, Kamut®
$1/4$ teaspoon	sea salt

Rinse and brown
chicken
Prepare gravy
Simmer chicken
with gravy

Preheat electric skillet to 350°. Add oil.
Recipe was developed using stainless steel electric skillet; others may require more oil.

1. Rinse chicken and pat dry with paper towel, leaving slightly moist. Roll each piece in flour. Place in hot skillet with meaty side down. Sprinkle with salt. Brown each side for 8–10 minutes until golden brown, using tongs to turn chicken (a fork releases meat juices and dries the meat out).
2. Whisk together gravy ingredients and add to skillet. Loosen any stuck chicken pieces. Cover with lid. Reduce heat to between simmer and 200° and simmer for 20–25 minutes. Check occasionally to confirm that gravy is only simmering (not boiling) and to loosen chicken that may be sticking to pan.

During Stage 2, use brown rice flour.

S₂c Pheasant & Gravy (Day 1 Recipe)

1. Cut up pheasant as you would a chicken. Soak several hours or overnight in salt water to remove wild game taste. Rinse and drain.
2. Prepare as in Step 1 of Country Fried Chicken and Gravy.
3. Transfer browned pheasant to covered casserole dish. Whisk together gravy ingredients and pour over pheasant. Cover and bake at 350° for 1 hour or until tender.

Yield: 4 servings   During Stage 2, use brown rice flour.

S₂ Easy Chicken Meal or Soup (Day 1 Recipe)

1 serving	chicken breast (or your favorite piece), skin removed
1 cup	thickly sliced celery
1 cup	chopped cabbage (large pieces)
¹/₄ teaspoon	sea salt
as desired	dill weed
1¹/₂ cups	water

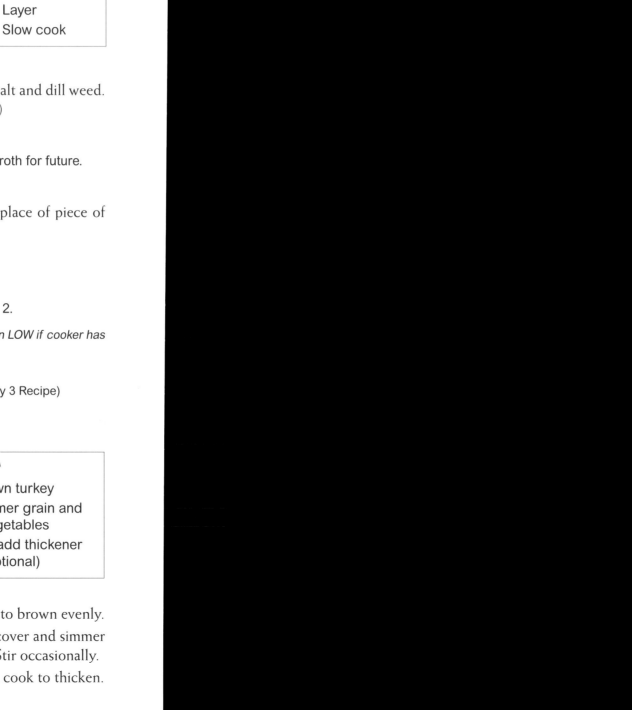

Recipes

> Layer
> Slow cook

Small-sized slow cooker.*

To Serve as a Meal:

1. Layer chicken, celery and cabbage in slow cooker. Sprinkle with salt and dill weed. Add water. (Cabbage will not be completely covered with water.)

2. Cook on LOW for 4 hours.

  Serve without broth as a meal, reserving and freezing broth for future.

To Serve as a Chunky Soup:

1. Use 4 oz. of deboned chicken breasts (or thighs) per serving in place of piece of chicken. Cut into bite-sized pieces and follow Step 1 above.

2. Cook on LOW for 4 hours.

  Serve as soup.

Yield: meal for one   One of my favorite recipes, especially during Stage 2.

Double, triple or quadruple recipe to cook in standard-size slow cooker. Cook on LOW if cooker has two settings.

☑ Millet or Quinoa Turkey Vegetable Stew (Day 3 Recipe)

1 pound	ground turkey breast
1 teaspoon	sea salt
1 cup	☑ Turkey Broth (page 134)
1¹/₂ cups	water
¹/₄ cup	hulled millet grain
	OR whole quinoa (rinse and drain)
1¹/₂ cups	sliced peeled parsnips
2 cups	cauliflower florets (small)
2¹/₂ cups	sliced carrots (peel if desired)
2 tablespoons	tapioca starch (optional)

Recipes

> Brown turkey
> Simmer grain and
>   vegetables
> Mix/add thickener
>   (optional)

1. In large skillet/pan, cook turkey and salt until done, stirring often to brown evenly.

2. Add liquids, grain and vegetables. Heat to boiling, reduce heat, cover and simmer for 15–20 minutes until grain is done and vegetables are tender. Stir occasionally.

3. If using starch, whisk with extra ¹/₂ cup of water. Add to stew and cook to thicken.

Yield: 6¹/₂ cups   6 Servings

☑ **Chicken/Broccoli Mac'n Cheese-Less** (Non-rotating Recipe[†])

2 cups	macaroni—spelt, br. rice, Kamut®		1/4 cup	diced red peppers[†]
2 cups	broccoli cuts			OR shredded carrots
1/4 cup	sesame oil (divided)			(Day 3 food)
1 pound	raw chicken chunks		1 1/2 tsp.	sea salt (divided)
1 cup	diced fennel		1/4 tsp.	dry mustard
as desired	dill		1 Tbsp.	fresh lemon juice[†]
1/4 cup	nuts—cashew, Brazil, macadamia		1 cup	☑ Chicken Broth (p.134)
	OR		1 cup	water
2 Tbsp.	sesame seeds		3 Tbsp.	flour—spelt, rice, Kamut®

1. In saucepan, bring water to boil. Add macaroni and 1/2 teaspoon of the salt; cook for 3 minutes. Add broccoli, reduce heat to medium, cover and cook for 2 more minutes until pasta is slightly under *al dente*. Drain.

2. Meanwhile, in large skillet, sauté chicken and fennel in 1 tablespoon of oil. Season with 1/2 teaspoon of salt and dill.

3. In blender, finely chop nuts (or grind seeds). Add red pepper (or carrots); blend. Add remaining 1/2 teaspoon of the salt, seasonings and lemon juice with small amount of the water. Blend until smooth, stopping to scrape sides and bottom of blender jar as needed. Add remaining water and broth. Blend before adding to skillet in Step 4.

4. After chicken is cooked, slide it to one side of skillet. Prepare roux in skillet by whisking flour and 3 tablespoons of the oil together. Cook for 1 minute. Gradually add blended mixture, stirring constantly. Cook to thicken, stirring often. Add pasta and broccoli. Cook for about 1 minute, stirring often. Remove from heat, cover and allow to "rest" for 1–2 minutes for sauce to set up and coat macaroni.

Recipes
Cook mac/broccoli in stages
Saute chicken/fennel
Blend nut (seed) mixture
Add ingred. in stages
"Rest"
Serve immediately

Yield: 8 cups   4 meal servings
This makes a delicious Stage 1 recipe to satisfy your desire for cheese.

[†]*This amazing, delicious recipe does not fit the rotation as outlined in this cookbook, however, I enjoy it on Day 1 without concern regarding the foods assigned to Day 2 or 3.*

"Reflect upon your present blessings, of which every man has many, not on your past misfortunes, of which all men have some."
—Charles Dickens

RECIPES

Entrées: Red Meats

Red meats offer that all-important protein required for healing. However, those with inflammatory health challenges (i.e., Fibromyalgia) may need to reduce their consumption of beef and pork because of the arachidonic acid present in them. Choosing the leanest cuts and/or taking high levels of vitamin E can reduce this inflammation. Also, the rotation offers venison and fish options if assistance is needed in limiting beef and pork.

Sondra's Hints

If using wild game, such as venison and rabbit, soak in salted water in refrigerator for a few hours or overnight to remove wild game taste; rinse and drain.

- - - - -

Meat cuts into strips easier if partially frozen.

S₂ Steak with Gravy

Meat Choices	**Day 2** $1^1/_2$# beef or buffalo round or minute steak	**Day 4** $1^1/_2$# pork cutlet	**Day 4** $1^1/_2$# venison cutlet or round steak

Ingredients for Gravy:

$1/_4$ cup flour	garbanzo bean flour	white bean flour
2 cups	water	
$1/_4$ teaspoon	sea salt	

Preheat (stainless steel) electric skillet to 350°. Add small amount of the Day's oil.

1. Roll meat in small amount of the Day's flour and place in hot skillet. Sprinkle with salt (and savory for beef) and brown for approximately 2 minutes on each side.

2. In 2-cup measure, whisk together gravy ingredients. Add to skillet. With stiff spatula, loosen meat pieces from skillet. Cover, reduce heat and simmer for 10–20 minutes. Round steak cuts, especially buffalo, tend to need extra cooking time.

See Roast & Broth (next page) for options to complement the meal. "Dress" foods with the gravy.

Flour and brown meat
Prepare gravy
Simmer

S₂ Roast & Broth

	Day 1 Beef or Buffalo	Day 4 Pork	Day 4 Venison
2–3 pounds	roast (arm, blade, rump, chuck, etc.)	shoulder roast uncured/unsmoked ham	roast
1 teaspoon	sea salt		
vegetable (optional)	1 onion, coarsely chopped	1 cup thickly sliced leeks	

Standard-sized slow cooker.

1. Sprinkle salt on all sides of meat. Add savory as desired to beef/buffalo. If desired, add onion or leek. Add about 1 inch deep of water.

2. Cook on LOW for 8–10 hours.

On Day 2 serve with potatoes ("dress" with broth), spaghetti squash and/or salad. On Day 4 serve with sweet potatoes, Basic Buckwheat or buckwheat pasta, asparagus and/or green beans ("dress" with broth).

Cooked Beef, Buffalo, Pork and Venison: After meal, pull or dice remaining meat. Package and freeze in desired servings.

Meat Broth: Strain broth, chill, remove fat and measure in desired portions as described in Roast Poultry & Broth (page 134).

Season meat
Add veggie & water
Slow cook
Freeze extra meat
  and broth

S₂ₗ  Easy Banquet Meal
(Day 4 Recipe)

2 med-sized	sweet potatoes, peeled
2 (6 oz.)	pork or lamb chops (trim off excess fat)
1 pound	asparagus spears, fresh or frozen

1. Fill bottom of steamer pan with water to about ¹/₂ inch from bottom of steamer insert. Heat to boiling.

2. In steamer pan insert, lay peeled (whole) sweet potatoes and sprinkle with salt. Place pork chops on top of potatoes and sprinkle with salt. Place insert pan over boiling water. Cover. Steam on medium-high for 25 minutes.

Layer potatoes & chops; steam
Add asparagus; cook

3. Add asparagus spears; sprinkle with salt. Cover and cook 10–15 minutes longer until tender.

 Dish onto plates arranging foods separately as this is not a stew.

Yield: 2 (meal) servings   During Stage 2, use a small portion of sweet potato.

S₂ₗ Squash & Meatballs (Day 4 Recipe)

1 (1³/₄–2 pounds)	acorn or butternut squash
1 pound	lean ground pork
¹/₂ cup	sliced leeks
¹/₄ teaspoon	garlic powder
¹/₂ teaspoon	sea salt (for meatballs)

Oven temperature—350°. Preheating not necessary.

> Prepare & bake squash
>
> Prepare & brown meatballs; add to squash & bake
>
> Freeze extra

1. Wash squash and cut in half lengthwise (core to core). Cut threads with scissors or curved, serrated grapefruit knife. Scoop out seeds with large spoon. Rinse. Sprinkle salt inside cavity. Place cut side down in covered casserole (deep enough to hold a filled squash half) Add about ¹/₄ cup of water. Bake uncovered for 20 minutes.

2. While squash is baking, gently mix remaining ingredients with your hands in a bowl. Score mixture into fourths; shape each section into 4 meatballs, creating 16. In large skillet, brown meatballs, turning often to brown on all sides. Drain browned meatballs on paper towels.

3. Remove squash from oven. Turn over and fill each cavity with meatballs, placing remaining meatballs beside them in casserole dish. Cover and bake for 30 minutes or until squash is fork tender and pork is at least 180° internal temperature.

> To serve, remove meatballs. Cut each squash portion in half crosswise. Serve each fourth squash with 4 meatballs. Complement the meal with green beans. Baste all with delicious drippings in casserole dish.

Yield: 4 servings   During Stage 2, enjoy this recipe on occasion.

S₂ Meatballs & Gravy (Day 4 Recipe)

1 pound	ground venison or lean pork
¹/₂ cup	sliced leeks
¹/₂ teaspoon	sea salt
¹/₄ teaspoon	garlic powder (optional)
3 tablespoons	pinto or white bean flour
1 cup	water OR ☑ Meat Broth (page 143)

> Prepare and brown meatballs
>
> Prepare roux; simmer
>
> Freeze extra

1. In bowl, use your hands to gently combine meat, leeks and seasonings. Score mixture into fourths; shape each section into 4 meatballs, creating 16.

2. In large (so not to crowd) skillet, brown meatballs (using small amount of oil for lean meat), turning often to brown on all sides. Remove to plate.

3. Prepare roux by whisking flour into meat drippings (add additional Day 4 oil if needed); cook for 1 minute. Gradually add liquid while whisking to blend. Return meatballs to skillet, cover and simmer for 20 minutes.

> Serve gravy over meatballs and peas or green beans.

Yield: 4 servings   During Stage 2, serve with only a small serving of peas.

S₂ ☑ **Stuffed Green Peppers** (Day 2 Recipe)

2 tablespoons	olive or sunflower oil
2 cups	chopped onion
1 cup	diced zucchini
	OR finely diced peeled eggplant
1¹/₂ cups	diced green pepper
3 cloves	fresh garlic, minced
1 pound	lean ground beef or buffalo
1¹/₂ teaspoons	salt
¹/₂ teaspoon	chili powder
¹/₂ teaspoon	dried red pepper flakes
1–1¹/₂ cups	tomato sauce or puree
1 (15 oz.) can	unsalted garbanzo beans (drained)
	OR
1¹/₂ cups	☑ Garbanzo Beans & Broth (page 105) (unsalted; drained)
8 medium-sized	Cubanelle (see page 78) or Bell peppers (~5 oz. each) (cut in half lengthwise, seeded)

Recipes
"Chop & Drop"
"Slide, Season & Cook"
Chop beans
Add beans and puree; simmer
Steam peppers & fill
Bake
Freeze extras unbaked

Preheat oven to 350° at about Step 3. Oil casserole dish.

1. In large skillet, "Chop & Drop" vegetables in order listed. "Slide, Season & Cook" meat and seasonings, stirring often.

2. Drain beans; pour onto large cutting board and "rock" knife (as you would for mincing garlic) to coarsely chop beans. (This step gives more of the appearance of rice that is standard in stuffed peppers.)

3. Add beans and tomato sauce/puree. Simmer for 5 minutes, stirring occasionally.

4. While vegetables and meat are cooking, prepare and steam peppers for 5-7 minutes. Peppers will be tender but not completely soft. Transfer peppers to cool water for a few seconds (just long enough to handle). Drain.

5. Arrange peppers inside up in oiled casserole dish. Fill peppers with hot filling. Bake for 10–15 minutes. If peppers and/or filling have cooled, baking takes longer.

Yield: 6 cups (filling)   8 servings
My favorite Day 2 recipe, especially during Stage 2.

Sondra's Hints

If meat is not lean, cook and drain, then add after veggies are cooked.

- - - - -

Freeze extras unbaked. Then bake at 350° from frozen state for about 1 hour in covered casserole dish OR about 30 minutes if thawed.

- - - -

After you get the "hang of it", this recipe can be completed in less than 1 hour. Oh, how sweet is the day that you enjoy the extras.

- - - - -

Fills 8 medium-sized peppers or 12 small-sized peppers.

S₂ ☑ Venison or Ham and Bean Stew (Day 4 Recipe)

1 pound	venison stew meat (~$1/2$-inch cubes)
	OR raw venison roast (trim and cut into ~$1/2$-inch cubes)
	OR fresh ham steak (uncured, unsmoked) (~$1/2$-inch cubes)
2 cloves	fresh garlic, minced
1 tablespoon	safflower oil
$3/4$–1 teaspoon	sea salt (divided)
1 cup	sliced leeks
4 cups	fresh stemmed or frozen green beans
1 teaspoon	chili powder (optional)
2 cups	☑ Venison or Pork Broth (page 143)
	OR water
2 cups	☑ Navy Beans & Broth (page 109)
2 tablespoons	white bean flour (optional)

Recipes

Brown meat

Add/cook veggies; simmer

Add/simmer beans and broth

Thicken if desired

Freeze extra; reheat slowly

1. In large pot or skillet, brown stew meat in oil, stirring often to brown meat evenly. Season with $1/2$ teaspoon salt while cooking.

2. Add garlic, leeks, green beans, chili powder and remaining $1/4$ teaspoon salt. Continue to cook for about 10 minutes, stirring often (add more oil if needed).

3. Add liquid, bring to boil, reduce heat, cover and simmer for 15 minutes or until green beans are close to desired doneness.

4. Add broth/beans and simmer for 5 more minutes.

5. If using flour, whisk with extra $1/4$ cup of water. Add to stew and cook to thicken.

Yield: $6^1/2$ cups   4 servings

S₂L Beef Stew (Day 2† Recipe)

1 pound	lean, tender cut beef stew meat (~$1/2$-inch chunks)
2 tablespoon	olive or sunflower oil
$1/2$ teaspoon	sea salt
1 cup	finely diced peeled eggplant
1 cup	coarsely chopped onion
2 cups	diced peeled potatoes
1 cup	diced zucchini squash (peel if desired)
$1/2$ cup	diced green peppers (optional)
2 cups	liquid—Beef Broth (page 143) or water
1 (14 oz.) can	diced tomatoes
$1/2$ cup	frozen peas† (optional)
1 tablespoon	potato starch (optional)

Recipes

Brown meat

"Chop & Drop"

Simmer w/ liquid & tomatoes

Optional: Add peas & thickener

1. Season meat with salt and $1/2$ teaspoon of summer savory (if desired). In large pot, brown meat in oil, stirring often to brown evenly.

continued ...

... continued

2. "Chop & Drop" vegetables except tomatoes and peas. Add more oil if needed.

3. Add liquid and tomatoes (hand crush some as adding to pot). Bring to boil, reduce heat, cover and simmer for 15 minutes or until vegetables are fork tender.

4. If using peas, add now. Also, if using starch, whisk with an extra $1/2$ cup water. Add to stew, stirring continuously until sauce thickens.

Yield: ~6 cups   4 servings

During Stage 2, enjoy on occasion or reduce/omit the potatoes and peas.

†*Peas are assigned to Day 4; omit eating them on Day 4 before and after eating on Day 2.*

S₂ₗ ☑ Stir-Fry Buckwheat & Vegetables (Day 4 Recipe)

1 tablespoon	safflower oil (divided)
1 clove	fresh garlic, minced
$1/2$ cup	sliced leeks
2 cups total	asparagus tips, sugar snap/edible pea pods (blanched)
1 cup	☑ Basic Buckwheat Groats, chilled (page 165)
as desired	sea salt
as desired	chili powder

In skillet, sauté garlic, leeks and vegetables until desired tenderness in small amount of oil; season as they cook. Add buckwheat, additional oil, sprinkle with seasonings and heat to serving temperature, stirring almost constantly.

Yield: 2$1/2$ cups   1 meal serving

During Stage 2, you might want to reduce the amount of buckwheat per serving.

S₂ₗ ☑ Stir-Fry Buckwheat & Vegetables with Meat
(Day 4 Recipe)

Follow recipe above, adding $1/2$ cup of cooked venison or pork chunks with buckwheat. If you don't have cooked meat, stir-fry thin raw venison steak or pork cutlet in a little oil before sautéing vegetables.

Yield: 3 cups   1 serving Follow same guidelines as recipe above.

S₂ Pork Chops (Day 4 Recipe)

In skillet, brown chops (season with salt and/or garlic powder) in a small amount of safflower oil for 2–3 minutes on each side. Add 1 cup of water, cover and simmer for 15–20 minutes until tender.

Brown & season
chops
Simmer

S₂ Easy Steak (Rabbit) Dinner (Day 2 Recipe)

1 pound	beef round steak, cut into strips
	OR
1 deboned	rabbit
⅓ cup	starch—arrowroot or potato (not potato flour)
	OR
½ cup	garbanzo bean flour
1 teaspoon	sea salt
2 cups	sliced onion
2 cups	green pepper strips
2 cups	sliced zucchini squash (peel if desired)
1 (28 oz.) can	diced tomatoes

Layer ingredients
Slow cook

Standard-sized slow cooker.

1. Place beef strips in slow cooker. Add thickener and seasonings. Stir to coat meat.

2. Layer vegetables in order listed on top of meat. <u>Do Not Stir</u>. Pour tomatoes and juice as evenly as possible over layers. <u>Do Not Stir</u>.

3. Cover and cook on HIGH for 4–5 hours or on LOW for 8–10 hours.

Serve over potato or garbanzo beans. Also, wonderful served over brown rice or millet if not following the rotation in this book.

Reheat leftover "Easy Dinners" slowly. The appearance is not as pretty when reheating, but taste is still wonderful. Often when this is leftover, I stretch the rotation and I enjoy them the next day (a Day 3) for lunch with millet.

Yield: 4 servings   Another of my favorite Day 2 recipes.
During Stage 2, choosing to serve with garbanzo beans is the best option.

S₂ Breaded Pork Chop (Day 4 Recipe)

¼ cup	Jerusalem artichoke flour
¼ teaspoon	paprika
¼ teaspoon	sea salt
8 (4–6 oz.)	boneless tenderized pork cutlets
	OR lean pork chops

Prepare coating
Coat chops
Bake

Preheat oven to 450°. Lightly oil stainless steel baking dish.

1. Rinse and pat dry chops with paper towel, leaving slightly moist.

2. In small bowl, combine flour and seasonings. Add a small amount to food storage bag, add a chop, hold closed (without extra air in bag) and shake to coat. Place in single layer in baking dish. Repeat for each chop, adding more coating as needed.

3. Reduce heat to 400°. Bake for 30–40 minutes (internal temp. of 180°).

 Freeze unused coating for future use.

Yield: 8 pork chops   8 servings

Scalloped Potatoes & Ham (Day 4† Recipe)

1 pound	ham steak (unsmoked and uncured), diced
3 cups	thinly sliced peeled potatoes† (rinse and drain)
1 cup	sliced leeks
3 tablespoons	potato starch†
2 tablespoons	chopped cashew, macadamia or Brazil nuts
1 teaspoon	sea salt
2 cups	water

Oven temperature—350°. Preheating not necessary. Oil a 3-quart covered casserole.

1. Layer potatoes, ham and leeks in casserole.
2. Combine potato starch, nuts, salt and $1/4$ cup water in blender. Blend on high until well blended, stopping to scrape sides and bottom as needed. Add remaining $1^3/4$ cups of water and blend for a couple seconds.
3. Pour nut mixture over layered ingredients. Lightly push any floating ingredients down into mixture. Cover and bake until potatoes are tender (about 45 minutes in shallow dish or up to $1^1/2$ hours in deeper dish).

Layer ingredients
Blend and add nut
  mixture
Cover and bake

Yield: ~3 cups   4 servings

Potatoes are assigned to Day 2; omit eating them on Day 2 before and after eating on Day 4.

 ☑ ## Pork & Bean Burritos (Day 4 Recipe)

4	☑ Day 4 tortillas or griddle breads (pages 186 & 184)
3 cups	fresh stemmed or frozen green beans
$1/2$ pound	lean ground pork
2 cups	☑ Mexican Medley Beans (page 108)

Preheat oven—350°. Casserole dish.

1. In saucepan, bring small amount of water to boil, add beans and season with salt. Cook for 3–5 minutes or until slightly under desired tenderness. Drain, reserving broth.
2. In skillet, cook meat and $1/4$ teaspoon of salt, stirring often to brown evenly. Add both beans. Simmer 5 minutes to blend flavors. (Sauce needs to be thick yet spreadable.)
3. Spread $1/2$ cup of mixture lengthwise on center third of each tortilla. Fold tortilla from each side over top of mixture. Transfer to dish in single layer with folded side down. Top with remaining mixture. Cover and bake until at serving temperature.

Simmer green beans
Brown meat
Add beans; simmer
Fill tortillas and bake

Yield: 5 cups sauce   4 burritos   4 servings

S₂  Stir-Fry Meal

	Day 1	**Day 2**	**Day 3**	**Day 4**
Meat, thin strips	chicken breast	sirloin or other tender cuts	turkey breast	tenderized pork or venison cutlet
See Stir-Fry Vegetables (page 82) for a wide selection of vegetable, nut, seed and seasoning choices.				

1. Choose and prepare your choice of ingredients in amounts desired.
2. Preheat skillet on medium; I prefer cast iron. Add oil after preheating.
3. Stir-fry meat, stirring often to brown evenly. Sprinkle with salt and/or seasonings.
4. Add vegetables and nuts/seeds with more oil if needed. Sprinkle with salt and/or seasonings. Stir often to cook vegetables evenly; best if left slightly crunchy. Add "last minute" vegetables. Cook an additional 30–60 seconds, stirring often. Serve immediately.

Stir-fry meat
Add/stir-fry veggies, nuts/seeds
Serve immediately

 Serve immediately with Brown Rice (Day 1), Amaranth (Day 2), Millet or Quinoa (Day 3) or Buckwheat Groats (Day 4).

Yield: Allow 3–4 ounces of meat, 2 cups of vegetables per serving.
During Stage 2, serve stir-fries with small servings of gluten-free grains.

S₂ₗ ☑ Pork/Venison & Buckwheat Pasta (Day 4 Recipe)

2 cups	fresh stemmed or frozen green beans
1 cup	liquid—water OR ☑ Meat Broth (pg. 143)
2 ounces	100% Buckwheat Soba Noodles (broken into 2-inch lengths)
¹/₂ cup	☑ cooked pork or venison chunks (pg. 143)

1. In saucepan, bring small amount of water to boil; add beans with salt. Cook for 3–5 minutes or until slightly under desired tenderness. Drain, reserving broth.
2. In medium-sized saucepan, bring liquid to boil, add broken noodles, reduce heat to medium-high and cook for 10 minutes, stirring often. Add more liquid if noodles begin to stick to bottom of pan.
3. Add green beans (with cooking liquid) and meat, reduce heat to medium, cover and simmer for 5 minutes to serving temperature. Stir often to prevent sticking.

Yield: 2¹/₂ cups 1 Serving During Stage 2, enjoy on occasion or reduce the amount of pasta used.

Simmer beans
Cook noodles
Add beans and meat; simmer

Travel Hint

A perfect travel meal to pack in a wide-mouth Thermos®. If you do so, cook noodles for only 8 minutes before continuing with the recipe as the noodles will continue to cook in Thermos®.

RECIPES

Entrées: Italian

"What?! No Cheese?! No Wheat?! But I love pizza, spaghetti and lasagna."
I once felt the same way but soon discovered that there is a substitute for
everything, including those things that satisfy the Italian taste bud. Enjoy
the similar tastes with allergen-free ingredients.

To shorten preparation time, many recipes in this section make use of two
cooking methods—"Chop & Drop" and "Slide, Season & Cook" (page 67).

 ## Pizza Crust

	Day 1	Day 1	Day 2	Day 4
	Kamut®	**Spelt**	**Amaranth**	**Buckwheat**
flour/starch	1$^1/_4$ cups Kamut® flour	1$^1/_4$ cups spelt flour	1 cup amaranth flour $^1/_2$ cup arrowroot starch	1$^1/_4$ cups White Buckwheat flour (page 171)
baking soda	$^5/_8$ teaspoon			
unbuffered vitamin C crystals	$^3/_8$ teaspoon			
sea salt	scant $^1/_4$ teaspoon			
water	$^1/_2$ cup	$^3/_8$ cup	$^1/_2$ cup	$^1/_2$ cup
oil	2 tablespoons of the Day's oil			

Preheat oven—350°. 12-inch pizza pan (Step 2).
See sauce recipes for toppings/baking directions.

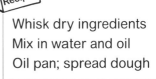

1. In mixing bowl, whisk together dry ingredients.
    Make a "well" in the center. Add water and oil.
    Stir, making sure all ingredients are moistened.

2. Using fingers, spread 1 teaspoon oil on pizza pan
    to within 1 inch of edge.

Whisk dry ingredients
Mix in water and oil
Oil pan; spread dough

3. With lightly oiled fingers, touch dough. If dough sticks, knead in 1–3 teaspoons
    of flour. Transfer dough to pan. Press dough out from center, maintaining even
    thickness in all directions. Push dough edge up on edge of pan. Dough will be about
    $^3/_8$ inch thick. If it appears thin in spots, press surrounding dough toward the thin
    area to remedy.

Yield: 1 (12-inch) pizza   8 slices

S₂ₗ 🥣 ☑ Spaghetti/Pizza Meat Sauce (Day 2 Recipe)

Version 1	Version 2	
1 teaspoon	1 tablespoon	olive oil
1 cup	1 cup	chopped onion
none	1 cup	diced green pepper
none	3 cups	your choice of Day 2 vegetables OR additional peppers and onion
2 cloves	4 cloves	fresh garlic, minced
1 pound	1 pound	lean ground beef or buffalo
1¼ teaspoons	1½ teaspoons	sea salt
¼ teaspoon	¼ teaspoon	summer savory
1½ teaspoons	2 teaspoons	dried basil
1 tablespoon	1½ tablespoons	dried leaf oregano
scant ¼ teaspoon	¼ teaspoon	crushed red pepper flakes
½ (28 oz.) can	½ (28 oz.) can	tomato puree
2 cups	2 cups	water

Pizza Toppings:

as desired	onion or green pepper slices
as desired	☑ Spaghetti Squash (page 80)

For Pizza: Preheat oven to 350°.

1. In large skillet, "Chop & Drop" vegetables in order listed. "Slide, Season & Cook" meat and seasonings, stirring often.

2. Add puree and water. Heat to boiling, reduce heat, cover and simmer for approximately 15 minutes, stirring occasionally.

Yield: 4 cups (Version 1) 6 cups (Version 2) This recipe served with Spaghetti Squash is a Stage 2 recipe without limitations. If served as pizza, limit to one or two pieces/serving.

Recipes

"Chop & Drop"

"Slide, Season & Cook"

Add puree and water; simmer

Freeze extra, see page 155

Meal Preparation Tips

For Spaghetti: Serve sauce over Spaghetti Squash. Begin baking the squash halves before beginning sauce. Or, temporarily transfer buckwheat from Day 4 and serve over purchased 100% buckwheat soba noodles.

- - - - -

For Pizza: While sauce is simmering, prepare and par-bake Amaranth Pizza Crust for 10 minutes. Spread 2 cups of warm sauce evenly over crust. Sprinkle with desired amount of peppers and/or onions. String spaghetti squash for a cheese-like appearance. Bake for 15–20 minutes.

S₂L 🥣 ☑ Amazing Spaghetti/Pizza Sauce (Day 2 or Day 4 Recipe)

The color of this sauce resembles what you would expect had it been made with yellow or low-acid tomatoes. The flavor is wonderful so don't discount this until you have tried it. Many of the ingredients can be temporarily moved between Days 2 and 4.

1 tablespoon	oil of the Day
1 cup	chopped onions
	OR sliced leeks
1 cup	diced green peppers
	OR sliced okra
2 cups	diced zucchini squash (peel if desired)
3 cloves	fresh garlic, minced
1 pound	lean ground meat of the Day—beef, buffalo, pork or venison
1¼ teaspoons	sea salt
4½ teaspoons	dried leaf oregano
2 teaspoons	dried basil
¼ teaspoon	crushed cayenne (red) pepper
1¾ cups	☑ Pumpkin Puree* (page 78)
	OR 1 (15 oz.) can of pumpkin
2½ cups	water

For Pizza: Preheat oven to 350°.

1. In large skillet, "Chop & Drop" your choice of vegetables and garlic. "Slide, Season & Cook" meat and seasonings, stirring often.

2. Add pumpkin and water. Heat to boiling, reduce heat, cover and simmer approximately 15 minutes, stirring occasionally.

Yield: 7 cups sauce

Since pumpkin and buckwheat are to be consumed in limited amounts during Stage 2, I suggest eating this recipe on either Day 2 or 4 with Spaghetti Squash (a food that can be easily moved to Day 4).

May substitute pumpkin with Puréed Butternut Squash, see page 191 for cooking directions.

Recipes	Meal Preparation Tips
"Chop & Drop" "Slide, Season & Cook" Add pumpkin and water; simmer Freeze extra, see page 155	**For Spaghetti:** On Day 2 or 4, serve sauce over Spaghetti Squash (page 80). Begin baking the squash halves before beginning sauce. On Day 4, serve over purchased 100% buckwheat soba noodles, cooking noodles while simmering the sauce. - - - - - **For Pizza:** Using Amaranth or Buckwheat Pizza Crust, follow the "Meal Preparation Tips" for recipe on previous page.

☑ **Chicken Spaghetti/Pizza/Creamed Chicken'n Biscuit**
(Day 1 Recipe)

1 cup	☑ Chicken Broth (page 134)
as indicated	liquid—water OR additional Chicken Broth
	1/2 cup for Pizza Sauce OR 1 cup for Spaghetti Sauce
4 cups	Day 1 vegetables (my favorites include fennel and broccoli)
1 cup	cooked chicken chunks (pages 130 & 134)
1/4 teaspoon	sea salt
3/4 teaspoon	ground cumin
	OR
1/2 teaspoon	dill weed
1 tablespoon	hulled sesame seeds
2 tablespoons	flour—spelt, brown rice, Kamut®

Simmer most ingredients
Blend seed mixture; heat to thicken
Freeze extra (see pg. 155)

For Pizza: Preheat oven to 350°.

1. In saucepan, combine broth, water, vegetables, chicken and seasoning. Bring to boil, reduce heat, cover and simmer for 3–5 minutes.

2. In blender, blend seeds and flour with 1/4 cup water on highest speed for 1–2 minutes, stopping to scrape sides as needed. Add to vegetable mixture and cook 2–5 minutes on low until sauce thickens and vegetables are cooked to your liking, stirring often.

 Meal Preparation Tips are on the next page.

Yield: 3 1/2 cups Spaghetti Sauce   2 servings
3 cups Pizza Sauce; enough for 1 (12-inch) pizza

 ☑ **Vegetarian Version** (Day 1 Recipe)

Follow directions for recipe above except:
- Omit chicken meat.
- Substitute water or vegetable broth in place of chicken broth.
- Increase vegetables to a total of 5 1/2 cups.
- Increase salt and other seasoning to your liking. (I like to add garlic powder even though it breaks rotation.)

 Meal Preparation Tips are on the next page.

Yield: 3 1/2 cups Spaghetti Sauce   2 servings
3 cups Pizza Sauce for 1 (12-inch) pizza

Meal Preparation Tips for Both Recipes on Previous Page

For Spaghetti: Heat the water for spaghetti (spelt, brown rice or Kamut®). While water is coming up to boil, prepare vegetables. Add spaghetti and salt to boiling water as you prepare this very quick sauce.

- - - - -

For Pizza: Begin with preparing vegetables. Then prepare Pizza Crust. Bake the crust for 10 minutes while preparing this very quick sauce. Spread warm sauce evenly over par-baked crust and bake for an additional 15–20 minutes.

- - - - -

Creamed Chicken'n Biscuits: To serve sauce over Day 1 biscuits, prepare vegetables for sauce. Set aside and mix biscuits. While biscuits are baking, prepare this very quick sauce.

Freezing & Reheating Pizza

To Freeze: Loosen slices from bottom of pan with metal spatula. Place pizza pan in freezer until frozen, approx. 30–60 minutes. After frozen, wrap each slice in food wrap and then place in freezer bag. Store in freezer where it will not be "knocked around" and damaged.

- - - - -

To Reheat: Thaw pizza in the refrigerator during the day or overnight. Carefully unwrap and transfer to (unoiled) baking sheet. Place baking sheet in cold oven. Turn oven to 300°. Check pizza occasionally to see if it is ready.

Toaster/Convection Oven

For reheating individual servings, a toaster oven is a great option. It is more efficient than heating up the oven for just one or two pieces of pizza. The convection oven feature is even better. See equipment list on www.canaryconnect.com.

S₂L Italian Tofu (Day 4† Recipe)

2 cups	fresh stemmed or frozen green beans
1/4 teaspoon	sea salt
1/4 teaspoon	dried minced garlic
1/4 teaspoon	dried basil†
1/2 teaspoon	dried leaf oregano
1 pinch	crushed cayenne (red) pepper†
1 cup	tomato puree†
8 ounces	tofu (drained and diced)

In saucepan, heat 1 cup of water to boiling. Add green beans and seasonings. Return to boil, reduce heat, cover and simmer 3–5 minutes. Add puree and simmer for 5 minutes. Gently stir in tofu. Heat to serving temperature.

Yield: 2 servings   If soy is not a known allergen, enjoy on occasion during Stage 2.

†These foods are assigned to Day 2; omit eating them on Day 2 before and after Day 4.

S$_{2L}$ Taco Pizza Sauce (Day 2 Recipe)

Sauce Ingredients/2 Pizzas:

2 tablespoons	olive oil
1 cup	chopped onion
1$^{1}/_{2}$ cups	thinly sliced peeled eggplant (page 73)
	OR diced zucchini (peel if desired)
2 cloves	fresh garlic, minced
1 pound	lean ground beef or buffalo
$^{1}/_{2}$ teaspoon	sea salt
$^{1}/_{2}$ teaspoon	dried leaf oregano,
$^{1}/_{2}$ teaspoon	chili powder
$^{1}/_{4}$ teaspoon	red pepper flakes
1 cup	tomato puree
1 cup	water

"Chop & Drop"
"Slide, Season & Cook"
Simmer
Prepare & par-bake crust
Add sauce; bake
Garnish w/ toppings
Freeze extra (page 155)

Pizza Toppings: Use desired amounts of diced onions, shredded lettuce, diced fresh tomatoes, Guacamole and/or Picante Sauce after baking.

Preheat oven to 350°. Prepare and chill Guacamole and Picante Sauce (page 98).

1. In large skillet, "Chop & Drop" your choice of vegetables and garlic. "Slide, Season & Cook" meat and seasonings, stirring often.

2. Add puree and water. Heat to boiling, reduce heat, cover and simmer for approximately 10 minutes, stirring occasionally.

3. While sauce is cooking, prepare and par-bake Amaranth Pizza Crust for 10 minutes. Spread 2 cups of warm sauce evenly over crust. (Freeze remaining 2 cups for future.) Continue baking for 15–20 minutes.

4. Prepare toppings. Cut pizza into 8 slices. Garnish each slice with toppings.

Yield: 4 cups sauce   2 (12-inch) pizzas   8 slices each
During Stage 2, limit pizza to one or two servings/day.

Vegetarian Pizza (Day 2[†] Recipe)

Preheat oven to 350°.

1. Prepare a $^{1}/_{2}$ recipe of the Vegetarian Lasagna (page 158) sauce except use only $^{1}/_{2}$ teaspoon of salt and add 4 pinches of crushed red pepper flakes. Prepare and par-bake Amaranth Pizza Crust for 10 minutes.

2. While crust is baking, wash/spin dry 4 oz. amaranth greens OR spinach leaves,[†] dice 1 green pepper and drain $^{1}/_{2}$ pound soft tofu[†]. Spread a thin layer of sauce on crust. Layer "greens" over sauce. Spread remaining sauce evenly over greens. Dot w/ crumbled tofu and sprinkle w/ peppers. Continue baking for 15–20 minutes.

Yield: 1 (12-inch) pizza   8 slices

[†]*See note for Vegetarian Lasagna on page 158.*

S₂ ☑ Meatballs in Tomato Sauce (Day 2 Recipe)

Ingredients for Meatballs:

1 pound	lean ground beef or buffalo
¼ cup	amaranth breadcrumbs (see www.canaryconnect.com for resource)
¼ cup	finely chopped onion
1 clove	fresh garlic, minced
1 teaspoon	Italian seasoning*
½ teaspoon	sea salt
½ teaspoon	crushed red pepper flakes

Ingredients for Sauce:

2 tablespoons	olive oil
1 cup	chopped onion
1 cup	thinly sliced peeled eggplant (pg. 73)
1 cup	diced green peppers
3 cloves	fresh garlic, minced
¾ teaspoon	sea salt
1 teaspoon	Italian seasoning*
1 (28 oz.) can	crushed tomatoes
1 (15 oz.) can	diced tomatoes
2 tablespoons	tomato paste
1 cup	☑ Beef Broth (page 143)
¾–1 oz.	fresh basil
as desired	liquid stevia†

> Combine, shape and bake meatballs
> "Chop & Drop"
> Add tomatoes, broth, meatballs (when cooked); simmer
> Add basil
> Freeze extra

Some ingredients in Italian seasoning may break rotation.

Begin meal preparation with baking spaghetti squash halves (page 80).

1. In bowl, use hands to gently combine ingredients for meatballs. Score mixture into 8 portions; shape each portion into 4 (1") meatballs. Place on baking sheet with sides (such as jelly roll pan). Bake for 25 minutes at 350° along side squash. If needed, drain on absorbent paper towels. Add to sauce in Step 3.

2. In large skillet, "Chop & Drop" vegetables and seasonings in order listed (holding fresh basil until Step 4).

3. Stir in tomatoes, paste and broth. Add meatballs when cooked. Bring to boil, reduce heat and simmer for approximately 15 minutes, stirring occasionally.

4. Wash and spin dry fresh basil. Pile up the fresh leaves, then tightly roll lengthwise and slice crosswise to make ribbon-like pieces. Add basil during last 5 minutes of simmering the sauce.

5. Taste. If a sweeter flavor is desired, add 5–10 drops of liquid stevia. However, realize that spaghetti squash is slightly sweet.

 Serve over spaghetti squash.

Yield: 8 cups   4–6 servings   One of my favorite recipes, especially during Stage 2.

†*Stevia is assigned to Day 4; omit on Day 4 before and after using on Day 2.*

Vegetarian Lasagna (Day 2[†] Recipe)

2 tablespoons	olive oil
1 cup	chopped onion
3 cups	thinly sliced peeled eggplant (see page 73)
1 cup	diced green pepper
5 cloves	fresh garlic, minced
1$\frac{1}{2}$ teaspoons	sea salt
4 teaspoons	dried leaf oregano
2 teaspoons	dried basil
$\frac{1}{2}$ (28 oz.) can	tomato puree
2 cups	water
as desired	fresh amaranth greens (page 238) OR fresh spinach[†] leaves
1 recipe	☑ Soy Lasagna Noodles[†] (page 159)
1 pound	soft tofu[†] (drained and crumbled)

"Chop & Drop"
Add puree and water; simmer
Layer ingredients
Bake
Freeze extra; thaw; reheat slowly

Preheat oven to 350° before layering lasagna.

To Prepare Sauce:

1. In skillet, "Chop & Drop" vegetables and seasonings in order listed. Stir in puree and water. Heat to boiling, reduce heat, cover and simmer approximately 10 minutes, stirring occasionally.

2. While sauce is simmering, prepare tofu and rinse/spin dry "greens".

To Prepare Lasagna:

3. In an 8-inch square baking dish, layer ingredients in the following order:
   - 1 cup of sauce, spread evenly
   - 2–3 layers of "greens"
   - 1 layer of Soy Lasagna Noodles
   - $\frac{1}{2}$ of the tofu
   - 1$\frac{1}{2}$ cups of sauce, spread evenly
   - 2–3 layers of "greens"
   - remaining tofu
   - 1 layer of Soy Lasagna Noodles
   - 2 cups of sauce to cover everything completely

4. Bake for 50–60 minutes or until sauce bubbles and ingredients are fork tender. Remove and allow to "rest" for 5 minutes before serving.

 Time Hint! To save time/energy, use packaged triple-washed baby spinach leaves.

Yield: 4 servings

[†]Tofu is assigned to Day 4; omit eating soy on Day 4 before and after eating on Day 2. If using spinach and wish to keep rotation, omit it on Day 3 before and omit all foods from Goosefoot Family #28 (beet, chard, quinoa, spinach) from Day 1 before and Day 3 after eating on Day 2 (see table below).

Rotation Cycle	Day 1	Day 2	Day 3	Day 4
1			omit spinach	omit spinach
2	omit Goosefoot Family	use spinach in recipes	omit Goosefoot Family	omit Goosefoot Family

Soy Lasagna Noodles (Day 4[†] Recipe)

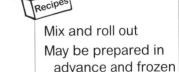

1¼ cups   soy flour (divided)
¼ tsp.   each: sea salt, garlic powder, dried basil[†]
½ tsp.   dried leaf oregano
¼ cup   water

> Mix and roll out
> May be prepared in advance and frozen

1. In a bowl, whisk together ¾ cup flour and seasonings. Add water. Stir to make moist ball. Divide into fourths.

2. Lightly flour rolling pin and rolling surface. Pat dough portion into rectangular shape, then roll out, working to keep noodle as rectangular as possible (4x8-inch size). Keep dough floured on both sides.

Yield: 4 noodles

[†]Basil is assigned to Day 2; omit eating basil on Day 2 before and after eating on Day 4.

S₂L Low Carb Lasagna (Day 2[†] Recipe)

1 teaspoon   olive oil
¾ cup   chopped onion
3 cloves   fresh garlic, minced
1 pound   lean ground beef or buffalo
1½ teaspoons   each: sea salt and dried basil
1 tablespoon   oregano
½ teaspoon   summer savory
½ (28 oz.) can   tomato puree
1 medium   eggplant
1 pound   soft tofu[†]

> Sauté onion & garlic
> Season & brown meat
> Add puree & water; simmer
> Sauté eggplant
> Layer ingredients
> Bake
> Freeze extra; thaw; reheat slowly

To Prepare Sauce:

1. In skillet, "Chop & Drop" onion and garlic. Add ground meat and seasonings, stirring often to brown evenly. Add puree and 2 cups of water. Heat to boiling, reduce heat, cover and simmer approximately 10 minutes, stirring occasionally.

2. While sauce is simmering, peel, slice and sauté eggplant for about 2 minutes on each side in additional oil. Drain on paper towel. Drain tofu.

To Prepare Lasagna: Preheat oven to 350° before layering.

3. In an 8-inch square baking dish, layer ingredients in following order:
   - 1 cup of sauce, spread evenly
   - ½ of the eggplant slices
   - ½ of the tofu (crumbled)
   - 1½ cups of sauce, spread evenly
   - remaining eggplant slices
   - remaining tofu (crumbled)
   - 2 cups of sauce to cover everything completely

4. Bake for 50–60 minutes or until sauce bubbles and ingredients are fork tender. Remove and allow to "rest" for 5 minutes before serving.

Yield: 4 servings   If soy is not a known allergen, enjoy on occasion during Stage 2.

[†]Tofu is assigned to Day 4; omit eating soy on Day 4 before and after eating on Day 2.

RECIPES

Entrées: Seafood

Some fish offer beneficial omega-3 fatty acids along with quality protein. However, they also contain toxins (i.e., mercury, PCBs [Polychlorinated Biphenyls], pesticides, herbicides). It is best to choose wild salmon caught in safe waters. Avoid farm-raised fish unless they are vegetable-fed and the streams feeding the area are free of chemical run-off. The highest mercury-containing fish to avoid are swordfish, shark, king mackerel, tilefish and some tuna. See www.canaryconnect.com for updates.

S₂c 🕐 Poached Fish Dinner

1/2 cup	liquid per serving—Day's vegetable broth* OR water
~5 oz.	Day's fish fillet per serving, seasoned with salt and the Day's seasonings
~2 cups	Day's vegetables per serving

1. In skillet with lid, heat liquid to boiling, carefully slide seasoned fish fillets into skillet, reduce heat, cover and begin to simmer while chopping the vegetables.

2. "Chop & Drop" vegetables. Sprinkle vegetables with salt and the Day's seasonings. Cover and continue to simmer until fish is flaky and vegetables are to desired tenderness (I prefer them slightly crunchy). Add liquid as needed.

 If desired, serve with the Day's starch (i.e., brown rice, amaranth, beans, quinoa, millet, buckwheat).

 *This is my favorite recipe for using the "Day's" vegetable broth made from steamed vegetables (page 69). However, a quality purchased brand may be used if breaking rotation is okay.

S₂c 🕐 Grilled Fish

1. Baste both sides of the Day's fish fillet (choose sturdy varieties) with small amount of the Day's oil. Sprinkle both sides with salt and the Day's seasonings.

2. Cook until flaky. I prefer an electric counter-top grill with thermostatic control (see next page). OR, use an electric skillet (see Orange Roughy recipe, page 163). OR, use grill pan (see 131).

3. Garnish according to the Day (i.e, Day 1 fresh parsley; Day 2 freshly squeezed lemon juice; Day 3 fresh cilantro; Day 4 freshly squeezed orange juice) and serve immediately.

Yield: 1 pound of fish equals 3 servings.

See guidelines above regarding choosing quality seafood.

S₂ᴄ Rainbow Trout (Baked or Grilled) (Day 3 Recipe)

To Bake:

- Rainbow Trout is cooked with head and tail intact.
- Rinse trout thoroughly. Sprinkle inside with small amount of salt.
- Place in shallow covered casserole dish that is large enough to keep fish flat. Cover and bake at 350° for 20 minutes or until trout is flaky and skin removes easily.

To Grill:

- Prepare trout the same as for baking except place trout in aluminum foil.* Fold ends and edges of foil around trout to make a folded seal.
- Place on counter-top electric grill preheated to the highest setting. Grill 10 minutes on first side, turn and grill 7 minutes on second side.

Counter-Top Grill

An electric thermostat-controlled counter-top grill is handy to grill fish filets, steaks, pork chops, etc. Look for a model that disassembles and reassembles easily for cleaning.

- - - - -

A non-stick coated grill is not recommended. These coatings contain formaldehyde that gives off toxic odors when cooking and leaches into the food.

See www.canaryconnect.com.

To Remove Skin & Bones for Serving:

- Using the edge of a fork, break through skin along backbone.
- Use two (2) table forks like tongs to pull skin off top of trout.
- Slide fork under meat to remove top fillet without bone. Fillet may come off in more than one piece.
- Carefully use fingers to pull bone up from tail. Look closely and remove any remaining small bones from bottom fillet.
- Turn fish over and remove skin from bottom fillet.
- Serve immediately with small amount of flaxseed oil or break rotation and sprinkle with garlic powder after using Clarified Butter.

See guidelines on page 160 regarding choosing quality seafood.

*Aluminum foil is okay to use on occasion in instances such as this when the skin of the fish protects the flesh (meat) (see page 257).

S₂ᴄ Salmon Patties (Day 3 Recipe)

8 ounces	☑ cooked salmon, flaked (season with salt during cooking)
1/2 cup	shredded carrots
1/4 cup	tapioca starch OR cornstarch
1 teaspoon	grapeseed oil

Preheat electric skillet to 350°. In bowl, gently combine salmon, carrots and starch with hands. Divide and shape into 6 patties. Cook for 3–5 minutes on each side until golden brown in oil. Serve immediately.

Yield: 2 servings   See guidelines on page 160 regarding choosing quality seafood.

S₂c Baked Fish

	Day 1	Day 2	Day 3	Day 4
Fish Choices:	halibut sole tuna steak	cod (scrod) pollack red snapper	flounder salmon steak	haddock mahi mahi ocean perch
Seasonings:	Choose from the Day's selections			
Other Ingredient Choices:	sliced celery sliced fennel water chestnuts almonds, pecans sesame seeds	sliced onion green pepper strips sliced zucchini sunflower seeds	thinly sliced carrots and/or parsnips	peas cashews
Garnish:	fresh parsley	fresh lemon juice	fresh cilantro	fresh orange juice

Preheat oven—350°.

Using your choice of ingredients:

- Place fish in covered casserole dish. • Sprinkle with salt and seasonings.
- Add other foods. • Drizzle with 1 teaspoon of the Day's oil per serving (optional). • Add 1–2 tablespoons of water per serving. • Cover and bake for 30 minutes or until easily flaked with fork. (Time depends upon thickness of fillet, if frozen or thawed and amount of other foods.) • Garnish and serve immediately.

Yield: Allow 1 pound of fish for 3 servings

See guidelines on page 160 regarding choosing quality seafood.

S₂ Spicy Baked Fish (Day 2 Recipe)

10 ounces	cod (scrod) or pollack fillet (2 servings)
½ cup	sliced onion
2 cups	sliced zucchini squash (peel if desired) OR
1 cup	sliced okra
1 (15 oz.) can	diced tomatoes
¼ teaspoon	each: sea salt, garlic powder, dried basil
½ teaspoon	dried leaf oregano

Sondra's Hints

Save juice from tomatoes for drinking or freeze it to use later in soup or stew.

- - - - -

If you desire a sauce to serve over potatoes or Basic Amaranth, omit draining tomatoes.

Place fillets in a shallow, covered casserole dish. Layer onions and squash or okra evenly over fillets. Drain tomatoes, reserving juice, and hand crush while pouring over vegetables. Sprinkle seasonings evenly. Cover and bake at 350° for 45 minutes or until fish is flaky and vegetables are tender.

Yield: 2 servings   See guidelines on page 160 regarding choosing quality seafood.

☑ **Shrimp Tofu Lasagna** (Day 4† Recipe)

4 cloves	fresh garlic, minced
1 cup	sliced leeks
2 teaspoons	safflower oil
1/4 cup	chopped macadamia or Brazil nuts
1/3 cup	kudzu starch
2 cups	water
1 teaspoon	sea salt
1 1/2 teaspoons	dried basil†
1 tablespoon	dried leaf oregano
3 cups	asparagus cuts/tips (fresh or frozen)
1 pound	☑ shrimp† (cooked, shelled and diced)
1 pound	soft tofu (drained and crumbled)
2 layers	☑ Soy Lasagna Noodles (page 159)

> Sauté garlic & onions
>
> Blend & add nut mixture
>
> Add asparagus & shrimp
>
> Layer ingredients
>
> Bake
>
> Freeze extra; thaw; reheat slowly

Preheat oven to 350° when beginning to layer lasagna (Step 4).

To Prepare Sauce:

1. In saucepan, sauté garlic and leeks in oil until soft.

2. In blender, blend nuts, kudzu and small amount of water on highest speed until well blended, stopping to scrape blender jar as needed. Add this mixture, the rest of water and seasonings to saucepan. Cook until thickened, stirring constantly.

3. Add asparagus and shrimp.

To Prepare Lasagna:

4. In an 8-inch square baking dish, layer ingredients in following order:
   - 1 cup sauce, spread evenly
   - 1 layer of lasagna noodles
   - 1/2 of tofu
   - 1 1/2 cups of sauce, spread evenly
   - remaining tofu
   - 1 layer of Soy Lasagna Noodles
   - 3 cups of sauce to cover everything completely

5. Bake for 50–60 minutes or until sauce bubbles and ingredients are fork tender. Remove and allow to "rest" for 5 minutes before serving.

Yield: 4 servings

†These foods are assigned to Day 2; omit on Day 2 before and after eating on Day 4.

S₂ **Orange Roughy** (Day 4 Recipe)

 Preheat electric skillet to 250°. Add small amount of safflower oil (or break rotation and use Clarified Butter). Add fillets and sprinkle with sea salt and tarragon. Cook 3–4 minutes per side until fish is flaky. Total cooking time depends upon thickness of fillets and if fillets are frozen or thawed.

 Serve with Cream of Asparagus Soup.

Yield: 1 pound of fish equals 3 servings This is my favorite fish dish.

S₂c ✓ **Salmon Millet Dinner** (Day 3 Recipe)

1/4 cup	dry hulled millet
1 cup	water
1/8 teaspoon	sea salt
2 cups	sliced fresh cauliflower
2 cups packed	fresh (cut) baby spinach (~3 oz.)
6 ounces	✓ cooked salmon, flaked
	(use 8 oz. salmon to yield 6 oz. cooked)

> Cook millet
> Add veggies and salmon; cook
> Freeze extra; thaw; reheat slowly

1. Add millet, water and salt to 3-quart saucepan. Bring to boil, reduce heat to medium, cover and simmer for 9 minutes.

2. Prepare vegetables. I use the triple washed baby spinach (approx. 2/3 of a 5 oz. bag). To "cut," pour out on cutting board and run a knife thru a few times. After millet has cooked for 9 minutes, remove lid and quickly layer vegetables and salmon. Do not stir. Return cover and simmer for an additional 10–11 minutes.

 Serve this very quick meal with raw carrot coins.

 I love the convection oven feature on my toaster oven to reheat this dish. See my recommendation on www.canaryconnect.com.

Yield: 3 cups 2 servings See guidelines on page 160 regarding choosing quality seafood.

RECIPES

Whole-Grain Cookery

Whole grains (pages 234–238) provide a rich array of nutrients (i.e., fiber, complex carbohydrates, minerals, vitamins B and E, protein). Their refined counterparts do not make similar contributions to our diet because the refining process strips them of most nutrients. Any vitamins or minerals added back in are usually in synthetic form (page 40). Grains are members of the Grass Family; some contain gluten and others are gluten-free (see page 235). Some of the Grass Family are common food allergens (i.e., wheat, corn, white rice), but many grains are easily tolerated (i.e., teff, millet, brown rice, wild rice).

Nongrains (pages 234–235, 238–240) are not true grains (they are not members of the Grass Family), but they act like grains and add a wonderful variety of low-allergenic foods to a nutrient-rich diet. For simplicity, all grains and nongrains in this section are referred to as "grains." It is important for people fighting *candida* to avoid all refined grains. Many also suggest avoiding gluten grains during Stage 2 of the Candida-Control Food Plan. During Stage 2, it is best to limit total consumption of any grains/nongrains to a few servings/day in order to maintain a low intake of carbohydrates. I have offered some guidelines on the recipes to help you incorporate these theories during your "Fight."

S₂CL ⏲ or 🥣 Basic Grains

Dry Grain	Assigned Day	Amount of Liquid/1 cup Grain	Simmering Time	Yield
Amaranth	Day 2	2 cups	30 minutes	$2^1/_4$ cups
Barley, hulled	Day 3	4 cups	45 minutes	$4^1/_2$ cups
Buckwheat Groats, unroasted	Day 4	2 cups	15 minutes	3 cups
Kamut®	Day 1	3 cups	$2^1/_2$ hours	3 cups
Millet, hulled	Day 3	2 cups	15 minutes	4 cups
Quinoa	Day 3	2 cups	15 minutes	4 cups
Rice—Brown Basmati, Long-& Short-Grain	Day 1	$2^1/_4$ cups	30 minutes	3 cups
Spelt	Day 1	3 cups	$2^1/_2$ hours	3 cups
Wild Rice	Day 3	$2^1/_2$ cups	40 minutes	3 cups

1. Before cooking grains, they should be rinsed to remove dirt and hulls.
   - Place measurement of grain in a $2^1/_2$ quart saucepan. Add water and gently stir.
   - Gently pour off and discard immature grains, hulls or other debris that floats.
   - Drain off water, using a fine-mesh strainer for smaller or medium-sized grains or a small-holed colander for larger grains such as spelt and Kamut®.
   - Work quickly, so the quick-cooking porous grains (quinoa, buckwheat, millet) do not absorb the rinsing water. This effects the texture of the cooked product.
   - For quinoa, repeat the process 2–3 times to remove the saponin layer (pg. 240).

2. In saucepan, combine grain, liquid such as water or vegetable/meat broth (see chart for amount) and $1/_4$ teaspoon (or more) salt with other Day's seasonings (some suggestions below):
   - $1/_2$ cup sliced leeks with buckwheat
   - $1/_2$ teaspoon caraway seed with millet
   - 1 teaspoon FOS (pages 46 and 243) with quinoa

3. Bring to boil, cover, reduce heat and simmer until tender (see chart for guidelines). Taste for doneness. Remove from heat and allow to "rest" for 5 minutes. Stir to fluff before serving.

 See "Helpful Hints" and "Equipment Tip" on next page.

Recipes
Rinse grain
Add liquid/ seasonings
Simmer
Freeze extra

Yield: see chart

During Stage 2, gluten-free grains (i.e., amaranth, buckwheat, millet, quinoa, brown rice, wild rice) and other higher carbohydrate foods (i.e., potatoes, acorn squash) can offer much desired energy. However, it is important to keep the carbs low by enjoying only ~$1/_2$–$3/_4$ cup of these per meal.

Helpful Hints for Grain Cookery

For best results, do not uncover or stir during cooking time. If it is necessary to check progress, do so quickly to minimize steam loss. DO NOT STIR as this will disrupt the even cooking of the grain. If tasting for doneness, use a fork to gently remove a small amount from surface of the grain. Different stoves/pans and altitude may require adjustments in time, temperature and liquid amount.

- - - - -

Freeze leftover cooked grains in single (or family–sized) servings or in amounts needed for use in various recipes such as Three Color Salad, Millet or Quinoa Pudding, soups and casseroles. This preplanning allows for more "Quick & Easy" meals and encourages you to stay on your rotational food plan, especially on those days when you need a cooking break.

- - - - -

My family and I love brown Basmati rice. The cooking fragrance is, "Mmm! Who is cooking popcorn?"

Fine Mesh Strainer

A fine-mesh strainer is very useful for washing small- to medium-sized grains such as quinoa, amaranth, teff, millet, rice and buckwheat.

- - - - -

They can also be used to strain meat broth or sift carob powder.

S₂ₗ Roasted Grains

Roasting intensifies the delicious taste of the grains and/or seasoning.

Rinse and cook grain as described in Basic Grains (page 165) except insert the following step before cooking.

Roasting Grain: Pour into cold, heavy-bottomed skillet. I prefer cast iron. For millet, add caraway seed if desired. Place skillet on range. Turn burner to medium-high. Roast, stirring almost constantly, for first roasting time as indicated in chart below or until the grain has become rather dry. Lower heat to medium low and continue to roast, stirring constantly for second roasting time as indicted in chart below or until you can smell an intense aroma. Be careful not to burn it.

Sondra's Hints

Roasted buckwheat groats, usually called Kasha, are available for purchase.

- - - - -

Other grains may be roasted following the same guidelines—"until grain becomes dry" and "until you can smell an intense aroma."

Grain	1st Roasting Time	2nd Roasting Time
Amaranth	6 minutes	4 minutes
Millet	4 minutes	4 minutes
Buckwheat	6 minutes	4–9 minutes

See Stage 2 guidelines on previous page.

S₂ₗ **Wild & Brown Rice with Herbs** (Day 1† Recipe)
Recipe depicted on front cover.

1 cup	dry brown rice
¹/₄ cup	wild rice†
2¹/₂ cups	water
¹/₄ teaspoon	sea salt
¹/₄ teaspoon	each: dried marjoram, dried rosemary, dried tarragon†
as desired	chopped pecans or almonds

 Follow directions for Basic Grains (page 165), adding the seasonings with the salt. Simmer for 40 minutes. Add nuts and stir.

Yield: 3 ³/₄ cups   During Stage 2, see note on page 165.

†*Wild rice is assigned to Day 3; omit it on Day 3 before and after eating on Day 1. Also, these spices break rotation but I do not concern myself with this minor rotation break; enjoy some "Spice in Life!"*

S₂ₗ **Brown Rice & Chard** (Day 1 Recipe)

 Follow directions for Basic Grains (page 165), laying 1–2 cups of chard (washed, torn into small pieces) on top of brown rice when simmering.

See Pilaf recipes on page 83 for more grain/vegetable combos.

 ☑ **Brown Rice & Almond Cereal** (Day 1 Recipe)

³/₄ cup	☑ cooked brown Basmati rice (page 165)
¹/₂ cup	Almond Milk (page 101)
	OR use purchased brown rice beverages (watch ingredients)
1 teaspoon	brown rice syrup
1 tablespoon	chopped almonds

 In saucepan, combine all ingredients and heat to serving temperature. Stir occasionally to prevent scorching. If desired, add a dash of ground cinnamon and more rice syrup. Serve for breakfast or dessert.

Yield: 1 serving

S₂ₗ **Oat Bran Cereal** (Day 3 Recipe)

1 cup	water
¹/₃ cup	oat bran
¹/₈ teaspoon	sea salt (or slightly less)

In saucepan, bring water to a boil. Add oat bran and salt, stir, reduce heat and cook for 1–2 minutes. Stir constantly to prevent boiling over or sticking. Cover, remove from heat and allow cereal to "rest" for 3–5 minutes to thicken.

Yield: 1 cup   1 serving   Enjoy small amounts on occasion during Stage 2.

S_{2L} Oatmeal (Day 3 Recipe)

3 cups	water
1¹/₂ cups	old fashioned rolled oats
¹/₂ teaspoon	sea salt

 In saucepan, bring water to a boil. Add oats and salt, stir and reduce heat to medium–high. Cook at a gentle boil for 5 minutes, stirring constantly. Remove from heat, cover and allow to "rest" for 3–5 minutes.

 Serve with oat milk, ground cinnamon, maple granules, flax seed oil and/ or diced apple.

Yield: 3 cups 3 servings Enjoy small amounts on occasion during Stage 2.

Oat Granola (Day 3 Recipe)

1 cup	rolled oats
1 cup	oat bran
¹/₄ cup	walnuts, chopped
2 tablespoons	maples granules (optional)
¹/₄ cup	liquid—water OR apple juice concentrate
¹/₂ teaspoon	alcohol-free cinnamon extract (optional)
2 tablespoons	Day 3 oil of your choice

> Combine dry
> ingredients
> Coat w/ liquids
> Bake
> Freeze extra

Preheat oven to 250°.

1. In a bowl, combine cereals, nuts and maple granules. Whisk together liquid, extract and oil. Gradually add to dry ingredients, stirring to evenly coat mixture.

2. Scatter mixture in a 9x13-inch baking dish. Bake for 45–60 minutes, stirring every 10–15 minutes until dry and slightly crunchy. Be careful not to burn. Cool completely. Store in freezer.

- • Eat plain for crunchy snack
- • Serve as topping on non-dairy frozen dessert
- • Enjoy as breakfast cereal served with Filbert Milk (page 101) or oat milk.
- • Enjoy as topping on baked apple: Peel and dice fresh apple. Place in oiled casserole bowl, sprinkle with ground cinnamon and bake at 350° until almost tender. Top with granola and bake for additional 5 minutes. Serve warm.

Yield: 2 cups 4 servings

> *If you have tried to do something and failed, you are vastly better off than if you had tried to do nothing and succeeded.*

S₂CL Slow Cooker Cereals

Cereal	Assigned Day	Amount of Dry Grain & Flour	Yield
Teff I	Day 1	$^1/_2$ cup brown teff grain	2 cups
Teff II	Day 1	$^1/_3$ cup br. teff grain + 2 T br. teff flour	2 cups
Kamut® or Spelt	Day 1	$^2/_3$ cup Kamut® or spelt kernels	2 cups
Amaranth I	Day 2	$^1/_2$ cup amaranth	2 cups
Amaranth II	Day 2	$^1/_3$ cup amaranth + 2 T amaranth flour	2 cups
Millet I	Day 3	$^1/_3$ cup hulled millet	2 cups
Quinoa I	Day 3	$^1/_3$ cup quinoa + 2 T quinoa flour	2–2$^1/_4$ cups
Quinoa II	Day 3	$^1/_4$ cup + 2 T quinoa	2–2$^1/_4$ cups
Buckwheat I	Day 4	$^1/_3$ cup buckwheat groats OR $^1/_3$ cup purchased Buckwheat Cereal	2 cups

Small-sized slow cooker.

1. For Kamut®, spelt and unroasted buckwheat groats, grind in chopper to make a coarse meal. For other grains, rinse according to Step 1 of Basic Grains (page 165).

2. Combine grains and/or flours with $^1/_4$ teaspoon salt and 2 cups liquid (water or 1$^3/_4$ cup water with $^1/_4$ cup nut milk). Cook on LOW overnight.

 Stir before serving. Enjoy this cereal plain or serve with toppings, such as raspberries or Pear Sauce for Day 1; sliced kiwi for Day 2; applesauce, cinnamon and/or diced apple for Day 3 or blueberries on Day 4.

Yield: See chart above   2 servings each   During Stage 2, enjoy small servings of the cereals using gluten-free grains (i.e., teff, amaranth, millet, quinoa, buckwheat) without fruit. Also, see "Sondra's Experience" on page 225.

Sondra's Hints

These recipes are designed for a 1.5 quart slow cooker. However, they can be easily doubled or tripled to cook in a standard-sized slow cooker.

- - - - -

By taking a few minutes to start slow cooker cereal before you go to bed, you can wake up to a very easy, delicious breakfast and enjoy the wonderful aroma of cooked cereal when you enter your kitchen in the morning.

Slow Cooker

When purchasing a slow cooker, look for one where the crock insert lifts out of the heating base, making it easier to clean.

S₂ₗ Stove Top Cereals

Cereal	Assigned Day	Amount of Dry Grain	Water	Simmering Time	Yield
Amaranth III	Day 2	$^1/_2$ cup amaranth seed	3 cups	35–45 min.	$1^3/_4$ cups
Millet II	Day 3	$^2/_3$ cup hulled whole millet	4 cups	20 min.	2 cups
Quinoa III	Day 3	$^1/_2$ cup whole quinoa $^1/_4$ tsp. FOS (optional)	$2^1/_2$ cups	20–25 min.	$2^1/_2$ cups
Buckwheat II	Day 4	6 Tbsp. buckwheat groats OR purchased Buckwheat Cereal	3 cups	10 min.	2 cups

Grind groats (Step 1 of Slow Cooker Cereals, page 169). For other grains, rinse following Step 1 of Basic Grains (page 165). In saucepan, heat water (may replace $^1/_4$–$^1/_2$ cup with nut milk) to boiling. Add grain and $^1/_4$ teaspoon of salt. Stir, reduce heat, cover and simmer (see chart), stirring occasionally.

Yield: See chart   2 servings   See Stage 2 note on previous page.

☑ Dill "Stove-Top" Stuffing   (Day 1 Recipe)

Vegetable Combination Choices:

$^1/_2$ cup each: diced celery and fennel

$1^1/_2$ cups finely chopped cabbage

$^1/_2$ cup diced celery with $^3/_4$ cup finely chopped cabbage

1 cup diced celery

1 tablespoon	sesame oil
2 cups	quick cooking Kamut® or spelt flakes (see _www.canaryconnect.com_)
1 teaspoon	each: sea salt and dill weed
$^1/_4$ cup	pecan pieces
1 cup	☑ Chicken Broth (page 134)
1 cup	water

1. In skillet, sauté vegetables in oil until just tender, stirring often. (Hold cabbage for Step 3.)

2. Add flakes, pecans, salt and dill. Continue to cook for about 5 minutes, stirring often. This "toasts" the flakes and enhances the flavors.

> Sauté veggies
>
> Add dry ingredients; cook
>
> Add liquids; simmer

3. Add liquids and cabbage (if using), stir, cover and cook on medium heat for 4–5 minutes or until flakes are done and liquid is absorbed. Stir and serve.

 This recipe has been a favorite of many guests. If you desire, you can double the amount of vegetables and/or pecans, add $^1/_2$ cup more liquid and little more salt.

Yield: 4 cups   8 servings

Stuffing   (Non Rotating† Recipe)

	neck and giblets from 1 roasting hen or turkey
2 1/2 cups	water
1/2 teaspoon	sea salt
4 cups	homemade or purchased* yeast-free bread (cubed and slightly dried)
1 1/4 cup	diced celery (also include celery leaves)
1/2 cup	chopped onions
1 teaspoon	dried rubbed sage
1/2 teaspoon	dried thyme
1/2 cup	sesame oil
	OR
1 stick	unsalted butter, melted

Cook & pull meat
Combine other
  ingredients
Crush bread
Bake

Oven temperature—350°. Preheating not necessary.   8-inch square baking dish

1. Remove fat and skin on neck and giblets. In saucepan, bring water to boil, add meat and salt, reduce heat, cover and simmer until tender (approx. 30–45 minutes).

 Sondra's Hints

Stuffing can be placed inside the cavity of a chicken or turkey. Allow ~30 min. more roasting time. Roast until internal temp. of stuffing is 180°.

2. Remove meat, cool enough to handle and pull/cut meat from bone and grizzle. Measure broth and add water to yield 1 cup.

3. In bowl, combine bread, vegetables and seasonings to evenly distribute spices. Pour broth and oil/butter evenly over mixture and stir to moisten. Use hands to smash, breaking the cubes into smaller crumbs. The liquid (if some remains) will be absorbed during baking. Transfer to baking dish. Bake for 35–40 minutes.

Yield: 8 servings

†This recipe breaks rotation. You can plan ahead to make modifications or, if only having occasionally as with holiday meals, enjoy without concern.

*See www.canaryconnect.com for resources for yeast-free bread.

S₂ₗ 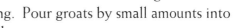 **White Buckwheat Flour**   (Day 4 Recipe)
How to Prepare Using Raw Buckwheat Groats

1. Before processing, sort through groats to remove debris and immature grains which otherwise would float to the top when washing. Pour groats by small amounts into fine-mesh strainer over sink and gently shake strainer to remove small debris.

2. In blender, blend on highest speed until finely ground, stopping occasionally to feel consistency and scrape sides of blender jar.

Yield: 2 cups groats = almost 2 1/2 cups flour

 Helpful Hint!

For best nutritional value, use flour immediately or store in refrigerator or freezer.

Prepare: Muffin Pans/Baking Dishes

Use same oil as used in recipe. If recipe does not give specific amount, begin with $1/4$ teaspoon oil. If recipe does not give specific instructions, follow:

- Using a $1/4$ teaspoon oil, drop a very small amount into each of 12 muffin cups. If you run out of oil, do not add more until after the next step.
- With fingers, spread oil in each cup to completely coat bottom and sides.
- Add more oil if needed to coat each cup.
- If recipe calls for muffin pan to be floured, immediately after oiling, sprinkle each cup with a small amount of flour, using same flour as in recipe.
- Immediately shake muffin pan quickly from side to side and front to back to distribute flour at least around the bottom. Amount of flour needed varies depending on the kind used, but it usually is 1 teaspoon for 6 muffin cups.
- Remove any excess flour by turning floured pan upside down over sink and tapping on bottom.

Use same procedure with baking dishes except drizzle $1/4$ teaspoon oil around in pan before spreading.

"Well"

Several recipes include instructions to make a "well" in the center of combined dry ingredients. To accomplish this, distribute dry ingredients in bowl so there is an indentation (hole) in the center where liquid ingredients will be poured. This helps to facilitate the thorough moistening of dry ingredients with less mixing.

S2L Soy Bread (Day 2[†] Recipe)

1 cup	soy flour[†]
$1/2$ cup	arrowroot starch
$2 1/4$ teaspoons	potato-based baking powder*
$1/2$ teaspoon	sea salt
2 tablespoons	soy oil[†]
1 cup	water

Combine
Bake
Freeze extra

Preheat oven to 375°.
Oil/flour bottom/sides of an 8-inch square baking pan.

1. In bowl, whisk together dry ingredients. Add water and oil. Mix thoroughly.

2. Transfer batter to prepared pan and spread evenly. Bake for 20 minutes. Bread is done when it sounds hollow when tapped on top surface. Cool 5–10 minutes.

 Serve for breakfast, with dinner (with or without wheat-free gravy) or as a snack.

Yield: 8 servings (Cut 4x2) If you do not have a known allergen to soy, you can enjoy soy bread on occasion during Stage 2.

[†]*Soy is assigned to Day 4; omit eating soy on Day 4 before and after eating on Day 2.*

*See www.canaryconnect.com for resource.

S₂CL Pancakes

	Day 1	Day 1	Day 1	Day 3	Day 3†	Day 4
	Kamut®	**Spelt**	**Teff**	**Quinoa**	**Rice/Oat**	**Buckwheat**
flour/starch	1½ cups Kamut® flour	2 cups spelt flour	½ cup brown teff flour	1 cup quinoa flour ⅜ cup tapioca starch	1 cup br. rice flour† ⅜ cup oat flour	1¾ cups White Buckwheat (page 171)
other ingred.					2 Tbsp. flaxmeal	
baking soda	1½ tsp.	1½ tsp.	½ tsp.	1 tsp.	1 tsp.	1½ tsp.
sea salt	scant ¼ tsp.	scant ¼ tsp.	2 pinches	scant ¼ tsp.	½ tsp.	scant ¼ tsp.
unbuffered vit. C crystals	½ tsp.	½ tsp.	¼ tsp.	½ tsp.	½ tsp.	½ tsp.
water	1½ cups	1½ cups	½ cup	1 cup	1 cup	1½ cups
Day's oil	2 Tbsp.	2 Tbsp.	2 tsp.	4 tsp.	¼ cup	2 Tbsp.
optional ingredients or fruit	1 cup	1 cup	⅓ cup	1 tsp. FOS 1 t. cinnamon		¾ cup fresh/frozen blueberries
	fresh/frozen raspberries					

Preheat griddle (see "Griddle," page 185). Lightly oil after preheating.

Mix
Cook
Freeze extra

1. In bowl, whisk together dry ingredients. Add water and oil. Stir with whisk until blended. Allow batter to "rest" for 30 seconds to thicken. Stir again.

2. Optional: Gently stir in fruit.

3. Pour batter onto griddle using small measuring cup (i.e., ⅛ cup). Cook until pancakes bubble (some smooth out) and are slightly dry around edges, approx. 1½–2 minutes. Turn. Cook until dry, approx. 1½–2 minutes.

If batter in bowl thickens (especially common with spelt, buckwheat and Kamut®) add small amounts of water. Add additional oil to griddle as needed.

Serve plain, with flaxseed oil and/or with allowed toppings for the rotation (i.e., pear sauce on teff, applesauce on quinoa).

Pancake w/o Fruit	Yield Dollar-Sized	Count/ Serving
Kamut®	30	5
Spelt	30	5
Teff	10	2
Quinoa	24	4
Rice-Oat	24	4
Buckwheat	21-24	4

During Stage 2, enjoy the gluten-free pancakes (i.e., teff, quinoa, rice/oat, buckwheat) without fruit. Also, see "Sondra's Experience" on page 225.

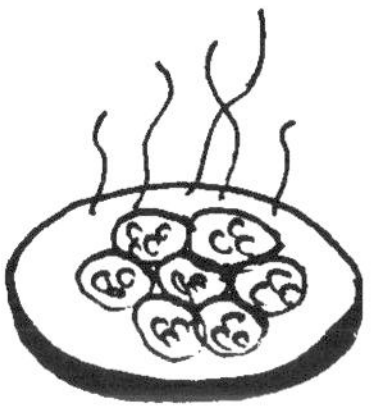

†Omit eating rice on Day 1 before and after eating on Day 3.

S₂CL Biscuits

Dropped biscuits are the quickest bread form—they take only 5–6 minutes to prepare and 10 minutes to bake.

	Day 1		Day 3	Day 4
	Kamut®	**Spelt**	**Oat**	**White Buckwheat**
flour	1¼ cups		1 cup	1¼ cups (page 171)
baking soda	½ teaspoon			
sea salt	scant ⅛ teaspoon		⅛ teaspoon	
vit. C crystals*	⅛ teaspoon			
optional			½ tsp. ground cinnamon	
water	½ cup + 2 Tbsp.	½ cup	⅓ cup	½ cup + 2 Tbsp.
Day's oil	1 tablespoon		2 teaspoons	1 tablespoon

	Day 2	Day 3
	Amaranth Garbanzo Bean	**Quinoa**
flour/starch	½ cup amaranth flour ¼ cup garbanzo bean flour ¼ cup arrowroot starch	¾ cup quinoa flour ¼ cup tapioca starch
baking soda	⅜ teaspoon (¼ teaspoon + ⅛ teaspoon)	
sea salt	⅛ teaspoon	scant ⅛ teaspoon
vit. C crystals*	⅛ teaspoon	
optional		1 teaspoon FOS ½ teaspoon ground cinnamon
water	⅓ cup	
Day's oil	2 teaspoons	

Directions for Dropped Biscuits:

Preheat oven—400°. Lightly oil baking sheet.

1. In bowl, whisk together dry ingredients. Make "well" in center.
   Add water and oil. Stir until dough clumps into ball and flour is well mixed.

2. Drop batter from rounded teaspoon onto baking sheet. Bake for 10 minutes.

Directions for Spelt or Kamut® Rolled Biscuits:

Preheat oven—400°. Ungreased baking sheet.

Perform Step 1 for Dropped Biscuits except use 1½ cups of flour.

2. Knead dough lightly on a floured board. Pat out to ½-inch thick using more flour as needed.

continued …

... continued

3. Cut out biscuits with biscuit cutter or drinking glass (~2$^1/_4$ inch). Form together remaining dough. Repeat to use all dough. Bake for 12 minutes.

 Serve biscuits for breakfast or snacks, with casseroles or other meals. Or, as dessert topped with unsweetened pear/applesauce and cinnamon.

*Use unbuffered vitamin C crystals

Biscuit	Yield
Amaranth Garbanzo Bean	10
Buckwheat	12
Kamut® Dropped	12
Kamut® Rolled	9
Oat	9
Quinoa	8
Spelt Dropped	12
Spelt Rolled	9

During Stage 2, enjoy the gluten-free biscuits (i.e., oat, amaranth garbanzo bean, buckwheat, quinoa) on occasion.

Mix
Drop OR
   knead/cut
Bake
Freeze extra

 French Toast (Day 1 Recipe)

1 large	egg
	OR 1 egg yolk with 1 tablespoon water
$^1/_8$ teaspoon	sea salt
dash	ground cinnamon (optional)
2 slices	homemade or purchased yeast-free bread
	(see www.canaryconnect.com for resources)

Preheat griddle (see "Griddle" on page 185).

 Lightly beat egg (or yolk with water), salt and cinnamon in shallow flat-bottomed bowl. Dip bread slices to coat on both sides. Cook for 2 minutes on each side until golden brown. Serve immediately.

 Serve with flaxseed oil, raspberries and/or pear sauce.

Yield: 1 serving

Flaxmeal Egg Substitute Directions
(Some muffins crumble without egg but the taste is unchanged.)

1. In saucepan, whisk flaxmeal (ground flaxseed) with water. If recipe does not indicate amount, use 1 tablespoon flaxmeal and $^1/_4$ cup water per egg.
2. Bring to boil, reduce heat to medium-high and boil for 1–2 minutes until consistency of egg white (color is not like egg white), whisking almost continuously. Set aside to cool before using in recipe.

Muffins

Oat Bran Muffins   (Day 3† Recipe)

3 cups	oat bran		2 large	eggs†
1 Tbsp.	baking powder			OR use Flaxmeal Egg Sub.
1/2 tsp.	salt			(page 175) using 2 Tbsp. flaxmeal
1 1/2 cups	unsweetened apple juice			with 3/8 cup water
1/4 cup	grapeseed oil		1/2 cup	raisins (optional)

 May use water for some of apple juice. These make great Christmas gifts.

†*Eggs are assigned to Day 1; omit them on Day 1 before and after eating them on Day 3.*

Kamut® or Spelt Muffins   (Day 1 Recipe)

2 1/2 cups	Kamut® or spelt flour
2 tsp.	baking soda
1/4 tsp.	sea salt
1/2 tsp.	unbuffered vitamin C crystals
1/4 cup	sesame oil
as indicated	liquid—pear juice or water
	1 7/8 cups for Kamut® (7/8 cup = 1 cup less 2 tablespoons)
	1 1/2 cups for spelt
1 cup	fresh or frozen raspberries (optional)

S₂CL Teff Muffins   (Day 1 Recipe)

1 cup	brown teff flour		2 Tbsp.	sesame oil
1 tsp.	baking soda		1 large	egg (optional)
1/4 tsp.	sea salt			OR Flaxmeal Egg Sub. (pg. 175)
1/4 tsp.	unbuffered vit. C crystals		1/2 cup	fresh/frozen raspberries (optional)
3/4 cup	water			

Quinoa Applesauce Muffins   (Day 3 Recipe)

1 3/4 cups	quinoa flour		1/2 tsp.	unbuffered vit. C crystals
1/2 cup	tapioca starch		1 cup	unsweetened applesauce
2 tsp.	baking soda		2/3 cup	water
1/2 tsp.	sea salt		2 Tbsp	grapeseed oil
2 tsp.	ground cinnamon (optional)			

S₂L Quinoa Muffins (No Fruit)   (Day 3 Recipe)

2 cup	quinoa flour		2 tsp.	ground cinnamon (optional)
1/2 cup	tapioca starch		1/2 tsp.	unbuffered vit. C crystals
2 tsp.	baking soda		1 1/2 cups	water
1/2 tsp.	sea salt		1/4 cup	grapeseed oil

continued ...

... continued

S₂ᴄʟ Buckwheat Muffins (Day 4 Recipe)

2 cups	Wh. Buckwheat Flour (page 171)		1³/₄ cups	water
2 tsp.	baking soda		¹/₄ cup	safflower oil
¹/₂ tsp.	sea salt		2 tsp.	orange extract (optional)
¹/₂ tsp.	unbuffered vitamin C crystals		1 cup	fresh or frozen blueberries (optional)
¹/₄ cup	kudzu starch OR			
1 tsp.	guar gum (add to liquid ingredients; whisk well before adding to dry ingredients)			

Directions for Muffins on pages 176–177:

Preheat oven according to chart.

Oil and flour the bottom and sides of muffin cups.

1. In bowl, whisk together dry ingredients except guar gum. Add liquids, guar gum, fruit sauce, egg/egg substitute and/or oil. Stir just to moisten dry ingredients. Gently smash larger lumps against side of bowl. Smaller lumps will bake out. For Oat Bran, allow to "rest" approx. 5 minutes to absorb liquid.

2. Optional: Gently stir in fruit.

3. Following chart below, portion batter into prepared muffin cups and bake until toothpick comes out clean.

4. Cool muffins in pan(s) on wire rack for 5 minutes. Take a sharp, thin knife around edges of muffins to loosen from sides. Turn out muffins.

Recipes

Mix ingredients (allow Oat Bran to "rest")

Portion batter

Bake; cool

Freeze extra

Chef

Is it Done?

Insert toothpick into center of bread, muffins and cakes. If done, toothpick comes out clean.

Muffin	Oven Temp.	Portion of Batter per Muffin Cup	Baking Time
Kamut®/Spelt	350°	rounded ¹/₄ cup	20–25 min.
Kamut®/Spelt w/ Raspberries	350°	scant ¹/₃ cup	25–27 min.
Teff	400°	rounded ¹/₄ cup	20 min.
Quinoa Applesauce	375°	rounded ¹/₄ cup	20–22 min.
Quinoa (No Fruit)	375°	scant ¹/₄ cup	20–22 min.
Buckwheat	375°	scant ¹/₄ cup	23–25 min.
Buckwheat w/ Blueberries	375°	scant ¹/₃ cup	24–25 min.
Oat Bran	425°	scant ¹/₃ cup	12–15 min.
Oat Bran w/ Raisins	425°	¹/₃ cup	12–15 min.

Yield: 12 muffins for all varieties except 6 for teff

During Stage 2, enjoy the gluten-free muffins without fruit (i.e., teff, quinoa, buckwheat) on occasion.

Also, see "Sondra's Experience" on page 225.

S₂CL Crackers

	Day 1 **Kamut®**	**Day 1** **Spelt**	**Day 1** **Brown Teff**	**Day 3** **Rye**
flour	1¼ cups	1¼ cups	1 cup + 2 Tbsp.	1⅓ cups
seeds			2 tablespoons sesame	2 teaspoons caraway
baking soda	½ teaspoon	½ teaspoon	1 teaspoon	½ teaspoon
sea salt	¼ teaspoon			
vit. C crystals*	¼ teaspoon			
water	½ cup	⅓ cup	½ cup	½ cup
Day's oil	2 tablespoons			

	Day 2 **Amaranth**	**Day 3** **Quinoa**	**Day 4** **Buckwheat**
flour/starch	1 cup amaranth flour ½ cup arrowroot starch	1¼ cups quinoa flour ⅓ cup tapioca OR cornstarch	1⅓ cups White Buckwheat flour (page 171)
seeds	⅓ cup sunflower OR use 3 Tbsp. more flour	2 teaspoons caraway	3 Tbsp. pumpkin OR use total of 1½ cups of flour
baking soda	1 teaspoon		
sea salt	¼ teaspoon		
vit. C Crystals*	¼ teaspoon		
water	½ cup		
Day's oil	2 tablespoons		

Amaranth Crackers are depicted with bowl of Chili on the front cover.

Preheat oven—350°. Place 1 teaspoon of oil on 10x14-inch baking sheet.
If using sunflower or pumpkin seeds, grind in small food processor/chopper.

1. In bowl, whisk together dry ingredients and seeds. Make "well" in center. Add water and oil. Stir until dough clumps into ball and flour is well-mixed. If dough is sticky, add between 1–3 teaspoons more flour. Mix.

2. Spread oil with fingers to within one inch of edges of baking sheet. (As dough is rolled out, it will push oil to edges.)

3. Transfer dough to center of baking sheet. With oiled fingers, press out evenly in all directions until it cannot be spread further, maintaining rectangular shape.

4. Lightly dust rolling pin with flour and roll dough out from center to edges. Press evenly in all directions to keep dough a uniform thickness.

5. If needed, use dull backside of table knife to press edges of dough to maintain rectangular shape. Continue rolling and shaping until dough is about ¼-inch thick and fills baking sheet. To help reduce the possibility of an extra-thin dough edge,

continued ...

... continued

use backside of table knife to gently push all four edges of dough to make edge thickness uniform with remaining dough.

6. Using a pizza cutter, cut dough into 96 squares (8x12). (Move pizza cutter slowly with a back and forth motion to help avoid tearing dough if cutter goes directly across a seed.) Use a sharp knife to separate crackers around outer edge.

7. Prick holes in each square with fork. If desired, salt top of crackers.

8. Bake for first baking time according to chart. Carefully remove outer circle of crackers if they are crispy. Return remaining crackers to oven for second baking time. TURN OFF OVEN and crisp crackers further during third baking time.

9. Place baking sheet on wire rack to cool. Store crackers in freezer. May be eaten straight from freezer without thawing.

Yield: 96 crackers   12 servings (8 crackers each)

*Use unbuffered vitamin C crystals.

Cracker	1st Baking Time	2nd Baking Time	3rd Baking Time
Amaranth	25 minutes	5 minutes	15 minutes
Buckwheat	25 minutes	5 minutes	15 minutes
Quinoa	23 minutes	5 minutes	15 minutes
Kamut®	22 minutes	5 minutes	10 minutes
Rye	35 minutes	5 minutes	15 minutes
Spelt	17 minutes	5 minutes	10 minutes
Teff	20 minutes	5 minutes	20 minutes

During Stage 2, enjoy small servings of gluten-free crackers (i.e., amaranth, teff, buckwheat, quinoa).

Also, see "Sondra's Experience" on page 225 regarding snacks.

Mix
Shape
Cut
Prick holes
Bake (3 stages)
Freeze extra

Cracker Preparation Hints

To make cracker prep faster, set up three workstations:

1. Mixing Area—recipe, ingredients, measures (dry and liquid cups and spoons), table knife, bowl, rubber spatula and whisk.

2. Rolling Area—baking sheet, rolling pin, pizza cutter, sharp knife, table fork and flour.

3. Baking/Cooling Areas—preheated oven, timer, metal spatula and cooling rack.

- - - - -

Recipes use a 10x14 inch baking sheet with low side edges. If yours is a different size, use ~140 sq. inches.

If your baking sheet has sides, be sure rolling pin fits all the way down onto surface on both the width and length of the sheet and that the handles clear the edge.

S$_{2L}$ Amaranth Buns (Day 2 Recipe)

1^3/$_4$ cups	amaranth flour
^{1}/$_2$ cup	arrowroot starch
1^1/$_2$ teaspoons	baking soda
^{3}/$_8$ teaspoon	unbuffered vitamin C crystals
^{1}/$_2$ teaspoon	sea salt
^{3}/$_4$ cup	water
3 tablespoons	olive OR sunflower oil

> Mix dry
> Add wet
> Portion; bake; cool
> (For Muffins: Follow
>   special directions)
> Freeze extra; thaw
>   at room temp.

Preheat oven—350°. Oil and flour baking dishes.

For Kaiser-sized Buns: Use 3 (~5-inch) baking bowls.

For Smaller-sized Buns (my preference): Use 5 (~3-inch) baking bowls.

1. In large bowl, whisk together dry ingredients. Make a "well" in the center.

2. In smaller bowl, whisk water and oil together for 15 seconds to disperse oil in water. Immediately add to the dry ingredients and mix thoroughly until evenly moistened (do not beat). Dough will be delicate and stiff but manageable.

3. To Portion: Press dough evenly and firmly into bottom of bowl. Use knife to cut into equal portions; lightly oil hands; shape portions; place in baking bowls.

4. Bake 30 minutes or until toothpick comes out clean. Turn buns out of bowls within 5 minutes after baking. Cool completely on a wire rack. Slice each bun in half horizontally. If centers are slightly doughy, lightly toast in toaster or toaster oven.

Yield: 3 or 5   During Stage 2, enjoy these buns on days when eating light on other carbs.

Amaranth Pumpkin Muffins (Day 2 Recipe)

1 Tbsp.	flaxmeal (egg substitute)		^{1}/$_2$ tsp.	ea: ground allspice & ginger
1^3/$_4$ cups	amaranth flour		^{1}/$_4$ tsp.	ea: ground nutmeg & cloves
^{1}/$_4$ cup	arrowroot starch		1 cup	☑ Pumpkin Puree (pg. 78)
^{1}/$_2$ tsp.	sea salt		^{1}/$_4$ cup	water
2 tsps.	baking soda		^{1}/$_4$ cup	olive oil
^{1}/$_2$ tsp.	unbuffered vitamin C crystals		2 Tbsp.	agave nectar

Preheat oven to 350°. Oil/flour bottom and sides of 12 muffin cups.

Prepare flaxmeal egg substitute (page 175).

1. In a bowl, whisk together the dry ingredients. Make a "well" in the center.

2. In small bowl, thoroughly whisk pumpkin, oil, agave nectar, water and flaxseed mixture. Add to dry ingredients and stir only until flour is evenly moistened. Do not beat. Batter is delicate and thick but spreadable.

3. Portion batter into cups (slightly more than ^{1}/$_4$ cup each). Using a small utensil, gently press batter down into each cup. Bake 30–35 minutes or until toothpick comes out clean. Turn oven off; leave muffins in oven for another 5–10 minutes.

4. Remove from oven to cool (covered with cloth) completely in the cups.

Yield: 12 muffins   Great recipe to try when challenging alternative "sugars."

S₂CL Buckwheat Bread/Buns (Day 4 Recipe)

¹/₂ cup	White Buckwheat Flour (page 171)
2 teaspoons	baking soda
¹/₂ teaspoon	unbuffered vitamin C crystals
2 cups	White Buckwheat Flour (page 171)
¹/₄ cup	kudzu starch OR
1 teaspoon	guar gum (omit during Stage 2, pg. 244)
¹/₄ teaspoon	sea salt
1¹/₂ cups	water
¹/₄ cup	safflower oil
1 cup	fresh or frozen blueberries (optional)

Recipes

Mix flour, soda & C
Combine ingred. in stages
Portion; bake
Freeze extra

Preheat oven to 350°. Oil and flour baking dishes.
For Bread: Use 1 (9x5-inch) loaf pan.
For Buns: Use 12 (~3-inch) baking bowls.

1. In small bowl, whisk together first listing of flour, baking soda and vitamin C. Set aside.

2. Set up stand mixer with beaters. In large mixer bowl, whisk together second measurement of flour, starch or guar gum and salt. Add water and oil. Mix on low (stir) speed to moisten flour. Then beat on medium (mix) speed for 2 minutes. Scrape sides with rubber spatula throughout mixing process.

3. Turn mixer to low, add set-aside flour mixture and continue to mix (scraping sides) until all flour is moistened. Then beat for 30 seconds on medium speed.

4. Optional: Gently stir in blueberries.

5. **For Bread:** Transfer batter to loaf pan. Spread evenly and smooth on top. Bake until toothpick comes out clean (55–60 minutes).

   For Buns: Portion rounded ¹/₄ cup of batter into each baking bowl. Spread evenly and smooth on top. Bake 40 minutes or until toothpick comes out clean.

6. Turn out of pans within 5 minutes of baking. Cool on wire rack. Slice bread and buns when slightly or completely cooled.

Stand Mixer

A stand mixer is preferred to prepare the Buckwheat and Kamut®/Spelt bread recipes. You have more control when mixing the dough than when using a hand-held mixer. Dough hook feature (as pictured) is very helpful for the Kamut®/Spelt recipes on the next two pages.

 Great for breakfast served toasted or untoasted. Bread without blueberries is delicious topped with Rhubarb Jelly.

Yield: 1 loaf (12 slices) or 12 (~3-inch) buns
During Stage 2, enjoy this bread on days when eating light on other carbs.

Kamut® or Spelt Bread/Buns/Dinner Rolls (Day 1 Recipe)

	Kamut®	Spelt
water	1¹/₂ cups	1¹/₄ cups
sesame oil	¹/₄ cup	
flour	¹/₂ cup Kamut®	⁵/₈ cup spelt
baking soda	1¹/₂ teaspoons	
unbuffered Vitamin C crystals	¹/₂ teaspoon	
flour	3 cups Kamut®	3 cups spelt
sea salt	³/₄ teaspoon	

(⁵/₈ cup = ¹/₂ cup +2 tablespoons)

Preheat oven—350°.
Oil/flour baking dishes.
For Bread: Use 1 (9x5-inch) loaf pan.
For Buns: Use 2 (10x14-inch) baking sheets.
For Dinner Rolls: Use 1 (8-inch) square baking pan.

Mix in stages
Portion; shape; bake
Cool; slice
Freeze extra

1. Measure water and oil in separate containers. Set aside. In small bowl, whisk together first listing of flour, baking soda and vitamin C. Set aside.

2. Set up stand mixer with dough hooks (see "Hints"). In large mixer bowl, whisk together the 3 cups flour and salt. Add water. Mix on low (stir) speed to moisten. Then beat mixture on medium (mix) speed for 3 minutes until dough becomes cohesive and climbs up hooks. Scrape sides throughout mixing process.

3. Add oil and mix on medium to mix oil into dough, scraping sides. Turn mixer to low, add Step 1 flour mixture and continue to mix (scraping sides) until all flour is moistened. Then beat for 30 more seconds on medium.

4. **For Bread:** With oiled hands, shape into smooth-topped loaf. Place in pan.
For Buns: With oiled hands, divide dough equally into 12 portions. Form into 4-inch bun shapes. Place on baking sheets, smooth side up.
For Dinner Rolls: With oiled hands, pinch off a 2-inch portion of dough. Form into roll shape. Place in pan, smooth side up. Repeat to prepare 16 rolls.

5. Bake according to time table below or until toothpick comes out clean:

	Kamut®	Spelt
Bread	55–60 min.	50–55 min.
Buns	15–18 min.	13–15 min.
Dinner Rolls	25 min.	20 min.

Hints!

No Dough Hooks: Reserve ¹/₂ cup flour from second listing and knead this flour into dough by hand after Step 3.

- - - - -

Re-oil hands as needed when shaping rolls/buns.

continued ...

... continued

6. **For Bread:** Turn bread out of pan within 5 minutes of baking. Cool on wire rack. Slice bread into $1/2$-inch slices when slightly or completely cooled.
   For Buns: Remove from baking sheet and cool on wire rack. Slice in half horizontally when slightly or completely cooled.
   For Dinner Rolls: Cut rolls along divisions. Remove from pan, pull apart and place in towel-lined basket. Serve warm.

Yield: 1 loaf of bread (12–16 slices); 12 buns; 16 dinner rolls

 ## Pecan Rolls—An Easter Treat (Day 1† Recipe)

Hot Cross Buns, a traditional Easter bread, may not be a option for you if you are avoiding yeast and wheat, but as I have always said—find a substitute. They can be made as rolls, in a braid or in coffeecake form. I hope they brighten your holiday.

Dough Ingredients:

Same ingredients as Kamut® or Spelt Bread/Buns/Dinner Rolls except:
- Use only $1^3/8$ cups of water for Kamut® and only $1^1/8$ cups of water for spelt;
- Add $1/4$ cup of brown rice sweetener.

Filling Ingredients:

1 Tbsp.	ground cinnamon†
$1/2$ cup	brown rice sweetener†
	OR
1 cup	FOS
$1/2$ cup	pecans, chopped

Glaze Ingredients:

1 Tbsp.	tapioca starch†
$1/4$ cup	brown rice sweetener
	OR
$1/2$ cup	FOS†
1 cup	water
$1/2$ tsp.	alcohol-free vanilla flavoring

Preheat oven—350°.
Oil/flour baking sheets; stainless steel does not need to be floured.
Follow Steps 1–3 (previous page), adding sweetener with flour mixture in Step 1.

4. If dough is sticky, knead in 1–2 tablespoons of flour by hand. Divide dough into two portions. On floured surface roll each portion into a 20x12-inch rectangle. Add more flour to top and bottom surfaces as needed.

5. Combine cinnamon and sweetener; spread over dough. Sprinkle with nuts. Roll lengthwise as for jelly roll. Seal edge (wetting with cold water) and cut in 1-inch slices. Place cut side down on baking sheet. Bake 12–15 minutes or until toothpick comes out clean.

6. While rolls are baking, combine glaze ingredients in saucepan. Heat on low until slightly thick. Stir often with whisk. Pour glaze over warm rolls.

Yield: 40 rolls

†*These foods are assigned to Day 3; omit them on Day 3 before and after eating on Day 1.*

S₂ₗ ⏱ Griddle Bread

Griddle bread is an excellent, easy-to-make substitute for sandwich bread and buns as well as a wonderful replacement for labor-intensive, time-consuming homemade tortillas. Because it is leavening-, preservative- and sugar-free, griddle bread is very useful for persons with CRC.

	Day 1	Day 2	Day 3	Day 4
	Teff	Amaranth OR Garbanzo Bean	Quinoa	Buckwheat Legume
1/3 cup	water			
1/4 cup flour	brown teff	amaranth (follow special directions) or garbanzo bean	quinoa	White Buckwheat (page 171) OR legume (see below)
oil as needed	sesame	sunflower	grapeseed	safflower

Optional Ingredients:

1–2 pinches	sea salt			
3 "sprinkles"	ground cumin	cayenne pepper	coriander	cayenne pepper
1 tablespoon	sesame seeds (+ 1–2 tsps. water)	sunflower seeds		chopped pumpkin seeds

Preheat griddle (see "Griddle" on next page). Lightly oil after preheating.

1. Measure water in a 1-cup liquid measure. Add flour and optional ingredients. Whisk together. Immediately pour onto griddle, using rings (beginning in the center and continue with increasing widening rings to create desired size).

2. Cook for length of time as indicated in chart. Flip and cook second side.

3. Cool slightly on cooling rack. Placing bread directly on a solid surface to cool (such as a plate) causes moisture build-up creating a soggy texture.

Recipes

Mix
Cook
Freeze extra; thaw at room temp.

Yield: 2 (5") or 1 (8") griddle bread

Flour	Cooking Time for 1st Side	Cooking Time for 2nd Side
brown teff	7 minutes	5 minutes
garbanzo bean, black bean, green lentil, red lentil	6 minutes	5 minutes
white buckwheat	5 minutes	5 minutes
quinoa	4 minutes	4 minutes

S₂L Amaranth Griddle Bread (Day 2 Recipe)

Preheat griddle and follow Step 1 as in Griddle Bread recipe on previous page.

Locate a lid that will cover the griddle or at least the 8-inch batter on the grill.

2. Cover with lid. Cook covered for 6 minutes. Turn, cover and cook for 2 minutes. Then uncover and cook for 3 more minutes.

3. Serve immediately or cool as described in Step 3 on previous page.

Yield: 2 (5") or 1 (8") griddle bread
During Stage 2, enjoy griddle breads on occasion, especially if you are craving a sandwich.

Griddle

Griddle is hot enough when water dances when sprinkled on surface.

- - - - -

I prefer a well-seasoned cast iron griddle; see www.canaryconnect.com for more info.

Sondra's Hints on Griddle Breads!

These recipes have been tested using an electric, non-stick coated griddle set between 375° – 400°.

- - - - -

Do not chop pumpkin seeds too fine as that creates a "meal" and changes the consistency.

- - - - -

Mix ingredients; immediately pour onto griddle.

- - - - -

If making multiple batches, scrape off residue and lightly re-oil griddle (a paper towel works well).

- - - - -

Since temperature of griddle surfaces vary, cooking times may need to be adjusted slightly for good results. The following tips will help insure success:
- Make sure griddle is thoroughly preheated.
- Measure water and flour accurately (see Appendix F).
- Cook bread longer on first side until dry around edges (many varieties curl slightly).
- If air bubble forms when cooking, break bubbles so batter falls to griddle and cooks.
- If bread is turned too soon and center surface is not done, cook on first side for 1–2 minutes more after second side is cooked.
- If still experiencing a doughy center, use slightly more water per recipe (start with 1 teaspoon).

- 8-inch griddle breads work well folded like tortillas for sandwiches such as Sloppy Joes, Fajitas, "salads" or nut/seed butter.

- Create a "veggie" sandwich by layering "greens" and thinly sliced veggies (i.e., cucumbers, zucchini) and/or sprouts.

- Use two 5" breads as a "sandwich" bun for your favorite meat or fish patty.

- Serve immediately for breakfast as a flat pancake topped with heated fruit sauce.

- Serve immediately for dinner topped with gravy.

S₂CL Tortillas

		Day 1		Day 2	Day 3	Day 4	
	Kamut®	Spelt	Brown Teff	Amaranth	Quinoa	Buck-wheat	White Bean
flour	1¹/₈ cups	1¹/₄ cups	¹/₂ cup	⁵/₈ cup	⁵/₈ cup	¹/₂ cup	¹/₂ cup
sea salt	¹/₂ teaspoon			¹/₄ teaspoon			
guar gum						¹/₂ tsp.	
water	¹/₂ cup			¹/₄ cup			
oil	no oil needed			¹/₂ teaspoon of the Day's oil			
~ ¹/₂ cup more flour is used for kneading and rolling							

Cooking Time/Side	40 sec.	45 sec.	45 sec.	45 sec.	45 sec.	40 sec.	45 sec.

Preheat unoiled griddle (see "Griddle" on pg. 185).

Mix
Knead; roll out
Brush off excess flour
Cook; cool
Freeze extra

1. In bowl, whisk together flour and salt. (If using guar gum, add; see Amaranth HH 1.) Make a "well" in center. Add water and oil. Stir until dough clumps together into a moist ball. If dough is too sticky for kneading, add 1 tablespoon more flour and stir in thoroughly.

2. Scatter 1 tablespoon of flour on rolling surface for Kamut®, teff, quinoa and buckwheat (2 tablespoons for spelt, amaranth and white bean). Transfer dough to floured surface and knead to work in as much of this additional flour as possible (see Amaranth HH 2). Dough texture should resemble Play Doh. Add more flour if needed. Form dough into ball and cut into equal portions (8 for Kamut® and spelt; 4 for teff, quinoa and buckwheat; 3 for white bean and 3 or 4 for Amaranth). Dust the cut surfaces of each portion with flour.

3. Lightly flour rolling pin and smooth rolling surface. Pat dough portion into circular shape; then roll out by pressing evenly from center out in all directions, keeping tortilla as round as possible. Keep dough floured on both sides, using up to 1 tablespoon of flour per tortilla. Flip (to flour) tortilla often, using a solid metal spatula. Feel surface occasionally for even thickness. Finished tortilla will be very thin and a diameter of 7–8" for Kamut®, spelt and quinoa; 6" for teff; 6 or 8" for amaranth (see Amaranth HH 3) and 6–7" for buckwheat and white bean.

4. Using a pastry brush, gently brush both sides to remove excess flour.

5. Cook on each side according to chart above. (See Amaranth HH 4 & Quinoa HH.)

continued ...

... continued

6. Cool on cooling rack for 1–2 minutes, then place between two layers of clean towel to continue cooling but not dry out (see General HH 8 and 9).

Yield: 8–Kamut® 8–spelt 4–teff 3 or 4–amaranth 4–quinoa 4–buckwheat 3–white bean During Stage 2 enjoy gluten-free tortillas (teff, amaranth, quinoa, buckwheat, bean) on occasion, especially when craving a sandwich.

Helpful Hints (HH) For Amaranth & Quinoa Tortillas

Amaranth Tortillas are more delicate so you may find the following helpful:

1. May add $1/2$ tsp. of guar gum (temporarily moved from Day 4 to Day 2) and start with only $1/2$ cup of flour.
2. If you have difficulty working additional flour into the dough, first cut into 3 or 4 equal portions, then knead about $1^1/2$ tsp. of flour into each portion.
3. Consider cutting dough into 3 portions and/or only rolling to 6 inches in diameter, making tortillas thicker so they should not tear as easily.
4. Cook the thicker 6-inch amaranth tortillas for 50–55 seconds per side. The tiny air pockets that form are normal.

- - - - -

Quinoa Tortilla: When cooking, the edge often curls up. This flattens out when cooking on second side.

- Serve whole or cut in half.

- - - - -

- Use your imagination to create a simple deli-like sandwich. For example: slivered cooked meat, "greens," "Mayo," sprouts, sliced/shredded vegetables (i.e., cabbage, tomatoes, cucumbers, zucchini, carrots).

- - - - -

- Serve with Sloppy Joes, Tacos, Burritos, Fajitas, "Salad" Sandwiches or nut/sesame butter.

- - - - -

- Create a "veggie" sandwich by layering "greens" and thinly sliced veggies.

General Helpful Hints on Tortilla Preparation

1. Before beginning tortilla preparation, assemble equipment and ingredients: **Mixing Area** (recipe, ingredients, mixing bowl, measuring equipment, rubber spatula, table knife and whisk); **Kneading/Rolling Area** (rolling surface, flour, rolling pin, pastry brush, table knife and solid metal spatula); **Cooking/Cooling Area** (preheated griddle, digital timer (times in seconds and best with memory function) and metal spatula, two cooling racks and cotton towel).

2. Measure ingredients accurately (see Appendix F: Measuring Tips).

3. If you tend to be a person with warm hands, run them under cool water and dry them before kneading. Hands that are too warm can cause dough to become sticky and difficult to handle.

4. Before flipping tortilla to flour underneath side, use solid metal spatula (slotted spatula can tear dough) to loosen edges and center

continued ...

... continued

of tortilla from rolling surface. To flip, place spatula under center of tortilla and your hand on top to support it. During this process, mend any cracked dough edges as they happen since tiny cracks will become large ones if left unrepaired.

5. It is best to start each tortilla with a clean surface and a small amount of fresh flour. Clean flour off rolling surface with metal spatula; then clean off spatula.

6. Transfer tortilla carefully to griddle by first lifting left side of tortilla with metal spatula (Diagram A). Then replace spatula with your left hand (Diagram B). Next place spatula under right side of tortilla (Diagram C). This will give adequate support as you use your hand and spatula to carry tortilla over and gently place it onto griddle (Diagram D). These directions are for a right-handed person. A left-handed person would do the opposite.

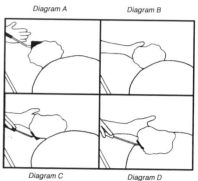

Diagram A   Diagram B

Diagram C   Diagram D

7. If your kitchen does not allow the rolling area to be inches away from the range, place a protective pad (i.e., small metal cooling rack) on counter surface near rolling area. Place hot griddle on protective pad, transfer tortilla as described above and immediately return griddle to range.

8. If you cook a tortilla too long on the griddle, it may help to cool it completely between layers of cotton cloth rather than partially cool on rack.

9. If you allow a tortilla to cool too long and become dry, follow these directions. First, place too-dry tortilla between layers of cloth. Then, place next cooked tortilla directly on top of dry tortilla without allowing it to cool on cooling rack. This will help the dry tortilla to regain a little moisture.

10. For easier cleanup, use a dry cloth to wipe dough particles and flour off the rolling surface and rolling pin before wiping with a wet cloth.

11. VERY IMPORTANT: Do not make tortillas on days of high humidity. The dough will tend to be sticky and adding too much flour to make it workable will result in tough tortillas.

12. **To Store:** Place tortillas in a flat food storage bag (1 flavor/bag and usually no more than 8/bag). Store flat in a safe place of freezer where other foods will not damage them.

13. **To Thaw and/or Reheat:** Transfer frozen tortilla to another bag; allow to thaw:
    - in refrigerator for a few hours.
    - at room temperature for approximately 30 minutes.
    - place on cold, unoiled griddle and turn on heat, allowing tortilla to thaw and heat slightly as griddle is heating; flip often.

14. Tortillas make great sandwiches for meals eaten away from home. Pack tortillas separately from fillings so tortillas do not collect moisture and fall apart when eating.

15. Double bag tortillas in dry climates (i.e., Colorado, Arizona).

RECIPES

The Sweets

The thought of eliminating refined sugars and flours from things like pies, cookies, cakes and ice cream can be daunting, especially when yeast in our bodies is "screaming" for those very foods. However, a healing food plan does not need to mean "no sweets." These recipes offer creative ways to make tasty treats that satisfy the "sweet tooth" without feeding the yeast. Some recipes are non-rotating, but special occasions, such as holidays and birthdays, warrant a special treat.

Enjoy the similar tastes with allergen-free ingredients.

Special Note: Stevia powder listed in these recipes is the pure form called white powder concentrate. For more information see Appendix D.

S₂CL ☑ Pumpkin Pie (Non-Rotating Recipe)

1 (9-inch)	☑ unbaked Pie Crust (page 192) (best if slightly frozen)
2 large	eggs
1³/₄ cups	☑ Pumpkin Puree (page 78)
	OR
1 (15 oz.) can	pumpkin
¹/₂ teaspoon	sea salt
1¹/₂ teaspoons	ground cinnamon
¹/₂ teaspoon	ground ginger
¹/₄ teaspoon	ground cloves
1 cup	liquid—water OR "milk" (rice beverage, soy, goat or Nut Milk)

> Mix
> Bake in crust
> Freeze extra

Sweetener Choice:
- ¹/₄ cup honey OR brown rice syrup
- scant ¹/₈ teaspoon stevia powder, increasing liquid to 1¹/₄ cups

Preheat oven—400°.

1. In bowl, slightly beat eggs. Add and whisk in pumpkin, salt and spices. Add your choice of sweetener and liquid. Stir to blend thoroughly.

2. Pour into unbaked crust. Bake for 15 minutes. Reduce temp. to 350° and continue baking for 50 minutes until knife blade comes out clean.

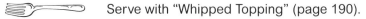 Serve with "Whipped Topping" (page 190).

Yield: 8 servings During Stage 2, you could enjoy this pie on occasion using the following choices: gluten-free crusts, stevia and any liquid except goat and rice beverage.

S₂ₗ Oatmeal Pie Crust (Day 3 Recipe)

1¹/₂ cups   uncooked old fashioned rolled oats
¹/₂ teaspoon   sea salt
¹/₄ cup   grapeseed oil
1 tablespoon   water

Preheat oven—450°. 8-inch pie pan.

1. Stir oats and salt. While stirring, gradually add oil to coat oats evenly.

2. Pour water evenly over mixture and stir again.

Combine dry ingred.
Add wet ingred.
Press in pie pan
Bake

3. Transfer to pan. Use hands to firmly press oat mixture evenly onto bottom/sides. Do not allow crust to be closer than ¹/₈ inch from lip of pan to prevent oil from bubbling over edge during baking.

4. Bake for 10 minutes, then cool for 10 minutes while allowing oven to cool down to 350° to bake Butternut Squash or Sweet Potato Pie (next page).

 Sondra's Hints!

This recipe was developed for use with Butternut Squash or Sweet Potato Pie. It has not been tested with other fillings but should work with pumpkin. This crust surprisingly holds together after the filling is baked in the crust.

Yield: 1 (8-inch) crust 8 servings During Stage 2, enjoy small amounts with a Stage 2 allowed filling.

S₂cₗ "Whipped Topping" (Non-Rotating Recipe)

1 pound   firm tofu (drain, discarding liquid)
¹/₂ cup   oil of your choice
2 teaspoons   alcohol-free vanilla flavoring
¹/₄–¹/₂ cup   "milk" (rice beverage, soy, goat or Nut Milk)

Sweetener Choice:

- ¹/₄ cup honey, br. rice syrup OR maple syrup, using ¹/₄ cup of "milk"
- ³/₄ cup powdered brown rice sweetener, using ¹/₃ cup of "milk"
- ¹/₈ teaspoon stevia powder, using ¹/₂ cup of "milk"

Blend ingredients in blender until smooth. Transfer to covered container and chill. Serve on pies, crisps and puddings.

Yield: 2²/₃ cups If you do not have a known allergy to soy, you could enjoy this topping on occasion during Stage 2, if you use stevia for sweetener and soy or nut milk for liquid.

 Sondra's Hints!

Extra topping may be frozen. Drop by tablespoons on baking sheets. After frozen, transfer to food storage bag. Thaws in minutes.

> *"True enjoyment comes from activity of the mind and exercise of the body; the two are ever united."* —Humboldt

Butternut Squash or Sweet Potato Pie (Non-Rotating† Recipe)

1 8-inch	☑ Oatmeal Pie Crust (previous page)
1 large	egg, lightly beaten
1 cup	☑ Pureed Butternut Squash OR Sweet Potatoes (recipe below)
1/4 teaspoon	sea salt
3/4 teaspoon	ground cinnamon
1/4 teaspoon	ground ginger
1/8 teaspoon	ground cloves
1/2 cup	unsweetened apple juice

Preheat oven—350°.

1. In bowl, mix egg, pureed vegetable and spices. Add apple juice and mix.

2. Pour mixture into prebaked/cooled Oatmeal Pie Crust. Bake 45–50 minutes or until knife comes out clean. Cool.

   May serve with "Whipped Topping" (page 190).

Yield: 1 pie   8 servings

†*With careful planning one can enjoy this non-rotating recipe, especially on holidays.*

Recipes
Mix
Bake
Freeze extra

Sondra's Hints!

Before freezing extra, cut pie into serving pieces.

- - - - -

To prepare with pie crusts on page 192, double this filling recipe. Bake for 65–70 minutes.

S₂ₗ Pureed Sweet Potatoes

1. Select firm potatoes with no sign of mold. Wash, peel and cut into small pieces.

2. Simmer in small amount of water until tender. Drain, reserving liquid.

3. Using an immersion blender (page 116) or potato masher, blend until creamy. Add drained liquid, if needed, to get the consistency of canned pumpkin. Measure into portions needed for pies. Use or freeze to be ready to prepare a pie in minutes.

Yield: 12 oz. sweet potato yields ~ 1 cup pureed

S₂ₗ Pureed Butternut Squash

1. Select ripe butternut squash. (Ripe squash has a medium tan color whereas unripe squash is off-white in color, sometimes with green lines.)

2. Wash squash, cut in half lengthwise. Scoop out seeds and strings.

3. Place cut side down in shallow baking dish. Add a small amount of water. Bake uncovered in oven at 350° for 30–60 minutes or until tender.

4. Allow squash to cool enough to handle. Scoop out soft flesh. Stir to blend. Measure into portions needed for pie. Use or freeze for later pies.

Yield: 2 small butternut squash yields about 1 1/2 cups pureed

S₂CL Pie Crust

	Day 1	Day 1	Day 2	Day 3	Day 4
	Kamut®	Spelt	Amaranth	Quinoa	Buckwheat
flour	1 cup	1 1/8 cups	3/4 cup	3/4 cup	3/4 cup
starch/gum if needed			1/4 cup arrowroot st.	1/4 cup tapioca st.	3/4 teaspoon guar gum
ice cold water	1/4 cup				
Day's oil	1/4 cup	1/4 cup	3 tablespoons	3 tablespoons	3 tablespoons
sea salt	1/4 teaspoon rounded		1/4 teaspoon		

8- or 9-inch pie pan OR 8-inch square baking dish for Tofu "Cheesecakes"

Chill a medium-sized bowl and whisk.

1. Combine dry ingredients in separate bowl, set aside.
2. In chilled bowl, whisk water, oil and salt until mixture is thick and an opaque, whitish creamy color.
3. Add flour mixture; stir until dough clumps into a ball. Some (i.e., buckwheat) are a little sloppy at first, but continue stirring for few seconds longer.
4. Oil pie pan or baking dish. With oiled fingers, transfer dough to pan. Press dough firmly into bottom and sides (bottom only for cheesecakes) as evenly as possible. Wipe outside of pan with damp cloth to remove excess oil.
5. Chill until ready to bake.
6. Bake according to filling recipe. For prebaked crust, pierce holes with fork around edges/bottom. Bake in 400° oven for 15–18 minutes. Cool before adding the filling.

Yield: 8 servings During Stage 2, use amaranth, quinoa or buckwheat crust for allowed fillings (see filling recipes for guidelines).

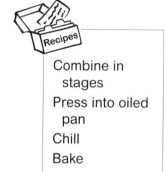

Combine in stages

Press into oiled pan

Chill

Bake

Helpful Hint

Water and oil needs to be cold for mixture to become thick and opaque. Oils which get cloudy and thick in refrigerator (i.e., olive, sesame) become most opaque.

S₂CL

Sweetener-Free Butternut Squash Pie (Non-Rotating Recipe)

Blend 2 slightly beaten eggs with 3 2/3 cups of Pureed Butternut Squash (page 191). Add salt/ spices as desired or as directed in Pumpkin Pie (page 189). Pour into ☑ unbaked Pie Crust (recipe above). Bake as directed in Pumpkin Pie.

Yield: 8 servings

Apple-Quinoa or Apple-Oat Crisp (Day 3 Recipe)

2 cups	apple slices
1 tsp.	ground cinnamon
sprinkle	nutmeg
4 tsp.	maple granules (optional)

Ingredients for Quinoa Topping:

1/2 cup	quinoa flour
4 pinches	sea salt
1/2 tsp.	ground cinnamon
sprinkle	nutmeg
4 tsp.	maple granules (optional)
1 Tbsp.	grapeseed oil
1 Tbsp.	water

Ingredients for Oat Topping:

1 cup	uncooked regular rolled oats
1/4 cup	oat bran
1/8 tsp.	sea salt
1/2 tsp.	ground cinnamon
sprinkle	nutmeg
4 tsp.	maple granules (optional)
5 tsp.	grapeseed oil

Preheat oven—425°. Oil 8-inch pie pan.

1. Toss apple slices with spices and maple granules. Layer in pan.

2. In bowl, whisk together dry topping ingredients.

3. **For Quinoa Topping**: Add oil and water. Stir to coat flour mixture evenly with liquids.

   For Oat Topping: Gradually add oil while stirring to moisten oatmeal evenly. May use hands to completely blend in oil.

4. Sprinkle crisp mixture evenly over apples. Bake for 18–20 minutes or until apples are tender.

Helpful Hint

Use eating-species of apples for more natural sweetness. The key ingredient is the cinnamon.

 Serve with Ice Cream (page 203).

Yield: 4 servings

BOTH CRISPS
Prepare fruit
Mix crisp; top
Bake

 ## Pear Crisp (Day 1 Recipe)

1 cup	sliced fresh pears (1 lg. or 2 med.)
3/8 cup	flour—brown teff, spelt, Kamut®
3 pinches	sea salt
2 teaspoons	sesame oil
2 teaspoons	water

Preheat oven—425°. Oil 8-inch pie pan.

1. Choose ripe, but not mushy pears.   Peel, slice and layer in pie pan.

2. In bowl, whisk together flour and salt. Drizzle oil and water over flour. Using a pastry blender, blend to moisten and form small dough balls. Sprinkle over pears.

3. Bake for 15 minutes or until pears are tender. Serve warm or cold.

Yield: 2 servings

S₂ₗ Carob Cake Brownies (Day 1†, 3† and 4 Recipe)

	Rice (Day 1†)	Quinoa (Day 3†)	Buckwheat (Day 4)
flour/starch	1½ cups brown rice flour	1½ cups quinoa flour + ½ cup tapioca starch	1½ cups White Buckwheat flour + 3 Tbsp. kudzu starch
carob powder,† sift after measuring	⅓ cup	½ cup	⅓ cup
baking soda	1½ teaspoons		
sea salt	¼ teaspoon		
unbuffered vitamin C crystals	½ teaspoon		
stevia powder†	¼ teaspoon		
water	1 cup	1¼ cups	1¼ cups
egg, slightly beaten	1 large		
Day's oil	2 Tbsp.	¼ cup	2 Tbsp. OR ¼ cup
optional			½ tsp. alcohol-free peppermint extract

Preheat oven—350°. Oil/flour 8-inch square baking dish.

1. In bowl, whisk together dry ingredients. Make a "well" in the center.

2. Add liquid (and egg) ingredients. Using an electric mixer, mix on lowest speed until dry ingredients are moistened. Then blend on mix speed for 20 seconds to make a creamy, cake-like batter. (OR stir to moisten dry ingredients and then beat by hand for 30 seconds.)

3. Spread evenly in pan. Bake for 25–30 minutes until toothpick comes out clean. The top will be a little dry and cracked.

4. Cool in pan on cooling rack, covered with towel. If desired, ice with Carob Icing (next page). Garnish iced Day 1 cake with chopped almonds and Day 3 with chopped walnuts.

Yield: 16 servings   During Stage 2, enjoy these desserts on occasion using stevia for the sweetener.

Mix ingredients
Spread in pan
Bake

Alternatives!

Substitute stevia w/ honey, using either 2 Tbsp. OR ¼ cup (reducing water by 1 Tbsp. for the ¼ cup).

- - - - -

Substitute kudzu w/ ¾ tsp. guar gum (mixing kudzu in w/ liquid ingredients).

†Carob and stevia are Day 4 foods; omit them for 4 days before and after on Day 1 or 3. Also make your own decision about omitting other members of the Legume and Composite Families for two days before and after eating Day 1 and 3 recipes but most are not concerned with this break in rotation, especially if enjoying recipe on occasion such as for a birthday.

S2c   **Carob Icing** (Day 4 Recipe)

1/4 cup	carob powder, sifted
2 teaspoons	kudzu starch
1/4 teaspoon	alcohol-free peppermint extract (optional)

Sweetener/Water Choices:

- 1/16 tsp. stevia powder with 1/2 cup water
- 2 tablespoons honey with 3/8 cup water (1/4 cup + 2 tablespoons)
- 1/4 cup honey with 1/4 cup water

 Sift Carob Powder!

Sometimes carob powder contains chunks of powder. To smooth, sift by placing into a fine-mesh strainer. (Have a bowl under it.) Then stir powder to work it through the mesh and into bowl.

 In saucepan, whisk together dry ingredients. Add sweetener/water and blend. Cook on medium heat until thickened, stirring almost constantly.

Yield: 1/2 cup   16 servings   During Stage 2, enjoy sweetened with stevia for the brownies on previous page.

Every Day Isn't Icing on The Cake

"Some days are shopping for ingredients. Some are collecting bowls and utensils. Some are pre-heating the oven. Others are mixing up the cake and baking it. These are the days we feel we are 'spinning our wheels'—but are we?

—For you can't ice the cake until it's baked!"

—Judy Beuter

 ☑ **Teff Pear Cake** (Day 1 Recipe)

1 cup	brown teff flour
1 teaspoon	baking soda
1/4 teaspoon	sea salt
1/4 teaspoon	unbuffered vitamin C crystals
1/2 cup	pear juice
1/4 cup	☑ Pear Sauce (page 102)
2 tablespoons	sesame oil

Combine
Spread in pan
Bake

Preheat oven—400°. Oil and flour the bottom/sides of a 9-inch pie pan.

1. In bowl, whisk together dry ingredients. Add juice, sauce and oil. Stir to just moisten dry ingredients.

2. Spread evenly in pan. Bake 20 minutes. Cool slightly. Cut into 8 wedges.

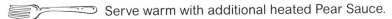 Serve warm with additional heated Pear Sauce.

Yield: 8 servings

Orange Buckwheat Cake (Day 4 Recipe)

1 1/2 cups	White Buckwheat Flour (page 171)
3 tablespoons	kudzu powder
	OR
3/4 teaspoon	guar gum*
1 1/2 teaspoons	baking soda
1/4 teaspoon	sea salt

Recipes

Mix ingredients
Spread in pan
Bake

Sweetener Choices:
- 1/16 teaspoon stevia powder
- 1–2 tablespoons honey

1 1/4 cups	freshly squeezed orange juice (or made from concentrate)
2 tablespoons	safflower oil
1/2 teaspoon	alcohol-free orange flavoring

Preheat oven—350°.

Oil/flour 8-inch square baking dish. Stainless steel does not need to be floured.

1. In bowl, whisk together dry ingredients. Make a "well" in the center.

2. Add oil and orange flavoring. Mix.

3. Add other liquids to dry ingredients. Stir to moisten evenly. Beat by hand for 20 strokes until you have a creamy, cake-like batter. <u>Do not over mix and do not use an electric mixer</u>.

4. Spread evenly in pan. Bake 20–22 minutes for stevia version OR 25–30 minutes for honey version or until toothpick comes out clean. Cool.

 Serve plain or ice with Orange Glaze. Cut 4x4.

 Yield: 16 servings

*To eliminate lumps, whisk guar gum into juice before adding to dry ingredients.

 Glaze for Orange Buckwheat Cake (Stevia or Honey Sweetened)

Sweetener Choices:
- 1/32 teaspoon stevia powder (1/4 of 1/8 teaspoon)
- 1 tablespoon honey

3/4 cup	freshly squeezed orange juice (or made from concentrate)
1 tablespoon	kudzu starch
1/4 teaspoon	unbuffered vitamin C crystals (optional)

 In saucepan, whisk together all ingredients except vitamin C crystals. Gently boil on low for 3–5 minutes, stirring constantly with whisk. Add vitamin C crystals and stir. Spread on slightly cooled cake.

Yield: 3/4 cup 16 servings

☑ **Granola Bars** (Day 1 and 3 Recipes)

	Almond-Sesame (Day 1)		**Oat-Apple** (Day 3)
1/4 cup	almonds OR pecans	2 Tbsp.	walnuts
2 cups	quick-cooking spelt OR Kamut® flakes*	2 cups	old fashioned rolled oats
		1/2 cup	oat bran
2 Tbsp.	hulled sesame seeds	1/4 cup	unsweetened coconut (optional)
1/2 tsp.	sea salt		
2/3 cup	☑ Pear Sauce Sweetener (page 102)	1/2 tsp.	sea salt
		2 tsp	cinnamon
2 Tbsp.	almond OR sesame oil	1/2 cup	apple juice concentrate
1 tsp.	alcohol-free almond extract	2 Tbsp.	grapeseed OR walnut oil

Preheat oven—350°. Oil 8-inch square baking pan with 1/2 teaspoon oil.

1. Set up food processor with knife blade. Pulse chop nuts for 15–20 seconds. Add flakes, salt and seeds. Pulse chop for 10–15 seconds.

2. In 1-cup measure, combine liquid ingredients. Add to processor. Pulse mix to combine and evenly coat flake mixture. Press evenly and firmly in pan.

4. Bake 25 minutes. Cool completely. Cut 4x2.

Pulse chop dry
Combine w/ liquid
Press in pan; bake

 Wrap extras individually to freeze. No thawing needed for quick breakfast, dessert or snack.

Yield: 8 servings

*Recipe developed using the quicker-cooking brands of flakes, see www.canaryconnect.com.

 Pear Custard (Day 1 Recipe)

1/4 cup	almonds	2/3 cup	pear juice
2/3 cup	water	1/2 teaspoon	alcohol-free almond extract
2 large	eggs	sprinkle	cinnamon
1/4 teaspoon	sea salt	sprinkle	nutmeg (optional)

Preheat oven to 350°. 8-inch square glass baking dish.

1. In blender, prepare "milk" with almonds and water (see Nut Milk on page 101 for directions). In bowl, beat eggs. Add rest of ingredients and nut milk. Stir.

2. Pour into 4 custard cups. Place cups in baking dish. Add room temperature water to baking dish so that water is 1 inch deep. Bake 40–45 minutes or until inserted knife comes out clean. Best served warm.

Prepare milk
Combine
Bake in custard cups

Yield: 4 (1/2 cup) servings

S₂ₗ Amaranth Carob Cookies (Day 2† Recipe)

1 cup	amaranth flour	³/₄ teaspoon	baking soda
¹/₂ cup	arrowroot starch	¹/₄ teaspoon	sea salt
¹/₄ cup	carob powder,†	¹/₂ teaspoon	stevia powder†
	sift after measuring	¹/₂ cup	water
¹/₂ teaspoon	unbuffered vitamin C crystals	2 tablespoons	Day 2 oil

Preheat oven—350°. Cookie sheets (oil in Step 3).

1. In mixing bowl, whisk together dry ingredients.

2. Add water and oil. Stir to moisten dry ingredients.

3. Oil cookie sheets. With lightly oiled fingers, form dough into 1-inch balls. Place about 2 inches apart. Flatten with fork or bottom of glass.

4. Bake 10 minutes. Immediately remove cookies to cooling rack.

Combine
Form balls, flatten
Bake
Freeze extra

Yield: 18 cookies   During Stage 2, enjoy on occasion.

†Stevia & carob are Day 4 foods, omit them on Day 4 before and after eating these on Day 2.

Amazing Sugarless Cookies (Day 1 Recipe)
Depicted on back cover.

My husband named these cookies after his first bite. Needless to say they are a hit!

1 cup	brown rice flour
1 teaspoon	baking soda
¹/₄ teaspoon	sea salt
¹/₄ teaspoon	unbuffered vitamin C crystals
1 cup	chopped almonds (optional)
¹/₃ cup	brown rice syrup
2 tablespoons	almond oil
1 teaspoon	alcohol-free almond extract (optional)
²/₃ cup	almond butter

Combine
Form balls, flatten
Bake
Freeze extra

Preheat oven—350°. Unoiled cookie sheets.

1. In bowl, whisk dry ingredients and almonds.

2. Combine syrup, oil and extract in 1-cup measure. Add mixture and almond butter to dry ingredients. Mix thoroughly. Batter will be a little stiff and slightly sticky.

3. Form dough into 1-inch balls. Place balls onto cookie sheets about 2¹/₂ inches apart. Flatten with fork or bottom of drinking glass to ¹/₄- inch thickness and 2-inch diameter. Dip fork or glass in water frequently to prevent dough from sticking.

4. Bake cookies for 8–10 minutes. Cool on cookie sheet to completely set up before transferring to cooling rack.

Yield: 3 dozen (2¹/₂ dozen w/o almonds)

Oatmeal Cookies (Day 3 Recipe)

2¹/₂ cups	rolled oats (divided)		¹/₂ tsp.	ground cinnamon
¹/₄ cup	tapioca starch		¹/₂ cup	Brazil or macadamia nuts
1 tsp.	baking soda		³/₄ cup	apple juice concentrate
¹/₄ tsp.	unbuffered vitamin C crystals		³/₄ cup	chopped walnuts
¹/₄ tsp.	sea salt			OR ¹/₂ cup additional oats

Preheat oven—350°.

1. In blender, blend 1 cup of oats on high to create flour (or use ⁷/₈ cup of oat flour).

2. In bowl, whisk together flour, starch, soda, C, salt and cinnamon.

3. In blender, blend Brazil or macadamia nuts to create nut butter. Add apple juice and blend on high a few seconds longer. Add this nut mixture to flour mixture. Stir until mixture forms a "sloppy" dough. Add rolled oats and walnuts and stir to form a soft batter.

4. Drop dough by rounded teaspoons onto cookie sheets about 2 inches apart. Bake 10 minutes. Immediately remove cookies to cooling rack.

Yield: 24 cookies

Blend oats
Combine ingred.
Prepare/add nut mixture
Add nuts/oats
Drop cookies
Bake

S₂L Pumpkin Cookies (Day 4† Recipe)

1¹/₃ cups	White Buckwheat flour (page 171)		¹/₂ tsp.	ground nutmeg
2 Tbsp.	kudzu starch		¹/₂ tsp.	ground ginger
¹/₁₆ tsp.	stevia powder		¹/₄ tsp.	ground cloves
1 tsp.	baking soda		¹/₄ cup	safflower oil
¹/₄ tsp.	unbuffered vit. C crystals		1 cup	canned pumpkin
¹/₄ tsp.	sea salt			OR ☑ Pumpkin Puree (pg. 78)
1 tsp.	ground cinnamon†		1 cup	chopped pumpkin seeds (optional)

Preheat oven—350°. Unoiled cookie sheets.

1. In bowl, whisk together dry ingredients. Make "well" in the center.

2. Add oil and pumpkin. Stir to moisten dry ingredients. If desired, stir in seeds.

3. Drop dough by rounded teaspoons onto cookie sheets. Bake 12 minutes. Immediately remove cookies to cooling rack.

Yield: 2 dozen   Enjoy these cookies on occasion during Stage 2.

Combine
Drop cookies
Bake; cool
Freeze extra

†Cinnamon is assigned to Day 3; most are not concerned with this break in rotation.

Zucchini Amaranth Cookies (Day 2 Recipe)

$1/2$ cup	amaranth flour
$1/4$ cup	arrowroot starch
$1/2$ teaspoon	baking soda
$1/4$ teaspoon	sea salt
$1/4$ teaspoon	unbuffered vitamin C crystals
$1/8$ teaspoon	allspice
2 small	kiwi, enough to create $1/4$ cup sauce OR fresh pineapple to create $1/4$ cup sauce
1 tablespoon	olive oil
$3/4$ cup	shredded zucchini squash (peeled optional)

Preheat oven—375°. Oil cookie sheets.

Whisk dry ingred.
Puree fruit
Combine in stages
Drop cookies
Bake

1. In bowl, whisk together dry ingredients.

2. Wash, peel and chunk kiwi or fresh pineapple. Blend in blender or with immersion blender to create a smooth sauce. Add with oil to dry ingredients. Stir thoroughly but do not beat. Mixture will be stiff. Add squash. Mix.

3. Drop by teaspoon onto cookie sheet. Flatten each cookie with fork to about 1 inch in diameter. Bake 18–20 minutes on upper rack of oven. Cool completely on cookie sheet to continue baking.

Yield: 15 cookies

Helpful Hints

Do not double batch because batter should not set.

- - - - -

The trick (for not doughy centers) is to make them small, flatten just enough, and bake as long as possible without burning.

- - - - -

Freeze extra. Thaw at room temp. Thawing in microwave creates soggy cookie.

S₂ Roasted Nuts (non-rotating recipe)

2 cups	nuts/seeds—almonds, Brazil nuts, cashews, filberts, macadamia nuts, pecans, pumpkin seeds, sunflower seeds and/or walnuts
$1/4$ teaspoon	sea salt, use more if desired
$1/4$ cup	water, agave nectar, honey, brown rice syrup, concentrated mixed fruit sweetener, 100% maple syrup OR use half sweetener and half water

1. Combine your choice of nuts/seeds in a 9x13-inch casserole dish.

2. Combine your choice of water and/or sweetener with salt. Pour evenly over nuts/seeds. Stir to coat evenly.

3. Bake at 250° for 1 hour, stirring every 15 minutes. Cool, stirring often to prevent sticking. When completely cooled, store in glass jar.

Coat nuts
Bake

☑ **Millet Pudding** (Day 3 Recipes)

Version 1	Version 2
1 cup sliced or diced peeled apple	
$^1/_4$ cup water	$^3/_4$ cup water
$^1/_2$ teaspoon ground cinnamon	
1–2 tablespoons chopped walnuts	
☑ 1 cup Millet Cereal 1 (page 169)	☑ 1 cup Basic Millet (page 165)
2 teaspoons tapioca starch 1 teaspoon alcohol-free vanilla flavoring	1 teaspoon alcohol-free vanilla flavoring

1. Layer apples, water, cinnamon, walnuts and millet in a 1-quart saucepan. Do not stir. Bring to boil over medium heat.

2. Reduce heat to low. Cover and simmer until apples are tender (approximately 15 minutes).

3. For (1): Dissolve starch in vanilla and 1 tablespoon of water. Add, stir and cook to thicken.
   For (2): Add vanilla and stir before serving.

Layer 1st 5 ingred; simmer
Thicken (1)
Freeze extras

 Serve warm (best) or cold for breakfast or dessert.

Yield (1): $1^2/_3$ cups   3 servings
Yield (2): $1^3/_4$ cups   3 Servings

 ☑ **Quinoa Pudding** (Day 3 Recipes)

Version 1	Version 2
☑ 1 cup Basic Quinoa (page 165) $^1/_2$ cup unsweetened applesauce $^1/_2$ cup water 2 tablespoons chopped walnuts $^3/_4$ teaspoon ground cinnamon 1 teaspoon alcohol-free vanilla flavoring	☑ 1 cup Quinoa Cereal I or II (page 169) $^1/_4$ cup unsweetened applesauce 1–2 tablespoons chopped walnuts $^1/_2$ teaspoon ground cinnamon 1 teaspoon alcohol-free vanilla flavoring

In saucepan, combine all ingredients. Simmer on low heat for 5–10 minutes to combine flavors. If desired, add more water.

 Serve warm or cold.

Yield (1): $1^1/_2$ cups   3 servings
Yield (2): $1^1/_4$ cups   2 servings

"Happiness is not a state to arrive at, but a manner of traveling."
—Margaret Lee Runbeck

Tofu "Cheesecake" (either Day 2 or 4† Recipe)

Carob	Blueberry
☑ 1 (8-inch) unbaked Amaranth OR Buckwheat Pie Crust (page 192)	
2 pounds soft tofu, drained	
$^1/_4$ cup carob powder $^3/_8$ cup honey ($^1/_4$ cup + 2 tablespoons) $^1/_2$ teaspoon sea salt 2 tablespoons dacopa (optional)	1 cup frozen blueberries (unthawed) $^1/_4$ cup honey $^1/_2$ teaspoon sea salt

Preheat oven—350°. Press crust recipe in bottom of 8-inch square baking dish.

1. With electric mixer or immersion blender, blend ingredients until thoroughly mixed and tofu is smooth.

2. Pour into unbaked crust. Spread batter evenly.

3. Bake for 60–65 minutes or until filling is done and knife comes out clean when inserted into center. Chill. Cut 4x4.

Yield: 16 servings

Combine
Bake in crust
Freeze extras

†All ingredients can easily be temporarily moved between Days 2 and 4.

S₂c 🕐 Carob Pudding (Day 4 Recipe)

$^1/_2$ cup	chopped macadamia OR Brazil nuts
$^1/_4$ cup	kudzu starch
2 cups	water
$^1/_8$ teaspoon	stevia powder OR
2 tablespoons	honey
$^1/_4$ cup	carob powder
$^1/_4$ teaspoon	alcohol-free peppermint extract (optional)

Prepare nut milk
Combine
Cook to thicken
Chill

1. Blend nuts, starch and small amount of water in blender on highest speed until well blended, stopping to scrape sides/bottom as needed. Add rest of water, blend a few seconds longer.

2. In saucepan, combine all ingredients. Cook over medium heat, stirring almost constantly, until thickened. Pour into custard cups. Chill.

Yield: 2$^1/_4$ cups 4 servings
During Stage 2, choose stevia for the sweetener.

> "The brain is as strong
> as its weakest think."
> —Eleanor Doan

The Frozen Treat We All Desire!

"I scream, you scream, we all scream for ice cream"—a favorite treat when I was a child. However, those (children and adults alike) with food allergies, CRC and/or lactose intolerance are not able to enjoy many commercial forms of ice cream. This recipe is very simple to make using a blender, a few basic ingredients and your imagination.

S₂c Ice Cream   Yield: 6 cups

2–2$^1/_4$ cups milk	rice beverage, goat or soy milk or Nut Milk (page 101)
Sweetener choices	$^1/_{16}$–$^1/_8$ teaspoon stevia powder 2 tablespoons – $^1/_4$ cup brown rice syrup 1 tablespoon – $^1/_4$ cup honey or pure maple syrup 2 tablespoons – $^1/_4$ cup FOS
Flavorings ideas	1–2 tsps. alcohol-free flavoring (maple, vanilla, almond, orange, etc.) $^1/_4$–$^1/_2$ teaspoon alcohol-free peppermint flavoring 2 Tbsp. carob powder with optional $^1/_8$ tsp. peppermint flavoring
Guar gum (optional)	1 teaspoon
Garnish ideas	chopped nuts—pecans, walnuts, almonds, etc. fresh or frozen (thawed) fruit—strawberries, raspberries, peaches, etc. milk-free, unsweetened carob chips

1. In blender, mix your choice of milk, sweetener (total 2$^1/_4$ cups milk and sweetener is needed), flavoring and guar gum.

2. Pour $^3/_4$ of mixture into ice cube trays and freeze until solid. When using stevia, freeze only $^2/_3$ of the mixture. Keep remaining mixture chilled in refrigerator.

3. When ready to prepare, set out frozen cubes at room temperature for 5 minutes. While cubes are standing, chill blender jar—fill $^1/_3$ of jar with cold water. Add some water ice cubes. Blend for a minute or so until jar is very cold to touch. Empty blender.

> **Recipes**
>
> Mix
> Freeze in ice
>   cube trays
> Chill blender jar
> Blend cubes

4. Add chilled mixture and 2 frozen cubes to blender jar and blend on highest speed until smooth. Continue to add 2 cubes at a time, blending until smooth. If using carob chips, add and blend with final cubes. Immediately serve in chilled bowls and your choice of garnish.

Helpful Hints

This has a texture and taste similar to real homemade ice cream. Extra may be frozen in single serving containers or popsicle containers. Thaw slightly before serving.

- - - - -

Guar gum is used to promote a smooth, soft texture and keep ice crystals from forming. Because of its highly absorbent character, guar gum thickens instantly when mixed with cold liquid. See notes regarding guar gum and leaky gut (page 244).

Facing holidays can be a challenge when all you see is candy with sugar, chocolate, peanut butter, etc. However, the following can easily satisfy the taste for sweets. Each piece can be individually wrapped in plastic wrap and then colored foil.

 ## Easy Can Do Kandee (non-rotating recipe)

$1/4$ cup	carob powder
$1/4$ cup	FOS (fructo-oligo-saccharides)
$1/2$ cup	almond butter
	OR cashew butter
	OR tahini

Coating Choices: as needed

> puffed amaranth
> sesame seeds
> shredded unsweetened coconut
> finely chopped nuts/seeds

Both Recipes

Combine
Form balls; roll
  in coating
Chill
Freeze extra

1. In bowl, whisk together carob and FOS.

2. Add nut butter or tahini and combine until a large ball is formed. Often a small amount of water is needed (i.e., 1–2 teaspoons for tahini or almond butter, 1–2 tablespoons for cashew butter). Add water gradually. Use hands for final mixing.

3. Form into 1-inch balls and roll in your choice of coating. Refrigerate until well chilled.

Yield: 24 Servings

 Helpful Hints

If too much water is added in Step 2, simply add small amounts of equal portions of carob and FOS.

- - - - -

If you have difficulty getting coating to stick, moisten hands with water before forming each candy ball.

- - - - -

For candy kiss shape, gently press coated ball into bottom of small funnel before refrigerating.

S₂ ## Carob Sunflower Candy
(Day 2[†] Recipe)

$1/3$ cup	carob powder[†]
$1/4$ teaspoon	stevia powder[†]
$1/4$ cup	water
$1\,1/3$ cups	sunflower seed butter
$1/2$ cup	ground sunflower seeds

1. In bowl, whisk together carob powder and stevia. Add water and mix until smooth. Add "butter" and mix thoroughly. Mixture will be sticky at first but will become firmer as you mix.

2. Shape into 1-inch balls. Roll in ground seeds. Chill and serve. May be frozen.

  Great to serve in place of fudge at holidays.

Yield: 48 servings

[†]*Carob & stevia are Day 4 foods, omit them on Day 4 before and after eating on Day 2.*

END NOTES

Chapter One: Understanding the Nature & Causes
of Candida-Related Complex

1. Jeanne Marie Martin, and Zoltan Rona, M.D., <u>Complete Candida Yeast Guidebook</u> (Rocklin: Prima Health, 1996) 14.
2. Bruce Miller, D.D.S., C.N.S., <u>Candida: The Nutrition Connection</u>, 3rd printing (Dallas: Bruce Miller Enterprises, 1997) 3-4.
3. Miller, <u>Candida</u> 9–10.
4. Martin 23–46.
5. William G. Crook, M.D., <u>The Yeast Connection Handbook</u> (Jackson: Professional Books, 1999) 1–5, 23–27, 31–89.
6. Bruce Miller, D.D.S., C.N.S., <u>Optiflora for a Healthy Colon</u> (Dallas: Bruce Miller Enterprises, 1998).
7. Miller, <u>Candida</u> 7.
8. Miller, <u>Candida</u> 7.
9. Miller, <u>Optiflora</u>.
10. Martin 15.
11. William G. Crook, M.D., and Marjorie Hurt Jones, R.N., <u>The Yeast Connection Cookbook</u> (Jackson: Professional Books, 1997) 25.
12. Don Colbert, M.D., <u>Toxic Relief</u> (Lake Mary: Siloam Press, 2001) 23.
13. Colbert 23.
14. Martin 15–16.
15. Colbert 23.
16. Martin 16.
17. Colbert 23.
18. Miller, <u>Candida</u> 7.
19. Paul F. Fulk, D.C., <u>The Candida Diet Cookbook</u> (Centerville: Dizzy Fish Creative Services, 1999) 3.
20. Marjorie Hurt Jones, "Leaky Gut—What Is It?," <u>Mastering Food Allergies</u> (July-Aug. 1995) 1.
21. Carol R. Dalton, N.P., <u>Yeast – What's The Problem</u>?, audio tape, Health Dynamics, 2001.
22. Dalton.
23. Martin 15.
24. Miller, <u>Candida</u> 11.
25. Colbert 23.
26. Martin 14.
27. Dalton.
28. Martin 15.
29. Dalton.
30. Fulk 2.
31. Martin 22–23.

continued ...

CHAPTER TWO: Understanding & Implementing
the Healing Strategies
for Candida-Related Complex

1. Jeanne Marie Martin, and Zoltan Rona, M.D., <u>Complete Candida Yeast Guidebook</u> (Rocklin: Prima Health, 1996) 20.
2. William G. Crook, M.D., <u>The Yeast Connection Handbook</u> (Jackson: Professional Books, 1999) 130.
3. Andrew Weil, M.D., <u>Eight Weeks to Optimum Health</u> (New York: Alfred A. Knopf, 1997) 37.
4. Crook 122–23.
5. Gardiner Harris, "Low Stomach Acidity," <u>Medical Nutrition</u> (Spring 1989).
6. Carol R. Dalton, N.P., <u>Yeast – What's The Problem</u>?, audio tape, Health Dynamics, 2001.
7. Weil 79.
8. Richard N. Firshein, D.O., <u>Reversing Asthma</u> (New York: Warner, 1996) 40.
9. Martin 56.
10. Martin 84.
11. Humbart Santillo, <u>Food Enzymes: The Missing Link to Radiant Health</u> (Prescott: Hohm Press, 1993) 77-78.
12. Paul F. Fulk, D.C., <u>The Candida Diet Cookbook</u> (Centerville: Dizzy Fish Creative Services, 1999) 3.
13. Martin 71–72.
14. Crook 136–137.
15. Martin 20.
16. Crook 136–130.
17. George Kroker, M.D., personal conversation at patient consultation, Feb. 1989.
18. James Balch, M.D., "Prescription for Nutritional Healing," Paul Barry Health Seminars, University of St. Thomas, St. Paul, 11 May 1996.
19. J. Randerson, "Microwaved Cooking Zaps Nutrients," <u>New Scientist</u> 25 Oct. 2003: 14.
20. C. Garcia-Viguera, "Phenolic compound contents in edible parts of broccoli inflorescences after domestic cooking," <u>Journal of the Science of Food and Agriculture</u> 83.14 (15 Oct. 2003), 16 March 2005 <http://www3.interscience.wiley.com/cgi-bin/abstract/106558884/ABSTRACT>.
21. Andrew Weil, M.D., Interview with Oprah Winfrey, <u>The Oprah Winfrey Show</u>, ABC, KCRG, Iowa City, 21 April 2000.

CHAPTER THREE: Understanding & Implementing
the Candida-Control Food Plan

1. William G. Crook, M.D., <u>The Yeast Connection Handbook</u> (Jackson: Professional Books, 1999) 115.
2. Gail Burton, <u>The Candida Control Cookbook</u> (New York: Penguin Books, 1989) 4.
3. C. Garcia-Viguera, "Phenolic compound contents in edible parts of broccoli inflorescences after domestic cooking," <u>Journal of the Science of Food and Agriculture</u> 83.14 (15 Oct. 2003), 16 March 2005 <http://www3.interscience.wiley.com/cgi-bin/abstract/106558884/ABSTRACT>.
4. J. Randerson, "Microwaved Cooking Zaps Nutrients," <u>New Scientist</u> 25 Oct. 2003: 14.
5. Bruce Miller, D.D.S., C.N.S., <u>Candida: The Nutrition Connection</u>, 3rd printing (Dallas: Bruce Miller Enterprises, 1997) 22.
6. Miller, <u>Candida</u> 23.
7. James F. Balch, M.D., and Phyllis A Balch, C.N.C., <u>Prescription for Nutritional Healing</u>, 2nd ed. (Garden City Park: Avery, 1997) 4.
8. Walter C. Willett, M.D., <u>Eat, Drink, and Be Healthy</u> (Simon & Shuster, 2001) as referenced in "Healthy Eating Pyramid," <u>Harvard School of Public Health Nutrition Source</u>, ed. President and Fellows of Harvard College, 28 March 2005 <http://www.hsph.harvard.edu/nutritionsource/pyramids.html>.
9. William G. Crook, M.D., and Marjorie Hurt Jones, R.N., <u>The Yeast Connection Cookbook</u> (Jackson: Professional Books, 1997) 24.

10. Burton 4.
11. Jennie Brand-Miller, Ph.D., Johanna Burani, M.S., R.D., C.D.E., and Kaye Foster-Powel, M. Nutr. & Diet., <u>The New Glucose Revolution</u> (New York: Marlowe & Company, 2003) 134.
12. Brand-Miller 146.

CHAPTER FOUR: Understanding & Implementing a Nutritional Support Program

1. Bruce Miller, D.D.S., C.N.S., <u>Candida: The Nutrition Connection</u>, 3rd printing (Dallas: Bruce Miller Enterprises, 1997) 4.
2. <u>Journal of the American College of Nutrition</u> 23.6 (2004): 669-682.
3. Jeanne Marie Martin, and Zoltan Rona, M.D. <u>Complete Candida Yeast Guidebook</u> (Rocklin: Prima Health, 1996) 85.
4. Bruce Miller, D.D.S., C.N.S., <u>Shaklee Discover the Difference</u>, 4th printing (Dallas: Bruce Miller Enterprises, 1998) 14.
5. Bruce Miller, D.D.S., C.N.S., <u>Immune System Nutrition</u>, Rev.Ed. (Dallas: Bruce Miller Enterprises, 1997) 4.
6. Miller, <u>Immune</u> 4.
7. Miller, <u>Candida</u> 22.
8. <u>Nutrition and You</u>, rev. ed. (Ashippun: Vita Books 2002) 6.
9. Martin 73–74.
10. Miller, <u>Candida</u> 22.
11. Martin 13.
12. <u>Nutrition</u> 7.
13. William G. Crook, M.D., <u>The Yeast Connection Handbook</u> (Jackson: Professional Books, 1999) 115.
14. Crook 115.
15. Miller, <u>Candida</u> 17.
16. Miller, <u>Candida</u> 16.
17. Miller, <u>Candida</u> 16.
18. Martin 74–75.
19. Miller, <u>Candida</u> 23.
20. Miller, <u>Candida</u> 24.
21. Miller, <u>Shaklee</u> 11.
22. Sherry Rogers, M.D., "Selenium for Cancer-Prevention" <u>Total Wellness</u> Aug. 2004: 4.
23. James F. Balch, M.D., and Phyllis A Balch, C.N.C., <u>Prescription for Nutritional Healing</u>, 2nd ed. (Garden City Park: Avery, 1997) 45.
24. Rogers 4.
25. Miller, <u>Candida</u> 26.
26. Miller, <u>Candida</u> 26.
27. Miller, <u>Candida</u> 26.
28. Miller, <u>Candida</u> 26.
29. <u>Nutrition</u> 8.
30. Miller, <u>Candida</u> 25.
31. Miller, <u>Candida</u> 25.
32 Miller, <u>Candida</u> 28.
33. Bruce Miller, D.D.S., C.N.S., <u>Optiflora for a Healthy Colon</u> (Dallas: Bruce Miller Enterprises, 1998).
34. Martin 67.
35. H. Hidaka, T. Eida, T. Takizawa, T. Tokunaga, and Y. Tahiro, "Effects of Fructooligosaccharides on Intestinal Flora and Human Health," <u>Bifidobacteria Microflora,</u> Abstract, 5.1 (1986): 37-50.

continued ...

... continued

36. R.C. McKellar and H.W. Modler. "Metabolism of Fructooligosaccharides by Bifidobacterium sp.," Applied Microbiology, Abstract, vol. 31 1989: (537-541.)

37. T. Mitsuoka, H. Hidaka, and T. Eida, "Effect of Fructooligosaccharides on Intestinal Microflora," Die Nahrung, Abstract, 31 5-6 (1987): 436.

38. H.W. Modler, R.C. McKellar, and M. Yaguchi, "Bifidobacteria and Bifidogenic Factors," Journal of Canadian Institute of Food Science and Technology 21.1 (1990): 29-41.

39. Hidaka, H., Y. Tashiro, and T. Eida, "Proliferation of Bifidobacteria by Oligosaccharides and Their Useful Effect on Human Health," Bifidobacteria Microflora, 10.1 (1991): 67.

40. Miller, Candida 27.

41. Miller, Candida 27.

42. Miller, Candida 27.

43. Steve Chaney, Ph.D., Shaklee Sets the Standard, audio tape, K&E Productions, 1999.

44. Steve Chaney, Ph.D, A Design for Living: Reducing Cancer Risk Factors, audio tape, K&E Productions, May 2000.

45. Marjorie Hurt Jones, R.N, "Leaky Gut: A Common Problem with Food Allergies," Mastering Food Allergies 8.5.75, Sept.-Oct. 1993: 1.

46. Crook 128.

47. Miller, Candida 28.

48. Bruce Fife, The Healing Miracles of Coconut Oil (Studio City: Health Wise Publications, 2003) 57.

49. Crook 130.

50. Crook 129.

51. Crook 131.

52. Crook 123.

53. Martin 65.

54. Martin 72.

55. Crook 130.

56. Martin 72–73.

57. Martin 67–68.

58. William G. Crook, M.D., Chronic Fatigue Syndrome and the Yeast Connection (Jackson: Professional Books, 1992) 256.

59. Crook, Chronic 256.

60. Fresh Flax Oil (Monument: Allergy Resources).

61. Eating Well with Flax Seed (West Des Moines: HyVee).

62. Beth Ann Meehan, "Linus Pauling's Rehabilitation," Discover Magazine, 14.1, Jan. 1993: 54.

63. Nutrition 9.

64. Vitamin Primer, The Weston A. Price Foundation, 12 March 2005, <http://www.westonaprice.org/basicnutrition/vitaminprimer.html>.

65. Carol R. Dalton, N.P., Yeast – What's The Problem?, audio tape, Health Dynamics, 2001.

66. Dalton.

67. Dalton.

68. Balch 45.

69. Martin 89.

CHAPTER FIVE: Understanding the Nature & Causes of Food Allergies

1. Natalie Golos, and Frances Golos Golbitz, Coping with Your Allergies (New York: Simon & Schuster, 1986) 85.

2. Alan Scott Levin, M.D., and Merla Zellerbach, The Type 1/Type 2 Allergy Relief Program (CA: Jeremy P. Tarcher, Inc., 1983) 96.

3. Marjorie Hurt Jones, "Leaky Gut—What Is It?," <u>Mastering Food Allergies,</u> X.4.86, July-Aug. 1995: 1.
4. Marjorie Hurt Jones, "Leaky Gut. A Common Problem with Food Allergies," <u>Mastering Food Allergies</u>, VIII.5.75, Sept.-Oct. 1993: 1.
5. Levin 18–19.
6. Jerry Springer, "Allergies—Making Kids Crazy," interview with Doris Rapp, M.D., videocassette, Multimedia Entertainment, 17 Dec. 1992.
7. Sherry Rogers, M.D., <u>The E.I. Syndrome</u> (Syracuse: Prestige Publishers, 1986) 283–309.
8. <u>Sidestepping Food Sensitivities</u> (Minneapolis: Good Earth Restaurants).

CHAPTER SIX: Understanding & Implementing the Mechanics of a Rotational Food Plan

1. Marjorie Hurt Jones, "Leaky Gut: A Common Problem with Food Allergies," <u>Mastering Food Allergies</u> 8.5.75 Sept.-Oct. 1993: 1.
2. Natalie Golos and Frances Golos Golbitz, <u>Coping with Your Allergies</u> (New York: Simon & Schuster, 1986) 85.

End Notes for Appendices are located at the end of each Appendix

BIBLIOGRAPHY

Bibliographical references for resources not indicated in the end notes.

<u>Amaranth—The Grain with a Future</u>. Naperville: Nu-World Amaranth, Inc.

<u>A History of Buckwheat</u>. Penn Yan: Birkett Mills.

Jones, Marjorie Hurt, R.N. <u>The Allergy Self-Help Cookbook</u>. Emmaus: Rodale Press, 2001.

Lewis, Sondra K., and Lonnett Dietrich Blakley. <u>Allergy & Candida Cooking Made Easy</u>. Coralville: Canary Connect Publications, 1996.

Rinkel, Herbert John, Theron G. Randolph, and Michael Zeller. <u>Food Allergy</u>. Springfield: Thomas, 1951.

Rockwell, Sally. <u>Coping with Candida Cookbook</u>. Rev. Ed. Seattle: By the author, 1986.

Truss, C. Orian, M.D. <u>The Missing Diagnosis</u>. Birmingham: By the author, 1982.

Wood, Rebecca. The New Whole Foods Encyclopedia. New York: Penguin Books, 1999.

Recipe Credits

A special thanks to Elva Waters of Iowa for developing the Sprout Salad recipe.

A special thanks to Judy Beuter of Iowa, my special organic chicken, beef and pork farmer, for sharing her Sweetener-Free Butternut Squash Pie recipe.

A special thanks to Gene D. of Ohio for sharing
the Pancake or French Toast "Maple Syrup" recipe.
He says it tastes "almost like the real thing." He found it with information from
the Candida Research and Information Foundation and added FOS for more sweetness.

The Lentil Casserole recipe was adapted from a recipe submitted by Katie R., MN.
She layers dry lentils, frozen lima beans and seasoned tator tots in a tall casserole,
then arranges the chops in a teepee on top and bakes it covered in the oven.

The Egg Soufflé recipe idea was from Deb Buhr of Sumner, Iowa.

Mayos, Creamy Italian Dressing, Garbanzo Bean & Potato Soup
and Easy Banquet Meal recipe ideas came
from The Yeast Connection Cookbook
by William G. Crook, M.D. and Marjorie Hurt Jones, R.N.

Pumpkin Cookies recipe idea
from The Complete Food Allergy Cookbook by Marilyn Gioannini

Soy Bread and Oatmeal Pie Crust recipe ideas
from Rotational Bon Appetité! by Hayes & Maynard

Mac'n Cheese-Less recipe idea
from Vegetarian Cooking School Cookbook by Danny & Charise Vierra

Creamy Tomato Soup and Chicken/Broccoli Mac'n Cheese-Less recipe ideas
from Rachel Ray on 30 Minute Meals with Rachel Ray

Lentil Patties and Pie Crust recipe ideas
from Marjorie Hurt Jones in Mastering Food Allergies newsletters

Amaranth Buns, Kamut® or Spelt Bread/Buns/Dinner Rolls and Ice Cream recipe ideas
from Allergy Cooking With Ease by Nicolette M. Dumke

Celery Soup recipe idea
from The EPD Patient's Cooking & Lifestyle Guide by Nicolette M. Dumke

APPENDIX A: Food Families

Foods are grouped based on biological origin. Each food family is assigned a name and number. List 1 provides an alphabetical listing of foods with their assigned number. List 2 groups the foods numerically. This list is especially helpful when using a rotational food plan, making it easy to avoid eating foods repetitively from the same family. The lists include non-edible plants because persons allergic to a plant may need to avoid foods from the same family, especially when it is in bloom. These lists were adapted from a compilation by Natalie Golos and used with her permission.[1]

List 1: Food Families (Alphabetical)

A

81	abalone
80	absinthe
41	acacia (gum)
46	acerola
79	acorn squash
41	adzuki beans
1	agar agar
12	agave
98	albacore
41	alfalfa
1	Algae Family
63	allspice
40b	almond
11	*Aloe vera*
54	althea root
30	amaranth
12	Amaryllis Family
94	amberjack
86	American eel
64	American Ginseng
68	American persimmon
117	Amphibians
41	anasazi beans
85	anchovy
85	Anchovy Family
65	angelica
65	anise
38	annatto
136	antelope
40a	apple
73	apple mint
40b	apricot

47	arrowroot, Brazilian (tapioca)
9	arrowroot (*Colocasia*)
17	arrowroot, East Indian (*Curcuma*)
19	Arrowroot Family
13	arrowroot, Fiji (*Tacca*)
4	arrowroot, Florida (*Zamia*)
19	arrowroot (*Maranta* starch)
16	arrowroot (*Musa*)
18	arrowroot, Queensland
80	artichoke flour
80	artichoke, globe
80	artichoke, Jerusalem
9	Arum Family
11	asparagus
2	*Aspergillus*
34	avocado

B

134	bacon
2	baker's yeast
6	bamboo shoots
16	banana
16	Banana Family
46	Barbados cherry
6	barley
73	basil
114	bass (black)
113	Bass Family
113	bass (yellow)
53	basswood

34	bay leaf
41	beans
132	bear
132	Bear Family
66	bearberry
24	Beech Family
137	beef
137	beef by-products
28	beet
74	bell pepper
73	bergamot
23	Birch Family
121	Birds
38	Bixa Family
114	black bass
41	black-eyed peas
21	black pepper
40c	black raspberry
80	black salsify
41	black turtle beans
22	black walnut
40c	blackberry
66	blueberry
93	bluefish
93	Bluefish Family
36	bok choy
80	boneset
98	bonito
79	Boston marrow
71	borage
71	Borage Family
40c	boysenberry
137	Bovine Family
6	bran

52	brandy	74	cayenne (red) pepper	76	coffee
47	Brazilian arrowroot	65	celeriac	55	cola nut
62	Brazil nut	65	celery	36	collards
25	breadfruit	65	celery leaf	80	coltsfoot
2	brewer's yeast	65	celery seed	36	colza shoots
36	broccoli	80	celtuce	71	comfrey
36	Brussels sprouts	81	Cephalopod	80	Composite Family
27	buckwheat	9	ceriman	5	Conifer Family
27	Buckwheat Family	80	chamomile	65	coriander (cilantro)
137	buffalo (bison)	52	champagne	6	corn
6	bulgur	28	chard	124	cornish hen
80	burdock root	79	chayote	6	corn meal
40d	burnet	137	cheese, goat	6	corn oil
137	butter	137	cheese, milk	6	corn products
31	Buttercup Family	40b	cherry	78	corn salad
79	buttercup squash	65	chervil	6	cornstarch
101	butterfish	24	chestnut	6	corn sugar
22	butternut	73	chia seed	6	corn syrup
79	butternut squash	124	chicken	80	costmary
		41	chickpea	54	cottonseed oil
	C	67	chicle	41	coumarin
36	cabbage	80	chicory	36	couve tronchuda
55	cacao	80	chicory, witloof	41	cowpea
60	Cactus Family	74	chili pepper	82	crab
6	cane sugar	36	Chinese cabbage	40a	crabapple
18	Canna Family		(napa)	66	cranberry
36	canola oil	64	Chinese Ginseng	114	crappie
79	cantaloupe	56	Chinese gooseberry	82	crayfish
37	caper	14	Chinese potato (yam)	52	cream of tartar
37	Caper Family	79	Chinese preserving	79	Crenshaw melon
74	*Capsicum*		melon	96	croaker
42	carambola	7	Chinese water chestnut	96	Croaker Family
65	caraway seed	24	chinquapin	79	crookneck squash
17	cardamon	11	chives	82	Crustaceans
80	cardoon	55	chocolate	79	cucumber
135	caribou	111	chub	65	cumin
41	carob	7	chufa	36	curly cress
41	carob syrup	40a	cider	39	currant
111	carp	65	cilantro (coriander)	79	cushaw squash
29	Carpetweed Family	34	cinnamon	87	cusk
1	carageen	2	citric acid	32	custard-apple
65	carrot	45	citron	32	Custard-Apple Family
65	Carrot Family	6	citronella	4	Cycad Family
65	carrot syrup	45	Citrus Family (Rue)		
79	casaba melon	81	clam		**D**
79	caserta squash	73	clary	103	dab
48	cashew	63	clove	80	Dacopa beverage
48	Cashew Family	41	clover		(dahlia)
47	cassava	81	cockle	80	dahlia (Dacopa
34	cassia bark	55	cocoa		beverage)
47	castor bean	55	cocoa butter	80	dandelion
47	castor oil	8	coconut	9	dasheen
112	Catfish Family	8	coconut meal	8	date
88	catfish (ocean)	8	coconut oil	8	date sugar
112	catfish species	79	cocozelle	135	deer
73	catnip	87	cod (scrod)	135	Deer Family
36	cauliflower	87	Codfish Family	40c	dewberry
104	caviar			65	dill

65	dill seed
56	Dillenia Family
73	dittany
95	dolphin
95	Dolphin Family
122	dove
122	Dove Family
52	dried "currant"
96	drum (saltwater)
116	drum (freshwater)
121	duck
121	Duck Family
1	dulse

E

17	East Indian arrowroot
68	Ebony Family
86	Eel Family
74	eggplant
77	elderberry
77	elderberry flowers
135	elk
80	endive
22	English walnut
80	escarole
63	eucalyptus

F

41	fava bean
65	fennel
41	fenugreek
78	fetticus
25	fig
13	figi arrowroot
23	filbert
34	filé
65	finocchio
104	Fishes (freshwater)
83	Fishes (saltwater)
44	Flax Family
44	flaxseed
65	Florence fennel
4	Florida arrowroot
103	flounder
103	Flounder Family
80	French endive
116	freshwater drum
117	Frog Family
117	frog (frogs' legs)
2	Fungi

G

41	garbanzo
27	garden sorrel
11	garlic
81	Gastropods
137	gelatin, beef
134	gelatin, pork

79	gherkin
5	gin
17	ginger
17	Ginger Family
64	ginseng
64	Ginseng Family
80	globe artichoke
6	gluten flour
137	goat
79	golden nugget squash
80	goldenrod
31	golden seal
121	goose
39	gooseberry
56	gooseberry, Chinese
28	Goosefoot Family
65	gotu kola
79	Gourd Family
6	graham flour
58	granadilla
52	grape
52	Grape Family
45	grapefruit
6	Grass Family
74	green pepper
61	grenadine
6	grits
74	ground cherry
7	groundnut
91	grouper
123	Grouse Family
123	grouse (ruffed)
41	guar gum
63	guava
125	guinea fowl
125	Guinea Fowl Family
41	gum acacia
41	gum tragacanth

H

87	haddock
87	hake
103	halibut
134	ham
129	Hare Family
101	harvestfish
101	Harvestfish Family
23	hazelnut
22	heartnut
66	Heath Family
84	Herring Family
54	hibiscus
22	hickory nut
134	hog
49	Holly Family
6	hominy
79	honeydew
77	Honeysuckle Family

25	hop
73	horehound
133	horse
133	Horse Family
36	horseradish
3	horsetail
3	Horsetail Family
79	Hubbard squash
66	huckleberry
73	hyssop

I

137	ice cream, goat
137	ice cream, milk
15	Iris Family
1	Irish moss

J

94	Jack Family
68	Japanese persimmon
80	Jerusalem artichoke
41	jicama
6	Job's tears
5	juniper

K

68	kaki
36	kale
6	Kamut®
1	kelp
41	kidney bean
56	kiwi berry
36	kohlrabi
1	kombu
41	kudzu
45	kumquat
41	kuzu

L

137	lactose
137	lamb
28	lamb's-quarters
134	lard
34	Laurel Family
73	lavender
41	lecithin
11	leek
41	Legume Family
45	lemon
73	lemon balm
6	lemon grass
72	lemon verbena
41	lentil
80	lettuce
41	licorice
11	Lily Family
41	lima bean
45	lime

53	linden
53	Linden Family
44	linseed
51	litchi
82	lobster
40c	loganberry
40c	longberry
79	loofah
40a	loquat
65	lovage
79	*Luffa*
51	lychee

M

26	macadamia
33	mace
98	mackerel
98	Mackerel Family
76	Madder Family
9	malanga
54	Mallow Family
46	Malpighia Family
6	malt
6	maltose
127	Mammals
48	mango
50	Maple Family
50	maple products
50	maple sugar
50	maple syrup
19	Maranta starch
73	marjoram
99	marlin
99	Marlin Family
49	maté
84	menhaden
12	mescal
137	milk, cow's
137	milk, goat's
6	millet
111	Minnow Family
73	Mint Family
6	molasses
2	mold
81	Mollusks
135	moose
2	morel
70	Morning Glory Family
25	mulberry
25	Mulberry Family
89	mullet
89	Mullet Family
41	mung bean
45	murcot
52	muscadine
2	mushroom
109	muskellunge
79	muskmelon

81	mussel
36	Mustard Family
36	mustard greens
36	mustard seed
137	mutton
63	Myrtle Family

N

14	ñame
36	napa cabbage
43	nasturtium
43	Nasturtium Family
41	navy bean
40b	nectarine
29	New Zealand spinach
74	Nightshade Family
41	northern beans
97	northern scup
33	nutmeg
33	Nutmeg Family
2	nutritional yeast

O

6	oat
6	oatmeal
88	ocean catfish
102	ocean perch
23	oil of birch
54	okra
137	oleomargarine
69	olive
69	Olive Family
69	olive oil
11	onion
128	opossum
128	Opossum Family
45	orange
20	Orchid Family
73	oregano
15	orris root
42	oxalis
42	Oxalis Family
81	oyster
80	oyster plant

P

8	palm cabbage
8	Palm Family
59	papaya
59	Papaya Family
74	paprika
62	paradise nut
65	parsley
65	parsnip
123	partridge
58	Passion Flower Family
58	passion fruit
6	patent flour

79	pattypan squash
32	pawpaw
41	pea
40b	peach
124	peafowl
41	peanut
41	peanut oil
40a	pear
22	pecan
40a	pectin
75	Pedalium Family
81	Pelecypods
73	pennyroyal
74	pepino
74	pepper, sweet, all colors
21	peppercorn
21	Pepper Family
73	peppermint
115	Perch Family
102	perch (ocean)
113	perch (white)
115	perch (yellow)
79	Persian melon
68	persimmon
124	pheasant
124	Pheasant Family
109	pickerel
122	pigeon (squab)
30	pigweed
109	pike
109	Pike Family
84	pilchard (sardine)
63	Pimenta
74	pimiento
10	pineapple
10	Pineapple Family
5	pine nut
41	pinto beans
21	*Piper*
48	pistachio
103	plaice
16	plantain
40b	plum
9	poi
48	poison ivy
48	poison oak
48	poison sumac
87	pollack
61	pomegranate
61	Pomegranate Family
94	pompano
6	popcorn
35	Poppy Family
35	poppyseed
97	porgy
134	pork
134	pork gelatin

74	potato		**S**		41	soybean	

74 potato
74 Potato Family
82 prawn
79 preserving melon
60 prickly pear
136 Pronghorn Family
26 Protea Family
40b prune
2 puffball
12 pulque
45 pummelo
79 pumpkin
79 pumpkin meal
79 pumpkin seed
114 pumpkinseed (sunfish)
40c purple raspberry
30 purslane
30 Purslane Family
80 pyrethrum

Q

124 quail
18 Queensland arrowroot
26 Queensland nut
40a quince
28 quinoa

R

129 rabbit
36 radish
80 ragweed
52 raisin
11 ramp
36 rape
40c raspberry, all colors
119 rattlesnake
6 raw sugar
41 red clover
40c red raspberry
135 reindeer
137 rennin (rennet)
118 Reptiles
27 rhubarb
6 rice
6 rice bran
6 rice flour
137 Rocky Mountain sheep
105 roe
80 romaine
40 Rose Family
102 rosefish
40a rosehips
54 roselle
73 rosemary
45 Rue Family
123 ruffed grouse
36 rutabaga
6 rye

S

80 safflower oil
15 saffron
73 sage
8 sago starch
99 sailfish
106 Salmon Family
106 salmon species
80 salsify
80 santolina
67 Sapodilla Family
62 Sapucaya Family
62 sapucaya nut
84 sardine
11 sarsaparilla
34 sassafras
115 sauger (perch)
137 sausage casings (beef)
134 sausage (pork)
73 savory
39 Saxifrage Family
81 scallop
80 scolymus
102 Scorpionfish Family
80 scorzonera
134 scrapple (pork)
91 sea bass
91 Sea Bass Family
88 Sea Catfish Family
27 sea grape
84 sea herring
96 sea trout
1 seaweed
7 Sedge Family
41 senna
75 sesame
75 sesame oil
105 shad
11 shallot
3 shavegrass
137 sheep
82 shrimp
96 silver perch
90 silverside
90 Silverside Family
98 skipjack
40b sloe
108 smelt
108 Smelt Family
81 snail
119 Snake Family
51 Soapberry Family
11 soap plant
103 sole
6 sorghum
27 sorrel
80 southernwood

S

41 soybean
41 soy products
79 spaghetti, vegetable
80 Spanish oyster plant
73 spearmint
28 spinach
29 spinach, New Zealand
6 spelt
96 spot
137 spray dried milk
47 Spurge Family
79 squash
81 squid
130 squirrel
130 Squirrel Family
55 Sterculia Family
80 stevia
79 straightneck squash
40c strawberry
41 string bean
104 sturgeon
104 Sturgeon Family
110 sucker
110 Sucker Family
137 suet
28 sugar beet
6 sugar cane
6 sugar, raw
73 summer savory
114 sunfish
114 Sunfish Family
80 sunflower meal
80 sunflower oil
80 sunflower seed
80 sunflower seed products
36 swede
65 sweet cicely
6 sweet corn
74 sweet pepper
70 sweet potato
134 Swine Family
100 swordfish
100 Swordfish Family

T

13 Tacca Family
75 tahini
41 tamarind
28 tampala
45 tangelo
45 tangerine
80 tansy
47 tapioca
9 taro
80 tarragon
57 tea
57 Tea Family

6 teff
41 tempeh
12 tequila
120 terrapin
73 thyme
92 tilefish
92 Tilefish Family
74 tobacco
41 tofu
74 tomatillo
74 tomato
41 tonka bean
74 tree tomato
6 triticale
106 trout species
2 truffle
98 tuna
79 turban squash
103 turbot
126 turkey
126 turkey eggs
126 Turkey Family
17 turmeric
36 turnip
120 Turtle Family
120 turtle species

U

36 upland cress

V

78 Valerian Family
20 vanilla
137 veal
79 vegetable spaghetti
79 vegetable sponge
135 venison
72 Verbena Family
40a vinegar

W

115 walleye
22 Walnut Family
36 watercress
79 watermelon
96 weakfish
131 whale
131 Whale Family
6 wheat
6 wheat flour
6 wheat germ
90 whitebait
107 whitefish
107 Whitefish Family
21 white pepper
113 white perch
6 whole wheat
6 wild rice
52 wine
40c wineberry

52 wine vinegar
23 wintergreen
73 winter savory
80 witloof chicory
76 woodruff
80 wormwood

X

23 xylitol

Y

14 yam
14 Yam Family
14 yampi
80 yarrow
9 yautia
2 yeast, brewer's
   or nutritional
113 yellow bass
94 yellow jack
115 yellow perch
49 yerba maté
137 yogurt
40c youngberry
47 yuca
11 yucca

Z

4 *Zamia*
79 zucchini

List 2: Food Families (Numerical)

Plant

1 Algae
   agar-agar
   carrageen (Irish moss)
   dulse*
   kelp (seaweed)
   kombu (seaweed)
2 Fungi
   baker's yeast
   brewer's or nutritional
      yeast
   mold (in certain
      cheeses)
   citric acid
      (*Aspergillus*)
   morel
   mushroom
   puffball
   truffle
3 Horsetail Family,
      Equisetaceae
   shavegrass (horsetail)*

4 Cycad Family,
      Cycadaceae
   Florida arrowroot
      (*Zamia*)
5 Conifer Family, *Coniferae*
   juniper (gin)*
   pine nut (piñon,
      pinyon)
6 Grass Family, *Gramineae*
   barley
      malt
      maltose
   bamboo shoots
   corn (mature)
      corn meal
      corn oil
      cornstarch
      corn sugar
      corn syrup
   hominy
      hominy grits
      popcorn

Job's tears
Kamut®
lemon grass
   citronella
millet
oat
   oat bran
   oatmeal
rice
   rice bran
   rice flour
rye
sorghum grain
   syrup
spelt
sugar cane
   cane sugar
   molasses
   raw sugar
sweet corn
teff
triticale

*One or more plant parts (leaf, root, seed, etc.) used as a beverage.

6 Grass Family (continued)
  wheat
    bran
    bulgur
    flour
      gluten
      graham
      patent
      whole wheat
    wheat germ
  wild rice

7 Sedge Family,
    Cyperaceae
  Chinese water chestnut
  chufa (groundnut)

8 Palm Family, *Palmaceae*
  coconut
    coconut meal
    coconut oil
  date
    date sugar
  palm cabbage
  sago starch
    (*Metroxylon*)

9 Arum Family, *Araceae*
  ceriman (*Monstera*)
  dasheen (*Colocasia*)
    arrowroot
  taro arrowroot
    (*Colocasia*)
    poi
  malanga (*Xanthosoma*)
  yautia (*Xanthosoma*)

10 Pineapple Family,
    Bromeliaceae
  pineapple

11 Lily Family, *Liliaceae*
  Aloe vera
  asparagus
  chives
  garlic
  leek
  onion
  ramp
  sarsaparilla*
  shallot
  yucca (soap plant)

12 Amaryllis Family,
    Amaryllidaceae
  agave
    mescal, pulque, and
      tequila

13 Tacca Family, *Taccaceae*
  Fiji arrowroot (*Tacca*)

14 Yam Family,
    Dioscoreaceae
  Chinese potato (yam)
  ñame (yampi)

15 Iris Family, *Iridaceae*
  orris root (scent)
  saffron (*Crocus*)

16 Banana Family,
    Musaceae
  arrowroot (*Musa*)
  banana
  plantain

17 Ginger Family,
    Zingiberaceae
  cardamon
  East Indian arrowroot,
    (*Curcuma*)
  ginger
  tumeric

18 Canna Family,
    Cannaceae
  Queensland arrowroot

19 Arrowroot Family,
    Marantaceae
  arrowroot (*Maranta
    starch*)

20 Orchid Family,
    Orchidaceae
  vanilla

21 Pepper Family,
    Piperaceae
  peppercorn (*Piper*)
    black pepper
    white pepper

22 Walnut Family,
    Juglandaceae
  black walnut
  butternut
  English walnut
  heartnut
  hickory nut
  pecan

23 Birch Family, *Betulaceae*
  filbert (hazelnut)
  oil of birch
    (wintergreen)
    (some wintergreen
      flavor is methyl
      salicylate)
  xylitol

24 Beech Family, *Fagaceae*
  chestnut
  chinquapin

25 Mulberry Family,
    Moraceae
  breadfruit
  fig
  hop*
  mulberry

26 Protea Family,
    Proteaceae
  macadamia
    (Queensland nut)

27 Buckwheat Family,
    Polygonaceae
  buckwheat
  garden sorrel
  rhubarb
  sea grape

28 Goosefoot Family,
    Cheopodiaceae
  beet
  chard
  lamb's-quarters
  quinoa
  spinach
  sugar beet
  tampala

29 Carpetweed Family,
    Aizoaceae
  New Zealand spinach

30 Purslane Family,
    Portulacaceae
  amaranth
  pigweed (purslane)

31 Buttercup Family,
    Ranunculaceae
  golden seal*

32 Custard-Apple Family,
    Annona species
  custard-apple
  papaw (pawpaw)

33 Nutmeg Family,
    Myristicacae
  nutmeg
  mace

34 Laurel Family, *Lauraceae*
  avocado
  bay leaf
  cassia bark
  cinnamon
  sassafras*
    filé (powdered
      leaves)

35 Poppy Family,
    Papaveraceae
  poppyseed

36 Mustard Family,
    Cruciferae
  bok choy
  broccoli
  Brussels sprouts
  cabbage
  cauliflower
  Chinese cabbage
    (napa)
  collards

*One or more plant parts (leaf, root, seed, etc.) used as a beverage.

36 Mustard Family (cont.)
    colza shoots
    couve tronchuda
    curly cress
    horseradish
    kale
    kohlrabi
    mustard greens
    mustard seed
    radish
    rape
    canola oil
    rutabaga (swede)
    turnip and turnip
      greens
    upland cress
    watercress

37 Caper Family,
    Capparidaceae
    caper

38 Bixa Family, *Bixaceae*
    annatto (natural yellow
      dye)

39 Saxifrage Family,
    Saxifragaceae
    currant
    gooseberry

40 Rose Family, *Rosaceae*
    a. pomes
      apple
        cider
          vinegar
        pectin
      crabapple
      loquat
      pear
      quince
      rosehips*
    b. stone fruits
      almond
      apricot
      cherry
      peach (nectarine)
      plum (prune)
      sloe
    c. berries
      blackberry
        boysenberry
        dewberry
        loganberry
        longberry
        youngberry
      raspberry (leaf)*
        black raspberry
        red raspberry
        purple raspberry
      strawberry (leaf)*
        wineberry

    d. herb
      burnet (cucumber
        flavor)

41 Legume Family,
    Leguminoseae
    alfalfa (sprouts)*
    beans
      adzuki
      anasazi
      black turtle
      fava
      lima
      mung (sprouts)
      navy
      northern
      pinto
      string (kidney)
    black-eyed pea
      (cowpea)
    carob*
      carob syrup
    chickpea (garbanzo)
    cloves
    fenugreek*
    garbanzo (chickpea)
    guar gum
    gum acacia
    gum tragacanth
    jicama
    kudzu (kuzu)
    lentil
    licorice*
    pea
    peanut
      peanut oil
    red clover*
    senna*
    soybean
      lecithin
      soy flour
      soy grits
      soy milk
      soy oil
      tempeh
      tofu
    tamarind
    tonka bean
      coumarin

42 Oxalis Family,
    Oxalidaceae
    carambola
    oxalis

43 Nasturtium Family,
    Tropaeolaceae
    nasturtium

44 Flax Family, *Linacaea*
    flaxseed*
    linseed oil

45 Rue (Citrus) Family,
    Rutaceae
    citron
    grapefruit
    kumquat
    lemon
    lime
    murcot
    orange
    pummelo
    tangelo
    tangerine

46 Malpighia Family,
    Malpighiaceae
    acerola (Barbados
      cherry)

47 Spurge Family,
    Euphorbiaceae
    cassava or yuca
      (*Manihot*)
      cassava meal
      tapioca (Brazilian
        arrowroot)
    castor bean
      castor oil

48 Cashew Family,
    Anacardiaceae
    cashew
    mango
    pistachio
    poison ivy
    poison oak
    poison sumac

49 Holly Family,
    Aquifoliaceae
    maté (yerba maté)

50 Maple Family
    maple sugar
    maple syrup

51 Soapberry Family,
    Sapindaceae
    litchi (lychee)

52 Grape Family, *Vitaceae*
    grape
      brandy
      champagne
      cream of tartar
      dried "currant"
      raisin
      wine
      wine vinegar
    muscadine

53 Linden Family, *Tiliaceae*
    basswood (linden)*

---

*One or more plant parts (leaf, root, seed, etc.) used as a beverage.

54 Mallow Family,
  Malvaceae
  althea root*
  cottonseed oil
  hibiscus (roselle)*
  okra
55 Sterculia Family,
  Sterculiaceae
  chocolate (cacao)*
  cocoa*
    cocoa butter
  cola nut
56 Dillenia Family,
  Dilleniaceae
  Chinese gooseberry
    (kiwi berry)
57 Tea Family, *Theaceae*
  tea*
58 Passion Flower Family,
  Passifloraceae
  granadilla (passion
    fruit)
59 Papaya Family,
  Caricaceae
  papaya
60 Cactus Family,
  Cactaceae
  maguey (Aguamiel)
  prickly pear
61 Pomegranate Family,
  Puniceae
  pomegranate
  grenadine
62 Sapucaya Family,
  Lecythidaceae
  Brazil nut
  sapucaya nut (paradise
    nut)
63 Myrtle Family,
  Myrtaceae
  allspice (Pimenta)
  clove
  eucalyptus*
  guava
64 Ginseng Family,
  Araliaceae
  American Ginseng*
  Chinese Ginseng*
65 Carrot Family,
  Umbelliferae
  angelica
  anise
  caraway
  carrot
    carrot syrup

celeriac (celery root)
celery
  seed & leaf*
chervil
coriander (cilantro)
cumin
dill
  dill seed
fennel*
  finocchio
    Florence fennel
gotu kola*
lovage*
parsley*
parsnip
sweet cecily
66 Heath Family, *Ericaceae*
  bearberry*
  blueberry*
  cranberry
  huckleberry*
67 Sapodilla Family,
  Sapotaceae
  chicle (chewing gum)
68 Ebony Family,
  Ebonaceae
  American persimmon
  kaki (Japanese
    persimmon)
69 Olive Family, Oleaceae
  olive (green or ripe)
  olive oil
70 Morning-Glory Family,
  Convolvulacea
  sweet potato
71 Borage Family (Herbs)
  Boraginaceae
  borage
  comfrey (leaf & root)*
72 Verbena Family,
  Verbenaceae
  lemon verbena*
73 Mint Family, *Labiatae*
  (Herbs)
  apple mint
  basil
  bergamot
  catnip*
  chia seed*
  clary
  dittany*
  horehound*
  hyssop*
  lavender
  lemon balm*
  marjoram

oregano
pennyroyal*
peppermint*
rosemary
sage
spearmint*
summer savory
thyme
winter savory
74 Nightshade (Potato)
  Family, *Solanaceae*
  eggplant
  ground cherry
  pepino (melon pear)
  pepper (Capsicum)
    bell, sweet (all colors)
    cayenne (red)
    chili
    paprika
    pimiento
  potato
  tobacco
  tomatillo
  tomato
  tree tomato
75 Pedalium Family,
  Pedaliaceae
  sesame seed
  sesame oil
  tahini
76 Madder Family,
  Rubiaceae
  coffee*
  woodruff
77 Honeysuckle Family,
  Caprifoliaceae
  elderberry
    elderberry flowers
78 Valerian Family,
  Valerianaceae
  corn salad (fetticus)
79 Gourd Family,
  Cucurbitaceae
  chayote
  Chinese preserving
    melon
  cucumber
  gherkin
  loofah (Luffa)
    (vegetable sponge)
  muskmelons
    cantaloupe
    casaba
    crenshaw
    honeydew
    Persian melon

*One or more plant parts (leaf, root, seed, etc.) used as a beverage.

79 Gourd Family (continued)
  pumpkin
    pumpkin seed & meal
  squashes
    acorn
    buttercup
    butternut
    Boston marrow
    caserta
    cocozelle
    crookneck &
      straightneck
    cushaw
    golden nugget
    Hubbard varieties
    pattypan
    summer
    turban
    vegetable spaghetti
    zucchini
  watermelon
80 Composite Family,
    Compositae
  absinthe
  boneset*
  burdock root*
  cardoon
  chamomile
  chicory*
  coltsfoot
  costmary
  dahlia (Dacopa
    beverage)
  dandelion
  endive
  escarole
  globe artichoke
  goldenrod*
  Jerusalem artichoke
    artichoke flour
  lettuce
    celtuce
  pyrethrum
  ragweed
  romaine
  safflower oil
  salsify (oyster plant)
  santolina (herb)
  scolymus (Spanish
    oyster plant)
  scorzonera
  southernwood
  stevia (sweet herb)
  sunflower
    sunflower seed, meal,
      and oil

tansy (herb)
tarragon (herb)
witloof chicory (French
  endive)
wormwood (absinthe)
yarrow*

Animal

81 *Mollusks*
  Gastropods
    abalone
    snail
  Cephalopod
    squid
  Pelecypods
    clam
    cockle
    mussel
    oyster
    scallop
82 Crustaceans
    crab
    crayfish
    lobster
    prawn
    shrimp

83 Fishes

84 Herring Family
    menhaden
    pilchard (sardine)
    sea herring
85 Anchovy Family
    anchovy
86 Eel Family
    American eel
87 Codfish Family
    cod (scrod)
    cusk
    haddock
    hake
    pollack
88 Sea Catfish Family
    ocean catfish
89 Mullet Family
    mullet
90 Silverside Family
    silverside (whitebait)
91 Sea Bass Family
    grouper
    sea bass
92 Tilefish Family
    tilefish
93 Bluefish Family
    bluefish

94 Jack Family
    amberjack
    pompano
    yellow jack
95 Dolphin Family
    dolphin
96 Croaker Family
    croaker
    drum
    sea trout
    silver perch
    spot
    weakfish (spotted sea
      trout)
97 Porgy Family
    northern scup (porgy)
98 Mackerel Family
    albacore
    bonito
    mackerel
    skipjack
    tuna
99 Marlin Family
    marlin
    sailfish
100 Swordfish Family
    swordfish
101 Harvestfish Family
    butterfish
    harvestfish
102 Scorpionfish Family
    rosefish (ocean perch)
103 Flounder Family
    dab
    flounder
    halibut
    plaice
    sole
    turbot
104 Sturgeon Family
    sturgeon (caviar)
105 Herring Family
    shad (roe)
106 Salmon Family
    salmon species
    trout species
107 Whitefish Family
    whitefish
108 Smelt Family
    smelt
109 Pike Family
    muskellunge
    pickerel
    pike

*One or more plant parts (leaf, root, seed, etc.) used as a beverage.

110 Sucker Family
    buffalofish
    sucker
111 Minnow Family
    carp
    chub
112 Catfish Family
    catfish species
113 Bass Family
    white perch
    yellow bass
114 Sunfish Family
    black bass species
    sunfish species
      pumpkinseed
    crappie
115 Perch Family
    sauger
    walleye
    yellow perch
116 Croaker Family
    freshwater drum

117 Amphibians

117 Frog Family
    frog (frogs' legs)

118 Reptiles

119 Snake Family
    rattlesnake
120 Turtle Family
    terrapin
    turtle species

121 Birds

121 Duck Family
    duck
      eggs
    goose
      eggs

122 Dove Family
    dove
    pigeon (squab)
123 Grouse Family
    ruffed grouse
    (partridge)
124 Pheasant Family
    chicken
      eggs
    cornish hen
    peafowl
    pheasant
    quail
125 Guinea Fowl Family
    guinea fowl
    eggs
126 Turkey Family
    turkey
    eggs

127 Mammals

128 Opossum Family
    opossum
129 Hare Family
    rabbit
130 Squirrel Family
    squirrel
131 Whale Family
    whale
132 Bear Family
    bear
133 Horse Family
    horse
134 Swine Family
    hog (pork)
    bacon
    ham
    lard
    pork gelatin
    sausage
    scrapple

135 Deer Family
    caribou
    deer (venison)
    elk
    moose
    reindeer
136 Pronghorn Family
    antelope
137 Bovine Family
    beef cattle
      beef
      beef by-products
        gelatin
        oleomargarine
        rennin (rennet)
        sausage casings
        suet
      milk products
        butter
        cheese
        ice cream
        lactose
        spray dried milk
        yogurt
      veal
    buffalo (bison)
    goat (kid)
      cheese
      ice cream
      milk
    sheep (domestic)
      lamb
      mutton
      Rocky Mountain
        sheep

Reference:

1. Natalie Golos and Frances Golos Golbitz, <u>If This is Tuesday, It Must be Chicken</u> (New Canaan, CT: Keats Publishing, Inc., 1983) 100–117.

APPENDIX B: Rotational Food Plan

The recipes in this cookbook follow the rotational food plan that follows with a few unassigned Fun Foods listed below (see explanation on page 64).

    5–pine nut   10–pineapple   17–ginger   20–vanilla   26–macadamia nut
    33–nutmeg   44 flax (oil, seed, meal)   50–maple   59–papaya
    62–Brazil nut   63–allspice and clove

Day 1 Foods

Grains & Flours

6	brown rice, spelt, Kamut® teff, wheat

Higher Carbohydrate Vegetables

36	turnip

Lower Carbohydrate Vegetables

6	bamboo shoots
7	Chinese water chestnut
28	chard
36	broccoli, cabbage, radish, collards, bok choy
65	celery, fennel, parsley*

Animal Protein

88	catfish
98	tuna
103	halibut, sole
124	chicken, chicken egg, Cornish hen, pheasant, quail

Fruits

40a	pear
40b	apricot, peach, nectarine
40c	raspberry, strawberry

Sweeteners

6	brown rice syrup 40a pear

Oils

40b	almond oil
75	sesame oil

Herbs & Spices

34	cinnamon*
36	dry mustard
65	dill, cumin, parsley*

Seeds & Nuts

22	pecan
40a	almond
75	sesame seeds

Day 2 Foods

Nongrains & Flours

19	arrowroot starch
30	amaranth
41	garbanzo bean flour (chickpea)
74	potato starch

Higher Carbohydrate Vegetables

41	garbanzo (chickpea), lima beans
74	potato 79 pumpkin**

Lower Carbohydrate Vegetables

11	onion
54	okra
74	tomato, peppers, eggplant
79	spaghetti, zucchini, patty pan and yellow squash, cucumber**
80	lettuce, radicchio

Animal Protein

82	shrimp, crab, prawn, lobster
87	cod (scrod), pollack
129	rabbit
137	beef, buffalo, plain yogurt
n/a	red snapper

Fruits

16	banana, plantain
45	grapefruit, lemon
56	kiwi 79 melons

Sweeteners

12	agave nectar

Oils

69	olive oil 80 sunflower oil
137	butter, ghee (clarified butter)

Herbs & Spices

11	garlic** 80 dahlia root (Dacopa)
73	oregano,** basil, marjoram, sage, rosemary, savory, thyme,
74	chili powder,** paprika cayenne (red) pepper

Seeds & Nuts

79	pumpkin seeds**
80	sunflower seeds

*Foods that float between Days 1 and 3   **Foods that float between Days 2 and 4

Day 3 Foods

Grains & Flours

6	barley, corn, millet, oat, rye, wild rice
28	quinoa
47	tapioca starch
52	cream of tartar (see page 252)

Higher Carbohydrate Vegetables

28	beets
36	rutabaga
65	parsnips

Lower Carbohydrate Vegetables

28	spinach
36	cauliflower, Brussels sprout, kale kohlrabi
65	carrots, parsley*

Animal Protein

103	flounder, turbot
106	salmon, trout
121	duck, goose
126	turkey, turkey egg

Fruits

34	avocado
40a	apple 40b plum, prune, cherry
52	raisin, grape

Sweeteners

28	FOS—NutriFlora™
40a	apple

Oils

8	coconut oil 22 walnut oil
52	grapeseed oil

Herbs & Spices

34	cinnamon,* bay leaf
65	parsley,* caraway, cilantro, coriander

Seeds & Nuts

22	walnut 23 filbert (hazelnut)

*Foods that float between Days 1 and 3

Day 4 Foods

Nongrains & Flours

1	agar agar, kombu
27	buckwheat
41	carob powder, kudzu (kuzu), legume flours, soy flour, guar gum
80	Jerusalem artichoke flour

Higher Carbohydrate Vegetables

41	peas, lentils, soy (tofu), beans (see family list on page 218)
70	sweet potato
79	pumpkin,** acorn, butternut & other starchy squash

Lower Carbohydrate Vegetables

11	asparagus, leeks 27 sorrel
41	green beans, bean sprouts, alfalfa sprouts
79	cucumber**
80	artichoke, dandelion

Animal Protein

87	haddock	130	squirrel
91	sea bass, grouper	134	pork
95	mahi mahi	135	venison
102	ocean perch	137	lamb, goat
n/a	orange roughy		

Fruits

27	rhubarb
45	orange, tangerine, tangelo
66	blueberry, cranberry

Sweeteners

27	buckwheat honey 41 clover honey
80	stevia

Oils

41	soy oil
80	safflower oil

Herbs & Spices

11	garlic** 80 tarragon
73	oregano,** peppermint
74	chili powder**

Seeds & Nuts

48	cashew 79 pumpkin seeds**

**Foods that float between Days 2 and 4

Foods for Day ___

Grains/Nongrains & Flours

Higher Carbohydrate Vegetables

Lower Carbohydrate Vegetables

Animal Protein

Fruits

Sweeteners

Oils

Herbs & Spices

Seeds & Nuts

Foods for Day ___

Grains/Nongrains & Flours

Higher Carbohydrate Vegetables

Lower Carbohydrate Vegetables

Animal Protein

Fruits

Sweeteners

Oils

Herbs & Spices

Seeds & Nuts

APPENDIX C: Rotational Meal Ideas

This appendix provides menu ideas that support the recipes and rotational food plan in this cookbook. The menus that fit Stage 2 are marked with an open bullet. Each menu falls into one of the following categories:

"Travel" or Lunch "At Work" Meal Ideas include a variety of foods that can be "carried" via insulated containers to keep them at the proper temperature (hot or cold).

Quick & Easy Meal Ideas can be prepared in approximately 30 minutes. The actual time varies somewhat depending on the quantity of vegetables being prepared. A few take slightly longer (average time is indicated).

Quick & Easy w/ Pre-Prep Meal Ideas can be prepared in 30 minutes or less with the use of advanced preparation. These pre-prep steps are often "extras" from other meals. The recipes in the cookbook alert you to the items that are suggested for pre-prep with this symbol ☑. Just a little advanced planning creates a wide variety of ideas.

Breakfast Ideas include foods such as cereals and breads (i.e., pancakes, muffins, biscuits) that make excellent breakfast choices along with ideas for adding vegetables and/or a protein source instead of eating only carbohydrates to start your day. Everyone's metabolism is different so you can adjust what you prepare for breakfast.

Snack Ideas for times between meals when you need a little something to carry you through.

Easy Meal Ideas take longer from start to finish, but often the actual time spent in the kitchen is very short. The longer time is usually due to cooking style and required cooking time (i.e., baking in the oven, slow cooker, simmering time to blend flavors).

Special Occasion Meal Ideas are for special times (i.e., brunches, potlucks, company). Healthy eating and rotation do not need to be "tossed out the window" for guests but sometimes it is okay to lax up on rotation and enjoy a treat.

Sondra's Experience

For Breakfast: When I was in the "throws" of fighting yeast and food allergies, I felt better if I ate the extra vegetables and protein sources from the previous evening's meal along with a small amount of carbohydrates. This also allowed me to have higher carbohydrate foods for my snacks.

- - - - -

For Snacks: I attempted to keep several varieties of crackers in the freezer.

Using the Rotation in This Cookbook

Spend time familiarizing yourself with the following:

- List of foods assigned to each Day in Appendix B (pages 221–223)
- Recipes, especially noting those that are "wetting your appetite"
- Meal planning ideas on the pages to follow, making note of those that appeal to your time for meal preparation. If your timing allows for meal preparation a few minutes here and there or in the morning (i.e., slow cooker meals) you might prefer those under the Easy Meal category. If you would rather prepare the meal in 30 minutes or less from start to finish, concentrate on the Quick & Easy ideas as well as the Quick & Easy w/ Pre-Prep Meal Ideas.

> Real situations do not always go as planned. Do not be too hard on yourself!

4 Steps to Enjoying Meals on Rotation

On a sheet of paper, prepare a chart with 5 columns and 6 rows, titled as below. Notice I am using the Dinner/Breakfast/Lunch rotation day format (see page 59) as it allows for breakfast when time is at a minimum and easier planning for lunches away from home.

	Day 1	Day 2	Day 3	Day 4
Dinner				
Breakfast				
Snack				
Lunch				
Snack				

1. Begin with your family meals. Depending upon your discoveries when doing the bullet list above, choose the category (or categories) of meals you desire to prepare (i.e., Quick & Easy, Easy, Quick & Easy w/ Pre-Prep Meal Ideas). Write in meal ideas for those family meals. Next, plan the lunches and breakfast meals using as much as possible of the "extras" from the evening meal. Select some snacks. Congratulations, this big step is done. Some may prefer to set up another 4 days but I suggest that you just repeat Days 1–4. (Special Note: when planning for the next grocery week, begin with the next rotation Day in the cycle.)

> **Success**
>
> Plan Your "Work"
> and
> Work Your Plan!

2. Using your plans, "flag" the recipes and create your shopping list.

3. Set your starting date, purchase your supplies and take the plunge.

4. **REPEAT ACTION STEP:** Repeat the steps a couple of days before your next shopping day. Evaluate your menu plans, expanding your horizons (choosing new recipes, altering/creating new menu plans).

 Seek Support

"Travel" or Lunch "At Work" Meal Ideas

(carry in insulated containers to keep warm/cold)

Day 1

o Chicken Turnip Soup w/ Teff Crackers OR Muffin

o Egg OR Chicken Salad on Teff Tortilla/Griddle Bread w/ chard celery sticks

o Tortilla Sandwich w/ "extra" Grilled or Roasted Chicken and chard fresh broccoli buds OR Coleslaw

o Easy Chicken Meal—take to work in a 1-quart slow cooker ready to plug in and cook for 4 hours

o All-in-One Salad (Chicken) w/ Teff Crackers or Muffin

o "extra" casserole OR soup

Day 2

o Day 2 soups w/ or w/o Amaranth Crackers
Cucumber slices

o Amaranth Tortilla w/ "extra" Roast Beef & tomato slices
green pepper strips

o Day 2 Mixed Salads tossed w/ Garbanzo Beans

o Potato Salad w/ "extra" Roast Beef & green pepper strips

o "extra" spaghetti or stew

o All-in-One Salad w/ Amaranth Crackers

Day 3

• Turkey Parsnip Soup w/ Pesto and Quinoa Crackers

o All-in-One Salad (Turkey or Salmon) w/ Qunioa Muffin

• Quinoa Tortilla w/ "extra" Roast Turkey & fresh spinach
Vegetable/Apple Salad

o Cauliflower Chowder
Carrot sticks

o 3 Color Salad w/ Quinoa Biscuit, Muffin or Crackers

• "extra" Turkey Loaf as sandwich on Quinoa Griddle Bread
raw cauliflower buds

Day 4

o Beans & Beans
Cucumber slices

o Quick Bean Soup
raw Jerusalem artichoke w/ Macadamia Nut "Mayo" as dip

• Cucumber & Pea Salad w/ "extra" Roast Pork

o Venison or Pork & Buckwheat Pasta

o Chili
Raw Jerusalem artichoke w/ Macadamia Nut "Mayo" as dip

o Lentil OR Split Pea Soup w/ "extra" Roast Pork OR Grilled Pork Chop (Lentil is better choice for Stage 2)
zucchini slices (floated from Day 2)

o All-in-One Salad w/ Buckwheat Crackers OR Biscuit

o *Indicates menus that fit Stage 2*
Food ideas that are capitalized indicate specific recipes in this book.

Quick & Easy Meal Ideas

Day 1

- Chicken Stir-Fry w/ pasta
- o Grilled Fish
  Cream of Broccoli Soup
- Pasta Primavera
- o Grilled Chicken Fillet
  Stir-Fry Vegetables
- o Denver Eggs
  Steamed Broccoli
- Vegetarian Spaghetti for Day 1
- o Poached Chicken Meal
- o Poached Fish Dinner

Day 2

- o Steak with Gravy
  mashed potatoes
  lettuce w/ Creamy Dressing
- o ground meat patty
  Creamed Potatoes
  tomato and zucchini slices
- o Sloppy Joes w/ Griddle Bread
  lettuce w/ Easy "C" Dressing
- o Taco Salad
- o Stir-Fry Vegetables (near the end
  add canned garbanzo beans)
- o ground meat patty OR minute steak
  amaranth pasta w/ Basil Pesto
  Sautéed Squash & Sunflower Seeds
- o Poached Fish Dinner

Day 3

- o Egg Drop Soup w/ Quinoa Biscuit
- o Turkey Patty
  wild rice pasta w/ flaxseed oil
  Steamed Spinach
- o Salmon Patty
  Basic Millet w/ Caraway
  spinach salad w/ Easy "C" Dressing
  raw carrot slices
- o Grilled Turkey Fillet
  Quinoa OR Millet Pilaf
  Brussels Sprouts (sautéed)
    OR Kale & Cauliflower
- Grilled Fish
  Steamed Parsnips
  Spinach or Kale w/ flaxseed oil
- o Poached Fish Dinner
  Basic Quinoa
- o Poached Turkey & Vegetable Meal

Day 4

- o Pork Cutlet w/ Gravy
  Peas
  Green Beans
- o Easy Meal Banquet
- o Pork Chop
  Baked Sweet Potato w/ flaxseed oil
  Sautéed Green Beans & Pumpkin
    Seeds
- o grilled venison steak
  Basic Buckwheat Groats
  Asparagus Spears
- Lentil Sloppy Joes (45 min.) w/
    Griddle Breads (sprout garnish)
  Roasted Asparagus Spears
- All-in-One Salad (w/ canned beans)
- o Poached Fish Dinner
- o Orange Roughy w/ Cream of
  Asparagus Soup

o *Indicates menus that fit Stage 2*
Food ideas that are capitalized indicate specific recipes in this book.

Quick & Easy w/ Pre-Prep Meal Ideas

Day 1

- Sesame Goulash
- Chicken Spaghetti
- Skillet Chicken Noodle Casserole
- Chicken/Broccoli Mac'n Cheese-Less
- o Grilled Chicken Broccoli Soup w/ Teff Crackers
- o All-in-One Salad for Day 1 (Chicken) w/ Teff Muffin
- o Chicken Salad Wrap w/ chard using one Teff Tortilla or Griddle Bread celery sticks
- o Chicken Collard Soup w/ crackers, muffin or biscuit (Teff for Stage 2)
- o Chicken Patty (use rice) Rice Pilaf and Steamed Broccoli

Day 2

- o Chef Salad w/ Amaranth Crackers
- Garbanzo Bean & Potato Soup green pepper strips
- o Vegetable or Nightshade Beef Soup using beans w/ Amaranth Crackers
- Tacos w/ Amaranth Tortillas
- Garbanzo Bean Patty w/ Garbanzo Bean Griddle Bread lettuce salad w/ Easy "C" Dressing

Day 3

- Millet OR Quinoa Turkey Vegetable Stew w/ Quinoa Biscuit
- o All-in-One Salad (Turkey) w/ Quinoa Muffin
- Turkey Parsnip Soup or Turkey Kale Soup w/ Quinoa Crackers or Muffin
- Turkey Salad w/ spinach on Quinoa Tortilla Beets
- Salmon Salad w/ spinach on purchased sourdough rye bread Vegetable/Apple Salad
- Quinoa Tortilla w/ Roast Turkey Kale & Cauliflower
- o Creamed Turkey on Quinoa Biscuit
- o 3 Color Salad OR 3 Color Stir-Fry
- o Salmon Millet Dinner
- o All-in-One Salad (Turkey/Quinoa)

Day 4

- o Stir-Fry Buckwheat & Vegetables with Meat
- Lentil Patty (45 min.) w/ Legume Griddle Bread Steamed Peapods
- o Ham & Bean Stew
- o Pork & Buckwheat Pasta
- Pork Fajita Sauteed Green Beans & Pumpkin Seeds
- o Venison & Buckwheat Pasta
- o Venison & Bean Stew
- Pork & Bean Burritos
- Black Bean Patty w/ Griddle Bread Roasted Asparagus Spears

o *Indicates menus that fit Stage 2*
Food ideas that are capitalized indicate specific recipes in this book.

Breakfast Ideas

See pages 28, 35, 59, 129, 168 and 225 for more ideas and
"Sondra's Experience" on page 225.

Day 1

o Teff Pancakes, Muffin or Cereal

• Kamut® or Spelt Muffins, Pancakes, Biscuits or Cereals.

• French Toast

o Purchased — hot rice cereals

• Purchased — puffed or flaked cold cereals (watch ingredients) w/ "Milks"

o Purchased puffed rice w/ "Milks"

• fresh fruit

• rice cake w/ almond butter OR tahini

o "extra" vegetable, fish, casserole and/or soup

o Hard-Boiled Egg w/ Teff "Bread"

o Scrambled Eggs w/ Bok Choy

o Denver Eggs

Day 2

o Amaranth Cereal

o Amaranth Griddle Bread (serve as pancake) w/ flaxseed oil

• Amaranth Griddle Bread w/ mashed kiwi (creating a sauce)

• fresh fruit

• Yogurt Delight

o "extra" vegetable, fish, casserole and/or soup

o Fried Potatoes w/ onions & green peppers

Day 3

o Quinoa Pancakes or Rice/Oat Pancakes

o Quinoa or Oat Biscuits

o Quinoa or Oat Cereals

o Millet Cereals

o Purchased — puffed millet cold cereal w/ "Milks"

• Purchased — hot barley cereal

• fresh fruit

o "extra" vegetable, fish, casserole and/or soup

• Millet Pudding

• Quinoa Pudding

Day 4

o Buckwheat Muffins, Pancakes, Bread or Cereal

o Lentils w/ pork chop or uncured bacon

• Split Pea Soup w/ pork chop or uncured bacon

o Stir-Fry Buckwheat & Vegetables

• fresh fruit

o "extra" vegetable, fish, casserole and/or soup

o Baked Sweet Potato OR butternut squash w/ flaxseed oil & pumpkin seeds

o *Indicates menus that fit Stage 2*
Food ideas that are capitalized indicate specific recipes in this book.

Snack Ideas

Day 1

o broccoli buds OR radishes

o celery stuffed w/ almond butter OR tahini

o brown rice cakes w/ tahini OR almond butter

o Teff Muffin

• Kamut® or Spelt Muffins

• Kamut® or Spelt Crackers

o Teff Crackers

• purchased — puffed Kamut®

• Almond-Sesame Granola Bars

• Amazing Sugarless Cookies

o almonds OR pecans

• fresh fruit

• Pear Crisp

Day 2

o green pepper strips

o cucumber slices

o zucchini slices

o sliced tomatoes

o Amaranth Crackers

o Soy Bread

o sunflower seeds

o Amaranth Carob Cookies

• Yogurt Delight

• Grapefruit Spritzer (on occasion)

• fresh fruit

Day 3

o carrot sticks

o cauliflower buds

o Quinoa Muffins

o Quinoa Crackers

o filberts or walnuts

• Oatmeal Cookies

• Oat OR Quinoa Biscuits w/ applesauce & cinnamon

• Apple Salad

• Apple Oat OR Quinoa Crisp

• Millet OR Quinoa Pudding

• fresh fruit

Day 4

o cucumber slices

o Buckwheat Muffin or Bread

o Buckwheat Crackers

o pumpkin seeds

o Carob Cake Brownies

• Buckwheat Bread w/ Rhubarb Jelly (my favorite)

• Blueberry Tofu "Cheesecake"

• Orange Buckwheat Cake

o Carob Pudding

o Soy Protein Shake

• Spritzer—3 varieties (on occasion)

• fresh fruit

o *Indicates menus that fit Stage 2*
Food ideas that are capitalized indicate specific recipes in this book.

Easy Meal Ideas

Day 1

o Oven Fried Chicken
  Brown Rice & Chard
  Coleslaw

• Chicken Patty (Spelt)
  Rice Pilaf
  Steamed Broccoli

o Easy Chicken Meal or Soup

o Baked Fish for Day 1
  Basic Brown Rice
  Stir-Fry Vegetables

• Roast Chicken
  Dill "Stove Top" Stuffing
  Steamed Collards

o Stir-Fry Chicken
  Basic Brown Rice

Day 2

o Spicy Baked Fish
  Garbanzo Beans & Broth
  Lettuce w/ Cr. Italian Salad Dressing

o Spaghetti Squash w/ Spaghetti Meat
    Sauce OR Meatballs in Sauce
  Lettuce w/ Lemon-Oil Dressing

o Easy Steak Dinner served over
    Garbanzo Beans & Broth
  cucumber slices

o Chili w/ green pepper strips

o Minestrone Soup w/ Baked Fish

• Pizza
  lettuce w/ Cr. Italian Salad Dressing

o Beef Stew

o Grilled Steak w/ small baked potato
  Artichoke w/ lemon oil dip

Day 3

o Spinach Chef Salad w/ Creamy
    Dressing and Quinoa Muffin OR
    Crackers

• Turkey Barley Soup w/ Rye Crackers

o Baked Fish
  Stir-Fry Vegetables
  rye pasta tossed w/ flaxseed oil &
    Cilantro Pesto

• Turkey Quinoa Pasta Stew
  Apple Quinoa Crisp

o Rainbow Trout
  Basic Millet OR Pilaf
  spinach salad w/ Creamy Dressing

Day 4

o Breaded Pork Chop
  Stir-Fry Vegetables
  Baked Beans

o Squash & Meatballs
  Green Beans

o Roast Pork OR Venison
  Basic Buckwheat Groats
  Green Beans OR Asparagus Spears

o Tomato-Free Chili
  Green Beans

• Tofu & Asparagus in Black Bean
    Sauce

o Lentil Casserole
  cucumber slices

o Amazing Spaghetti Sauce w/
    buckwheat soba pasta or
    mung bean pasta

o *Indicates menus that fit Stage 2*
Food ideas that are capitalized indicate specific recipes in this book.

Special Occasion Meal Ideas

Day 1

- BRUNCH—Breakfast Brunch
  Squares
  celery stuffed w/ almond butter
  Dacopa
- COMPANY—Oven Fried Chicken
  Wild & Brown Rice w/ Herbs
  Steamed Broccoli and/or Coleslaw
  Pear Custard
  Dacopa
- o POTLUCK—
  Oven Fried Chicken (cold)
  Coleslaw
  sparkling mineral water

Day 3

- BRUNCH—Egg Soufflé
  carrot sticks
  Biscuits w/ applesauce
    OR Apple Crisp
  Pau D'Arco Tea
- EASY THANKSGIVING FEAST—
  Cranberry Spritzer (from Day 4)
  Roasted Turkey
  Dill "Stove Top" Stuffing (from Day 1)
  Steamed Broccoli, Cauliflower and/
    or carrots (broccoli from Day 1)
  Apple Salad
  Kamut® Dinner Rolls (from Day 1)
  Pumpkin Pie
  Dacopa
- LUNCHEON w/ GRANDPARENT—
  Chowder (cauliflower/salmon)
  raw carrot slices
  Oat Granola Bar
  Iced Pau D'Arco tea

Day 2

- o COMPANY—Grilled steak
  baked potato w/ Cr. Italian Salad
    Dressing (replaces sour cream)
  Artichoke w/ lemon oil dip
  lettuce w/ Cr. Italian Salad Dressing
  Carob Amaranth Cookies
  sparkling mineral water
  Dacopa
- COMPANY—Tofu Lasagna
  lettuce w/ Lemon-Oil Dressing
  Zucchini Amaranth Cookies
  Iced Pau D'Arco tea
- o PICNIC—grilled hamburgers w/
    Catsup and Amaranth Bun
  Potato Salad OR Kidney Bean Salad
  mixed greens, cucumber & tomato
    w/ Cr. Italian Salad Dressing
  Carob Amaranth Cookies
  sparkling mineral water

Day 4

- o CHILI FEAST—
  Choice of 1 or more of the following:
  —Mexican Medley Beans
  —Tomato-Free Chili
  —Veggie Chili
  raw vegetables floated/moved from
    other Days
  Carob Cake Brownies
  Dacopa
- COMPANY—
  Shrimp Tofu Lasagna
  Blueberry Tofu "Cheesecake"
  Dacopa

o *Indicates menus that fit Stage 2*
Food ideas that are capitalized indicate specific recipes in this book.

APPENDIX D: Know Your Ingredients

If you are eating on rotation, allergic to foods such as wheat and corn or are simply interested in diversifying, alternative grains/nongrains, starches and sweeteners offer several options. This appendix provides brief descriptions about these lower allergen foods, including their nutritional properties and interesting stories about their origin and uses today. They are listed in alphabetical order within each subgroup: Grains, Nongrains, Starches, Alternative "Sugars" and Miscellaneous Foods. These foods are available in health-food stores and from mail-order sources (see resource list on www.canaryconnect.com). A growing number of these foods are now also available in large local and chain grocery stores.

Introduction to Grains & Nongrains

Whole grains have been staple foods for thousands of years in almost all cultures. Today they are a common source of carbohydrates and an inexpensive source of protein.

Whole grains are seeds that contain three natural components:
- bran layer: a tough coating rich in fiber and minerals that protects the grain
- germ: contains vitamin E, essential fatty acids and proteins that provide food for the plant seed to sprout and develop a root system
- endosperm: the starchy bulk layer of the grain, rich in complex carbohydrates and proteins, that nourishes the seedling during the early growth period before the leaves begin photosynthesis

Barley, bamboo shoots, corn, Kamut®, millet, oat, rice, rye, sorghum, spelt, sugar cane, molasses, teff, triticale, wheat and wild rice are all part of the Grass Family though all are not true cereal grains. Buckwheat, quinoa and amaranth come from separate families and are differentiated as nongrains, even though they act like and are prepared like a grain in whole and flour form.

Refined grains have been degermed or polished, which removes the germ and bran layers and lowers the nutritional value. For example, "pearled" barley is a refined product that has undergone six scourings between Carborundam wheels. As a result, the barley loses between 74% to 97% of its protein, fat, fiber and minerals.[1] Another example of a refined grain is the white (wheat) flour prevalent in American diets. Wheat loses up to 80% of its nutrients in the refining process. Even though these products are advertised as "enriched", more than twenty nutrients have been removed and only four are added back—thiamin, niacin, riboflavin and iron.[2] Refined flours are also subjected to a bleaching process which destroys the essential amino acids or protein.

An Understanding of Gluten

Some flours have gluten, a type of protein that makes bread rise. The gluten-containing grains are wheat and other wheat relatives (spelt and Kamut®), rye and barley. There is a debate if oat is gluten or gluten-free (see short discussion on www.canaryconnect.com).

Celiacs are unable to digest gluten. The undigested gluten erodes the intestinal villi and can cause abdominal symptoms (i.e., gas pain, bloating, cramping).[3] The intestinal villi are very important for the absorption of soluble nutrients in our body. Celiacs continuing to ingest gluten show signs of malnourishment regardless of the quality of their diets.

According to the Rodale Research Center, all grains and grain-like foods do contain some traces of gluten. However, the essentially gluten-free grains and nongrains should be tolerated by celiacs. The gluten in these foods is bound and unavailable to enter into reactions within the body.[4] These grains/nongrains are amaranth, buckwheat, corn, millet, quinoa, rice, sorghum, teff and wild rice.

Grains

Kamut® (Grass Family, #6)

Kamut® (pronounced Kah-moot) is a gluten-containing grain related to durum wheat. Kamut® is higher in nutritional value than other strains of wheat, with 30% more protein than common wheat varieties and a higher percentage of most minerals, especially magnesium and zinc. Kamut® contains higher levels of 16 of the 18 amino acids found in wheat and has significantly higher levels of all of the major fatty acids. Many wheat-sensitive persons can tolerate Kamut®, especially on a rotational basis, however, a food challenge is recommended (see pages 33, 52 and 62).

It is believed that Kamut® originated near the Tigris and Euphrates in ancient Egypt. In 1949, a U.S. airman stationed in Portugal was given 36 kernels and told that they were gathered from an Egyptian pyramid excavated tomb. Intrigued, the airman mailed the seeds to his father, a Montana wheat farmer, who germinated 32 of the seeds and within 6 years had 1,500 bushels.* It received some local attention at the county fair as "King Tut's Wheat," but eventually the novelty diminished, and it went to cattle feed. Kamut® was all but forgotten until 1977, when a Montana agricultural scientist and wheat farmer, Bob Quinn, Ph.D., and his father searched to find some of the ancient grain. For the next ten years, they carefully selected and propagated it on their Montana ranch and named (and registered a trademark for) the grain Kamut®, an ancient Egyptian word for wheat.

Unlike modern-day wheat, Kamut® has not been hybridized and "scientifically improved." Since it is self-pollinating, it can grow in a field right next to common wheat and not interbreed or "cross" with it. The plants grown today are replications of the ancient ones. Kamut® has a wonderful, rich and almost-buttery taste. It is commonly found as whole grain berries, flakes, puffed cereal, prepared breakfast cereal, a flour and pastas. Kamut® flour resembles finely ground cornmeal and produces golden brown baked goods. The pasta has a delicious firm texture. The flakes have an appearance similar to oatmeal and can be cooked as hot cereal or used for recipes such as granola bars and "stove-top" stuffing.

*The source of the kernels is questionable since there is no documentation that ancient and mummified seeds found in the pyramids are able to grow.

Millet (Grass Family, #6)

Millet is a small, yellow, gluten-free seed. It has the most complete protein of all true cereal grains and is rich in iron, potassium, calcium and B-vitamins. When cooked, millet has alkaline properties, making it one of the best grains good for healing gastrointestinal irregularities and thrush. Many who do not tolerate other grains can eat millet without experiencing allergic reactions.

The millet plant is hardy, surviving most growing conditions and appearing in 6,000 variations around the world. Today, it is a major food source in Asia and North Africa.

Millet is available as a hulled grain, a flour, flakes and puffed cereal. Since millet turns rancid quickly after hulling, it should be stored in the refrigerator or freezer. Millet can be cooked to a range of textures, from soft and dry to creamy. Dry roasting millet before cooking enhances its flavor and helps to blend in the flavors of other combined foods. Millet flour can be used in baking, but being gluten-free, it must be used with egg, another binding agent or a gluten grain for the end product to hold together. Herbs, spices, broths and fruits enhance the light sweet flavor of millet.

Rice (Grass Family, #6)

Rice is a gluten-free grain and the second most-produced food in the world. Natural rice is a great source of B-vitamins and very popular with people who cannot tolerate wheat. There are many varieties available in a range of colors.

Rice originated in India, Southeast Asia and China around 4000 B.C. Today it is grown in many parts of the world, including the United States.

Brown rice is available in many forms including whole grain, flour, puffed, rice cakes, flakes, pastas and creamy hot cereal. Brown rice flour has a drier consistency than wheat flour. Choose brown rice products over white as the processed white rice products have the natural vitamins and fiber removed. Rice has a rather plain flavor that provides an excellent canvas waiting to be colored with other foods and spices; the only limiting factor is the imagination of the cook.

Spelt (Grass Family, #6)

Spelt is a gluten-containing grain related to wheat. It is among the first original, natural grains known to man. One of spelt's most outstanding features is its high nutritional value. It contains all of the basic materials for a healthy body, including fats, carbohydrates, vitamins, trace elements, minerals and up to 40% more protein and 65% more of several amino acids than commercial wheat. Spelt is particularly rich in B-vitamins and in polyunsaturated fats (essential fatty acids). The nutrients in spelt dissolve rapidly in liquid and require a minimum amount of digestive work. Many wheat-sensitive persons tolerate this delicious grain but since spelt and wheat are closely related[5] a food challenge is recommended (see pages 33, 52 and 62).

Mentioned by name in the Bible, spelt originated in central Asia and was brought to Europe more than 9,000 years ago. Today, it remains very popular in Europe where it is considered a "gourmet" food. Spelt is not a hybrid like commercial wheat. It can be grown without fertilizer and pesticides, requires a minimum amount of care and grows in varying terrains and any climate, even those with difficult winters. Due to its resistance, spelt is not sensitive to typical grain diseases. The spelt kernel is tightly surrounded by a strong husk or hull, which must be removed before the grain can be used for cooking. This protective covering guards the spelt grain against all types of pollutants in the air, even radioactive fallout. It also protects the grain during storage, ensuring the freshest possible product after dehulling and milling.

Spelt has a nutty flavor similar to whole wheat. It may be found in several forms such as whole grain, flour, flakes and pasta as well as white spelt flour. The whole-grain spelt flour is an excellent substitute for whole-wheat flour in recipes (see Appendix G: Substitutions). Since white (refined) flours are not recommended for those with CRC, all recipes in this cookbook use whole-grain spelt flour.

Teff (Grass Family, #6)

Teff is an ancient, gluten-free grain. The overall nutrition of teff is superior to all cereal grains, including spelt, having as much as five times the amount of iron, calcium and potassium. Teff is high in copper, zinc and protein as well as soluble and insoluble fiber. The word teff means "lost" and is appropriate since the seeds are very tiny. The smallest of the grains, it takes 150 teff grains to equal one wheat kernel. Because teff is in a subgroup by itself, separate from other members of the Grass Family, many who do not tolerate other grains can eat teff without experiencing allergic reactions.

Teff comes from Ethiopia where it has been used and loved for thousands of years. When Wayne Carlson was a Public Health worker in Ethiopia, he learned about and enjoyed eating teff. Upon returning to the United States, he missed having teff in his diet. Mr. Carlson found a valley in southwestern Idaho with a terrain and climate similar to that of Ethiopia and successfully grows teff there today. There are many varieties of teff, but only brown, ivory and red are grown in the United States. Because the grains are easily lost in the fields, harvesting is very labor intensive. Teff is also cultivated in Kenya and Australia for its hay.

Teff grain is dried for cooking into cereal or for grinding into flour. Teff's mild, pleasing, slightly molasses-like flavor is so delicate and versatile it allows the flavor of other ingredients to come through. Cooked teff grain has a gelatinous texture. Brown or red teff makes a rich porridge and ivory teff makes a milder creamy cereal. The flour can be used in crackers, tortillas, muffins, pancakes and desserts. Most teff recipes contain ingredients such as gluten-containing grain, eggs, starch, sweetener and/or milk. However, this book includes several recipes that do not contain these extra ingredients. Some of my favorite teff recipes include crackers, pancakes and as breading on Oven Fried Chicken.

Wild Rice (Grass Family, #6)

While wild rice is a member of the Grass Family (#6), it is in a different subgroup from rice and is technically an aquatic grass seed, not a true cereal grain. It is brown-black in color, very thin and can be as long as one inch in length. Wild rice has a greater concentration of B-vitamins, magnesium and zinc than cultivated rice, is low in fat and has one of the highest protein contents among grains. It is also rich in carbohydrates, which are easily converted to energy in the body.

Wild rice is indigenous to the lakes and rivers of Minnesota and Canada where it is still harvested today. It has been a staple food of the Chippewa Indians and an important part of their heritage for centuries. Because wild rice is harvested by hand, its price reflects its scarcity and labor-intensive processing. Considered a gourmet food by many, wild rice aficionados maintain that it is well worth the cost.

Wild rice is available in the whole grain and in 100% wild-rice pasta. It has a very strong flavor so a little goes a long way when it is included in recipes. As it cooks, the grain opens to show a soft white-gray inside against a curling brown-black cover. A favorite wild-rice recipe is Wild and Brown Rice with Herbs (depicted on the front cover).

Nongrains

Amaranth (Pigweed Family, #30)

Amaranth is a gluten-free seed (nongrain). As small as poppy seeds, amaranth seeds range in color from tan to black. They contain a high level of vegetable protein, a good balance of amino acids and are especially high in lysine. Lower in carbohydrates than grains, amaranth is rich in vitamins and minerals, including vitamin B complex, iron, calcium and phosphorus. Many who are allergic to grains tolerate it, however, if you are allergic to the pigweed pollen, you could have a sensitivity to amaranth.

Amaranth originated with the Aztecs in Mexico and South America. In 1521, Cortez banned amaranth as part of his quest to destroy the Aztec culture and it nearly vanished. However, in 1972 a botanical team found it growing wild in Mexico. They collected some of the seeds and were successful in growing it in the United States. Amaranth was also known in ancient China and today China is its major producer. Amaranth means immortality and is appropriately named considering its history.

Amaranth seeds can be ground into flour for baking, dried for cooking or used as a thickening agent. Amaranth can be purchased in many forms, including whole seed, flour, roasted bran flour, puffed (popped) and amaranth breadcrumbs. Amaranth has a nutty, slightly sweet flavor that is intensified if the seed is dry-roasted before cooking. Too many black seeds can add a bitter taste. The cooked whole seeds have a gelatinous texture and are coated with a thick, shiny film that makes them shimmer, giving the appearance of caviar. Puffed amaranth, very high in dietary fiber, is used as a breading, snack or texturizer in recipes such as cookies or granola. Amaranth flour is very fine and delicate and can be used for crackers, tortillas and griddle breads as well as buns and muffins.

The home gardener can grow amaranth for the nutritious leaves. As the leaves are harvested (picking from the heavy center stalk), they grow back and the plant produces fewer seeds.

Buckwheat (Polygonaceae—sometime known as Buckwheat—Family, #27)

Buckwheat is a gluten-free nongrain and is not related to wheat. Buckwheat is a blood-building food that neutralizes toxic acidic wastes. The fruit of the plant is a triangular-shaped seed covered with a protective hard outer black hull. This fruit, called groats, is white with hints of green, gray and tan. Buckwheat groats are rich in B-vitamins, especially thiamin and riboflavin, have large amounts of vitamin E, are rich in phosphorus and potassium and are high in iron and calcium. Buckwheat is the best food source of rutin, a bioflavonoid, which functions in the body to strengthen the walls of the blood vessels and help prevent arteriosclerosis. A good source of protein, buckwheat has seven usable amino acids, is especially high in lysine and is best complemented by combining with peas and beans.

Originally, buckwheat came from the plains of China and Siberia. The Chinese cultivated this ancient nongrain for hundreds of years before traders took it from Asia to Europe. Then early-American settlers transported it to the United States. By the 1800s it was an important crop in the United States, but wheat and corn became more widely used and buckwheat faded in popularity. Buckwheat is the basis of many delicious whole-food dishes in Asia and Europe (piroshki, kasha varnishkas, kasha knishes) and in Japanese cuisine, mostly in the form of a pasta called soba. A field of fragrant blossoms attracts many bees to produce buckwheat honey, which is darker and stronger in flavor than clover honey.

When getting used to the flavor of buckwheat, begin by eating raw groats. Buckwheat has a strong earthy flavor, which is enhanced with roasting. Roasted buckwheat groats (called kasha) become deep brown in color with a strong aroma and flavor. There are three grades of buckwheat flour: whole grain, dark and light. Whole-grain flour is made by grinding groats still covered with the protective outer black hull. Dark buckwheat flour is also made by using hull-covered groats with additional hulls added for additional fiber. Commercial light buckwheat flour is made from groats with most of the hulls removed. Buckwheat groats are very porous, cook quickly, and can be used as a cereal, in stir-fry or as a potato substitute.

If a reaction to whole-grain or dark buckwheat flour occurs, it may be because the hard outer hull has not been removed and it is adding too much fiber to the diet; the White Buckwheat Flour (see page 171) may prove a better choice. Allergic reactions to buckwheat may also be due to sensitivity to the weed "dock."

Quinoa (Chenopodium or Goosefoot Family, #28)

Quinoa (pronounced keen-wah) is a gluten-free nongrain and is tolerated by many who are allergic to grains. Other members of this family are spinach, beets, chard and lamb's-quarters. Quinoa is a complete protein source, containing all eight essential amino acids and is high in lysine. The National Academy of Sciences has called quinoa "one of the best sources of vegetable protein in the vegetable kingdom." The essential amino acid balance is close to the ideal set by the United Nations Food and Agriculture Organization. Quinoa protein is equal in quality to that of dried milk and close to that of mother's milk. Quinoa is high in vitamin E, B-vitamins, calcium, phosphorus and iron. It is a strengthening food, easily digested and versatile.

Quinoa, meaning "the mother grain," has been cultivated in the Andes Mountains of South America since 3000 B.C. and was named by the Inca Indians for its life-giving properties. They used the whole plant in their daily life. Young plants supplied deep, green, leafy vegetables. The seeds were their staple nourishment. The stalks were used for fuel in high altitude areas where wood was unavailable. The Incas realized quinoa's life-giving properties to such an extent that they encouraged pregnant and lactating mothers to eat quinoa every day for healthy babies and an adequate milk supply. Also, if needed, mothers made a thin gruel for their babies from cooked quinoa flour to supplement their milk. Quinoa was so important to the Incas that it was considered sacred, and as part of their ceremonial rights, the Inca ruler planted the first row each year with a gold planting stick.

In 1982, Steve Gorad, founding president of the Quinoa Corporation, traded an Andean farmer the shirt off his back for quinoa seeds. This launched the Colorado quinoa growing program under the supervision of Colorado State University.

Quinoa seeds have a coating called saponin, which functions as a natural repellent to insects and birds and protects the seed from the high intensity of the altiplano sun. Before cooking, the seeds should be washed two or three times to remove this unharmful, bitter, saponin coating. Interestingly, the Incas saved the foam from washing quinoa to use as shampoo. To remove the bitter saponin coating so the seed can be ground into flour, the Quinoa Corporation developed a system of belts along which they jostle the whole seeds. This method, called pearling, uses friction rather than chemicals to buff off the saponin.

Quinoa has a slightly bland character that can easily be enhanced with vegetables, fruits, meats, etc., to create a delicious, light, fluffy dish. The subtle, nutty taste makes it a great side dish with almost any meal or a pleasant addition to soups, salads and casseroles. Quinoa can be considered a fast food within whole-grain cookery since the seeds cook very quickly. As the whole quinoa cooks, the germ (outside of the grain) unfolds, disclosing a glistening translucent partial spiral. Black quinoa is considered a delicacy like wild rice.

Starches

Arrowroot (Arrowroot Family, #19)

Arrowroot is an edible starch made from the rootstocks of the Maranta arundinacea plant. It is a fine, silky white powder with a faint licorice aroma. Its fine texture allows it to thicken quickly when cooked at low temperatures. When boiled in water, it yields a transparent, odorless, pleasant-tasting jelly. It can also be used as a binding agent, especially in baked goods made from non-gluten flours. Being almost pure starch, arrowroot supplies no vitamins and is very low in protein. It is easily digested and excellent for use by persons requiring a bland, low-salt and/or low-protein diet.

"True" arrowroot is native of Guyana and western Brazil. The plants reach a height of 5–6 feet and have large, arrow-shaped leaves and a few short-stalked white flowers. The plants are harvested when the root tubers are gorged with starch just before the plant's dormant season. The peeled roots are grated in water, dried to a powder and then purified by several washings.

Kudzu (Kuzu) (Legume Family, #41)

Kudzu (also spelled kuzu) is an oriental culinary thickener. Usually sold in a white chunk form, kudzu is a starch powder, which may be used for the same thickening purposes as arrowroot or tapioca starch and as a gelling agent like agar and gelatin.

Kudzu is a tenacious, perennial vine, which thrives in the rugged, volcanic, mountainous terrain and rural regions of Japan, other areas of eastern Asia and in the southeastern United States. For centuries, skilled craftsmen have followed a time-honored process, which takes over 100 days, to extract the kudzu starch. The roots are hand harvested at full maturity during the cold winter months. They are then crushed and the resulting mash is washed and filtered several times, using pure mountain water. The resulting kudzu cakes are set in wooden boxes to dry naturally and are then crumbled into a chunky powder.

In the United States, the primary use of kudzu is for thickening puddings, gravies, clear soups, sauces and jellied fruit desserts. The root adds a subtle sweetness and smoothness to sauces, desserts and confections. Grinding chunks into a powder in the blender makes accurate measuring simpler.

Tapioca (Spurge Family, #47)

Quite nutritious and digestible, tapioca starch is prepared from the root of the cassava plant. The cassava plant is native to the West Indies and to South America. It became a common food in Asia during the 19th century.

Tapioca granules and starch flour are used as a thickener in soups, sauces and puddings. When cooked, granular tapioca swells, thickens and becomes translucent. The familiar granular "pearl" form of tapioca is commonly used in puddings. The fine white tapioca starch flour, similar in behavior and consistency to cornstarch or arrowroot, is used as a binder in baked goods. Tapioca starch flour may be labeled as tapioca starch or tapioca flour.

Alternative "Sugars"

Agave Nectar (Amaryllis Family, #12)

Agave nectar is a natural sweetener extracted from the pineapple-shaped core of the Blue Agave, a cactus-like plant native to Mexico. It is best known for its use in making tequila. With a 90% fruit sugar and 10% glucose content, agave nectar absorbs slowly into the body, decreasing the highs and lows associated with sucrose (sugar) intake, making this a good sweetener for those with CRC as well as for diabetics.

FOS—Fructo-oligo-saccharides (Chenopodium or Goosefoot Family, #28)

FOS (Fructo-oligo-saccharides), a prebiotic, is a fine white powder, about half as sweet as regular sugar with no aftertaste or bitterness. FOS naturally occurs in small amounts in a variety of fruits, vegetables and grains.[6] It is produced commercially by using natural sugar (sucrose, common table sugar) and a special enzyme, which adds an extra molecule to the sucrose. The resulting FOS molecule is too large for humans to digest,[7] making it essentially noncaloric and having no effect on blood sugar. Over ingestion of FOS (5 teaspoons/day for men, 6 teaspoons/day for women) may result in diarrhea.[8] For more information, see Chapter Four.

Honey (Food Family depends upon source of honey)

Raw (unprocessed) honey, the most commonly used natural sweetener, is 99% naturally predigested and requires little additional processing by the digestive tract, resulting in quick absorption and an energy boost in the body. Since honey is seventy-five percent glucose and fructose, it can upset the blood sugar level as much as sugar does. The darkness or lightness of this thick, sticky syrup indicates how strongly it is flavored by its plant source and how rich it is in mineral content. Darker honeys have a much stronger, more distinctive flavor and contain higher levels of minerals such as iron, copper, sodium, potassium, magnesium, manganese, calcium and phosphorus. In addition, honey contains small amounts of C and B-vitamins, bee protein, enzymes and pollen. Consider avoiding honeys with a base plant source to which you are allergic.

Honey generally is the least chemically-contaminated sweetener available because bees exposed to pesticides usually do not make it back to the hive. Labeling such as "U.S. Grade A" or "Fancy" refers to the level of filtration used in processing and does not give any indication of quality or freedom from chemical contamination. Honey can come from many different floral sources. For rotational purposes, it is very important to know the source of any honey used and to purchase only honey that is labeled with this information. Read the label carefully because it is a common practice to mix different source honeys to create a marketed brand. Also, the least processing is the best for honey. Avoid honey subjected to heat or chemicals or that comes from beehives sprayed with antibiotics or other chemicals. Choose honey that is labeled "undiluted" because some marketed honey is diluted with corn syrup.

Due to its ability to absorb and retain moisture, honey has a "keeping" quality, which retards the drying out that occurs in baked goods. The flavor of baked goods made with honey is actually better the day after baking. Because using honey as a sweetener will add an additional flavor factor to the end product, it is better to use a lighter, more mildly flavored honey when baking.

Almost all honey naturally crystallizes over time. It is easy to liquefy honey by placing the container in a pan of warm water (not hot) until the crystals disappear. This process does not affect the taste or purity of the honey.

Maple Granules and Maple Syrup (Maple Family, #50)

Maple granules are a dehydrated form of 100% pure maple syrup. Maple syrup, a concentrate of maple-tree sap, has long been used as a mainstay natural-food sweetener. Because it is in a family by itself it can easily be assigned and moved to any day in a rotational food plan.

Rice (Brown) Syrup (Grass Family, #6)

Brown rice syrup is an opaque golden liquid with a consistency similar to honey. It has a pleasant, lightly sweet taste and is 20% as sweet as sugar and is excellent to use when only a touch of sweetness is needed.

Quality brown rice syrup (see www.canaryconnect.com) is made by grinding organic brown rice into a meal, cooking it to a slurry and mixing it with a small amount of natural cereal enzymes (less than 1%). This process converts the starches to complex natural sugars (maltoses). The liquid is then squeezed from the slurry and cooked until thickened.

Brown rice syrup may be used to top your favorite pancakes, rice cakes or breads. One of my favorite desserts is the Amazing Sugarless Cookies sweetened with brown rice syrup.

Stevia (Composite Family, #80)

Stevia is a very concentrated, natural herbal sweetener, 100 times sweeter than sugar. With a faintly licorice-like flavor, the white powder extract is the purest form of stevia and is most commonly used in cooking and baking. It is listed in the recipes as stevia powder (see www.canaryconnect.com for suggested brands). It is also available in a liquid extract and as crumbled stevia rebaudiana leaves. Stevia rebaudiana is a small shrub which grows wild near the southern border of Brazil. While a teaspoon of white stevia extract powder has the same sweetening power of 24 cups of sugar, it contains only eight calories. Since it is not absorbed by the body and has such a low caloric content, stevia does not trigger a rise in blood sugar levels. It has been researched extensively since 1899 and found to be completely nontoxic. Stevia has been used effectively in treatment plans for diabetes, high blood pressure and infections, as well as in weight-loss programs.

Stevia has long been used by the Guarani Indian tribes to sweeten teas and foods. In the city of Birigui, Brazil, stevia is so popular that it is used to sweeten milk shakes, juices and coffee in almost all bars and restaurants. The Japanese are using stevia to sweeten their diet foods since all artificial sweeteners are banned in Japan due to their toxic effects. Stevia has not been approved for marketing as a sweetening agent in the United States, but it is available as an herbal supplement.

Stevia is stable at any temperature and is very useful for sweetening everything from beverages to cereals and baked products. Generally only $1/4$ teaspoon of the pure powder extract is needed to sweeten a whole recipe; adding too much stevia can cause a bitter taste. For a cup of tea, a few drops of the liquid form is sufficient. Because of its high potency as a sweetener, it is best to move cautiously at the beginning, starting with slightly less than is called for until you learn how much to use to satisfy your personal taste.

Special Note: Some brands of stevia powder have filler ingredients that may not be acceptable for one using a Candida-Control and/or Rotational Food Plan.

Miscellaneous Foods

Carob (Legume Family, #41)

Carob, an excellent substitute for chocolate or cocoa, is a high-protein, low-fat, low-calorie, caffeine-free tropical bean with three times the calcium as milk. Unlike cocoa, which has a naturally bitter taste, carob's natural sweetness allows you to use much less sweetener while still having the rich cocoa-brown color and consistency. Carob powder is slightly lighter in color than cocoa, but its aroma and flavor are very similar, costing about one-fifth as much as chocolate. Many believe the "locust" mentioned in the Bible as the food John the Baptist ate were carob pods, which is why carob is still known as St. John's bread.

The carob tree is an evergreen, which can reach a height of 50 feet and is found in hot, rainy climates, primarily near the shores of the Mediterranean Sea. Carob trees are also found in the semiarid regions of the United States. The trees require very little pruning, need no spraying because they are remarkably free from fungal diseases and insect pests and generally need no fertilization until the tree begins bearing fruit. The fruit is a fat leathery pod, which contains brown seeds in a sweet pulp. Carob powder in raw or toasted form contains the entire seedpod except for the seeds. The pod is processed into pulp, dried, toasted and pulverized into the final product. Carob seeds are extensively used in the manufacture of gum tragacanth, a widely used food additive. In addition, they are used for animal feed and algarroba oil, which is used for medicinal purposes. Carob seeds, uniform in weight, are thought to have been the original carat weight used by jewelers.

Carob can be used to make baked goods, in place of cocoa. Commercial "carob chips" usually include other ingredients, which are not on the Candida-Control Food Plan.

Clarified Butter (Ghee) (Bovine Family, #137)

Clarified butter (also known as ghee) is the pure oil derived from butter when milk solids are separated and removed and the water is cooked out (butter is over 16% water). Since it does not contain the milk sugar, it is a versatile, beneficial oil even for persons on a dairy-free regimen. Clarified Butter is commercially available under the product name Ghee. However, it is relatively simple to make (see page 97).

In India and the Middle East, ghee has been a staple oil and a practical way to preserve butter for centuries. Often called "royal oil," ghee was used as a medicinal supplement for healthy skin, mental alertness, good digestion and improved memory and was renowned for its rejuvenating properties. Traditional herbal remedies were usually mixed into a small amount of ghee before eaten, allowing herbs to be assimilated into the cells more quickly.

Since clarified butter is a pure oil it may be used as you would other oils. Use it for sautéing and frying since it does not burn or smoke like other oils. Experiment with it, with or without herbs, as a topping for baked potatoes, spaghetti squash, amaranth pasta or fish. Take it along when dining out.

Flax Seeds, Meal and Oil (Flax Family, #44) (For more info, see Chapter 4, page 48.)

Flaxseeds are flat ovals and range in color from light to dark reddish brown or yellow. Flaxmeal (ground flaxseeds) can be purchased or made by grinding the seeds in a blender. They are brown in color and a good source of dietary fiber. Flaxseed oil has a fairly bright yellow color, relatively little odor and a light buttery taste. If you rotate flaxseed, it may be placed on any day because it is in a family by itself.

Flaxseed and flaxseed oil have been used for 5,000 years. However, it is only recently that the extent of its beneficial effects has been uncovered. Flaxseed oil is common in Europe and was common in the United States until the beginning of World War II. Flax is an annual plant grown mostly in the colder regions of the world. Because of the cool, long days common to its northern latitudes, Canada is the world leader in high-quality flax production.

Whole or ground flaxseed can be cooked in water to create a flour binder for use as an egg substitute in baking. Flaxseed oil is excellent for use in salad dressings or to drizzle on foods for a buttery taste (i.e., pancakes, biscuits, cooked vegetables). It can be blended half-and-half with butter or clarified butter to form a "soft" spread.

Heat, light and air (oxygen) must be eliminated during processing and storage for flaxseed oil to maintain its freshness. Flaxseed oil should have an expiration date on the container. Store flaxseed/meal as well as the oil in refrigerator or freezer so it does not go rancid.

Guar Gum (Legume Family, #41)

Guar gum is a fine white powder derived from the seed pod of the guar plant, Cyamopsis tetragonolobus. Guar gum adds fiber to foods and is used commercially as a binder in non-gluten flour baked goods to help them rise and hold moisture. It is also used in the production of ice cream to promote a smooth, soft texture and to keep ice crystals from forming. Because of its highly absorbent character, guar gum thickens instantly when mixed with cold liquid. Since guar gum may actually increase permeability of the intestinal tract, persons with leaky gut should avoid using it.[9]

Kombu (Algae Family, #1)

Kombu is a seaweed that is rich in potassium, calcium and vitamins A and C. It also contains B-vitamins. It has a high sugar content. See page 104 for more information.

Salt

Sea salt is processed from ocean water. "Real Salt" is a mined sea salt, which was originally deposited on the floor of an ancient ocean long before the advent of chemicals (i.e., herbicides, pesticides). It is best to choose (sea or real) salt that is free of dextrose, an additive much more commonly found in table salt.

Tahini (Pedalium Family, #75)

Tahini is a light colored butter made by grinding raw whole or skinned sesame seeds. It has its own interesting flavor, different from the flavor of plain sesame. Tahini can be used to replace peanut butter or jelly as a spread on your favorite muffin or pancake. In addition, it can be used as an egg substitute in baked goods.

Vitamin C Crystals

The texture of unbuffered vitamin C crystals resembles salt. They can be labeled as crystals or unbuffered. The unbuffered crystal form of vitamin C is differentiated from the buffered form of vitamin C in that the buffered form can be used to reduce allergic reactions (see page 56). When purchasing a vitamin C crystal product, be sure to choose a brand that is free of your food allergens.

Unbuffered vitamin C crystals are used for two purposes in recipes. In baking, they act as a leavening agent when used in combination with baking soda, a good substitute for corn-based baking powder. In "mayos" or salad dressings, their tart taste makes them a good replacement for vinegar or citrus juice.

References:

1. Sheila Phillips, <u>Natural Foods Primer: Grains</u>.
2. Phillips.
3. Marjorie Hurt Jones, R.N., <u>Super Foods</u> (Coeur d'Alene: Mast Enterprises, 1990) 27.
4. Marjorie Hurt Jones, R.N., "New Foods and How to Use Them," <u>The Human Ecologist</u>, 52 Winter 1991: 1.
5. Harold M. Friedman, M.D., Robert E. Tortolani, M.D., John Glick, M.D., and Richard T. Burtis, M.D., "Spelt is Wheat," <u>Allergy Proceedings</u>, 15.4 July-Aug. 1994: 217-218.
6. Peter J. Perna, Ph.D., <u>Fructooligosaccharides (FOS) An All Natural Food Which Promotes Bifidobacteria and Lactobacillus</u> (Broomfield: NutraFlora) 1.
7. Perna.
8. Perna.
9. Jones, Marjorie Hurt, R.N., "Leaky Gut—What Is It?," <u>Mastering Food Allergies</u>, X.44.86 July-Aug. 1995: 7.

APPENDIX E: Cook's Glossary

Al dente: describes pasta and/or vegetables that are slightly firm

Bake: to cook in the oven

Beat: to vigorously stir a mixture until smooth, with hand or electric mixer

Blanch: to partially cook in simmering water or over steam for the purpose of halting the natural breakdown of fruits and vegetables. After cooking/steaming, food is transferred to cool water to stop the cooking process. Used to prepare some vegetables for use in stir-fry, salads or for freezing. Also used to loosen skin from certain foods (i.e., tomatoes, peaches).

Blend: to combine ingredients creating a smooth mixture

Broil: to cook foods by placing them just a few inches over or under a hot heat source

Carry-Over Cooking: see pages 81 and 127

Chill: to cool a food or combination of foods quickly by immersing in cold water or placing in the refrigerator

Chop: to cut foods into small pieces (approx. $1/4$–$1/2$ inch). If using a knife instead of a food chopper, choose a knife with a triangular blade. Hold the knife handle with one hand and rest the other hand on the knife's tip. Rock the knife up and down, moving back and forth in an arc, until food is in pieces of desired size OR see garlic (page 74).

Chop & Drop: see page 67

Coat: to use a food (i.e., a seasoning mixture) to cover another food

Core: to remove the center of a fruit or vegetable

Cube: to cut foods into small cubes (approx. $1/2$–1 inch). Begin by slicing food lengthwise; then cut across the lengths to create cubes of desired proportions.

Cut in: to mix fat (butter, solid or liquid oil) into flour with fork, knife or pastry blender

Dash: a sprinkle of seasoning (much less than $1/8$ teaspoon), such as that achieved by gently shaking a seasoning bottle

Deglaze: to make a gravy or broth from the browned drippings of cooked meat by adding liquid to the pan, stirring and briefly heating

Dice: to cut foods into cubes (approx. $1/4$ inch). Begin by slicing foods lengthwise, then cut across the lengths to create irregular cubes.

Drippings: the particles and juices from cooking meats and/or vegetables

Drizzle: to pour a thin stream of liquid over food

Fillet: a boneless piece of meat, fish or poultry; to remove such a piece for cooking

Fold: to gently combine ingredients without stirring

Fry: to cook food in fat (i.e., oil) over medium-high heat

Garnish: to decorate finished dish with attractive, edible ingredient

Glaze: to spread a mixture on a food for the purpose of giving it a glossy appearance

Grill: to broil food over heat source

Knead: to press and stretch dough using your hands in a "fold toward, push away, quarter turn" action to work flour into dough and/or make dough smooth and elastic

Lightly Steamed: to briefly cook foods in a small amount of simmering water to set color and allow to become slightly tender (as in blanching). May use steamer basket, steamer pan or saucepan.

Mince: to finely chop foods (i.e., garlic, fresh herbs)

Par-bake: to partially bake, as with a pizza crust

Peel: to remove the skin of fruits and vegetables

Pinch: a small measure of a seasoning that can be held between your thumb and index finger

Poach: to cook by covering food in simmering liquid (i.e., fish, poultry, eggs)

Prick: to use a fork to make holes in a food before baking (i.e., pie crusts, crackers)

Pull (meat off bones): removing cooked meat from bone in a pulling fashion

Puree: to make a food into a smooth mixture by pressing through a sieve or using a food processor or blender

"Rest": to allow food to sit for a few moments. Serves two purposes: 1) allows batter (i.e., pancakes) or other food product (i.e., lasagna) to set-up; 2) allows juices of meats to run back through the meat so that they do not run out when the meat is cut (this keeps the meat moist).

Ribbon Cut: see page 136

Roast: to cook in oven

Roux: a mixture of flour and fat that is cooked for one minute to enhance the nutty flavor of the flour while removing the starchy taste. The next step is to add a liquid and cook to thicken sauce or gravy.

Sauté: to cook briefly in a small amount of fat over medium heat, stirring regularly

Season: to use spices and seasonings to flavor food

Shred: to cut food into long, thin pieces

Sift: to shake dry ingredients through a sieve, adding air and combining multiple ingredients together. Also used to remove chunks (i.e., carob powder).

Simmer: to cook foods at a gentle bubble

Slide, Season & Cook: see page 67

Sprinkle: to measure a small amount of food by shaking

Steam: to cook foods over simmering water in a steamer basket, steamer pan or saucepan

Stir-fry: to sauté over medium heat while stirring constantly (meats should be thinly sliced and some vegetables need to be blanched before beginning to stir-fry)

Toss: to combine ingredients gently

Well: an indentation in a mixture of dry ingredients; liquid ingredients are then placed in the well, allowing for more even distribution

Whisk: to quickly stir ingredients with a fork or whisk to make a smooth, airy mixture

APPENDIX F: Measuring How-To's

For most recipes (i.e., casseroles, salads, soups), amounts given are a guide. After preparing these recipes a couple of times, exercise your creative skills and adjust the quantities using the "handful/sprinkle" method of measuring. In contrast, accurate measuring is the best guarantee of success in baking "breads," especially when using gluten-free flours and thickeners.

Suggested Measuring Tools

1. At least one set of dry-measuring cups ($^1/_4$, $^1/_3$, $^1/_2$ and 1 cup). If possible, include a $^1/_8$–cup measure (note: some are sold as coffee measures, which are only approximately $^1/_8$ cup).

Dry Measures

2. At least one each (1-cup and 2-cup) clear liquid measures. They can be also used to measure cooked meats and diced fresh vegetables. Choose a brand with easy-to-read markings and that nest inside of each other for convenient storage.

Liquid Measure

Liquid Measure

3. A 4-cup and/or 8-cup batter bowl are handy for measuring large amounts. These can double also as mixing bowls.

4. At least one set of long-handled measuring spoons (1 tablespoon, 1 teaspoon, $^1/_2$ teaspoon, $^1/_4$ teaspoon and $^1/_8$ teaspoon). The long handles (approx. 5 inches in length) work well for getting small amounts of spices, etc. out of narrow-neck bottles. I prefer to take the set apart and store the individual spoons on separate small hooks conveniently located in the mixing area of my kitchen. The $^1/_8$ teaspoon measure is perfect for measuring small amounts of stevia.

Measuring Spoons

Accurate Measuring Guidelines

A. For dry ingredients (i.e., flour, starch), use dry measuring cups ($^1/_4$, $^1/_3$, $^1/_2$ and 1 cup).

1. Choose measuring cup appropriate to amount to be measured.

2. Fill cup a little over full with ingredient, especially on backside (side nearest handle).

3. Using a table knife held vertically, move backside (straight edge) across top of measuring cup to level off ingredient. Have some type of container underneath to catch excess.

Measuring Dry Ingredients

B. To measure small amounts of dry ingredients such as starch, leavening agents (i.e., vitamin C crystals, baking soda, baking powder), salt, seasonings, etc., use a set of measuring spoons (1 tablespoon, 1 teaspoon, $^1/_2$ teaspoon, $^1/_4$ teaspoon, $^1/_8$ teaspoon).

    1. Choose measuring spoon appropriate to amount to be measured.

    2. Dip measuring spoon into ingredient until a little over full, especially on backside (side nearest handle).

    3. Using a table knife held vertically, move backside (straight edge) across top of spoon to level off ingredient. Have some type of container underneath to catch excess.

Special Note: Salt and seasonings often do not need to be measured as accurately. Simply shake spoon gently to level ingredient.

C. To measure stevia powder in amounts smaller than $^1/_8$ teaspoon:

    1. Fill $^1/_8$ teaspoon measure with stevia and level it off.

    2. To measure $^1/_{16}$ teaspoon, using tip of a thin-bladed knife, divide stevia in half. The stevia will hold its form enough to then take tip of knife and push half of the $^1/_8$ teaspoon ($^1/_{16}$ teaspoon) of stevia out of measuring spoon and into bowl, etc.

Measuring
Stevia

    3. To measure $^1/_{32}$ teaspoon, divide the $^1/_{16}$ teaspoon amount in half and then only push off one fourth of amount in the $^1/_8$ teaspoon measure.

Special Note: When first learning to measure in these very small amounts, push measurement into a separate container before adding ingredient to mixing bowl.

D. To measure very small amounts of dry ingredient such as salt or seasonings, use the pinch method. A pinch is the amount pinched between index finger and thumb. Recipes in this cookbook are based on an approximate equivalent of 10 pinches of salt per $^1/_4$ teaspoon.

E. To measure liquid ingredients (i.e., water, juice, syrup, oil, broth), use a clear liquid measuring cup with markings to indicate the fractional divisions of the measure.

    1. Place liquid measure on a level table or counter.

    2. Bend down so your eyes are level with red lines on measure.

    3. Liquids are measured at bottom of the meniscus (ma-NIS-cus). The meniscus is the saucer-like depression along the top edge of the liquid. Add liquid gradually until the meniscus is lined up with desired mark on liquid measuring cup.

Measuring
Liquid Ingredients

    4. The difference in amount of liquid measured at top versus bottom of the meniscus is only a small amount and does not make a significant difference in many recipes. However, in many gluten-free baked products the difference in amount of liquid can cause doughy centers, etc. This simple measuring tip is easy to learn and can make all the difference in your success with gluten-free baking.

    5. Some liquid measures are designed to be read from the top.

F. Use measuring spoons to measure small amounts of liquid ingredients, but be careful that measured liquid does not "round up" on spoon and add additional liquid.

Measuring Abbreviations

To assure accurate interpretation of measurements, I used abbreviations only when space was an issue. Below is a list of common abbreviations. Those bolded are used in this cookbook.

For tablespoon:
T. OR Tbs. OR **Tbsp.**

For teaspoon:
t. OR **tsp.** OR teas.

For cup: c. OR C

For pint: pt.

For quart: qt.

For gallon: gal

Measuring Hints

When measuring syrup-style sweeteners (i.e., agave nectar, rice syrup, honey), lightly coat the measuring utensil with oil first. This makes the removal of the syrup from the utensil much easier. If the recipe calls for oil, simply measure the oil before the syrup. If the recipe does not call for oil, use water on the measuring utensil. (However, water does not work as well as oil.)

- - - - -

Oils that become thick at refrigerator temperatures (i.e., olive, sesame) are easier to measure if you store them in a wide-mouth jars. This enables you to measure the thicker consistency of these oils by spooning them out rather than warming to reliquefy them and then pouring them out.

Measuring Equivalents

Below are simple fractional equivalents to assist when measuring (i.e., $^3/_8$ teaspoon, $^5/_8$ teaspoon, $^7/_8$ cup, etc.) and/or preparing one-half or double a recipe:

1 gallon	=	4 quarts OR 8 pints OR 16 cups
1 quart	=	2 pints OR 4 cups
1 pint	=	2 cups
1 cup	=	16 tablespoons
$^7/_8$ cup	=	14 tablespoons OR 1 cup less 2 tablespoons
$^1/_2$ cup	=	8 tablespoons
$^1/_3$ cup	=	$5^1/_3$ tablespoons OR 5 tablespoons + 1 teaspoon
$^1/_4$ cup	=	4 tablespoons
$^1/_8$ cup	=	2 tablespoons
1 tablespoon	=	3 teaspoons
$^1/_2$ tablespoon	=	$1^1/_2$ teaspoons
$^7/_8$ teaspoon	=	$^1/_2$ teaspoon + $^1/_4$ teaspoon + $^1/_8$ teaspoon
$^3/_4$ teaspoon	=	$^1/_2$ teaspoon + $^1/_4$ teaspoon
$^5/_8$ teaspoon	=	$^1/_2$ teaspoon + $^1/_8$ teaspoon
$^3/_8$ teaspoon	=	$^1/_4$ teaspoon + $^1/_8$ teaspoon
$^1/_8$ teaspoon	=	one half of a $^1/_4$ teaspoon
$^1/_{16}$ teaspoon	=	one half of a $^1/_8$ teaspoon OR one-fourth of a $^1/_4$ teaspoon
$^1/_{32}$ teaspoon	=	one fourth of a $^1/_8$ teaspoon

APPENDIX G: Substitutions

This appendix is designed to assist you in making substitutions to best fit your rotational and personal desires. There are substitute ideas for milk, leavening agents, flour, starch, thickening agents, dry herbs, sugar and eggs.

These listings are a compilation from several sources and personal experience. It is important to note that when substitutes are used for many ingredients in a recipe (i.e., flour, sugar, egg, baking powder, liquid), it is often necessary to test, adjust and retest the new version to get a quality product.

Milk Substitutes

Those with CRC are to omit milk at least during Stage 2 of the Candida-Control Food Plan. Also, dairy is a common food allergen. This presents a lack of beverage options as well as a dilemma with milk-based soups and casseroles and some baked products.

For a beverage ideas, see pages 29, 100 and 101.

For a milk substitute in baking:

- Use an equal amount of water for the required amount of milk or buttermilk. When substituting water in a pancake recipe, start by using an equal substitution amount. Cook one pancake to test for thickness and then, if needed, make adjustments in remaining batter—add more water to thin batter or add more flour to thicken batter.
- Use an equal amount of fruit juice for listed amount of milk, especially good for also adding sweetness.

For hot or cold breakfast cereals, use from the wide variety of prepared "milks" (i.e., oat milk, br. rice beverages, soy milks) OR "milk" prepared from seeds and/or nuts (page 101).

For soups, use Brazil, Cashew or Macadamia Nut Milk.

For creamy-based casseroles such as Chicken/Tuna Noodle Casserole, use Sesame Milk or add blended sesame seeds to casserole mixture as done in the Skillet Chicken Noodle Casserole (page 136).

For custards and puddings, use Almond, Cashew, Brazil or Macadamia Nut Milk.

Many of the recipes in this cookbook have the milk substitute proportions and preparation steps incorporated into the recipe so you do not need to make the nut milk separately.

Prepared soy milks in powder and liquid form are commercially available. However, soy is a common food allergen so always rotate during the healing stages. Choose only organic

continued ...

... continued

and GMO-free soy milks and read labels to avoid unacceptable ingredients (i.e., barley malt). Also, note that some packaging is corn-based.

Leavening Agent Substitutes

The most common leavening agents are baker's yeast and baking powder. Baker's yeast is a common food allergen and/or often creates a problem for those with CRC. If you tolerate baker's yeast, you may add the Fungi Family to your choice day in the rotation.

Baking powder is a leavening agent with two parts: Acid and Alkaline. It is the reaction between these that causes food to rise. Often the ingredients of a non-alum baking powder are calcium acid phosphate, baking soda and cornstarch. Since corn is a common food allergen, using baking powder (especially on a daily basis) may create a problem.

There is potato-based baking powder (see www.canaryconnect.com) but this can be a problem for those with sensitivities to the Nightshade Family (#74) and it breaks rotation if used daily. If you choose to use this product on one day of your rotation, use:

$1^1/_2$ teaspoons potato-based baking powder for 1 teaspoon of baking powder

Another leavening option is to make your own baking powder by using:

> 1 teaspoon of baking soda
> 2 teaspoons of some type of starch or flour
> 2 teaspoons of cream of tartar

Mix the three ingredients together and store in an air-tight container. This mixture may cause problems for persons with CRC because cream of tartar is made from the fermented residue in wine barrels, however, you might be able to use the mixture for one day of your rotation. To convert recipes, use:

$1^1/_2$–$1^3/_4$ teaspoons of above mixture for 1 teaspoon of baking powder

Perhaps the best option for those with CRC and food allergies is the use of unbuffered, corn-free vitamin C crystals combined with baking soda. It seems to contain the least allergenic substances and is tolerated my most even when consumed everyday. Almost all of the recipes in this cookbook that require a leavening agent use this combination.

To convert recipes, use:

$1/_4$ teaspoon of vitamin C crystals
+ 1 teaspoon of baking soda
for $1^1/_2$–2 teaspoons of baking powder

Special Notes

This vitamin C/baking soda option seems to add more salt flavor than baking powder so reduce salt amount when converting other recipes.

- - - - -

Since most of the baked goods recipes call for vitamin C crystals and baking soda, this is one combination of ingredients that is not rotated. If you have reactions when using vitamin C crystals, research the source and attempt to find a variety of sources to fit the rotation.

Wheat Flour Substitutes in Baking

For 1 Cup (refined) Wheat Flour

1 cup amaranth flour with ~$1/4$ cup of starch

$1/2$ cup barley flour

$3/4$ cup brown rice flour + $1/4$ cup sweet rice flour

1 cup buckwheat flour

$3/4$ cup garbanzo (chickpea) or other bean flours

1 cup millet flour

$1 1/3$ cups oat flour

1 cup quinoa flour with addition of a starch

$7/8$ cup brown rice flour

$1 1/4$ cups rye flour

Caution During Stage 2

Omit the following flours
during Stage 2
of the Food Plan:

barley
oat
rye
Kamut®
spelt
sweet rice flour (use
sparingly at all times)

For 1 Cup Whole-Grain Wheat Flour

1 cup Kamut® flour

spelt flour—increase flour amount by 20–25%

OR use $3/4$ of liquid amount with 1 cup of spelt flour

Starch Substitute: $1/4$ tsp. guar gum for 1 Tbsp. starch (add guar gum w/ liquid)

Thickening Substitutes

For 2 tablespoons of wheat flour OR 1 tablespoon of cornstarch use:

1 teaspoon of guar gum.

1 tablespoon of the following:

Starch: arrowroot, kudzu, tapioca, potato (Kudzu produces a slightly thinner gel than other starches and is clear, not cloudy like cornstarch)

Flour: bean, nut, brown rice

The measurements listed above are designed to thicken 1 cup of liquid for sauces. Double listed amount when thickening pudding.

Preparation Guidelines: Whisk starch/flour in cool or room temperature liquid (not hot) to dissolve. Add gradually to hot food, stirring constantly. Cook only to thicken, as prolonged cooking breaks down the thickening capability.

Herbs—Substituting Fresh for Dry

Most recipes in this cookbook use dried herbs. Some recommend CRC patients to avoid dried herbs during early stages of treatment as molds collect on the herb leaves (and teas) during the drying process. I personally feel that mold can be present just as much on fresh herbs (unless you grow your own and use only freshly picked). However, if dried herbs are a problem for you, use fresh herbs by substituting:

1 tablespoon of fresh for 1 teaspoon of dried herbs

To prevent fresh herbs from gathering mold before being used, wash, gently spin dry, mince and freeze them.

Sugar Alternatives

Honey, Rice Syrup or Maple Syrup: Substitute $^3/_4$ cup of honey, brown rice syrup or maple syrup for 1 cup sugar, along with reducing the liquid by $^1/_8$–$^1/_4$ cup. Also see page 198 for substituting honey for stevia.

Agave Nectar: Substitute $^3/_4$ cup of agave nectar for 1 cup of sugar along with reducing liquid by $^1/_3$ cup.

Fruit Juice: Substitute 1 cup fruit juice for 1 cup of sugar and 1 cup of liquid.

Stevia: Omit sugar, using $^1/_4$ teaspoon of stevia powder (pure white powder concentrate) per $1^1/_2$ cups of flour listed in recipe.

*FOS: Omit the listed measurement of sugar and substitute with double the amount of FOS. Liquid may need to be adjusted (lowered) since FOS causes baking doughs to become sticky. FOS does not dissolve as readily as sugar.

*Dry Brown Rice Sweetener: Use 1 cup brown rice sweetener to replace 1 cup of sugar. Since it is made from rice syrup, dough tends to be a little sticky so reduce liquid amount slightly, starting with 2 tablespoons less liquid per 1 cup of sweetener used.

*Dry Concentrated Fruit Sweetener: Use $1^1/_4$ cups of dry fruit sweetener for 1 cup of sugar.

*Liquid Concentrated Fruit Sweetener: Use $^2/_3$ cup of liquid fruit sweetener for 1 cup sugar and reduce liquid by $^1/_3$ the amount sweetener used. (For example, if 1 cup of the fruit sweetener is used, reduce liquids by $^1/_3$ cup. If $^2/_3$ cup of fruit sweetener, reduce liquid by $^1/_4$ cup less 1 teaspoon.)

*See www.canaryconnect.com for brands and resources.

Helpful Hints!

Honey browns more easily than sugar so decrease the oven temp by 25° and bake on the middle oven rack.

Add a pinch of baking soda to baked goods to help neutralize honey's natural acidity.

- - - - -

Since honey and other syrup-style sweeteners are 20–50% sweeter than sugar, recipes in this cookbook have been developed using less than the suggested substitutions.

- - - - -

Rice syrup baked products do not brown as much as those with sugar.

- - - - -

When baking with agave nectar, reduce oven temperature by 25°.

- - - - -

Since reducing "sugars" are necessary during three of the four stages (omitted totally during Stage 2) of the Candida-Control Food Plan, I recommend reducing alternative sugars as well. When using syrup-style sweeteners, replace some of the sweetener with water using the following formula:

Replace $^1/_4$ cup syrup-style sweetener with a scant 3 tablespoons of water.

Miscellaneous Substitutes (listed in the helpful hints or within the recipes)

Egg Substitutes

Eggs are needed in recipes for three main reasons: (1) flavor, (2) binding quality and (3) leavening quality. Since eggs are a common food allergen, most of the recipes in this cookbook are developed without eggs or list an egg substitute alternative.

To Replace 1 Egg in a Recipe Use: **Good For**

2 tablespoons starch (i.e., arrowroot, kudzu, tapioca) or bean flours with 2 tablespoons water Dip food product into starch solution before coating with breading.	binding the breading
1 tablespoon whole or ground flaxseed with $^1/_4$ cup water See page 179 for preparation.	binding & leavening
1 tablespoon flaxmeal with 3 tablespoons water Mix and add to recipe.	leavening
1 tablespoon psyllium seed husk mixed with 3 tablespoons of water Let it stand briefly before adding to recipe.	binding
1 tablespoon tahini with 3 tablespoons of water	binding
1 tablespoon lecithin granules with 3 tablespoons water	binding
$^1/_4$ cup tofu	binding
1 tablespoon garbanzo bean flour with 1 tablespoon oil	binding
1 teaspoon plain unflavored gelatin dissolved with 3 tablespoons water Place in freezer. Take out when thickened and beat until frothy.	binding
*$1^1/_2$ tablespoons water, $1^1/_2$ tablespoons oil & 1 teaspoon baking powder Mix well until somewhat frothy. For best results, prepare and add this substitute after you have mixed everything else in the batter.	binding & leavening
2 teaspoons baking powder mixed with 2 tablespoons water For a second egg, add only 1 tsp. baking powder with 2 tablespoons water.	binding & leavening
*$^1/_2$ teaspoon baking powder, 2 tablespoons flour and $1^1/_2$ teaspoons oil	binding & leavening
**3 tablespoons thick pureed fruit	binding
**2 tablespoons apricot mixture (see recipe below)	binding

**Apricot Mixture for Egg Replacer

Measure 1 cup of dried apricots into a bowl. Cover with boiling water and let stand until fruit is soft. Puree in blender or food processor. Cover and store in refrigerator. (Source: *Coping with Candida Cookbook* by Sally Rockwell.)

To replace 1 egg white, dissolve 1 tablespoon plain unflavored gelatin in 1 tablespoon water. Whip. Chill and whip again.

*Reminder that baking powder contains cornstarch so use only on your corn-assigned day in the rotation or avoid these substitutes if sensitive to corn.

**Omit these options during Stage 2 of Candida-Control Food Plan.

Also, see www.canaryconnect.com for a list egg replacement products available for purchase.

APPENDIX H: Helpful Gadgets & Equipment

Having and properly using the correct equipment is by far one of the best ways to save time in the kitchen. Within the recipes there are a few Equipment Tips, indicated by criss-crossing whisk/spoon. If you do not have this equipment, you may desire to gradually add it to your kitchen. For some, I have recommend brands, see www.canaryconnect.com for a listing.

My suggested list of helpful equipment and gadgets includes the following:

- **Mixing and Cooking Utensils**, including mixing bowls, heat-resistant rubber spatulas or spoonulas (page 66), whisk, metal spatulas, tongs, pastry brush, rolling pin, vegetable peeler

- **Measuring** Supplies (page 248)

- **Colander** for draining many things including beans

Colander

- Fine Mesh **Strainer** (page 166)

- **Salad Spinner:** great to quickly remove washing water from "greens" and other vegetables and fruits. One that has a small inside basket for delicate fruits/vegetables is nice for berries and fresh herbs.

Vegetable Brush

- **Broth/Fat Separator** (page 134)

- **Vegetable Brush** to scrub the skins of vegetables and fruit

- **Cutting Boards** can be used for several food preparation purposes (i.e., chopping vegetables and slicing meat, rolling dough like tortillas, kneading and cutting dough like biscuits). I suggest that you have several different styles for different purposes. The pebble-like-surfaced acrylic cutting board is good for chopping vegetables. An over-the-sink style is handy for limited kitchen space. A smooth-surfaced cutting board is best for dough preparation. A non-porous surface is a must for cutting meat and its best if it is dishwasher safe. I recommend that you never use the same cutting board for raw meat as other things, especially raw vegetables. Whatever you choose, a wooden cutting board is the worst sanitation problem in a family kitchen. Since wood is porous, any liquids or juices from food products, especially meats, can seep down into the board's surface.

- Sharp **Knives** with non-wooden handles designed for purpose needed—paring (for peeling), chef knives (chopping/mincing vegetables, see page 74, garlic), fillet and carving (for cutting cooked/raw meats, page 131)

Chef Knife

- Digital **Timer**, preferably one that times in seconds and has a memory function to use when preparing tortillas

Digital Timer

- **Blender** (page 101)
- **Immersion Blender** (page 116)
- Stand **Mixer** with Beaters and Dough Hooks (page 181)
- **Food Processor/Chopper:** a great time saver for chopping (i.e., onions), slicing (i.e., potatoes) and shredding (i.e., cabbage); many can double as dough mixer and nut chopper
- **Cast Iron Cookware**, especially a **Griddle** (page 185) for tortillas, pancakes, etc., a **Skillet** for stir-fries, simple meats (cooked without sauces) and a **Grill Pan** (page 131) for grill cooking meats (grilled chicken on front cover). Pre-seasoned cast iron cookware may be purchased; however, additional seasoning and care tips are available on www.canaryconnect.com. One of the benefits of cast iron is that, when well-seasoned, its surface becomes almost non-stick.

Food
Processor

- **Stainless Steel Cookware** (without non-stick coating), especially skillets, saucepans and larger pots for soups, all with lids. A **Steamer Pan** (double-boiler style pan with holes in the top pan to allow steam in bottom pan to cook vegetables in the top without water touching the vegetable) and/or a **Steamer Basket** (collapsible basket that fits inside saucepan) can also be handy for cooking vegetables.
- **Stainless Steel Bakeware** (without non-stick coating), including baking (cookie) sheets and an 8-inch square pan
- **Glass Bakeware** (without non-stick coating), including an 8-inch square pan, pie pans and covered casseroles dishes in a variety of sizes
- **Slow Cookers** (page 169): small-sized (~1½ quart) for cooking smaller amounts like slow-cooker cereals as well as standard-sized (they come in a variety of sizes/shapes and some with programmable features, see www.canaryconnect.com)
- **Toaster/Convection Oven** (page 155) Toaster Ovens are preferred over microwaves as microwaves can drastically reduce the levels of valuable nutrients from foods. One study showed microwave cooking can eliminate 95% of the antioxidants from a food.[1]
- Counter-Top **Grill** (page 161) or **Grill-Pan** (page 131)
- **Food Storage Containers:** I recommend using glass containers (canning jars come in a variety of sizes) for storing foods in the refrigerator and freezer as much as possible. Plastic containers can leach "plastizers" into food products, adding additional toxins for our bodies to detoxify.
- **Food Storage Wraps:** Avoid using waxed paper, as it is often dusted with cornstarch. As with plastic containers, it is best to avoid/limit the use of plastic food wraps/bags. Also, avoid aluminum foil directly touching food as aluminum toxicity leads to forms of dementia. Cellophane, a plant fiber product may be the best option. See www.canaryconnect.com for more info.

Reference:

1. Randerson, J. "Microwaved Cooking Zaps Nutrients." New Scientist 25 October 2003: 14.

APPENDIX I: Helpful Hints

Throughout the book are many "Helpful Hints" that provide additional information. Most hints relate to the recipes and can make food preparation go more smoothly. Some hints are for one specific recipe while others are more general and can be applied to multiple circumstances. Many of these hints are denoted with a chef's hat, though some are simply found in the text itself. This appendix offers a few additional hints as well as listings of the general hints found throughout the book.

Hints Concerning Oven Temperatures

The oven temperatures listed within the recipes are given in degrees Fahrenheit. At times you may find a recipe from another source which does not list a specific oven temperature but which instructs you to use a "slow" or other level of oven. The chart at right gives the temperature ranges associated with these descriptions to aid you in adapting recipes.

Temperature	Descriptive Term
250° – 275°	very slow
300° – 325°	slow
350° – 375°	moderate
400° – 425°	hot
450° – 475°	very hot
500° – 525°	extremely hot

Hints Concerning Vegetables

Hints Concerning Red Meat and Poultry

Turning Meats: Use tongs rather than fork to turn meats as fork lets the juices escape, drying out the meat.

Hints Concerning Beans

Freezing cooked beans, 104
Lentils (mashing), 121
Use of kombu, 104
Storing, 103
Cooking, 104, 105

Lentils (soaking), 111
Beans (mashing), 120
Relieving intestinal gas, 104
Testing for doneness, 104

Hints Concerning Pasta, Grains and Breads

Fruited Muffins: To prepare muffins without fruit for Stage 2 CRC person as well as with fruit for others, fill muffin cups for desired quantity without fruit then stir fruit into remaining batter before filling cups.

Buckwheat flour (storing), 171
Millet (storing), 236
Toothpick test, 177
Preparing muffin tins/baking dishes, 172
Purchasing roasted buckwheat groats, 166
Reheating quinoa pasta, 119
Griddle Breads, 185
Cooking whole grains, 166
Rice pasta (flavor solution), 89
Working "bread" dough w/o dough hooks, 182

Perfect pasta, 88
Pancake topping, 102
"Breads" especially for children, 122
When batter is too thick, 173
Freezing cooked grains, 166
Tortillas, 187–188
Shaping rolls/buns, 182
Brown Basmati rice, 166
Salmon/Quinoa combination, 89

Hints Concerning Nuts/Seeds

Chopped Nuts: Many recipes call for small amounts (i.e., 2 tablespoons) of chopped nuts. To save time, chop 1 or more cups of each kind. Store chopped nuts in freezer.

Tolerating nuts, 35, 99
Chopping pumpkin seeds, 185

Ground sesame seeds, 136

Hints Concerning Storage

Grains and flours, see "Hints Concerning Pastas, Grains and Breads"
Coatings, 133, 138, 148
Nuts, see "Hints Concerning Nuts/Seeds"
Food storage wraps, 257

Salad Dressings, 96
Food storage containers, 257

Hints Concerning Freezing

Also see Recipe Index (freezing food hints).

Beans (cooked), 104
Guacamole, 98
Leeks, 76, 77
Pie, 191
"Whipped Topping", 190

Grains (cooked), 166
Ice cube trays (use of), 99
Onions, 77
Pizza, 155

continued ...

Hints Concerning Thawing Foods

Always thaw foods (except "breads") for at least a day in the refrigerator. Thawing at room temperature can lead to a food-born illness. In a "pinch" you can thaw foods (i.e., soups, beans) stored in glass jars by setting jar into a container of warm water. The water should cover as much of the jar as possible without "floating" the jar or reaching the lid. Change the water as it cools. As soon as the food nearest the edge of the jar thaws, you should be able to gently slide the food out into a saucepan to continue thawing it over low heat, stirring often.

Hints Concerning Reheating

Warm tortillas, griddle breads and pancakes on an un-oiled, cast iron griddle, flipping food often. I usually place the food on a cold griddle so the food gradually warms as the griddle warms. You can also warm slowly in a 300° convection/ toaster oven.

Muffins or similar bread products (i.e., buns) can be warmed slowly in a convection/ toaster oven or sliced in half and toasted on griddle as mentioned for tortillas.

For casseroles-style foods (i.e., lasagna) that you would not stir, it is best to reheat slowly in a covered (or uncovered) casserole dish in a 300° oven or toaster/ convection oven. I especially like using the convection feature on my toaster oven for these as it warms food in about half the time without it "drying out."

To reheat soups, beans and products that can be stirred, warm them in a saucepan over medium heat, stirring occasionally.

Miscellaneous Hints

If you have sensitive skin, it is advisable to wear plastic gloves when handling jalapeño peppers. Also, be careful not to get the jalapeno juice in your eyes or open cuts.

APPENDIX J: Assistance Beyond This Book

Assistance is available beyond this book to help you with your healing and with following a preventative lifestyle. Visit www.canaryconnect.com for information, resource links and to sign up for the FREE e-mail newsletter, e-CCNews (Canary Connect News).

If you do not have Internet access, send a request* for "ACC info pricelist" along with a business-sized, self-addressed, stamped envelope to:

Canary Connect Publications
A division of SOBOLE, Inc.
605 Holiday Road
Coralville, IA 52241-1016

Speaking & Consultation Services:

Sondra is available for radio and public speaking on several health-related topics. She is also available for personal consultations, usually by phone. Call the "order line" number below or e-mail (see website for e-mail address) for availability and charges.

To order Books or
Products call

WholeApproach

1-888-889-7320 or order
online at:
wholeapproach.com

The views expressed are those of the author; and not necessarily those of
WholeApproach, Attogram Corp. or any of its distributors. Nothing in this publication
shall be construed as a statement or claim for any specific product.

SUBJECT INDEX

RECIPE & FOOD INDEX

My Favorite Recipes

Personal Healing Action Plan

About the Authors

Sondra Lewis has a BS degree in home economics education from Western Illinois University, Macomb, Illinois and two years of graduate studies from the University of Northern Iowa, Cedar Falls, Iowa.

She was diagnosed in 1988 and 1989 with yeast-related health issues including Candida-Related Complex (CRC), food allergies, Chronic Fatigue Syndrome and Multiple Chemical Sensitivities/Environmental Illness (MCS/EI). Before her diagnosis, she was a home economist, educator and an assistant manager in college food service.

Sondra used her expertise and personal healing experience to develop the rotational food plan, the corresponding recipes and healing action plans in this book.

Her interests include cooking, gardening, walking, reading, Bible study, watching ice skating and helping others help themselves. She lives with her husband, Bob, in Coralville, Iowa. Sondra is currently developing recipes for her next cookbook.

Dorie Fink received a BA in American Studies and licensure to teach grades K-6 from Mary Washington College, Fredericksburg, VA. Before becoming a mom, she taught both 4th and 5th grade. She now lives in Iowa City, Iowa with her husband and two sons.

Dorie's interest in yeast-related health issues began when her mother-in-law was diagnosed with CRC. Since then, she has supported several friends and family members dealing with the effects of yeast overgrowth, including her younger son who has food allergies and asthma. She is grateful for Sondra's invaluable help and support in these endeavors.

Along with mothering and with encouraging her husband in his graduate studies and teaching, Dorie enjoys reading, gardening, Bible study and friendships.

Synergism at It's Best!

Webster defines synergism as a "cooperative action of discrete agencies such that the total effect is greater than the sum of the effects taken independently."

Lonnett (editor of the earlier editions of this book) and I knew no better way to describe our relationship.

Dorie and I are the same. We often are thinking the same thoughts. And our separate ideas combine to work so perfectly together that we know their source comes from far beyond us.

We have enjoyed working together on this project. Our friendship has grown through this professional relationship. Be on the watch for more books by the two of us, www.canaryconnect.com.

**God Bess You
On Your Healing Journey!**

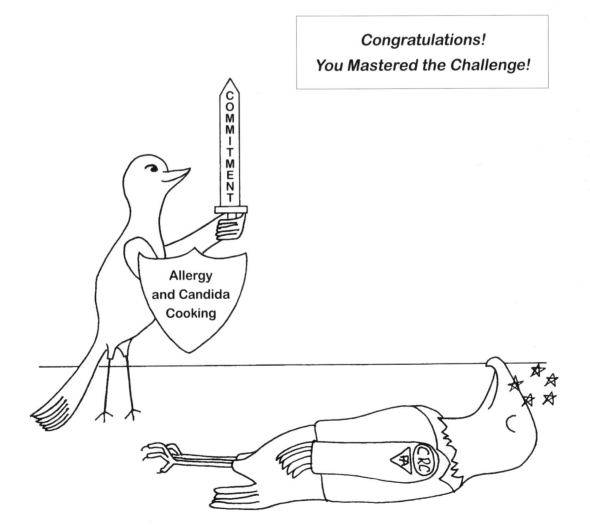